Read & Think
SPANISH
PREMIUM Fourth Edition

Read & Think
SPANISH

PREMIUM Fourth Edition

The editors of
Think Spanish
magazine

New York   Chicago   San Francisco   Athens   London   Madrid
Mexico City   Milan   New Dehli   Singapore   Sydney   Toronto

1 2 3 4 5 6 7 8 9   LCR   27 26 25 24 23 22

ISBN   978-1-260-47459-6
MHID   1-260-47459-3

e-ISBN   978-1-260-47460-2
e-MHID   1-260-47460-7

McGraw Hill books are available at special quantity discounts to use as premiums and sale promotions, or for use in corporate training programs. To contact a representative, please visit the Contact Us pages at www.mhprofessional.com.

McGraw Hill Language Lab App

Audio recordings for select readings (see page 239 for full list) and flashcards for all vocabulary lists are available to support your study of this book. Go to www.mhlanguagelab.com to access the online version of this application. Also available for iPhone, iPad, and Android devices. Search "McGraw Hill Language Lab" in the iTunes app store or Google Play App store for Android.

Contents

Introduction   xi

Cultura

Los vejigantes	*Festival of Saint Loiza, Puerto Rico*	4
¿Quién es el jíbaro?	*The pride of Puerto Rico*	5
De tapeo	*The art of eating tapas in Spain*	6
La siesta en Argentina	*Benefits of the siesta*	8
Pescando con "caballos"	*Peru's ancient fishing techniques*	10
Los alebrijes	*Mexican folk art*	12
La pollera panameña	*The national costume of Panama*	14
El gaucho	*The Uruguayan cowboy*	16
La carretanagua	*Myths and legends from Nicaragua*	18
El rodeo y los "huasos"	*Chilean rodeo and cowboys*	19
Boticas mexicanas	*The Mexican pharmacies*	20
Un país lleno de música	*Music and culture in Paraguay*	22
Piedras misteriosas	*Mysterious stones in Costa Rica*	24
Examina tu comprensión	*Test your comprehension*	26

Viaje

El barrio gótico de Barcelona	*The Gothic Quarter in Barcelona*	30
Humacao	*The pearl of Puerto Rico*	31
Colonia del Sacramento	*The cobblestone streets of Uruguay*	32
Verano en enero y febrero	*Summer in January in Argentina*	34
Mallorca y sus castillos	*Castles off the coast of Spain*	36
Un paraíso en el Caribe	*Caribbean paradise, Dominican Republic*	38
Varadero, arenas blancas	*Cuba's white sand beaches*	40
Cali, ¡qué ciudad!	*Discover a new city in Colombia*	42
El turismo rural	*Countryside travel in Spain*	43
San Miguel de Allende	*Mexican colonial city*	44
Tulum, la ciudad sobre el mar	*Mexico's ancient walled city*	45
Vinos y Bodegas	*Uruguayan wine country*	46
Bocas del Toro	*The islands of Panama*	48
Isla de Taquile	*Peru's most beautiful island*	50
Examina tu comprensión	*Test your comprehension*	52

Tradición

La quinceañera — Mexico's "sweet 15" birthday party — 56

Chichicastenango — Traditions of a Guatemalan town — 57

La Pachamama — Peru's celebration of "Mother Earth" — 58

El uso de las plantas medicinales — Argentinian healing plants — 60

Una Navidad en Paraguay — Christmas in Paraguay — 61

La gritería — Christmas traditions in Nicaragua — 62

Gaspar, Melchor y Baltasar — The three wise men of Puerto Rico — 64

7 de julio San Fermín — Pamplona's running of the bulls — 66

¡Viva el novio! ¡Viva la novia! — Spanish wedding traditions — 68

Castillos en el aire — Human towers in Spain — 70

La leyenda de la Colosuca — Honduran folklore and legends — 72

Día Internacional del Libro — Spain's celebration of books — 73

Otávalo — An Ecuador village traditions — 74

Examina tu comprensión — Test your comprehension — 76

Celebración

La Mamá Negra — Ecuador's most famous fiesta — 80

El Salvador del Mundo — The patron saint of San Salvador — 81

El Día de los Muertos — Day of the Dead, Mexico — 82

Festeja su independencia — Chile's Independence Day — 84

¡Menudo tomate! — La Tomatina festival, Spain — 86

El baile del palo de mayo — Dance of the May Pole, Nicaragua — 88

Celebración del mercado medieval — Medieval market celebration in Spain — 89

La Virgen de la Candelaria — Celebration in the Peruvian high plains — 90

La Pascua y Semana Santa — Holy Week in Argentina — 92

Un lento retorno — Easter celebrations in Cuba — 93

La fiesta con más Gracia — Spanish neighborhood festivities — 94

El carnaval de Cádiz — Mardi Gras on the coast of Spain — 96

Celebración de Navidad — Christmas in Colombia — 98

Noche del fuego en Salamina — A night of lights and magic — 100

San Pedro de Macorís — Dominican Republic's carnaval — 101

Examina tu comprensión — Test your comprehension — 102

Personas

La magia de García Márquez	*Colombia's celebrated author*	106
Las hazañas de Rita Moreno	*Puerto Rico's famous actress*	107
Diego Rivera	*Prolific Mexican artist and muralist*	108
Frida Kahlo	*Mexico's legendary female painter*	110
Celia Cruz	*Beloved Cuban salsa singer*	112
Rubén Darío	*Talented Nicaraguan poet*	113
El Che Guevara	*Argentina's renowned activist*	114
Unamuno, el eterno poeta	*Spanish writer, philosopher, and poet*	116
Hispanos para la historia	*Anthony Quinn, Mexico's adored actor*	117
Andrés Segovia	*The father of the classical guitar*	118
Galeano	*Radical Uruguayan journalist*	120
María Félix	*Mexico's beloved film actress*	122
Examina tu comprensión	*Test your comprehension*	124

Deportes

El arte de imitar a los pájaros	*Paragliding in Argentina*	128
Acampando en San Felipe	*Camping in Baja California, Mexico*	129
Surfing en Costa Rica	*The best beaches and waves*	130
Escalando el Nevado Sajama	*Scaling Bolivia's highest peak*	131
El fútbol	*Soccer Argentina style*	132
El jai alai	*Popular sport from Spain*	134
Sierra Nevada, el paraíso blanco	*Skiing in Spain*	136
Conociendo Guatemala a caballo	*Exploring Guatemala on horseback*	137
El senderismo en el Perú	*Trekking through Peru*	138
Examina tu comprensión	*Test your comprehension*	140

Música

Bailando al son de merengue	*The sounds of The Dominican Republic*	144
Los instrumentos musicales	*Musical instruments of Venezuela*	145
El arte flamenco	*The Spanish art of Flamenco*	146
El reguetón está "rankeao"	*Dance music in Puerto Rico*	148
El tango: pasión en la pista	*Passion in the streets of Argentina*	150
Las sevillanas	*Expressive Spanish dances*	152
El mariachi	*Mexico's popular mariachi*	154
Los gamberros universitarios	*University musicians in Spain*	155
El candombe	*Traditional music in Uruguay*	156
La música andina	*Peru's music of the Andes*	158
Las danzas tradicionales	*Traditional dances of El Salvador*	160
La Tamborrada	*Spain's drum festival*	162
Orishas	*Cuban Hip Hop*	163
Examina tu comprensión	*Test your comprehension*	164

Historia

El cinco de mayo	*Celebration of the Battle of Puebla*	168
Los hijos del sol	*Incan history and civilization*	170
La historia del toreo	*History of bullfighting, Spain*	172
La independencia de Colombia	*The independence of Colombia*	174
Un símbolo de la nación	*The Chilean flag, symbol of a nation*	176
La bandera de México	*The flag of Mexico*	177
San Juan	*Puerto Rico's distinctive capital city*	178
Las ruinas de Tiwanaku	*Ancient ruins in Bolivia*	180
Una pieza de historia	*A piece of history, Honduras*	181
Los garifunas	*The Garifuna culture in Belize*	182
La Virgen de Guadalupe	*Mexico's Virgen of Guadalupe*	184
Viaje a una ciudad histórica	*A historical city in Uruguay*	186
Examina tu comprensión	*Test your comprehension*	188

Geografía

El Parque Nacional Darién	*Panama's largest national park*	192
Las islas Galápagos	*Galapagos Islands, Ecuador*	194
El jurumí	*Paraguay's giant anteater*	196
Paisajes diversos	*Bolivia's diverse regions*	198
Paisajes, flora y fauna	*Landscapes of Venezuela*	200
Las ballenas de Valdez	*Argentina's Valdez Peninsula*	202
La Reserva de El Vizcaíno	*Baja California's desert reserve*	203
Orquideario	*Beautiful orchids of Nicaragua*	204
Lluvia de ranas en El Yunque	*Puerto Rico's tropical frogs*	205
La laguna de San Ignacio	*Whale migration in Mexico*	206
Examina tu comprensión	*Test your comprehension*	208

Gastronomía

El dulce de papaya	*Sweet papaya in Puerto Rico*	212
El mate	*Traditional Argentinian tea*	213
El dulce de leche	*A sweet treat in Argentina*	214
La deliciosa papa	*The delicious potato grown in Peru*	216
Recetas con papas	*Mexican potatoes*	218
Ensalada de yuca	*Yucca salad, Cuba*	219
Camarones en salsa blanca	*Shrimp in white sauce, Mexico*	220
Carnitas	*Typical Mexican pork dish*	221
Sangría, la bebida del verano	*Spain's drink of summer*	222
La chicha	*Ceremonial drink of Ecuador*	223
El turrón	*Popular Spanish Christmas treat*	224
Tradicional comida	*Traditional food of Guatemala*	225
La "dieta mediterránea"	*The benefits of a Mediterranean diet*	226
Un delicioso postre: flan de huevo	*Latin America's popular dessert, flan*	227
Examina tu comprensión	*Test your comprehension*	228

Conversación

Un ejemplo de salud sustentable *An example of sustainable health* 232
El desafío de criar hijos bilingües *The challenge of bilingual children* 234
Recomendaciones de un amigo *Travel recommendations from a friend* 236
Para luchar contra la inequidad *The fight against inequity* 238
Sabiduría indígena *Wisdoms from the jungles* 240
El sueño de la casa propia *Owning your own home in Cuba* 242
Examina tu comprensión *Test your comprehension* 244

Costumbres

Tiendas de productos alimenticios *Hispanic stores and foods* 248
Programas de televisión *Learning Spanish with television* 249
El mes de la herencia hispana *Hispanic Heritage Month* 250
El Día de los Muertos *Halloween and Day of the Dead* 252
Estados Unidos con salsa *Learning to dance the Salsa* 254
La huella del español por Texas *The Spanish mark on Texas* 256
La cara latina de Miami *Population growth in Miami* 258
Guayaberas *Latin America style* 260
Talavera poblana *Mexican pottery traditions* 262
Examina tu comprensión *Test your comprehension* 264

Respuestas 266
Audio Recordings 271

Introduction

Read & Think Spanish is an engaging and non-intimidating approach to language learning. A dynamic, at-home language immersion, *Read & Think Spanish* is intended to increase Spanish fluency while teaching you about life and culture in Spanish-speaking countries.

This language learning tool is designed to build on and expand your confidence with Spanish, presenting vocabulary and phrases in meaningful and motivating content emphasizing all four language skills: reading, writing, speaking, and understanding the spoken language.

Read & Think Spanish brings the Spanish language to life! Our diverse team of international writers is excited about sharing their language and culture with you. Read a travel narrative from Spain and a documentary on Colombian folk music. Explore the geography of the Amazon and the jungles of Costa Rica. And don't forget, while you are enjoying these intriguing articles, you are learning Spanish.

Read & Think Spanish is used by educators and students of all ages to increase Spanish fluency naturally and effectively. Using this as a complement to classroom study or as a self-study guide, you will actively build grammar and develop vocabulary.

The cultural information provided in each chapter creates a deeper understanding of the traditions and cultures in Spanish-speaking countries and in turn fosters greater interest and success with learning Spanish. Each article is accompanied by a bilingual glossary. You can read and learn without stopping to look up words in a dictionary or phrase book.

Read & Think Spanish accommodates a range of skill sets from beginning to advanced:

• **Beginning:** We recommend that the student have the equivalent of one semester of college- or high-school-level Spanish. Your previous experience with Spanish may have been through studies at a private or public school, self-study programs, or immersion programs. *Read & Think Spanish* will allow you to immerse yourself in the language and the culture, and your understanding of sentence structure and use of verbs will be reinforced.

• **Intermediate:** As an intermediate student, you will learn new vocabulary and phrases. You will notice increased fluency and comprehension. You will also learn nuances about the language and the culture as you experience the authentic writing styles of authors from different countries.

• **Advanced:** The advanced student will continue to gain valuable information, as language acquisition is a lifelong endeavor. The diverse topics from a team of international writers offer you the opportunity to learn new vocabulary and gain new insight into the language and the people.

Whatever your current skill level, *Read & Think Spanish* is an effective, fun, and accessible way to learn Spanish. Experience the enthusiasm that comes with learning a new language and discovering a new culture. Read, speak, enjoy—think Spanish!

About the Author

Read & Think Spanish is based on articles from *Think Spanish,* an online language learning magazine and memberhip that was published by Second Language Publishing. The writers for *Think Spanish* are native Spanish speakers, including college and high school Spanish instructors, travel experts, and journalists. Articles in this book were coordinated under the direction of Kelly Chaplin, founder of Second Language Publishing.

Guidelines for Success

Read & Think Spanish is divided into chapters guiding you through the cultures and traditions of different Spanish-speaking countries. At the end of each chapter is a "Test your comprehension" section. This section encourages development of reading comprehension and the understanding of written Spanish in different voices.

It is not necessary for you to read *Read & Think Spanish* from start to finish or in any certain order. You can read one chapter at a time or pick an article or chapter that is of particular interest to you. You can complete the test questions by article or by chapter. This flexibility allows you to go at your own pace, reading and re-reading when needed. The high-interest articles encourage enthusiasm as you study and make the material more enjoyable to read.

• Read through the article to get the general idea of the story line. Do not get frustrated if the first time through you do not fully understand the vocabulary.

• After you gain an understanding of the article, read through the story again and focus on vocabulary that is new to you. Notice how the vocabulary is used in context.

• Practice reading the article aloud.

• If you have access to an audio recorder practice recording the articles or ask a fluent speaker to record them for you. Listen to the recording and notice how your listening comprehension improves over time.

Repeat, Repeat, Repeat! This is especially important for memorizing important parts and forms of words. Sometimes only active repetition will secure your memory for certain hard-to-retain items. Frequent vocal repetition impresses the forms on your "mental ear." This auditory dimension will help you recognize and recall the words later. With *Read & Think Spanish* you have the opportunity to repeat different learning processes as often as you'd like and as many times as you want. Repeat reading, repeat listening, and repeat speaking will aid in your overall success mastering the Spanish language.

Custom Bilingual Glossary

A custom bilingual glossary is provided next to each article to facilitate ease and understanding while reading in Spanish. With uninterrupted reading, comprehension is improved and vocabulary is rapidly absorbed.

Every article contains new grammar, vocabulary, and phrases as well as repetition of previous vocabulary and phrases. The repetition throughout the articles enhances reading comprehension and encourages memorization. The articles are written in different perspectives. Most articles are written in third person while some are written in first person. This change of voice allows you to recognize verbs as they are conjugated in different tenses.

Spanish instructors often recommend that students "create an image" or associate foreign words with something familiar to enhance memorization of new vocabulary. As you are learning new vocabulary with *Read & Think Spanish*, however, you will not have to "create" these images. The images will be automatically created for you as the story unfolds. Take your time as you are reading and imagine the story as it is written, absorbing the new vocabulary. If a vocabulary word is particularly difficult, try focusing on an image in the story that the word represents as you say the word or phrase aloud.

Verbs in the glossary are written first in their conjugated form as they appear in the article as well as in their infinitive form.

For example: **salimos/salir:** we went/to go

aportaban/aportar: they carried/to carry

Test Your Comprehension

The test questions provided at the end of each chapter are designed to further develop your reading comprehension skills and ensure your overall success with Spanish. In addition to determining the general meaning of the article by word formation, grammar, and vocabulary, you will also learn how to use context to determine meaning. Understanding context allows you to make educated "guesses" about the meaning of unfamiliar words based on the context of a sentence, paragraph, or article. Answers are provided at the end of the book and within each chapter.

Read & Think
SPANISH
PREMIUM Fourth Edition

Los hombres son como los astros, que unos dan luz
de sí y otros brillan con la que reciben.

José Martí

Cultura

Los vejigantes
PUERTO RICO

vejigantes: men or women dressed in costumes (like monsters)
pueblo: town
habitantes: inhabitants
ya que muchos: since many
esclavos: slaves
traídos a la isla: brought to the island
la conquista española: the Spanish conquest
se asentaron/asentar: were settled/ to settle
libertad de religión: religious freedom
se encargaron: took care
convertirlos/convertir: convert them/ to convert
cristianismo: Christianity

nacen/nacer: are born/to be born
mantener: to keep
mezclada: mixed
moros: Moors
no eran/ser: were not/to be

Santiago Apóstol: Patron Saint of Loiza
salen a la calle/salir: they go to the street/to go out
para asustar a los jóvenes: to scare young people
usualmente: usually
se visten/vestir: they are dressed/ to dress
mamelucos: overalls
colores brillantes: brilliant colors

mangas: sleeves
parecen alas: look like wings
lo más impresionante: the most impressive
máscaras: masks
hechas de coco: made of coconut
se corta/cortar: is cut/to cut
en 45 grados: in 45 degrees
se saca la fruta de adentro: the fruit inside is taken out
más dura: the hardest
se talla/tallar: is carved/to carve
cara grotesca: ugly, grotesque face
dientes: teeth
bambú: bamboo
cuernos: horns
tallo: stem
racimos: bunches, clusters
guineo: banana

razas: races

Loiza es un **pueblo** al noreste de Puerto Rico. Sus **habitantes** son de descendencia africana **ya que muchos** de los **esclavos traídos a la isla** durante **la conquista española se asentaron** allí. Los esclavos no tenían **libertad de religión** y los españoles **se encargaron** de **convertirlos** al **cristianismo**.

Los vejigantes **nacen** como una forma de **mantener** su religión **mezclada** con la religión cristiana. Ellos representan a los **moros** que **no eran** cristianos.

Durante las fiestas de **Santiago Apóstol** el 25 de julio, los vejigantes **salen a la calle para asustar a los jóvenes**. **Usualmente**, las personas **se visten** con **mamelucos** grandes y de **colores brillantes**.

Las **mangas parecen alas**. **Lo más impresionante** son las **máscaras** que usan. Están **hechas de coco**. El coco **se corta en 45 grados**. Luego **se saca la fruta de adentro** y la parte **más dura** del interior. En el exterior **se talla** una **cara grotesca**, pintada también de colores brillantes. Los **dientes** se hacen de **bambú** y los **cuernos** del **tallo** de los **racimos** de **guineo**.

Los vejigantes son parte de la tradición puertorriqueña y de la integración de diferentes **razas** en nuestra cultura.

¿Quién es el jíbaro?
PUERTO RICO

El **jíbaro** es el **orgullo** de Puerto Rico. Representa al hombre **trabajador** del **campo**. Su figura simboliza la honestidad y el **sentimiento** de **lucha** del pueblo puertorriqueño.

El jíbaro es **humilde. Viste pantalones anchos, camisas holgadas a medio abrochar** y un **sombrero de paja**, la pava, sobre su cabeza para **cubrirse del sol candente** del Caribe. La pava también **se ha convertido** en símbolo de nuestro país. El jíbaro es **luchador**, **pobre**, pero **lleno de sueños. Contra viento y marea**, **se mantiene fuerte**. Así es el pueblo de Puerto Rico. Así es el puertorriqueño y el jíbaro se mantiene vivo **para recordarnos lo que somos**. Nuestro **famoso compositor**, Rafael Hernández, **supo** de su importancia y le escribió una **canción**: El Jíbaro.

jíbaro: Puerto Rican peasant	
orgullo: pride	
trabajador: hard worker	
campo: field, the country	
sentimiento: feeling	
lucha: fight, battle	

humilde: humble
viste pantalones anchos: wears wide pants
camisas holgadas a medio abrochar: half-buttoned, loose shirts
sombrero de paja: straw hat
cubrirse del sol candente: to cover himself from the hot sun
se ha convertido/convertir: has become/to become
luchador: fighter
pobre: poor
lleno de sueños: filled with dreams
contra viento y marea: against all odds (idiom)
se mantiene fuerte/mantener: keeps himself strong/to keep
para recordarnos lo que somos: to remind us of what we are
famoso compositor: famous composer, song writer
supo/saber: knew/to know
canción: song

CULTURE NOTE

Traditionally a *jíbaro* was a poor mountain man (as in the American hillbilly)—someone from the mountains, in *el campo* or *"la isla"* as they refer to the heart of the island in Puerto Rico. Not all residents of the interior of the island were *jíbaros*. Some were *hacendados* from well-to-do families. The *hacendados,* who considered themselves *españoles*, were well educated, often completing their education in Europe, and had servants. Music was a major component in the development of the *jíbaro* persona. *Jíbaros* made their own entertainment and most of the time that meant music. With strong Spanish roots, the *jíbaros* became poets, composers, and great storytellers. A variety of instruments contribute to the rich variety of folk music found in Puerto Rico. Some of the most popular include the percussion instruments called *tambours* (hollowed tree trunks covered with stretched-out animal skin), *maracas* (gourds filled with pebbles or dried beans and mounted on handles), and a variety of drums whose original designs were brought from Africa.

De tapeo
ESPAÑA

Ir de tapas es una **costumbre culinaria** a la que pocos **amantes del buen comer se niegan**. Estos platos, tan pequeños como **vistosos**, **han sobrevivido a través de los siglos** y son, sin duda, los reyes de la vida social española.

Aunque las recetas y **modalidades** varían **según** la región donde las comamos, las **normas** del **tapeo son compartidas** por todos los españoles: **acudir en grupo**, **pedir** varias tapas para **comerlas con el resto**, beber un **vinillo** para **alegrar el alma** y **hablar sin parar**. De hecho, si se observa a las personas que están **alrededor** de una mesa con tapas **parece que muestren** un elegante **desprecio** hacia la comida y es que, en realidad, **se da prioridad** al **gesto** y a la buena **charla** entre amigos.

La existencia de las tapas **se la debemos** al **rey** Alfonso X ya que fue **bajo sus órdenes** que los **mesones** castellanos empezaron a servir las **copas y jarras** de vino **acompañados con** algo de comida. Con esta nueva norma, el monarca **pretendía** que el alimento **se empapara** del alcohol y el vino **no subiese tan rápido a la cabeza** de los **asiduos** a las **tabernas**, **evitando** así **peleas** y otros **alborotos**.

ir de tapas: to go around to the bars eating tapas (popular expression)
costumbre culinaria: culinary custom
amantes del buen comer: lovers of good food
se niegan/negarse: they refuse to do something/to refuse to do something
vistosos: colorful, spectacular
han sobrevivido/sobrevivir: they have survived/to survive
a través de los siglos: throughout the centuries

aunque: although
modalidades: forms, types
según: according to
normas: rules
tapeo: eating tapas
son compartidas/compartir: they are shared/to share
acudir en grupo: to go in groups
pedir: to ask for
comerlas con el resto/comer: eat them with the rest of the group/to eat
vinillo: diminutive of vino (wine)
alegrar el alma: to cheer up one's soul
hablar sin parar: to talk non-stop
alrededor: around
parece que muestren/mostrar: it seems like they show/to show
desprecio: scorn, contempt
se da prioridad: priority is given
gesto: gesture
charla: chat, talk

se la debemos/deber: we owe it/to owe
rey: king
bajo sus órdenes: under his orders
mesones: inns
copas y jarras: glasses and pitchers
acompañados con: together with
pretendía/pretender: he pretended/to pretend
se empapara/empaparse: it got soaked/to get soaked
no subiese tan rápido a la cabeza: it didn't go to their heads, to get drunk
asiduos: regular customers
tabernas: taverns
evitando/evitar: avoiding/to avoid
peleas: fights
alborotos: disturbances

A pesar de ser un **manjar apto para todos los bolsillos**, las tapas y su relación con la **alta alcurnia** no es poca, pues deben también su nombre a otro monarca. **Cuenta la leyenda** que el rey Alfonso XIII, de visita en la provincia de Cádiz, decidió entrar en el Ventorrillo del Chato—una **venta** que hoy en día aún existe para **refrigerarse** y **descansar un rato**. El **camarero** le llevó una copa de **jerez** al monarca y cuando la depositó en la mesa una **ventisca de arena** entró por la ventana.

Muy **avispado**, el **mozo** tuvo la idea de **tapar** la copa con una **loncha de jamón** para evitar que la arena (o algún **bichito volador**) **arruinara** el vino, **disculpándose** ante el rey por "**colocar** una **tapa**" para proteger el jerez. Le gustó tanto el **ingenioso sobrenombre** a Alfonso XIII que al rato pidió otra copa de jerez "pero con otra tapa igual". Los miembros de la Corte que **le acompañaban** imitaron el **pedido** y, desde entonces, la historia cuenta que la comida que acompaña a la bebida en los **aperitivos** recibe el nombre de tapas.

De las lonchas de jamón o queso que constituían las primeras tapas de la historia se ha pasado a una variedad tal que **supera toda imaginación**. **Chocos, patatas bravas, aceitunas rellenas, boquerones, croquetas, champiñones al ajillo, embutido, pescaíto frito, sepia a la plancha, gambas, tigres, bombas, chistorra** o **pulpo a la gallega**, son algunas de las **más demandadas**. Como **acompañamiento**, no puede faltar el vino o la sangría, aunque cada vez más, se está **imponiendo** la **cerveza**. **¿Alguien se apunta** a unas auténticas tapitas?

me tiraría: I would lie on (the bed)
descansar: to rest
ratito: little while, time
modorra: drowsiness
sueño: sleep
almorzar: lunch

extendida: widespread
pueblos: small towns
aunque: although
menos: less

palabra: word
proviene/provenir: it came from/
  to come from
correspondía/corresponder:
  it corresponded/to correspond
mediodía: midday
relacionamos/relacionar:
  we relate/to relate
en realidad: in fact, actually
reposo: rest
acompañado/acompañar:
  accompanied/to accompany
suele seguir: usually follows
disfruta/disfrutar: enjoys/to enjoy
duerme/dormir: sleeps/to sleep
se relaja/relajarse: he relaxes/to relax

holgazanería: laziness
estudios: studies
afirman/afirmar: they affirm/to affirm
mitad: middle
ayudan/ayudar: they help/to help
recuperar: to recover, regain
descargar ansiedades: to relieve anxieties
desbloquear: to unblock
mente: mind
altas temperaturas: high temperatures
agotador: exhausting
se convierte/convertir: it becomes/
  to become
excusa perfecta: perfect excuse
resguardarse: to take shelter
no perder fuerzas: not lose strength

La siesta en Argentina
ARGENTINA

Zzzzzzzzzzz... ¡Cómo **me tiraría** a **descansar** un **ratito**! ¡Qué **modorra**! ¿A quién no le da **sueño** luego de **almorzar**?

La siesta es una costumbre **extendida** en la mayoría de las provincias del interior de Argentina y en muchos **pueblos** de Latinoamérica, **aunque menos** en las grandes ciudades.

La **palabra** siesta **proviene** del latín *sixta*, que significa "la sexta hora del día"; entre los romanos **correspondía** al **mediodía**, las horas comprendidas entre las 13 y las 16 hs. Nosotros **relacionamos** a la siesta con el sueño pero **en realidad**, la siesta es el **reposo** (**acompañado** o no del sueño) que **suele seguir** a la comida del mediodía. El que **disfruta** de una siesta entonces, **duerme** un rato o simplemente **se relaja** unos instantes luego del almuerzo.

Los detractores de esta costumbre la relacionan con **holgazanería** pero, en realidad, existen varios **estudios** que **afirman** que unos minutos de relax en la **mitad** del día **ayudan** a **recuperar** energías, **descargar ansiedades**, **desbloquear** la **mente** y estimular la creatividad. En lugares con **altas temperaturas**, donde el clima del mediodía es **agotador**, la siesta **se convierte** en la **excusa perfecta** para **resguardarse** del calor excesivo y **no perder fuerzas**.

Pero, como en todo en la vida, el **equilibrio** es fundamental, ya que el **prolongado descanso vespertino podría alterar** el **ciclo normal** del sueño. Los especialistas recomiendan siestas de entre 15 y 30 minutos **diarios** y **nunca más** de 40.

En las grandes ciudades **suele escucharse** la **queja** famosa de "**no tengo tiempo** para la siesta" porque en la mayoría de los **casos** se la **confunde** con la acción de "**meterse en la cama** a dormir"; **sin embargo**, un simple relax de 20 minutos en algún sofá **basta** para **aliviar** tensiones, **descansar** y seguir con las actividades. Otras investigaciones **aseguran** que el efecto **reparador** de este descanso **previene** el **envejecimiento** y **alarga la vida**. De hecho, los efectos inmediatos de una buena siesta **se reflejan** en la **luminosidad** de la **cara** y en el buen humor. ¿**Descansamos** un rato?

equilibrio: balance
prolongado/ prolongar: extended/ to extend
descanso: break
vespertino: evening
podría alterar: it could alter, modify
ciclo normal: normal cycle
diarios: daily
nunca más: never more

suele escucharse/escuchar: usually hears/to hear
queja: complaint
no tengo tiempo: I have no time
casos: cases
confunde/confundir: confuses/ to confuse
meterse en la cama: get into bed
sin embargo: however
basta/bastar: it will be enough/ to be enough
aliviar: to relieve, soothe
descansar: to rest
aseguran/asegurar: assured/to assure
reparador: restorative, invigorating
previene/prevenir: it prevents/ to prevent
envejecimiento: aging
alarga la vida: it prolongs life
se reflejan/reflejar: it reflects/to reflect
luminosidad: luminosity
cara: face
descansamos/descansar: we rest/to rest

CULTURE NOTE
In the USA most people believe that the origins of the *siesta* are most commonly traced to Mexico. In reality, it is the traditional daily sleep of the Southern region of Alentejo, in Portugal. It was adopted by Spain and then by influence became a tradition in South America, Central America, and Mexico. However, the original concept of a *siesta* was merely that of a midday break. This break was intended to allow people time to spend with their friends and family. In recent years, studies have suggested a biological need for afternoon naps. An afternoon nap seems to be an instinctive human need. The studies have shown that there is a strong biological tendency for humans to become tired and possibly fall asleep in the middle of the afternoon. A *siesta*, or a slightly longer nap, can often satisfy this desire for sleep and allow a person to wake up feeling refreshed and much more alert. The main benefit of the *siesta* is mood improvement and some improved thinking ability. Just as your mother told you when you were a grumpy toddler: "Go take a nap."

pescando: fishing
se encuentra/encontrarse: there is/ to be
caleta: small beach
llamada/llamar: called/to call
pescadores: fishermen
siguen/seguir: they keep/to keep
costumbre: custom
antepasados: ancestors
mar: sea
rústicos: rustic
botes: small boat
hechos de: made of
caña: cane
caballitos: little horses
balsilla: small raft
a simple vista: at first sight
resistente: resistant
furia marina: marine fury
herencia: heritage
habitó/habitar: it inhabited/to inhabit
zona costera: coastal area
fecha: date
humildes: humble, poor
se ganan la vida/ganar: they earn their living/to earn
sacando/sacar: taking out/to take out

medio de transporte: means of transportation
aparecía/aparecer: it appeared/ to appear
grabado: engraved
lengua: language
llegaron/llegar: they arrived/to arrive
colonizadores: colonists
reino: kingdom
fueron rebautizados/rebautizar: they were rebaptized/to rebaptize
se montaban/montar: they got in/ to get in
miden/medir: they measure/ to measure
de largo: long
de ancho: width
de forma alargada: elongated shape
materia prima: raw material or matter
embarcación: boat
crece/crecer: it grows/to grow
cerca: near
ha alcanzado/alcanzar: it has reached/ to reach
desarrollo: development
es cortada/cortar: it is cut/to cut
luego: afterwards
ponerla/poner: put it/to put
secar: to dry
arena: sand

Pescando con "caballos"
PERÚ

A 450 kilómetros al norte de Lima, en el departamento de La Libertad, **se encuentra** una famosa **caleta llamada** Huanchaco donde los **pescadores** del lugar **siguen** la **costumbre** de sus **antepasados** al salir al **mar** en unos **rústicos botes hechos de caña** llamados "**caballitos** de totora".

Esta frágil **balsilla a simple vista** pero **resistente** a la **furia marina** es la **herencia** de la cultura mochica, que **habitó** esta **zona costera** del Perú hace más de 1.200 años. Desde esa **fecha**, los **humildes** pescadores de este lugar **se ganan la vida sacando** los frutos del mar de esta forma.

Este **medio de transporte** ya **aparecía grabado** en las cerámicas pre-incas. Se les llamaba *tup* en **lengua** mochica, pero cuando **llegaron** los **colonizadores** españoles a este **reino fueron rebautizados** como "caballitos", por la forma en que los indígenas **se montaban** en ellos para salir al mar. Los caballitos **miden** entre tres y cuatro metros **de largo** por metro o metro y medio **de ancho**, y son **de forma alargada**. La **materia prima** para hacer esta pequeña **embarcación** es la caña de totora que **crece cerca** de esta caleta de pescadores. Una vez que la totora **ha alcanzado** su máximo **desarrollo es cortada** desde su base para **luego ponerla** a **secar** en las **arena** de la playa.

De allí, manos expertas **prensan** los **carrizos tejiendo** una **popa** ancha hasta **finalizar** con una **fina proa arqueada en punta**. Este ritual de construcción **continúa llevándose a cabo** desde hace **siglos**.

Muy de madrugada, como **caballeros** en sus **corceles** los *huanchaqueros* o pescadores salen **en busca** del **jurel**, **chita** o **corvina**. Observar a los pescadores **navegando hábilmente** en sus míticos caballitos es un **espectáculo** turístico.

Los **curtidos** hombres regresan del mar antes del **mediodía** con sus **canastillas repletas** de **pescados** cuando la **pesca** es buena. Luego, las embarcaciones **son puestas de pie** en la arena como **vigilantes mirando hacia** el mar.

Lamentablemente esta actividad **parece extinguirse** por el **escaso** interés de las nuevas generaciones. Muchos de los **hijos** de los *huanchaqueros* viajan a Lima a **buscar** un futuro mejor. El **desaliento** también **tiene que ver** con la poca pesca **debido a** la actual presencia de **barcos arrastreros** que **arrasan** con todo los peces que **encuentran a su paso**. La dificultad por encontrar los totorales hoy día por la **acelerada** urbanización de Huanchaco también **está actuando en contra** para que, **en un futuro próximo**, esta **milenaria actividad pesquera pueda quedar sólo en recuerdo**.

---

prensan/prensar: they press/to press
carrizos: a riverbank plant
tejiendo/tejer: weaving/to weave
popa: stern
finalizar: to finish
fina: fine
proa: bow (in a boat)
arqueada: bent, curved (arch shape)
en punta: pointy
continúa llevándose a cabo: it continues to be carried out
siglos: centuries

muy de madrugada: very late in the night or very early in the morning
caballeros: horseback riders
corceles: steeds
en busca: in search of
jurel: scad
chita, corvina: types of fish
navegando/navegar: sailing/to sail
hábilmente: skillfully
espectáculo: show

curtidos: hardened
mediodía: midday, noon
canastillas: small baskets
repletas: full
pescados: fish
pesca: fishing
son puestas de pie: they are stood up
vigilantes: guards, watchmen
mirando/mirar: looking at/to look at
hacia: towards

lamentablemente: unfortunately
parece/parecer: it seems/to seem
extinguirse: to die out
escaso: scarce
hijos: children
buscar: to look for
desaliento: discouragement
tiene que ver: it has to do
debido a: due to
barcos arrastreros: trawling boats
arrasan/arrasar: they destroy/ to destroy
encuentran/encontrar: they find/ to find
a su paso: in their way
acelerada: accelerated, fast
está actuando/actuar: it is acting/ to act
en contra: against
en un futuro próximo: in the near future
milenaria: thousand-year-old
actividad pesquera: fishing activity
pueda quedar sólo en recuerdo: it can only remain as part of the past

último: last
volví/volver: I returned/to return
querer: to want
traerme: to bring with me
valija: valise, bag
llena de: full of
alebrijes: name of a typical Mexican craft, artisanry
lindos: pretty, nice
parecen salidos de: they seem to come from
cuento fantástico: fantastic story
aunque: although
pueden encontrarse/encontrar: they can be found/to find
casi todo el país: almost all of the country
madera: wood
cartón: cardboard
papel maché: paper mache

criaturas: creatures
suelen mezclarse: they usually mix
ejemplares: copies, examples
tortugas: turtles
mariposas: butterflies
sapos: frogs
elaborados/elaborar: made/to make
manos mágicas: magic hands
vivos: lively
llamativos: bright, colorful

leyendas: legends
se disputan/disputar: they dispute/ to dispute, to compete for
dicen/decir: they say/to say
salen/salir: they go out/to go out
árboles: trees
cuevas: caves
nubes: clouds
sostienen/sostener: they hold, maintain/to hold, to maintain
derivan/derivar: they derive/to derive
enfermó/enfermar: he fell ill/to fall ill
extraña: strange
afección: condition
lo dejó inconsciente: it left him unconscious
cama: bed

Los alebrijes
MÉXICO

En mi **último** viaje a México, **volví** a entusiasmarme y a **querer traerme** la **valija llena de alebrijes**. ¡Es que son tan **lindos** y tan coloridos que **parecen salidos de** un **cuento fantástico**! Los alebrijes son artesanías características de México, especialmente de Oaxaca **aunque pueden encontrarse** en **casi todo el país**. Los hay de **madera**, de **cartón** y de **papel maché**.

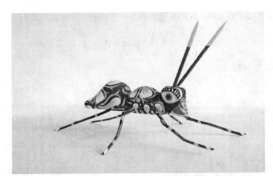

Son figuras de animales o **criaturas** fantásticas. En general **suelen mezclarse** dos o más animales, aunque también existen **ejemplares** de las clásicas **tortugas**, **mariposas**, escorpiones y **sapos**. Parecen **elaborados** por **manos mágicas**, con colores muy **vivos** y **llamativos** y formas que impactan por la perfección de su manufactura.

Existen varias **leyendas** que **se disputan** su invención y origen. Algunos **dicen** que son demonios que **salen de los árboles**, de las **cuevas**, ríos y **nubes**. Otros **sostienen** que **derivan** de las máscaras de animales características de Oaxaca. Pero la leyenda que tiene más adeptos los relaciona con Pedro Linares, un hombre de la ciudad de México, que a los 30 años **enfermó** de una **extraña afección** que **lo dejó inconsciente** en la **cama** durante varios días.

En su agonía **soñaba con** un bosque extraño donde había animales desconocidos y fantásticos: **burros con alas** de mariposa, **gallos** con **cuernos de toro**, leones con **cabezas de águila** y perros con **patas de araña**, entre otros. Un **ruido ensordecedor gritaba** el nombre de "alebrijes" y él en su esfuerzo por **salir de aquella pesadilla despertó** de la enfermedad. Cuando **se repuso** totalmente y recordó su sueño, **quiso** que su familia y todas las personas conocieran a estos animales que lo habían **salvado**. **Valiéndose de** sus habilidades como **cartonero**, **moldeó** esas extrañas criaturas que tanto **admiraba**.

Hoy en día, los alebrijes **no sólo** forman parte de la cultura popular mexicana **sino también** del arte contemporáneo con **reconocimiento** internacional.

soñaba con/soñar: he dreamed of/to dream
burros con alas: donkeys with wings
gallos: roosters
cuernos de toro: bull horns
cabezas de águila: eagle heads
patas de araña: spider legs
ruido ensordecedor: deafening noise
gritaba/gritar: screamed/to scream
salir de aquella: to get rid of that
pesadilla: nightmare, bad dream
despertó/despertar: he woke up/to wake up
se repuso/reponerse: he recovered/to recover
quiso/querer: he wanted/to want
salvado/salvar: saved/to save
valiéndose de: making use of
cartonero: cardboard-maker or seller
moldeó/moldear: he molded/to mold
admiraba/admirar: he admired/to admire

hoy en día: nowadays
no sólo...sino también: not only ... but also
reconocimiento: recognition

CULTURE NOTE

To communicate well with people of other countries, you must learn to speak well, right? Yes, but speaking isn't everything. Your gestures and other nonverbal actions matter too. The United States and Mexico are relatively different in nonverbal cues because of historical and cultural differences. Mexico is a high-contact culture. People tend to stand closer, touch frequently, and maintain good eye contact. In Mexico, when greeting someone for the first time the handshake is the customary greeting. Longtime friends may engage in a full embrace, which is called the *abrazo*. Women tend to greet with a kiss on the cheek rather than an *abrazo*. When meeting with someone, eye contact is important in Mexico. Not making eye contact implies boredom or disinterest. Certain gestures in America mean different things in Mexico. In Mexico, placing your hands in your pockets is considered impolite. It suggests that you are keeping a secret or hiding something from the person with whom you are talking. Standing with your hands on your hips is considered challenging and hostile to another Mexican. Understanding even a few key gestures from different cultures can make you a better communicator. So next time you travel, be culturally sensitive. Find out the local gestures, and let your body talk.

mojito: a traditional Cuban drink
pertenencia: belonging
vestimentas: clothing
trajes típicos: typical outfits, folk outfits
sobresale/sobresalir: she stands out/ to stand out
distinguidos: distinguished
la lleva/llevar: she wears it/to wear
derrocha/derrochar: she brims over/ to brim over
gracia: grace
andar: walking
atrae/atraer: she attracts/to attract
miradas: looks
se topa/toparse: she runs into/to run, bump into
camino: way

si bien: even though
país: country
existen/existir: there are/to be
principalmente: mainly
tipos: kinds
vestir de diario: everyday dress, everyday clothes
encajes: lace
gala: full dress
se usa/usar: it is used/to use
festejos: holidays
motivos: reasons
elaborada: elaborated
acompañando: together with
según: depending on

ancha: wide
confeccionada: made
tela: fabric
algodón: cotton
suele usarse: it is usually used
ambas: both
blusas: blouses
pegada: tight
suelta: loose
pueden ser/poder: they can be/can

La pollera panameña
PANAMA

La pollera es a Panamá, lo que el **mojito** es a Cuba, el tango a la Argentina, o el carnaval a Brasil: un orgullo, un símbolo de nacionalidad, identidad y **pertenencia**. Entre las **vestimentas** y **trajes típicos** del mundo, la pollera panameña **sobresale** como uno de los más espectaculares y **distinguidos**. La mujer que **la lleva derrocha gracia** en sus movimientos, elegancia en su **andar** y **atrae** las **miradas** de todo aquel con quien **se topa** en su **camino**.

Si bien hay variaciones en todas las regiones del **país**, **existen principalmente** dos **tipos** de polleras: la pollera montuna, que es la de **vestir de diario** o de trabajo; y la pollera de **encajes** o de **gala**, que es la que **se usa** para **festejos** o **motivos** importantes y que es una versión más **elaborada** de este vestido nacional. **Acompañando** a la pollera y, **según** el caso, las mujeres completan la vestimenta con diferentes accesorios.

La pollera montuna, **ancha** y **confeccionada** con **tela** calicó (de **algodón**), **suele usarse** con basquiñas o chambras: **ambas** son **blusas**, **pegada** al cuerpo la primera, y más **suelta** la segunda, que **pueden ser** blancas o de color.

Este **conjunto puede terminarse** con el **cabello** con **trenzas** y flores naturales, con un **sombrero de paja** o con **peinetas doradas** y algunos trembleques (flores **hechas a mano** que pueden ser de diferentes materiales, desde un **fino alambre enroscado** hasta **escamas** de **pescado** y **seda**).

La pollera de encajes, la más **lujosa** y delicada, ancha y con dos o tres divisiones, está muy decorada con **lanas** y **cintas**. Se usa con una blusa **amplia** de **lino** y también está confeccionada con **bordados** y encajes. Para vestir sus cabellos, las mujeres **lucen** este traje con peinetas importantes que pueden ser de **oro** y trembleques (generalmente blancos), en el resto de la cabeza.

Este **vestido de gala se adorna** con gran cantidad de **joyas**: **cadenas**, **aros**, **pulseras**, **anillos** y **hebillas** son sólo algunas de ellas, que pueden ser de oro, perlas o **piedras preciosas**. Los **zapatos se llaman** chapines y pueden ser de **satén** o **terciopelo**, en general, muy **planos** y con una hebilla de oro, encajes y cintas.

Históricamente no hay muchos **archivos**, ni **detalles** exactos que **revelen** el origen de la pollera panameña, **aunque** algunos **reconocen** sus **raíces** en España.

conjunto:	ensemble, set
puede terminarse/terminar:	it can end/to end
cabello:	hair
trenzas:	braids
sombrero de paja:	straw hat
peinetas:	accessory to hold up the hair
doradas:	golden
hechas a mano:	handmade
fino:	thin
alambre:	wire
enroscado:	coiled
escamas:	scales
pescado:	fish
seda:	silk
lujosa:	luxurious
lanas:	wools
cintas:	bands, strips
amplia:	large, wide
lino:	linen
bordados:	embroidery
lucen/lucir:	they wear/to wear with grace
oro:	gold
vestido de gala:	full dress
se adorna/adornar:	it is decorated/to decorate
joyas:	jewelry
cadenas:	chains
aros:	hoops, earrings
pulseras:	bracelets
anillos:	rings
hebillas:	buckles
piedras preciosas:	gems
zapatos:	shoes
se llaman/llamarse:	they are called/to be called
satén:	satin
terciopelo:	velvet
planos:	low, without heel
archivos:	files
detalles:	details
revelen/revelar:	they reveal/to reveal
aunque:	although
reconocen/reconocer:	they recognize/to recognize
raíces:	roots

El gaucho
URUGUAY

Se lo conoce como *cowboy* en Norteamérica, como llanero en Venezuela y como gaucho en la pampa argentina y en el Uruguay. Es, simplemente, el habitante típico de las zonas rurales en el continente americano. En Uruguay, el gaucho es una figura importante del folclore nacional ya que simboliza la **libertad** y la individualidad. Las representaciones poéticas del gaucho lo describen como el ideal de **valentía** e independencia. Pero **más allá** de cómo lo presenten la música, la literatura, y la **pintura**, este **personaje constituye** un símbolo importante dentro de la cultura uruguaya.

Si nos acercamos a la realidad, el gaucho es el **hombre de campo** que trabaja **principalmente arreando ganado**. En su imagen **estereotípica**, siempre **está acompañado** de un **caballo** que, además de servirle de transporte, es una de las pocas posesiones materiales que **se asocian** con el **modo de vida** gauchesco. **En la actualidad**, el caballo **sigue siendo** una pieza fundamental de las actividades que el gaucho **realiza** en el campo.

Tradicionalmente, el gaucho **contaba** también entre sus posesiones con el **facón** y las boleadoras, que le servían como **arma** y como **herramienta** de trabajo. El facón es un **cuchillo** largo que los gauchos **llevan** en la **espalda**, **colgando** del **cinturón**, para múltiples usos, ya sea para defensa personal, para comer, o para **cuerear** las **vacas**. Hoy en día siguen usándolo, principalmente, a la hora de trabajar. Las boleadoras son dos **piedras redondeadas** unidas por una **cuerda hecha** con **cuero trenzado**.

Una **hendidura** que **recorre** el exterior de las piedras **permite atar** la cuerda **de forma que** las piedras estén bien **aseguradas** y **no se escapen**. Los gauchos las **utilizaban** para **atrapar** al ganado **cimarrón** o salvaje y para **cazar ñandúes**. Actualmente las boleadoras ya no se usan porque el ganado es doméstico con lo cual este instrumento resulta innecesario.

El gaucho sigue siendo fácilmente **distinguible** por sus **vestimentas**. Usa bombachas o chiripá (un **pantalón de pierna ancha ajustado** a la **cintura** con una **faja** o **cinto**) que puede ser de **tela** o cuero con decoraciones en **plata** u otros metales. El **atuendo** se complementa con una **camisa** y **pañuelo al cuello**. Lleva también un **sombrero de ala ancha sujetado** al **mentón** con una **cinta** que le permite **cabalgar sin temor** a **perderlo**. El **abrigo** tradicional es el poncho, que resulta ideal para **mantener** el **calor** en las **madrugadas** frías en las que sale a cabalgar. En los pies usa **botas** de cuero, también **pensadas** para las **cabalgatas**, ya que debe **proteger** los pies y **piernas** del continuo **roce** con los **estribos**. Cuando no está encima de su caballo, el gaucho **puede verse** usando **alpargatas,** un tipo de calzado **llegado** de Europa.

En Montevideo, un museo **rinde homenaje** a la figura del gaucho. Allí se pueden **apreciar** representaciones tradicionales de este personaje durante sus **horas de ocio**, ya sea jugando a la taba (un juego típico del campo), tomando mate, o **fumando** un **cigarro armado** por él mismo.

En Tacuarembó, uno de los departamentos norteños del país, se conmemoran las **costumbres** gauchescas con la Fiesta de la Patria Gaucha en el mes de febrero o de marzo. Durante su celebración, a la que muchos de sus **asistentes concurren a caballo**, se realizan actividades tradicionalmente asociadas con las **tareas** del campo. Está presente la música folclórica con sus guitarras, así como el **asado con cuero**, y varias **pruebas de destreza** como las **jineteadas**, las domas y las cabalgatas. Este tipo de fiestas contribuye a **fomentar** la identidad nacional uruguaya, dentro de la que el gaucho conserva, aún hoy, un lugar **destacado**.

distinguible: easy to distinguish
vestimentas: clothing
pantalón: pants
de pierna ancha: wide leg
ajustado: tight
cintura: waist
faja: girdle
cinto: belt
tela: fabric
plata: silver
atuendo: attire
camisa: shirt
pañuelo: handkerchief
al cuello: around the neck
sombrero de ala ancha: wide-brimmed hat
sujetado: fixed
mentón: chin
cinta: lace
cabalgar: to ride
sin temor: without fear
perderlo/perder: losing it/to lose
abrigo: coat
mantener: to keep
calor: heat
madrugadas: early mornings
botas: boots
pensadas: thought, intended
cabalgatas: horseback rides
proteger: to protect
piernas: legs
roce: rubbing, friction
estribos: stirrups
puede verse: it can be seen
alpargatas: canvas sandals, espadrilles
llegado/llegar: arrived/to arrive

rinde homenaje/rendir homenaje: they pay homage/to pay homage
apreciar: to appreciate
horas de ocio: spare time
fumando/fumar: smoking/to smoke
cigarro: cigarrette
armado/armar: assembled/to assemble

costumbres: customs
asistentes: the public
concurren/concurrir: they converge/ to converge, to meet
a caballo: riding a horse
tareas: tasks
asado con cuero: beef that is roasted in its hide over an open fire
pruebas de destreza: skill contests
jineteadas: breaking-in (horses)
fomentar: to promote
destacado: outstanding

La carretanagua

NICARAGUA

Nicaragua es un país **muy arraigado** a tradiciones ancestrales, las cuales están presentes en **casi todas** sus costumbres y cultura. Muchas de estas tradiciones **encierran profundas creencias** en **personajes fantasmagóricos** o **brujas**, como La Mocuana, La Llorona y La Cegua. Pero **quizás** el **más conocido** y **temido** es el fantasma de La Carretanagua: una **desvencijada carreta tirada por flaquísimos** y **viejos bueyes** y **conducida** por La Muerte misma. La "Muerte Quirina", un terrorífico **esqueleto envuelto** en un **sudario** de **sábanas blancas**, **cargando** su **guadaña amenazadora** y **rodeada de calaveras**.

Algunos **aseguran** haber **padecido** una horrible **fiebre** luego de haberla visto, otros el haber perdido el habla por varios días. Dicen que **recorre** las **calles oscuras**, alrededor de la una de la **madrugada**, haciendo mucho **ruido** a su paso ya que **se trata de** una **carreta vieja** y **destartalada**. Los que la **oyen** pasar temen **asomarse** por las ventanas y **encontrarla** es que según la superstición, el día siguiente de haberla visto, está marcado con la muerte de alguno de los de su pueblo. La misteriosa carreta **se mueve** muy rápido y al llegar a las **esquinas desaparece**, **reapareciendo** sobre otra calle atemorizando a animales y creando **desasosiego** y **mucho miedo** entre la gente.

La Carretanagua (o Carreta Nagua) es un símbolo muy fuerte en la mitología y folklore nicaragüense, en la que **se amalgama** un **pasado doloroso** y una imaginación creativa y supersticiosa. Con ella **se recuerda** a las persecuciones y torturas que sufrían los indios a manos de los conquistadores. Dicen que en los tiempos de la colonia, en el Siglo XVI, los españoles llegaban a medianoche en carretas **buscando** oro y **riquezas** y **sacando** a los indios de sus **caseríos**; se los llevaban como esclavos **encadenados** a sus carretas. El mito de la Carretanagua **parece** haber nacido también de la necesidad de los nicaragüenses de **darle** forma material y concreta a un fenómeno tan incontrolable como la muerte.

El rodeo y los "huasos"
CHILE

"¡¡Arre!!" Entre todas las fiestas y **juegos** tradicionales, el rodeo es uno de los más **emocionantes**, **alegres** y **coloridos** de Chile. Se **originó** hace muchos años como consecuencia del **duro trabajo** de los **campesinos** y su necesidad de **ordenar** el **ganado**. Cada **primavera** los animales son **traídos** desde los **cerros**, donde pasan el **invierno**. Este trabajo debe ser realizado por los hombres más **fuertes** y **hábiles** en el **manejo del caballo** y del **lazo**: los huasos. Viven principalmente en valles fértiles o en **granjas** con tierras cultivadas y su **tarea** es **conducir** a los animales **bordeando** precipicios, cruzando ríos, **bajando y subiendo pendientes** hasta llegar al corral. En esta **travesía** muchos **vacunos** **se espantan** y **descarrían** por lo que los huasos tienen que correr **velozmente** tras ellos, **atajarlos** con sus lazos y **unirlos** otra vez al grupo.

Cada año se celebra en Chile el Campeonato Nacional de Rodeo. Este juego ha **ganado** mucha fama (algunas rivalidades) ya que aquí se **pone a prueba** la capacidad, **fortaleza física** y **destreza** de estos *cowboys* chilenos, que se caracterizan por su **orgullo**, **seguridad** y **picardía**. El colorido de sus **vestimentas** y la de sus caballos reflejan el espíritu de tradición: sombreros, pantalones generalmente **rayados**, **botas de cuero**, **espuelas adornadas** y **mantas** o ponchos de colores vistosos. El rodeo consiste básicamente en imitar el trabajo de estos campesinos: atajar y controlar al ganado. Los **jinetes** corren de a pares. El **novillo** que va a ser corrido se lleva a una **pista circular** con **portones** que permiten su entrada y salida. Para comenzar, un arreador con grito **estridente** provoca la **carrera** del animal que busca la salida del corral. Entonces, los huasos deben tratar de alcanzarlo y detenerlo en un punto determinado, **señalado** con una **bandera**. Con espíritu deportivo, el **fallo del jurado** es riguroso y estricto. Este paisaje de fiesta se completa con la música, los bailes tradicionales y **por supuesto**, con una gastronomía especial típica del lugar.

juegos: games
emocionantes: exciting
alegres: joyful
coloridos: colorful
originó/originar: started/to start
duro trabajo: hard work
campesinos: country men, farmers
ordenar: to arrange, put in order
ganado: livestock
primavera: spring
traídos/traer: brought/to bring
cerros: hills
invierno: winter
fuertes: strong
hábiles: skillful
manejo del caballo: handling the horses
lazo: lasso
granjas: farms
tarea: task
conducir: to take
bordeando/bordear: going round/to go round
bajando y subiendo: going down and going up
pendientes: slopes, inclines
travesía: trip
vacunos: cattle
se espantan/espantar: they get scared/to scare, to frighten
descarrían/descarriar: they go astray/to separate, to go astray
velozmente: quickly
atajarlos/atajar: intercept them, stop them/to intercept, to stop
unirlos/unir: join them/to join

ganado/ganar: it gained/to gain
pone a prueba: put to the test
fortaleza física: physical strength
destreza: skill
orgullo: pride
seguridad: confidence
picardía: craftiness
vestimentas: clothing
rayados: striped
botas de cuero: leather boots
espuelas adornadas: decorated spurs
mantas: blankets
jinetes: riders, horsemen
novillo: young bull
pista circular: circular court
portones: big gates
estridente: noisy, strident
carrera: race
señalado/señalar: marked/ to mark
bandera: flag
fallo del jurado: jury verdict
por supuesto: of course

Boticas mexicanas
MÉXICO

Antes de la llegada de los españoles a América, el **mundo indígena ya contaba con** un **desarrollado conocimiento** de las propiedades **curativas** de la fauna y flora locales con el que **habían desarrollado** procedimientos terapéuticos sistemáticos. **Prueba de** ello son **obras** como el Herbario, **escrito por** Martín de la Cruz y Juan Badiano, que **demuestra** la manera en que los indígenas nahuas **habían establecido cuadros clínicos bien definidos para identificar** síntomas de **enfermedades**. Estas enfermedades eran **tratadas con drogas** curativas que **se aplicaban** en forma de **polvos**, pociones, **ungüentos**, **emplastos** y **parches**.

En los dos **siglos siguientes** a la conquista española, **se produjeron** avances **surgidos de** la combinación del **saber médico** europeo y el indígena y **se escribieron** más textos médicos. **Pero pronto se hizo patente** la necesidad de contar con preparadores de medicinas que **combinaran** conocimientos médicos y de botánica con técnicas de laboratorio. Así fue como **surgieron** los **boticarios**, antecesores de los actuales **químicos farmacéuticos**.

Puesto que en la Nueva España, al igual que en Europa, **se regulaba** el **ejercicio** de las profesiones por **gremios**, **para mediados** del siglo XVII **se constituyó** el real Tribunal del Protomedicato como **examinador** de la labor de **barberos**, **parteras**, **cirujanos**, boticarios y **boticas**.

Las boticas eran establecimientos donde **se preparaban** los remedios **prescritos** por los **médicos**. **De acuerdo a** una costumbre **iniciada por** los árabes, eran visitadas regularmente por autoridades especializadas para **constatar** que las preparaciones farmacéuticas **se hicieran** de acuerdo a las fórmulas establecidas, inspeccionar las **pesas** y medidas **empleadas**, **quemar** las medicinas que **se encontraran alteradas** y **vigilar** la vigencia de las tarifas de los medicamentos.

---

antes de llegada: before the arrival
mundo indígena: indigenous world
ya contaba con: already had
desarrollado: developed
conocimiento: knowledge
curativas: healing
habían desarrollado: had developed
prueba de: proof of
obras: works
escrito por: written by
demuestra/demostrar: shows/to show
habían establecido: had established
cuadros clínicos: clinical profiles
bien definidos: well-defined
para identificar: in order to identify
enfermedades: diseases
tratadas con drogas: treated with drugs
se aplicaban/aplicar: were applied/ to apply
polvos: powders
ungüentos: ointments, salves
emplastos: poultices, dressings
parches: plasters, patches

siglos siguientes: following centuries
se produjeron/producir: took place/ to take place
surgidos de: emerged from
saber médico: medical knowledge
se escribieron/escribir: were written/ to write
pero pronto: but soon
se hizo patente: became obvious
combinaran/combinar: combined/ to combine
surgieron/surgir: appeared/to appear
boticarios: pharmacist, drugist
químicos farmacéuticos: pharmacists

puesto que: given that
se regulaba/regular: was regulated/ to regulate
ejercicio: practice, exercise
gremios: guilds, unions
para mediados: towards the mid
se constituyó/constituirse: was formed/to form
examinador: examiner
barberos: barbers
parteras: midwives
cirujanos: surgeons
boticas: chemists, druggists

se preparaban/preparar: they prepared/to prepare
prescritos: prescribed
médicos: doctors
de acuerdo a: according to
iniciada por: started by
constatar: (to) check, (to) confirm
se hicieran/hacer: were done/to do
pesas: weights
empleadas: used, utilized
quemar: (to) burn
se encontraran alteradas: were found to be altered (adulterated)
vigilar: (to) watch

Ya para el siglo XVIII, los boticarios **necesitaban** contar con un título legal para **ejercer** su profesión. **Para obtenerlo** necesitaban haber estado **bajo la tutela** de un maestro boticario **calificado** por un periodo de cuatro años, **saber** latín perfectamente, **tener nociones** de **física** y **química**, **aprobar** un curso teórico-práctico de botánica en el Real Jardín Botánico y presentar un examen ante el Protomedicato, **además de** contar con una constancia de **limpieza de sangre** y una **fe de bautismo**.

Las boticas en la Nueva España **podían ser privadas** e **instalarse** en cualquier **calle** de la ciudad **o bien encontrarse** en hospitales y conventos. Su relevancia **no se limitaba a** medicamentos: su **amplia gama** de productos **las convertía** en importantes centros para sus comunidades. También **proveían** a éstas de ingredientes estratégicos para **recetas de cocina** y **secretos de belleza**, **piedras preciosas**, algunas frutas, **raíces**, metales como **hierro**, **plomo** y **acero**, **sales**, **semillas**, **gomas**, **aceites**, **jarabes** y aguas.

En la Ciudad de México aún es posible encontrar boticas que **datan de** la década de 1940. Desafortunadamente **varias de ellas** están **enfrentando** serios problemas **para cumplir** con los estrictos requisitos sanitarios y la **feroz competencia** de las grandes **cadenas** farmacéuticas. Pocas son las que **han logrado combinar** la tradición con la modernidad. Entre ellas se encuentra la famosa Farmacia París, **ubicada** en el centro histórico de la ciudad, en **lo que fuera** el noviciado del Real Convento de San Agustín, uno de los conventos más grandes y exquisitos del **virreinato**.

La Farmacia París **se fundó** en 1944 y, conservada como **negocio familiar**, se encuentra en su tercera generación. Su **surtido** es tan grande que los defeños **están dispuestos a cruzar** toda la ciudad para ir a ella, puesto que **vende** desde fórmulas magistrales, medicamentos **elaborados específicamente** para cada individuo por un farmacéutico, hasta productos de herbolaria y homeopatía. Como si eso fuera poco, también vende artículos de perfumería y belleza, **tratamientos** dermatológicos, productos químicos y **envases**, instrumental médico, **quirúrgico** y de laboratorio, materiales ortopédicos, **libros especializados** en medicina e incluso **juguetes educativos.**

---

necesitaban/necesitar: needed/to need
ejercer: (to) practice
para obtenerlo: in order to obtain it
bajo la tutela: under the tutelage
calificado: qualified
saber: to know
tener nociones: to have notions
física: physics
química: chemistry
aprobar: to pass
además de: in addition to
limpieza de sangre: purity of bloodline
fe de bautismo: baptism certificate

podían ser privadas: could be private
instalarse: (be) installed, set up, settled
calle: street
o bien encontrarse: or (be) found
no se limitaba a: wasn't limited to
amplia gama: wide range
las convertía: made them into
proveían/proveer: provided/to provide
recetas de cocina: cooking recipes
secretos de belleza: beauty secrets
piedras preciosas: gemstones
raíces: roots
hierro: iron
plomo: lead
acero: steel
sales: salts
semillas: seeds
gomas: gums
aceites: oils
jarabes: syrups

datan de: date back to
varias de ellas: several of them
enfrentando/enfrentar: facing/to face
para cumplir: to conform, to abide
feroz competencia: cutthroat competition
cadenas: chains
han logrado combinar: have managed to combine
ubicada: located
lo que fuera: which was
virreinato: viceroyalty

se fundó/fundar: was founded/ to found
negocio familiar: family business
surtido: selection, supply, stock
están dispuestos a cruzar: are willing to cross
vende/vender: (it) sells/to sell
elaborados específicamente: prepared specifically
tratamientos: treatments
envases: containers
quirúrgico: surgical
libros especializados: specialized books
juguetes educativos: educational toys

Un país lleno de música
PARAGUAY

La **palabra "música" proviene del griego antiguo** *mousikē* que **quiere decir** "el arte de las **musas**". **Según** esta definición la música **sería** el arte de **organizar sensible** y **lógicamente sonidos** y silencios, **en forma armónica**, **melódica** y **rítmica**.

Como toda manifestación artística, es un producto cultural, **que tiene como objetivo expresar sentimientos**, **pensamientos** o ideas. Es un **estímulo** con varias funciones: **entretener**, **comunicar** o **ambientar** un **lugar**.

Para Paraguay y su **gente**, la música es una de las formas de expresión que **más los identifica** y con la que **tienen más apego**. Los instrumentos más populares son **el arpa** y la guitarra, y los **géneros** más **difundidos** son la **canción paraguaya** o purajhei**, la polca** y la guarania.

Esta última es una forma de canción paraguaya **creada**, en 1925, por el músico José Asunción Flores, **quien**, **con el propósito de encontrar** una música que **tradujera** el carácter del **pueblo** paraguayo, **combinó ritmos lentos** y melodías, **a veces** melancólicas y a veces **de carácter heroico**, **dando lugar a bellas canciones**.

La polca es **otro** de los géneros famosos. Es una danza y una canción de **movimiento rápido** y **acompasado** que tiene la **particularidad** de combinar **varios** ritmos, **diferenciándose así de** la polca europea.

---

palabra: word
música: music
proviene de: comes from
griego antiguo: ancient Greek
quiere decir: means
musas: muses
según: according to
sería/ser: would be/to be
organizar: to organize
sensible(mente): sensibly
lógicamente: logically
sonidos: sounds
en forma ... : in a ... way
armónica: harmonious
melódica: melodious
rítmica: rhythmical

como toda manifestación: as every manifestation
que tiene como objetivo: whose objective it is
expresar: to express
sentimientos: feelings
pensamientos: thoughts
estímulo: stimulus
entretener: to entertain
comunicar: to communicate
ambientar: to create atmosphere in, to liven up
lugar: place

gente: people
más los identifica: identifies them the most
tienen más apego: (they) feel more attachment to
arpa: harp
guitarra: guitar
géneros: genres
difundidos: spread
canción: song
paraguaya: Paraguayan
polca: polka

esta última: the last one
creada: created
quien: who
propósito de encontrar: for the purpose of finding
tradujera/traducir: would translate/ to translate
pueblo: people
combinó/combinar: (he) combined/ to combine
ritmos: rhythms
lentos: slow
a veces: sometimes
de carácter heroico: of a heroic nature
dando lugar a: producing
bellas: beautiful
canciones: songs

otro: another
movimiento: movement(s)
rápido y acompasado: fast and rhythmic
particularidad: peculiarity
varios: several
diferenciándose así de: differing in this way from

La canción paraguaya o *purajhei* es un **tipo de** música **derivada de** la polca paraguaya, **pero** con una **cadencia más lenta** que la **anterior**, y **cuyos textos generalmente** son en guaraní o jopará, una combinación de guaraní y español.

Otro género musical tradicional es la zarzuela, **inspirado** en la **zarzuela** española, **que tuvo** su **época** de **esplendor** en los **años** 50s y 60s pero que **luego fue perdiendo** popularidad.

El rasguido doble es otro tipo de música, **bien diferente**: un tipo de canción paraguaya derivado de la habanera (música **típica** de Cuba), de **gran difusión hacia fines del siglo** XIX y **principios** del XX. Su **nombre** proviene del **hecho** de que **se acompaña** con el **"rasguido"** de la guitarra y **se dan "dos" golpes** con la **mano derecha, cada dos compases**.

En cuanto a la danza, **no sólo existen** las polcas; también están las polcas galopadas. **Las primeras se bailan en parejas** y **las segundas, llamadas** *galoperas,* se bailan en grupo, de **mujeres más precisamente, llamadas** *galoperas* que **giran** en **círculos balanceándose de un lado a otro**. Otra variante es la danza de la botella, **donde** la **bailarina principal** baila **hasta con diez botellas en la cabeza**. También existen los *valseados*, que son la versión local de los **valses**.

Con todos estos **ejemplos podemos concluir** que el pueblo paraguayo, ¡**lleva** la música en la **sangre**!

tipo de: type of
derivada de: derived from
pero: but
cadencia: cadence
más lenta: slower
anterior: previous
cuyos: whose
textos: words, lyrics
generalmente: generally

inspirado: inspired
zarzuela: *traditional Spanish operetta*
que tuvo/tener: which had/to have
época: time, period
esplendor: splendor
años: years
luego: later
fue perdiendo: gradually lost

bien diferente: very different
típica: typical, traditional
de gran difusión: widely spread
hacia fines del siglo: towards the end of the century
principios: beginning
nombre: name
hecho: fact
se acompaña/acompañar: (it) is accompanied/to accompany
rasguido: strumming
se dan dos golpes: (the player) strikes (the guitar) twice
mano derecha: right hand
cada dos compases: every second beat

en cuanto a: as for
no sólo existen: there aren't only
las primeras: the formers
se bailan/bailar: are danced/to dance
en parejas: in pairs
las segundas: the latter
llamadas: called
mujeres: women
más precisamente: more exactly
giran/girar: go around/to go around, to spin
círculos: circles
balanceándose: swaying
de un lado a otro: from side to side
donde: where
bailarina principal: main (female) dancer
hasta con: with up to
diez: ten
botellas: bottles
en la cabeza: on her head
valses: waltzes

ejemplos: examples
podemos concluir: we can conclude
lleva/llevar: carries/to carry
sangre: blood

sin revelar: undisclosed
cada: each
país: country
los suyos: its own
esconde/esconder: hides/to hide
pasadas: past
quizás: perhaps
algún día: some day
se descubran/descubrir: will be
  discovered/to discover
tal vez: maybe
permanezcan ocultas/permanecer:
  will stay hidden /to stay
para siempre: forever
creo/creer: (I) think/to think
justamente: precisely
en desconocer: in not knowing
bolas de piedra: stone balls
hasta hoy: (up) until today
antiguas: old

se trata de: they are
cientos: hundreds
esferas: spheres
fueron encontradas/encontrar:
  were found/to find
selva: jungle
distintos parajes: various spots
al aire libre: in the open (air)
enterradas: buried
hasta: up to
casi: almost
toneladas: metric tons
peso: weight
hechas/hacer: made/to make
pulidas: polished
salieron/salir: (they) came from/
  to come from
las hizo/hacer: made them/to make
las puso allí/poner: put them there/
  to put
significan/significar: (they) mean/
  to mean
preguntas: questions
sin respuesta: without [an] answer
alientan/alentar: nourish/
  to nourish, to encourage
búsqueda: search

fueron removidas/remover: were
  removed/to remove
sitios: sites
actualmente: presently,
  at the moment
decoran/decorar: adorn/to adorn,
  to decorate
jardines: gardens
museos: museums
edificios: buildings

Piedras misteriosas
COSTA RICA

Misterios, secretos, enigmas **sin revelar**. **Cada país** tiene **los suyos**, cada región **esconde** intimidades **pasadas** que **quizás algún día se descubran** o **tal vez permanezcan ocultas para siempre**. **Creo** que parte de la magia reside, **justamente**, **en desconocer** sus orígenes, sus detalles. Las **bolas de piedra** de Costa Rica son, **hasta hoy**, uno de los tantos misterios de las civilizaciones **antiguas**.

Se trata de cientos de **esferas** que **fueron encontradas** en la **selva** costarricense, en **distintos parajes**, **al aire libre** o **enterradas**. Son de varias dimensiones: las hay de diez centímetros **hasta** más de dos metros de diámetro y **casi 15 toneladas** de **peso**. Están **hechas** en piedra, muy **pulidas**, casi sin imperfecciones. ¿De dónde **salieron**? ¿Quién **las hizo**? ¿Quién **las puso allí**? ¿Qué **significan**? **Preguntas sin respuesta** que **alientan** el espíritu de **búsqueda** de investigadores, historiadores y arqueólogos.

Las esferas **fueron removidas** de sus **sitios** originales y, **actualmente**, **decoran jardines** públicos, **museos**, **edificios** oficiales y colecciones privadas.

Se descubrieron en el sur del **país**, en el Delta del Diquís, la Península de Osa y la Isla del Caño. Fue **a fines de** la **década de los treinta**, **por casualidad**, cuando la compañía United Fruit **buscaba terrenos para desarrollar** plantaciones de bananas. **Desde entonces** y durante muchos años, estas **tierras fueron trabajadas, niveladas** y **explotadas** por esta **empresa** norteamericana, que **se ocupó de sacar** todos los obstáculos **de su camino** —**montículos** o **plataformas** donde **se apoyaban** las esferas, pequeños **muros** y las esferas **en sí**—, **para construir caminos, diques, zanjas** y **sistemas de riego**. Fue **recién** después de 10 años de su **descubrimiento** que alguien **se preocupó de comenzar** un **estudio sobre** ellas.

Los arqueólogos **estiman** que las piedras **fueron ubicadas** por los indígenas de la zona entre el 300 A.C y 300 D.C., pero su **trabajo escultórico no ha podido ser datado aún. En cuanto a** su **utilidad** o **significado** algunos **piensan** que fueron jardines astronómicos que tenían el **fin de medir** los **ciclos agrícolas**. Otros **creen** que **servían** para establecer el rango social **dentro de** una tribu. **Lo cierto es** que, **a pesar de todas** las investigaciones que **se hicieron** y **se siguen haciendo**, muchos de los enigmas originales **siguen sin resolverse**: ¿cómo **fueron trasladadas**?, ¿cómo **lograron** ese **pulido** casi perfecto?, ¿para qué y cómo **las usaban**?, ¿**se conocerán** estas respuestas **algún día**?

se descubrieron/descubrir: they were discovered/to discover
país: country
a fines de: towards the end of
década de los treinta: the thirties
por casualidad: by chance
buscaba/buscar: was looking for/ to look for
terrenos: land
para desarrollar: to develop
desde entonces: since then
tierras: lands
fueron trabajadas/trabajar: were worked/to work
niveladas/nivelar: leveled/to level
explotadas/explotar: exploited/to exploit
empresa: company
se ocupó de sacar: took upon itself the removal of
de su camino: in its way
montículos: mounds
plataformas: platforms
se apoyaban/apoyarse: were resting/to rest
muros: walls
en sí: themselves
para construir: (in order) to build
caminos: roads
diques: dams
zanjas: ditches, channels
sistemas de riego: irrigation systems
recién: only
descubrimiento: discovery
se preocupó de comenzar: bothered to start
estudio sobre: study on

estiman/estimar: estimate/to estimate
fueron ubicadas/ubicar: were placed/to place
trabajo escultórico: sculptural work
no ha podido ser datado aún: hasn't been dated yet
en cuanto a: as for
utilidad: usefulness
significado: meaning
piensan/pensar: think/to think
fin de medir: purpose of measuring
ciclos agrícolas: agricultural cycles
creen/creer: believe/to believe
servían/servir: (they) served/to serve
dentro de: within
lo cierto es: the truth of the matter is
a pesar de todas: despite all
se hicieron/hacer: was done/to do
se siguen haciendo: continues to be done
siguen sin resolverse: are still not solved
fueron trasladadas/trasladar: were (they) moved/to move
lograron/lograr: did (they) achieve/ to achieve
pulido: polish(ing)
las usaban/usar: did (they) use them/to use
se conocerán … /conocer: will … be known/to know
algún día: some day

Examina tu comprensión

Los vejigantes, página 4

1. ¿Cuál es el país de origen de los habitantes de la ciudad de Loiza?

2. El festival del 25 de julio representa ¿las mezclas de qué grupos?

3. ¿Qué se utiliza para hacer las máscaras vejigantes?

De tapeo, página 6

1. Además de comer, ¿cuáles son las normas de la tradición de las tapas?

2. ¿En qué provincia tiene lugar la leyenda de la tapa?

3. Cuando la tormenta de arena golpeó, ¿qué gran idea tuvo el camarero y por qué?

4. Describa o enumere los diferentes tipos de tapas.

La siesta en Argentina, página 8

1. ¿Cuál es el origen de la palabra siesta?

2. ¿Cuáles son algunos de los beneficios de la siesta para la salud?

3. Los expertos recomiendan una siesta ¿de cuántos minutos diarios?

Pescando con "caballos", página 10

1. En Huancacho los pescadores mantienen la costumbre preincaica de sus antepasados ¿haciendo qué?

2. ¿Durante cuántos años fue usado este antiguo barco pesquero?

3. Esta valiosa costumbre está en peligro de extinción debido ¿a qué tres cosas?

Test your comprehension

Los alebrijes, página 12

1. ¿De qué material están hechos los alebrijes?

2. ¿Qué tipos de figuras se representan en el arte alebrije?

3. Hay varias leyendas con respecto al origen de los alebrijes. ¿Cuál de ellas tiene más seguidores?

La pollera panameña, página 14

1. ¿Cuáles son los dos tipos diferentes de polleras y cuándo se usan?

2. ¿Qué materiales se usan para hacer las flores que se llevan en el sombrero de paja?

3. ¿Cómo se llaman los zapatos que se usan con la pollera y de qué tela están hechos?

4. ¿Cuál es el origen de la pollera?

El gaucho, página 16

1. ¿Qué simboliza el gaucho?

2. ¿De qué están hechas las boleadoras y qué propósito tienen?

3. Describa la ropa tradicional del gaucho.

El rodeo y los "huasos", página 19

1. ¿Por qué comenzó el rodeo?

2. ¿Qué tres cosas son puestas a prueba durante un rodeo?

Viajar es imprescindible y la sed de viaje,
un síntoma neto de inteligencia.

Enrique Jardiel Poncela

Viaje

ciudad: city
contrastes: contrasts
después de: after
paseo: walk
Barrio Gótico: Gothic Quarter
nos hace olvidar: makes us forget
altos edificios: high buildings
ruido: noise
coches: cars
es debido a: it is due to
posee/poseer: owns/to own, to possess
saber: to know
ocupa/ocupar: occupies/to occupy
lo que: what
hace siglos: centuries ago
torres semicirculares: semicircular towers
muralla: wall, battlement

podemos continuar: we can continue
su construcción: its construction
comenzó/comenzar: began/to begin
siglo XIII: 13th century
fachada: facade
el complejo de la Catedral: the cathedral complex
comprende/comprender: comprises/to comprise
palacios medievales: medieval palaces
desde allí: from there
recorrido: path
agradable: pleasant
paseo: walkway
cubierto: covered
llegaremos/llegar: we'll arrive/to arrive
Puente de los Suspiros: Bridge of Sighs
a continuación: next
veremos/ver: we'll see/to see
palacio: palace
Ayuntamiento: Town Hall
está rodeada/rodear: is surrounded/to surround
pasear: to take a walk
seguiremos/seguir: we'll follow/to follow
estrecha: narrow
llena de: full of
tiendas: shops
llegar: to arrive
una de las más nobles: one of the most honored, more aristocratic
para aquellos que quieran ver: for those who want to see
vista panorámica: panoramic view

consejo: advice
calzado cómodo: comfortable footwear

El barrio gótico de Barcelona
ESPAÑA

Barcelona es una **ciudad** de **contrastes**. Y **después de** visitar la ciudad moderna, un **paseo** por su **Barrio Gótico nos hace olvidar** los **altos edificios** y el **ruido** de los **coches**. El nombre de esta zona **es debido a** los monumentos góticos que **posee**. Pero es interesante **saber** que este barrio **ocupa lo que** fue, **hace siglos**, una antigua ciudad romana. Aquí, podemos visitar la "Plaza Nova", con dos **torres semicirculares** de la antigua **muralla** romana.

Podemos continuar nuestro paseo con una visita a la Catedral. **Su construcción comenzó** en el **siglo XIII**, y su **fachada** es del siglo XIX. **El complejo de la Catedral comprende** tres **palacios medievales**: Cases dels Canonges, Casa del Degà y Casa de l'Ardiaca. **Desde allí**, tenemos un bonito **recorrido**: después del Cloister, un **agradable paseo cubierto**, **llegaremos** al **Puente de los Suspiros** y a la Plaza de San Jaume. **A continuación**, **veremos**, en esta plaza, dos edificios: el "Palau de la Generalitat" o "**Palacio** de la Generalidad" y el **Ayuntamiento**. La Plaza de San Jaume **está rodeada** de estrechas calles, ideales para **pasear**. A continuación, **seguiremos** una **estrecha** calle **llena de tiendas**, para **llegar** a la Plaza del Rey. Esta plaza es **una de las más nobles** de Barcelona. Aquí, podemos visitar el Museo de Historia y también el Mirador del Rei Martí, **para aquellos que quieran ver** una **vista panorámica** del Barrio Gótico.

Y un **consejo**: ¡el **calzado cómodo** es esencial!

Humacao
PUERTO RICO

"**La perla del oriente**" o "La ciudad **gris**" son algunos de los nombres con los que **se conoce** el pueblo de Humacao, Puerto Rico. Esta pequeña **localidad**, **ubicada** en la **costa este** de la isla, **toma su nombre** del indio **taino** que la gobernaba **en tiempos de la conquista española**. Los nativos de este pueblo se denominan **humacaenos**.

Humacao tiene **cerca de** 59.000 habitantes **repartidos por** sus 15 **vecindarios**. Este pueblo es **rico** en **playas hermosas**. Uno de los hoteles más famosos y exclusivos de la isla **se encuentra** allí, el Hotel Palmas del Mar. Humacao también posee museos y un **enorme** observatorio **desde** donde se pueden ver las **galaxias más lejanas**. En Humacao se produce café, **arroz**, tabaco y **aceite de castor** pero su **mayor industria**, evidentemente, es el turismo.

El 8 de diciembre se celebran las **fiestas a la Santa Patrona**: La Inmaculada Concepción de Maria. El **primer fin de semana** de septiembre todos los humacaenos y **visitantes disfrutan** del **Festival de la Pana** durante el que **se organizan** eventos musicales, **deportivos** y culturales, y durante el que **se cocinan** muchas **recetas típicas**. ¿**Hechas** con que? Con pana, **por supuesto**. La **próxima vez** que **vengan** a Puerto Rico, visiten nuestra "perla del oriente".

la perla del oriente: the pearl of the orient (east)
gris: gray
algunos: some
nombres: names
se conoce/conocerse: it's known/ to be known
localidad: locality, town
ubicada: located
costa este: east coast
toma su nombre/tomar: takes its name/to take
taino: natives from the island of Puerto Rico
en tiempos de la conquista española: in times of the Spanish conquest
humacaenos: natives from Humacao

cerca de: close to
repartidos por: spread about
vecindarios: neighborhoods
rico: rich
playas hermosas: beautiful beaches
se encuentra/encontrarse: it is located/to be located
enorme: huge
desde: from
galaxias más lejanas: farthest galaxies
arroz: rice
aceite de castor: castor oil
mayor industria: main industry

fiestas a la Santa Patrona: Patron Saint celebrations
primer fin de semana: first weekend
visitantes: visitors
disfrutan/disfrutar: enjoy/to enjoy
Festival de la Pana: The Breadfruit Festival
se organizan/organizar: they are organized/to organize
deportivos: sports
se cocinan/cocinar: they are cooked/ to cook
recetas típicas: typical recipes
hechas: made
por supuesto: of course
próxima vez: next time
vengan/venir: they come/to come

pasear: to go for a walk
calles empedradas: cobblestone streets
placer: pleasure
disfrutan/disfrutar: they enjoy/
  to enjoy
tanto...como: both ... and
lugareños: locals
cualquier: any
estación: season

fines de semana: weekends
se llena/llenarse: it gets plenty/
  to get plenty
cruzan/cruzar: they cross/to cross
ropa: clothes
confeccionada: made
lana: wool
cuero: leather
asimismo: likewise, in the same way
puestos: stands
artesanía: craft
se ubican/ubicarse: they are located/
  to be located
alrededor: around
posavasos: coasters
repujado: embossed
caja: box
alfajores: South American cookie
pendientes: earrings
amatista: amethyst
guantes: gloves
gorro: hat
hechos a mano: handmade
quizás: perhaps
incluso: even
juguetes de madera: wooden toys
todos los gustos: any taste, all tastes

compras: shopping
lo mejor: the best
hacer una parada: to stop
aunque: although
tales como: such as
caseras: homemade
carne asada: roasted meat
cazuelas: stewing pans
ensopados: soups
empanados: breaded
fritos: fried
postres: desserts
elegir: to choose
solicitados: popular, in great demand
caminata: long walk
almuerzo: lunch
recuperar fuerzas: to get energy or
  strength back

gustan de/gustar de: they like/to like
están de suerte: they are lucky
fue fundada/fundar: to be founded/
  to found
ganar: to gain

Colonia del Sacramento
URUGUAY

Pasear por las **calles empedradas** del barrio viejo de Colonia del Sacramento es un **placer** del que **disfrutan tanto lugareños como** turistas en **cualquier estación** del año.

Los **fines de semana**, Colonia **se llena** de argentinos que **cruzan** en barco desde la cercana Buenos Aires a disfrutar el ritmo tranquilo de sus calles y plazas. Los turistas recorren las tiendas de productos típicos, generalmente **ropa confeccionada** con **lana** o **cuero**. **Asimismo**, visitan los **puestos** de **artesanía** que **se ubican alrededor** de las plazas, en los que es difícil decidirse: ¿Unos **posavasos** de cuero **repujado** o una **caja** de **alfajores**? ¿Unos **pendientes** en **amatista** o unos **guantes** y **gorro** de lana **hechos a mano**? **Quizás incluso** unos **juguetes de madera** para los niños, hechos por artesanos locales. Hay para **todos los gustos**.

Después de las **compras** de la mañana, **lo mejor** es **hacer una parada** en alguno de los restaurantes locales. **Aunque** son pequeños preparan deliciosos platos típicos, **tales como** pastas **caseras**, **carne asada**, pescados y otros productos del mar, en **cazuelas** y **ensopados** o **empanados** y **fritos**. Para los **postres**, uno puede **elegir** flan con dulce de leche o ensalada de frutas con helado. Si bien estos dos postres son sólo dos de las opciones disponibles, son también, sin lugar a dudas, los más **solicitados**. Después de la **caminata** y el **almuerzo**, nada mejor que una siesta para **recuperar fuerzas**.

Por la tarde, los que **gustan de** la historia **están de suerte**. Colonia del Sacramento **fue fundada** por los portugueses en 1680 como forma de **ganar** territorio americano a los españoles.

Colonia es, pues, la ciudad más **antigua** del Uruguay **actual** y **ha sido nombrada** como *Patrimonio Histórico de la Humanidad* por la UNESCO gracias a su valor cultural. Como tal, **cuenta con** varios museos. Uno de los mejores es el Museo de los **Azulejos**, que **posee** una hermosa colección de *azulejos* portugueses. Uno de los aspectos más interesantes del museo es el **edificio** en el que **está alojado**: una casa antigua y bien preservada, de **paredes anchísimas** y **puertas** y **techos bajos**, característicos de la **época**.

Colonia tiene también algo que **ofrecer** a los **enamorados**. Muchas parejas de novios eligen celebrar aquí su **boda** por la belleza de su **iglesia principal**, la Iglesia Matriz, la más antigua del país. **Si bien** es pequeña y simple, el **entorno** de las calles empedradas y los siglos de historia que **la rodean le dan un aire especial**. No es raro **toparse**, al **pasar** cerca de la iglesia, con un grupo de **festejantes tirando arroz** a los **novios**. Quienes quieran **pasar** la **luna de miel** en Colonia tienen una buena opción en los hoteles antiguos de la ciudad que, con sus patios internos y sus **fuentes**, sus **portones** de **hierro forjado** y sus **enredaderas**, **proporcionan** un **ambiente** romántico único.

Al **atardecer**, la opción más popular es ir a comprar unos **bizcochos** en la **panadería** y salir, con el mate **bajo el brazo**, a caminar por el **puerto** en compañía de amigos o familia. Situado sobre el Río de la Plata, el pequeño puerto **alberga botes** y **barcos veleros**, turistas que deciden **llegar por mar** con su propio transporte, o lugareños que disfrutan **saliendo** a **pescar río arriba**. El puerto es también el sitio ideal para ir a pescar y son muchos los que **aprovechan** la oportunidad. Pero tanto para navegantes como para pescadores y turistas, **deleitarse** con la **puesta del sol** sobre el río, entre los barcos, es siempre el **cierre** perfecto para un fin de semana en Colonia de Sacramento.

---

antigua: old
actual: nowadays
ha sido nombrada/nombrar: it has been nominated/to nominate
cuenta con/contar con: it has/to have
azulejos: tiles
posee/poseer: it has/to have
edificio: building
está alojado: it is housed
paredes: walls
anchísimas: very wide
puertas: doors
techos: ceilings
bajos: low
época: period, time

ofrecer: to offer
enamorados: lovers
boda: wedding
iglesia principal: main church
si bien: although
entorno: environment
la rodean/rodear: they surround it/ to surround
le dan un aire especial: they make it special
toparse: to bump into
pasar: to walk by
festejantes: the people celebrating
tirando/tirar: throwing/to throw
arroz: rice
novios: the bride and groom
pasar: to spend
luna de miel: honeymoon
fuentes: fountains
portones: hall doors
hierro forjado: wrought iron
enredaderas: creeper, climbing plant
proporcionan/proporcionar: they provide/to provide
ambiente: atmosphere

atardecer: evening, dusk, sunset
bizcochos: cake
panadería: bakery
bajo el brazo: under one's arm
puerto: harbor
alberga/albergar: it harbors/to harbor
botes: small boats
barcos veleros: sailing boats
llegar por mar: to arrive by sea
saliendo/salir: leaving/to leave
pescar: to fish
río arriba: up the river
aprovechan/aprovechar: they take advantage of/to take advantage of
deleitarse: to take delight
puesta del sol: sunset
cierre: close

Verano en enero y febrero
ARGENTINA

Explotó el **calor**, los **días son mucho más largos** y en la **calle** se ven **minifaldas, escotes** y **bermudas**. La **temporada alta estival** en Argentina se vive con **alegría** y con la mirada puesta en el mar. **Miles de familias** preparan su **equipaje** en el que **nunca falta** el **traje de baño**, la **toalla** y el **bronceador, listos** para unas vacaciones en la **playa**.

La provincia de Buenos Aires **ofrece** múltiples **opciones** para los turistas decididos a pasar unos días sobre la **arena**. **A no más de** 400 kilómetros de la capital, se encuentran las **principales ciudades balnearias**. Mar del Plata, Pinamar, Cariló o Villa Gessell **son algunas** de las más **concurridas**.

Con un **mar** con temperatura para **valientes**, pero con playas **anchísimas** y largas, estas ciudades se caracterizan **no sólo** por una costa generosa **para disfrutar** durante el día, **sino también** por una gran diversidad de entretenimiento y **salidas nocturnas**.

Mar del Plata es **la más grande** y la que cuenta con más **desarrollo. Caminar** o hacer *footing* por la **rambla** a la **vera del mar, sentarse a mirar** las **destrezas** de los **surfistas** o **tirarse** como un **lagarto al sol** son algunas de las **actividades diurnas**.

Por las noches, puede verse a **gente colorada por el sol**, **probando suerte** en el casino, **haciendo cola para entrar** en alguno de los **espectáculos teatrales** o **disfrutando de un café** en algunas de las **terrazas al aire libre**, siempre y cuando el **viento marino** lo permita. Pinamar y Cariló con un aire más señorial, combinan la playa con el **bosque**, la **arena amarilla** con la **madera oscura** de los **árboles**. Una **mezcla mágica** para quienes buscan **relajarse** y **pasar unos días** al lado del mar **en plena naturaleza**.

Y para los **adolescentes** que quieren divertirse, las playas ventosas pero **menos frías** de Villa Gessell son la mejor opción. **Allí**, durante el día, se pueden realizar todo tipo de actividades y **deportes** playeros, **mientras** que por la noche es el momento de **acudir** a recitales, **espectáculos callejeros** y **discotecas** para **bailar hasta el amanecer**.

gente colorada por el sol: sunburned people
probando/probar: trying/to try
suerte: luck
haciendo cola para entrar: making a line to enter
espectáculos teatrales: theatre shows
disfrutando de un café/disfrutar: enjoying coffee/to enjoy
terrazas al aire libre: outdoor balcony or terrace
viento marino: ocean wind
bosque: forest
arena amarilla: yellow sand
madera oscura: dark wood
árboles: trees
mezcla mágica: magical mix
relajarse: to relax
pasar unos días: to spend days
en plena naturaleza: in the middle of nature

adolescentes: teenagers
menos frías: less cold
allí: there
deportes: sports
mientras: whereas
acudir: to go
espectáculos callejeros: street shows
discotecas: discotheques, clubs
bailar hasta el amanecer: dance until dawn

CULTURE NOTE

More and more people have realized that you do not have to be in college to "study abroad." People of all ages and all walks of life are discovering the benefits and enjoyment of turning a vacation into an opportunity to study Spanish. Learning Spanish is more than learning the world's second most-used language. It can also turn an average vacation into an extraordinary one, making friends from all over the world while truly immersing yourself in another culture. The global boom in cultural tourism has resulted in a vast selection of language schools and tour packages. The company we turn to again and again is AmeriSpan. They customize each program to fit your needs. They have various language programs all around the world, for all ages and all Spanish levels, from beginning to advanced. You can read about their programs and in-depth destination reviews at: www.amerispan.com. *¡Buen viaje!*

Mallorca y sus castillos
ESPAÑA

Las **Islas Baleares**, archipiélago **situado** en el Mar Mediterráneo, **son conocidas** por su **belleza** pero, **sobre todo**, por ser un **destino** turístico de **interés** internacional. Sus **instalaciones** hoteleras y sus playas son el primer objetivo  **para aquellos que buscan sol** y **diversión**. Pero en estas islas y, especialmente en Mallorca, existen **antiguos** monumentos y castillos, **cuya** visita es **de obligado cumplimiento**.

Comenzando desde el Castillo de Alaró, situado en la **cumbre de la montaña** que lleva el **mismo nombre**, en la **Sierra** Tramuntana, hasta castillos como el del Rey o el de Santueri, Mallorca tiene una **variada** oferta turística y cultural.

A tres kilómetros de Palma de Mallorca (**principal ciudad** de la isla de Mallorca) y a unos 140 metros de **altitud**, **rodeado** por un **bosque de pinos**, está el **castillo gótico** de Bellver (significa "buena **vista**"), muy peculiar **debido a** su forma totalmente circular. **Fue construido** en el año 1300, aproximadamente. El rey Jaime I, **aquejado** de tuberculosis, **quiso** construir este castillo para **descansar** en un **entorno sano**. El **corto periodo** de **tiempo empleado** para la construcción de este castillo (40 años), dio **como resultado** su peculiar **estilo arquitectónico**.

Un gran patio circular forma el centro del castillo, **alrededor del que se encuentran habitaciones** y **salas**. Tiene cuatro **torres**, **la mayor** y con base circular, **se llama** la Torre del **Homenaje**; el resto tienen forma de **herradura**. **De hecho**, este es el **único** castillo de planta circular de toda Europa. **Actualmente**, las **piedras** de este castillo son muy blancas. El motivo de tan peculiar aspecto es que en el **pasado**, **concretamente** en el siglo XIX, **tuvieron que limpiar** la **fachada** del castillo, pues **había sido quemado** como **método de desinfección** para **acabar** con una **plaga de peste**.

Este castillo ha tenido múltiples usos. **En un principio**, fue la residencia de Jaime II de Mallorca, pero **posteriormente fue utilizado** como **refugio** contra la plaga de peste; como **puesto de defensa** contra los ataques del **ejército** turco; como escenario para fiestas y representaciones teatrales, o incluso como **cárcel** hasta el siglo XX. **Pasear** sobre la **ancha** circunferencia de la **parte superior** del castillo y **mirar hacia abajo**, hacia el patio interior, es realmente espectacular.

En el interior del Castillo de Bellver interior se encuentra el Museo de la Ciudad, que **abarca** la historia de esta isla desde la Prehistoria hasta la **Edad Media**. Sin duda, lo que más **vale la pena** es la espectacular panorámica que **nos ofrece**.

alrededor del que: around which
se encuentran/encontrarse: there are/to be
habitaciones: rooms
salas: halls
torres: towers
la mayor: the biggest
se llama/llamarse: it is called/to call
homenaje: tribute
herradura: horseshoe
de hecho: in fact
único: unique
actualmente: nowadays
piedras: stones, rocks
pasado: past
concretamente: specifically
tuvieron que/tener que: they had to/to have to
limpiar: to clean
fachada: facade
había sido quemado/quemar: it had been burnt/to burn
método de desinfección: method of disinfection
acabar: to finish
plaga de peste: bubonic plague

en un principio: at first
posteriormente: later
fue utilizado/utilizar: it was used/ to use
refugio: refuge, shelter
puesto de defensa: place of defense
ejército: army
cárcel: prison, jail
pasear: to walk, to go for a walk
ancha: wide
parte superior: top
mirar hacia abajo: to look downwards

abarca/abarcar: it includes/to include
Edad Media: Middle Ages
vale la pena: it is worth it
nos ofrece/ofrecer: it offers us/to offer

Un paraíso en el Caribe
REPÚBLICA DOMINICANA

En los últimos años, la República Dominicana **se ha convertido** en uno de los **principales destinos** del Caribe, **tanto** para los turistas **procedentes de** América **como** para los europeos. Y **no es de extrañar**, pues cuenta con su exotismo caribeño, con el carácter **abierto** y **acogedor** de sus **gentes** y con un **entorno** natural de increíble **belleza**.

La isla española, que **pertenece** a las Grandes Antillas, está dividida en dos zonas: la República Dominicana y Haití. La República Dominicana ocupa **dos tercios** de la **superficie** de la isla, la cual está **formada** en un 80 **por ciento** por **montañas**. La montaña más alta es Pico Duarte, con unos 3.170 metros. La geografía de este país es muy diversa: **desde planicies** semidesérticas **a** valles con **bosques tropicales**. **Así**, algunos turistas **prefieren** las playas de **arena dorada** que **se extienden** sobre un tercio de la costa dominicana. Es en esta zona donde **se encuentran** los principales centros turísticos. La provincia de Barahona **incluye** cascadas, montañas y unas extensas playas de agua **cristalina**. **Entre** sus hábitats naturales está el Lago Enriquillo, el más grande de las Antillas.

La Romana fue un gran **puerto azucarero** hasta los años 70. Allí **encontraremos** Casa de Campo, uno de los **balnearios** más famosos del mundo. Y si **queremos** visitar Altos de Chavón, el pueblo de los artistas, **disfrutaremos** de un entorno similar a los pequeños pueblos del sur de Francia, a la **orilla del río** Chavón.

---

en los últimos años: in the last few years

se ha convertido/convertirse: it has become/to become

principales: main

destinos: destinations

tanto...como: both ... and

procedentes de: arriving from, coming from

no es de extrañar: it is hardly surprising

abierto: open

acogedor: warm

gentes: people

entorno: environment

belleza: beauty

pertenece/pertenecer: it belongs/ to belong

dos tercios: two thirds

superficie: surface

formada/formar: formed/to form

por ciento: percent

montañas: mountains

desde...a: from ... to

planicies: plains

bosques tropicales: tropical forests

así: so

prefieren/preferir: they prefer/ to prefer

arena dorada: golden sand

se extienden/extenderse: they get extended/to get extended

se encuentran/encontrarse: they are found/to be found

incluye/incluir: it includes/to include

cristalina: crystal clear

entre: among

puerto azucarero: sugar port

encontraremos/encontrar: we will find/to find

balnearios: natural spas

queremos/querer: we want/to want

disfrutaremos/disfrutar: we'll enjoy/ to enjoy

orilla del río: river bank

Para los **amantes** de la costa, Playa Grande pone a su disposición unas 300 hectáreas de vegetación de 1.500 metros de playa. También pueden disfrutar de su campo de golf a **orillas del mar**. Pero no debemos **olvidar** Punta Cana, con sus playas de agua **azulada**, y **muy próxima** a Playa Grande está Bávaro, con sus hoteles, a pocos minutos del aeropuerto de Punta Cana.

Otro tipo de visitantes prefiere visitar el interior, pues **piensan** que aquí pueden encontrar el **verdadero encanto** de la República Dominicana. La isla **está atravesada** por tres impresionantes **cordilleras**, **paralelas** en **sentido** Este-Oeste. Por un lado, está la Cordillera Central, que se extiende desde Haití hasta San Cristóbal, cerca de Santo Domingo. En esta cordillera se encuentra el Pico Duarte. Por otro lado, más al norte, se encuentra la Cordillera Septentrional, que atraviesa el valle de Cibao, donde están las **antiguas minas de oro**. Por último, la Cordillera Oriental se encuentra en el Este y es la más pequeña. Un **dato reconfortante** es que en **la mayoría de** las islas caribeñas no hay **serpientes venenosas** ni insectos **cuya picadura** o **agujón** sean una **amenaza** vital. Si usted planea visitar la República Dominicana, **tenga en cuenta** que, aunque su **lengua** oficial es el español, en las principales zonas turísticas muchos dominicanos hablan inglés y **alemán**, y **algunos** conocen también el francés y el italiano. Pero si usted decide visitar la zona interior, allí los residentes solamente hablan español, así que es conveniente que usted tenga unos **conocimientos** básicos de este **idioma**.

Entre los principales atractivos de la República Dominicana destacan su clima subtropical, con una **temperatura media** de 28 **grados centígrados** y sus playas de agua azul turquesa, con palmeras que ofrecen una reconfortante **sombra**. **Además de** su **envidiable entorno natural**, en los últimos años el Departamento de Turismo dominicano **ha incrementado** la **oferta** de **nuevas** formas de turismo.

amantes: lovers
orillas del mar: seashore
olvidar: to forget
azulada: bluish
muy próxima: very close

piensan/pensar: they think/to think
verdadero: true
encanto: charm
está atravesada/atravesar: it is crossed/to cross
cordilleras: mountain ranges
paralelas: parallel
sentido: sense
antiguas minas de oro: ancient gold mines
dato: piece of information
reconfortante: comforting
la mayoría de: most of
serpientes venenosas: poisonous snakes
cuya: whose
picadura: bite
agujón: sting
amenaza: threat
tenga en cuenta/tener en cuenta: take into account/to take into account
lengua: tongue, language
alemán: German
algunos: some of them
conocimientos: knowledge
idioma: language

temperatura media: average temperature
grados centígrafos: degrees Celsius
sombra: shade
además de: as well as
envidiable: enviable
entorno natural: natural environment
ha incrementado/incrementar: it has increased/to increase
oferta: offer
nuevas: new

Varadero, arenas blancas
CUBA

La **privilegiada ubicación** de Cuba hace que sus **playas** transparentes y **cálidas** sean una atracción para turistas de **todo el mundo** durante los 365 días del año. Varadero, **conocida como** "la playa preferida por su sol", **se encuentra** en Matanzas, provincia cuyas costas **descansan** en el océano Atlántico y el Mar Caribe. En Varadero, el sol **ilumina** la **arena** durante unas 12 horas diarias y la temperatura es de, aproximadamente, 25 **grados centígrados**. **Al oeste**, esta provincia limita con La Habana; al este, con Villa Clara, y al sudeste, con Cienfuegos.

¿Por qué son tan especiales las playas de Varadero? ¿Qué las diferencia de las otras **orillas cubanas**? Sus **fondos marinos**. **Poseen** más de 40 clases de corales, una increíble diversidad de **peces**, **langostas**, **camarones**, **cangrejos**, tortugas y casi un **centenar de moluscos**. En este pequeño **paraíso** cubano, la arena es blanca y **fina** y la costa, de 22 kilómetros de longitud, **despliega** una **paleta de azules** inimaginables en el horizonte. Aunque en Varadero la belleza del Caribe se despliega a cada paso, cada una de sus playas ofrece particularidades que las **distinguen**. Playa Coral **nos ofrece** más de 30 especies de corales, mientras que Cueva de Saturno es una caverna en la que **podemos encontrar estalactitas y estalagmitas**. Las Mandarinas posee una variada **fauna marina** en la que **abundan** los peces coralinos, las **morenas** y los **meros**.

Playa Caribe **nos invita** a la aventura ya que en ella se encuentran los secretos y misterios de un **antiguo barco alemán** que **naufragó** en la costa cubana. Por su parte, Punta Perdiz posee uno de los ecosistemas más diversificados del Mar Caribe y **se ubica** en la popular **Bahía de Cochinos**.

Por último, El Cenote tiene un gran **lago** y **grietas** en las que es posible **sumergirse** hasta 25 metros. Es importante **destacar** que esta playa se encuentra en la Ciénaga de Zapata, uno de los mayores y mejor preservados **humedales** de la región.

Pero Varadero no es sólo sus playas. A aquellos interesados en **tomar contacto** con las **raíces populares** de la región, posiblemente les interesará visitar la Cueva de Ambrosio en la que se encuentran **dibujos rupestres realizados** por aborígenes y, **se supone**, también por **esclavos**. La Casa de la Cultura también **nos permite aproximarnos** a la cultura popular cubana ya que es allí donde los artistas locales **exponen** sus **mejores obras**. Además, los **fines de semana** es posible ver **obras de teatro** y **espectáculos**. **Y si** de **aprender** a bailar **se trata**, este centro cultural ofrece **clases de baile** dictadas por profesores que **brindan** sus servicios a los turistas.

En el Museo Municipal de Varadero la ciudad **guarda viejos secretos**. Allí **se exhiben piezas claves** de la cultura y la historia. La arquitectura del museo **rescata** el **estilo** tradicional de muchas construcciones de la zona **combinando** la textura de la **madera** con colores vibrantes. **Sin lugar a dudas**, Varadero, este pequeño paraíso cubano, nos ofrece la posibilidad de **disfrutar** de unas de las playas **más hermosas** del mundo y de la **riqueza** y **encanto** de la cultura del Caribe.

por último: finally
lago: lake
grietas: fissures, cracks
sumergirse: to immerse oneself, to dive
destacar: to stress, to emphasize
humedales: wetlands

tomar contacto: to contact
raíces populares: popular roots
dibujos rupestres: cave drawings
realizados/realizar: made/ to make
se supone/suponer: it is supposed/to suppose
esclavos: slaves
nos permite/permitir: it allows us/to allow
aproximarnos/aproximarse: approaching/to approach
exponen/exponer: they expose/ to expose
mejores obras: best art pieces, best works
fines de semana: weekends
obras de teatro: theatre works
espectáculos: shows
y si: and if
aprender: to learn
se trata/tratarse: it is about/ to be about
clases de baile: dance classes
brindan/brindar: they offer/ to offer

guarda/guardar: it preserves/ to preserve
viejos secretos: old secrets
se exhiben/exhibir: they are exhibited/to exhibit
piezas claves: key pieces
rescata/rescatar: it rescues/ to rescue
estilo: style
combinando/combinar: combining/to combine
madera: wood
sin lugar a dudas: without a doubt
disfrutar: to enjoy
más hermosas: most beautiful
riqueza: wealth
encanto: charm

Cali, ¡qué ciudad!
COLOMBIA

Algunos la llaman "**la sucursal del cielo**". **Quizás se deba a** su **clima primaveral durante** todo el año, a la **alegría** de su **gente** o al espíritu de fiesta que se siente en **cada rincón** de la **ciudad** y que estalla en los últimos días del año durante la Feria de Cali.

En Cali la temperatura **mínima apenas toca** los 19°C y la máxima **llega** a los 34°C. La temperatura media en la ciudad es de 26°C y la ciudad **se encuentra** a más de 1000 metros **sobre el nivel del mar**. En la región **se conoce** a sus habitantes por su carácter **amable**, **alegre** y **relajado**. El clima **hace que** los **domingos** todos **salgan a pasear** a la costa y, si el día **lo permite**, **darse un chapuzón** en el **río** Cauca. Por las **noches**, durante todo el año **se respira** el clima de fiesta. **Al caer la tarde** los bares **se abren** y la música **toma** la **calle**. Todos **quieren salir** a **bailar** o, al menos, a **dar una vuelta**.

Aunque muchos la llaman "la capital de la rumba", es importante **destacar** el peso que su economía y su industria tienen en la economía del **país** y el gran **aporte** que su cultura significa para las industrias culturales.

Cali **se destaca además** por ser el segundo núcleo urbano de Colombia por su **cantidad** de habitantes. Además, **posee** un importante centro industrial y comercial. **Cuenta con** una importante oferta educativa que moviliza las migraciones de **jóvenes** que **llegan para cursar** sus estudios **probar suerte** en el **mercado laboral**.

---

algunos: some
la llaman/llamar: call it/to call
la sucursal del cielo: heaven's branch
quizás: perhaps
se deba a/deberse a: is due to/ to be due to
clima primaveral: spring-like climate
durante: during
alegría: joy
gente: people
cada rincón: every corner
ciudad: city

mínima: minimum
apenas: barely
toca/tocar: touches/to touch
llega/llegar: reaches/to reach
se encuentra/encontrarse: is/to be (located)
sobre el nivel del mar: above sea level
se conoce/conocer: are known/ to be known
amable: friendly, kind, nice
alegre: joyful
relajado: relaxed
hace que: makes, causes
domingos: Sundays
salgan a pasear: go out for a walk
lo permite: allows it
darse un chapuzón: to go for a dip
río: river
noches: nights
se respira/respirar: one breathes/ to breathe
al caer la tarde: at sunset
se abren/abrir: open/to open
toma/tomar: takes/to take
calle: street
quieren salir: want to go out
bailar: to dance
dar una vuelta: to go out for a while, to go around

destacar: to highlight
país: country
aporte: contribution

se destaca/destacarse: stands out/to stand out
además: in addition
cantidad: amount, number
posee/poseer: has/to have
cuenta con/contar con: has/to have
jóvenes: young people
llegan/llegar: arrive/to arrive, to come
para cursar: to study, to take courses
probar suerte: to try their luck
mercado laboral: job market

El turismo rural

ESPAÑA

Durante los últimos años, el turismo rural **ha llegado a ser** en España una alternativa al turismo convencional. Pero, ¿Cuál es la **principal** característica del turismo rural? El **entorno**, la **ausencia** de **multitudes**, el relax y la posibilidad de practicar actividades como hacer **rutas en bicicleta**, **colaborar** en las **tareas** de una **granja** o en los **cultivos**, o simplemente hacer **senderismo**.

Hablando de España, **hay dos tipos de alojamientos rurales**: las casas rurales y los hoteles rurales. **En cuanto a** las casas rurales, es posible **alquilar toda la casa**, normalmente **durante un fin de semana como mínimo**, o alquilar una **habitación los días que queramos**. **Tanto** las casas **como** los hoteles rurales son **antiguos edificios reconstruidos**, **viejas casas de pueblo** e **incluso pequeños castillos**.

El **ambiente** de las casas rurales es **amigable**. Normalmente existe la posibilidad de **degustar** la gastronomía típica **de cada lugar**. Muchas casas rurales tienen **piscina**, principalmente en la zona mediterránea y sur de la península.

Hoy en día, **podemos encontrar** mucha información en internet, simplemente **escribiendo** en un **buscador** las palabras "casa rural" o "turismo rural", **debido a** la gran oferta existente.

¡Esta es **una de las mejores formas de olvidar** el **estrés** y el teléfono móvil! Aunque sólo sea durante dos días, **respirar aire puro** y **ver preciosos paisajes nos ayuda, no sólo física, sino mentalmente**.

durante los últimos años: during the last years
ha llegado a ser: has become
principal: main
entorno: environment, scene
ausencia: absence
multitudes: crowds, multitudes
rutas en bicicleta: bicycle routes
colaborar: to collaborate, to help
tareas: jobs, tasks
granja: farm
cultivos: crops
senderismo: hiking

hablando de/hablar: talking about/ to talk
hay dos tipos de alojamientos rurales: there are two types of rural lodging
en cuanto a: as for, with regard to
alquilar: to rent
toda la casa: the entire house
durante un fin de semana: for a weekend
como mínimo: as a minimum
habitación: room
los días que queramos: as many days as we want
tanto...como: both ... and
antiguos edificios: old buildings
reconstruidos: reconstructed
viejas casas de pueblo: old village houses
incluso: even
pequeños castillos: small castles

ambiente: atmosphere
amigable: friendly
degustar: to taste
de cada lugar: from every place
piscina: swimming pool

hoy en día: nowadays
podemos encontrar: we can find
escribiendo/escribir: writing/to write
buscador: search engine
debido a: due to

una de las mejores formas de olvidar: one of the best ways to forget
estrés: stress
respirar aire puro: to breathe clean air
ver preciosos paisajes: to see wonderful landscapes
nos ayuda/ayudar: helps us/to help
no sólo física, sino mentalmente: not only physically, but mentally

Glossary	
pequeña ciudad mexicana: small Mexican city	
carretera: road	
clima: climate	
moderado: moderate	
no muy fríos: not very cold	
no alcanzan/alcanzar: they do not reach/to reach	
extremadamente altas: extremely high	
localidad: locality, city	
atmósfera: atmosphere	
agradable: pleasant	
jubilados: retired people	
hoy en día: nowadays	
acoge/acoger: it welcomes/ to welcome	
estudiantes: students	
visitan/visitar: they visit/to visit	
personas jubiladas: retired people	
siguen sintiéndose atraídas: keep on feeling attracted	
expatriados: expatriates	
viviendo/vivir: living/to live	
podemos/poder: we can/can	
encontrar: to find	
mercados: markets	
deseemos/desear: we wish/to wish	
mercadillo al aire libre: open air market	
reúne/reunir: it gathers/to gather	
alrededores: surrounding areas	
asistir: to attend	
hay infinidad: there are a great number, many	
piezas artesanales: handmade pieces	
procedentes de: coming from	
cualquier lugar: any place	
mejores aspectos: best aspects	
junto con: together with	
comodidades: comforts	
grandes urbes: big cities	
invitan/invitar: they invite/to invite	
visitarla: to visit it	
sin importar: it doesn't matter	
época del año: time of year	
elijamos/elegir: we choose/to choose	
estancia: stay	
inolvidable: unforgettable	

San Miguel de Allende
MÉXICO

San Miguel de Allende es una **pequeña ciudad mexicana** situada, por **carretera**, a poco más de una hora del aeropuerto de León, y a unas cuatro horas al norte de la ciudad de México. Su altitud es de 1.908 metros y su **clima** es **moderado**: inviernos **no muy fríos** y veranos que **no alcanzan** temperaturas **extremadamente altas**.

Esta bonita **localidad**, de **atmósfera** colonial y **agradable** temperatura, fue durante los años 70 el lugar ideal para los **jubilados** de Estados Unidos y Canadá. **Hoy en día** San Miguel **acoge** a numerosos **estudiantes** que **visitan** la ciudad para estudiar español y arte. Las **personas jubiladas siguen sintiéndose atraídas** por esta ciudad y, de hecho, hay unos 2.000 **expatriados viviendo** aquí.

Es fácil vivir en San Miguel. Aquí, **podemos encontrar** excelentes **mercados** en los que comprar todo aquello que **deseemos**. Cada martes, un gran **mercadillo al aire libre reúne** a muchos vendedores de los **alrededores**. La ciudad ofrece variadas actividades culturales. En agosto podemos **asistir** al festival de música de cámara y en invierno al festival de jazz, entre otros muchos. **Hay infinidad** de galerías de arte y probablemente las mejores tiendas de artesanía de México, con **piezas artesanales procedentes de cualquier lugar** del país.

En San Miguel se reúnen los **mejores aspectos** de la pequeña ciudad **junto con** las **comodidades** de las **grandes urbes**. Sus variados restaurantes, sus mercados, el teatro y sus exposiciones de arte nos **invitan** a **visitarla sin importar** la **época del año** que **elijamos**. ¡Nuestra **estancia** aquí será **inolvidable**!

Tulum, la ciudad sobre el mar
MÉXICO

Hace muchísimos años, los mayas **descubrieron** un **paraíso a orillas de** las **aguas azules y cristalinas** del mar Caribe y allí, sobre un **acantilado** de doce metros de altura sobre el **nivel del mar**, **construyeron** una gran ciudad **amurallada**, una **fortaleza rodeada** por una enorme **pared**. **La llamaron** Tulum, que en su **lengua** quiere decir: **muro, cerco, muralla**.

Alcanzó su **esplendor alrededor** del año 1200 DC y hasta la llegada de los conquistadores españoles fue un **puerto mercante** próspero y eficiente, **basado** principalmente en el **trueque**. La **gente común vivía** fuera de esta ciudad **sagrada** y sólo algunos privilegiados como **sacerdotes**, matemáticos, **ingenieros** o astrónomos vivían **dentro** de ella ya que **se los consideraba seres superdotados**. Uno de los mayores **legados** de estos **eruditos** fue el Calendario maya.

LA CIUDAD POR DENTRO

Toda la ciudad **se extiende** a lo largo de seis kilómetros sobre la costa. Existen muchas construcciones de las cuales algunas fueron **dedicadas** a la **veneración**, y otras fueron **edificios administrativos** o **lugares de residencia**.

El edificio más importante es llamado el Castillo: **edificado** sobre rocas es el más alto de la ciudad y fue construido durante diferentes **etapas** de la civilización maya. Fue principalmente utilizado para rituales religiosos y, por su **grandeza**, hacía las veces de faro para los **barcos mercantes** que **navegaban** a lo largo de la costa. Otras de las construcciones relevantes son el Templo de los Frescos, el cual tuvo una gran importancia social y religiosa, y el Gran Palacio o Casa de las Columnas, una estructura de tres **niveles** que **contaba** con numerosas **cámaras pequeñas** y fue habitado por los nobles superiores de la sociedad.

Tulum **deslumbra** por su **belleza, tamaño, fuerza** e historia. Es un lugar para **no perderse**.

hace muchísimos años: many years ago
descubrieron/descubrir: they discovered/to discover
paraíso: paradise
a orillas de: on the banks of
aguas azules y cristalinas: blue and crystalline waters
acantilado: cliff
nivel del mar: sea level
construyeron/construir: they built/to build
amurallada: walled
fortaleza: fortress
rodeada: surrounded
pared: wall
la llamaron/llamar: they named it/to name
lengua: language
muro, cerco, muralla: wall

alcanzó/alcanzar: it reached/to reach
esplendor: magnificent
alrededor: around
puerto mercante: merchant port
basado: based
trueque: barter
gente común: common people
vivía/vivir: they lived/to live
sagrada: sacred
sacerdotes: priests
ingenieros: engineers
dentro: inside
se los consideraba/considerar: they were considered/to consider
seres superdotados: gifted beings
legados: legacies
eruditos: erudite

se extiende/extenderse: it extends/to extend
dedicadas: dedicated, devoted
veneración: veneration
edificios administrativos: administration buildings
lugares de residencia: places of residence

edificado: built up
etapas: stages
grandeza: greatness
barcos mercantes: merchant boats
navegaban/navegar: they sailed/to sail
niveles: levels
contaba/contar: it counted/to count
cámaras pequeñas: small chambers

deslumbra/deslumbrar: it dazzles/to dazzle
belleza, tamaño, fuerza: beauty, size, strength
no perderse/perder: not to miss/to miss

vino: wine	
está de moda/estar de moda: it is	
fashionable/to be fashionable	
amantes: lovers	
ya... o: whether... or	
bebida: drink, beverage	
buscan/buscar: they look for/	
to look for	
sabores: flavors	
olores: scents, aromas	
poco conocidos: lesser-known	
a pesar de: in spite of	
trayectoria: path, course	
caldos: wines	
estaba destinada a/destinar: it was	
meant for/mean, to intend	
consumo: consumption	
ha sido únicamente: it has been only	
bodegas: wineries	
han comenzado/comenzar: they have	
started/to start	
vender: to sell	
en el exterior: abroad	
cambio: change	
mercado: market	
suministrar: to provide	
población: population	
abastecer: to supply	
consumidores: consumers	
ajustes: adjustments	
empresas: companies, businesses	
enfrentarse a: to face	
requería/requerir: it demanded/	
to demand	
se vieron obligadas a: they were	
forced to	
cerrar: to close down	
puñado: handful	
tamaño: size	
quedaron en pie/quedar en pie: they	
were left standing/to be left standing	
aun así: even then	
manejaban/manejar: they were	
handling/to handle	
en ocasiones: sometimes	
unirse: to join together	
nivel mundial: worldwide level	

Vinos y bodegas
URUGUAY

El **vino está de moda**, y los **amantes** del vino, **ya** sea en países de larga tradición vinícola **o** en países donde esta **bebida** es todavía un producto exótico, **buscan** nuevos **sabores** y **olores** en vinos **poco conocidos** y originales. **A pesar de** la larga **trayectoria** que tiene el vino en Uruguay, sus **caldos** son poco conocidos, ya que tradicionalmente la producción del país **estaba destinada** a **consumo** local. **Ha sido únicamente** en las dos últimas décadas que las **bodegas** uruguayas **han comenzado** a producir vino para **vender en el exterior.**

El **cambio** de **mercado** ha tenido numerosas repercusiones a nivel nacional. Pasar de **suministrar** vinos para tres millones de personas (la **población** de Uruguay) a **abastecer** a mercados como Alemania, Estados Unidos o Brasil, con cientos de millones de **consumidores,** no es fácil. Para ello, las bodegas uruguayas han tenido que hacer varios **ajustes.** Al comienzo, muchas de las pequeñas **empresas** familiares no pudieron **enfrentarse** al cambio tecnológico que **requería** producir en mayor cantidad y **se vieron obligadas a cerrar.** Sólo un **puñado** de empresas, las más establecidas o de mayor **tamaño, quedaron en pie.** Pero **aun así**, estas compañías **manejaban** volúmenes tan pequeños que **en ocasiones** tuvieron que **unirse** para poder competir a **nivel mundial.**

Como en la ocasión en la que se presentaron **conjuntamente** para participar en una **feria** internacional de bebidas y **alimentos**, o aquella otra en la que las mayores bodegas **trabajaron juntas** para producir un vino en común y abastecer así un gran **pedido**.

La estrategia de **desarrollo** que las bodegas utilizaron también estuvo determinada por su tamaño. Las bodegas uruguayas **pronto se dieron cuenta de** que, **debido a** su pequeña capacidad de producción, no iban a poder competir en volumen con otros países productores de vino, sobre todo teniendo en cuenta la enorme producción de sus vecinos, Argentina y Chile. Uruguay decidió **apuntar** entonces **a** la calidad. La **política vitivinícola** del país fue trabajar **concentrándose** en **mejorar** a todo **nivel**: no sólo producir mejores vinos sino también mejorar y modernizar la **presentación**, **cuidando** la calidad del material y el **diseño** de las **botellas**, los **corchos** y las **etiquetas**.

También se procedió a mejorar las **uvas,** sustituyendo viejos **viñedos** por nuevas **cepas** importadas. Los vinos uruguayos utilizaban tradicionalmente varios tipos de uva, incluyendo las **francesas** merlot y cabernet sauvignon y las **alemanas** gewürztraminer y riesling. Pero las uvas tannat han sido, **sin lugar a dudas**, las que han determinado la marca característica del vino uruguayo. De origen francés, se plantan **en la actualidad únicamente** en Uruguay. Con esa uva insignia, muchas bodegas **salieron a competir** y el **esfuerzo ha dado sus frutos**: los vinos uruguayos **han logrado hacerse con** numerosos **premios** y **reconocimientos** en **concursos** regionales e internacionales.

conjuntamente: together
feria: fair
alimentos: food
trabajaron/trabajar: they worked/ to work
juntas: together
pedido: order

desarrollo: development
pronto: soon
se dieron cuenta de: realized
debido a: due to
apuntar...a to bet on
política vitivinícola: wine production policy
concentrándose/concentrarse: focusing/to focus
mejorar: to improve
nivel: level
presentación: presentation, appearance
cuidando/cuidar: paying attention to/ to pay attention to
diseño: design
botellas: bottles
corchos: corks
etiquetas: labels

uvas: grapes
viñedos: vineyards
cepas: vines
francesas: French
alemanas: German
sin lugar a dudas: without a doubt
en la actualidad: nowadays
únicamente: only
salieron a competir: started to compete
esfuerzo: effort
ha dado sus frutos/dar frutos: it has given its results/to give results
han logrado/lograr: they have managed/to manage
hacerse con: to get
premios: prizes
reconocimientos: honors, awards
concursos: competitions, contests

lugareños: locals
tienen un dicho: have a saying
llega a visitarnos: comes to visit us
se queda/quedarse: stays/to stay
años: years
aunque: although
puede parecer: may seem
condimentada: seasoned
pizca: pinch
orgullo: pride
pequeño paraíso: small paradise
saben/saber: know/to know
algo tiene de verdad: there is some
   truth to it

tesoros perdidos: lost treasures
playas: beaches
aguas tornasoladas: iridescent waters
apacibles: placid
de ensueño: dreamlike
bosques: woods, forests
parece no tener fin: doesn't seem
   to have an end

últimos: last
siglos: centuries
han anclado/anclar: have anchored/
   to anchor
barcos: ships
cruceros: cruise ships
hoy: today
ha resultado/resultar: has been/to be
desde siempre: always
imán: magnet
desde: from
mundo: world
ha quedado inscripta: remains etched
de madera: wooden
mezcla: mixture
vocablos: words, terms
al hablar en: when speaking
lengua: tongue, language
estilo de vida: lifestyle

arena blanca: white sand
cálidas: warm
mil azules: [a] thousand blues
se encuentran enmarcadas en: (they)
   form part of
aún no: not yet
empresas turísticas: tourist companies
lugar: place
para poder acceder a: to (be able to)
   access
hay que: it is necessary, one has to
canoas: canoes
medio de transporte: [a] means
   of transportation
cruzar: (to) cross
a pie: on foot, walking

Bocas del Toro

PANAMÁ

Los **lugareños** de Boca del Toro **tienen un dicho**: "Quien **llega a visitarnos** por tres días, **se queda** tres **años**". **Aunque** la frase **puede parecer condimentada** con una **pizca** de **orgullo** local, quienes han visitado este **pequeño paraíso** de Panamá **saben** que **algo tiene de verdad**.

Piratas, **tesoros perdidos**, **playas** de **aguas tornasoladas**, comunidades locales **apacibles**, flora y fauna **de ensueño**, corales, **bosques**, arte, cultura, gastronomía... La lista de razones para visitar Bocas del Toro **parece no tener fin**.

En los **últimos** cinco **siglos** de historia, allí **han anclado barcos** de conquistadores españoles, piratas, traficantes de esclavos, constructores, exportadores de productos locales y **cruceros** internacionales. Por diferentes razones, **hoy** fundamentalmente comerciales, Bocas del Toro **ha resultado desde siempre** un **imán** para quienes llegan **desde** los puntos más remotos del **mundo**. Mucha de esta diversidad cultural **ha quedado inscripta** en los detalles de su colorida arquitectura **de madera**, en la **mezcla** de **vocablos** típicos del inglés, francés y español que se usan **al hablar en** la **lengua** local, y en el **estilo de vida** de sus habitantes.

Las playas de Bocas del Toro tienen **arena blanca** y aguas cristalinas, **cálidas**, de **mil azules. Se encuentran enmarcadas en** espacios naturales **aún no** explotados por **empresas turísticas**. Una característica del **lugar** es que **para poder acceder a** las diferentes playas **hay que** utilizar **canoas** como **medio de transporte** o **cruzar** el bosque **a pie**.

Esto permite al visitante **disfrutar de** una experiencia pura, tranquila, en **pleno** contacto con la naturaleza, sin el **bullicio** de las multitudes y los **carteles** de **marcas** comerciales **invadiendo** el paisaje.

Estas costas **ofrecen olas para todos los gustos**. Algunas son ideales para hacer surf, otras **para remar**, otras **para zambullirse** y **bucear** y otras simplemente **para tomar sol** y **relajarse** con el **arrullo del mar**. Algunas playas **cuentan con** pequeños **paradores** que ofrecen **refrescos** y delicias **hechas con** productos típicos de la zona.

Los bosques tropicales de Bocas del Toro también se caracterizan por su tranquilidad y poca explotación turística. **Se los puede atravesar** en canoa, **a caballo**, en bicicleta o simplemente a pie. **Cualquiera que sea** la opción del visitante, **se recomienda pedir consejo a** los **guías locales**, **ya que** muchos **senderos** no están **señalizados**. **Recorrer** estos bosques, **ya sea de día o de noche**, permite disfrutar de los colores, perfumes y **sonidos** que **guarda** el bosque. **Descubrir** frutos y flores de colores **se vuelve** un **juego** que no tiene fin y **solo** es interrumpido por los **curiosos animalitos** que **salen de sus escondrijos para saludar a** los visitantes.

Si se lo compara con otros **destinos** del Caribe, Bocas del Toro posee el **encanto** de aquellas comunidades que aún ofrecen productos **desarrollados** artesanalmente y servicios turísticos **atendidos por sus propios dueños**. El clima tropical, la **belleza** de los escenarios naturales y la riqueza cultural del lugar **hacen que uno se enamore de**l lugar, **se olvide de**l **reloj** y simplemente **decida extender** su **estadía**.

---

disfrutar de: to enjoy
pleno: full
bullicio: noise, racket
carteles: billboards
marcas: brands
invadiendo: invading

ofrecen/ofrecer: offer/to offer
olas: waves
para todos los gustos: for every taste
para remar: for rowing
para zambullirse: for diving
bucear: swimming under water
para tomar sol: for sunbathing
relajarse: relaxing
arrullo: murmur
mar: sea
cuentan con/contar con: have/to have
paradores: stands
refrescos: soft drinks, cold drinks
hechas con: made with

se los puede atravesar: (they) can be crossed
a caballo: on horseback
cualquiera que sea: whichever is
se recomienda/recomendar: it is recommended/to recommend
pedir consejo a … : ask … for advice
guías locales: local guides
ya que: for, since
senderos: paths
señalizados: marked (with signs)
recorrer: walking about
ya sea: whether
de día o de noche: during the day or at night
sonidos: sounds
guarda/guardar: has in store/ to have in store
descubrir: discovering
se vuelve/volverse: becomes/to become
juego: game
solo: only
curiosos animalitos: inquisitive little creatures
salen de sus escondrijos: come out of their hiding places
para saludar a: to greet

si se lo compara: if we compare it
destinos: destination
encanto: charm
desarrollados: developed
atendidos por: run by, operated by
sus propios dueños: the owners themselves
belleza: beauty
hacen que uno se enamore de: make one fall in love with
se olvide de/olvidarse: forget/to forget
reloj: clock
decida extender: decide to extend
estadía: stay

Isla de Taquile
PERÚ

isla: island
situada: located
lado peruano: Peruvian side
allí: there
viven/vivir: live/ to live
alrededor de: around
conocidos como: known as
hablan/hablar: speak/ to speak
lengua indígena: indigenous language
mundo entero: whole world
ropas: clothes, clothing
tejidas a mano: hand woven
entre: among
artesanías de mejor calidad: best quality handicrafts
hombres: men
mujeres: women
niños: children
hilan/hilar: spin/ to spin
tejen/tejer: weave/ to weave
vestimentas: pieces of clothing
cinturón: girdle, sash
algunos: some
son usados como/usar: are used as/ to use
calendarios: calendars
para registrar: to register
complejos: complex
ciclos: cycles
anuales: annual, yearly
cada: each

Taquile es una **isla situada** en el **lado peruano** del lago Titicaca. Esta islita tiene 5,5 por 1,6 kilómetros de extensión, y **allí viven alrededor** de 1700 personas. Sus habitantes, **conocidos como** taquileños, **hablan** la **lengua indígena** quechua. Los taquileños son famosos en el **mundo entero** por sus textiles y **ropas tejidas a mano**, las cuales están consideradas **entre** las **artesanías de mejor calidad** de todo Perú. Todas las personas en la isla – **hombres**, **mujeres** y **niños** – **hilan** y **tejen**.

Las **vestimentas** taquileñas más características son el chullo y el **cinturón** tejido. **Algunos** cinturones **son usados como calendarios**, **para registrar** los **complejos ciclos anuales** de las actividades sociales, religiosas y **agrícolas** de **cada** familia.

El chullo es mucho más que un **gorro: informa** a la comunidad de la posición social de un hombre. Si el chullo tiene una parte **blanca** en su **base**, el hombre es **soltero; si tiene rojo**, el hombre es **casado**. Un **líder comunitario** tiene un chullo con **orejeras** y colores más brillantes.

Los taquileños viven **modestamente**, en armonía con su **tierra**. **No hay** autos **ni calles** en Taquile. La **única entrada** a la isla es una **empinada escalera de piedra** de más de 500 **peldaños que sube desde** el lago. No hay **caballos** ni **burros**, **ni siquiera** llamas o alpacas; **toda carga se lleva sobre** los **hombros**.

La sociedad taquileña está **basada en** el colectivismo y la **vieja moral incaica**. Como **prueba** de la **honestidad**, la isla no tiene policía ni prisión: **cualquier** problema que **surge** en la comunidad **es resuelto por** líderes **electos anualmente**. La **vida** comunitaria y la **toma de decisiones de forma colectiva** es la **clave** para una vida **pacífica** en esta **pequeña** isla.

---

gorro: hat, cap
informa/informar: (it) informs/ to inform
blanca: white
base: base
soltero: single
si: if
tiene/tener: (it) has/to have
rojo: red
casado: married
líder comunitario: community leader
orejeras: earflaps
modestamente: modestly
tierra: land
no hay: there are no
ni calles: or streets
única: only
entrada: access, entry
empinada: steep
escalera de piedra: stone staircase
peldaños: steps
que sube desde: which climbs up from
caballos: horses
burros: donkeys
ni siquiera: not even
toda carga: all loads
se lleva/llevar: is carried/to carry
sobre: on
hombros: shoulders

basada en: based on
vieja moral incaica: old inca morals
prueba: proof
honestidad: honesty
cualquier: any
surge/surgir: arises/to arise
es resuelto por: is solved by
electos anualmente: elected annually
vida: life
toma de decisiones: decision making
de forma colectiva: collective(ly)
clave: key
pacífica: peaceful
pequeña: small

Examina tu comprensión

El barrio gótico de Barcelona, página 30

1. Siglos atrás, ¿qué era el barrio gótico?

2. ¿Cuál es el nombre del puente ubicado aquí?

3. ¿Qué consejo se da al final del artículo?

Colonia del Sacramento, página 32

1. ¿Qué podría encontrar para comprar o comer en Colonia del Sacramento?

2. ¿Qué debería hacer después de comprar un bizcocho?

Verano en enero y febrero, página 34

1. A medida que los días se vuelven más calientes, ¿qué se ve en las calles de Argentina?

2. Describa algunas actividades favoritas para el día y la noche.

3. ¿Qué ciudad es la más grande y más desarrollada?

4. ¿Qué dos ciudades crean un lugar mágico para relajarse y por qué?

Mallorca y sus castillos, página 36

1. ¿Por qué son las Islas Baleares un popular destino turístico? ¿Dónde se encuentran?

2. Las piedras del castillo ahora son muy blancas. ¿Por qué?

Test your comprehension

Un paraíso en el Caribe, página 38

1. Nombre cuatro entornos geográficos en este país.

2. ¿Qué encontrará en La Romana?

3. Un aspecto reconfortante de la mayoría de las islas del Caribe es la falta de algunas criaturas. ¿Cuáles son?

Varadero, arenas blancas, página 40

1. ¿Qué hace que las playas de Varadero sean tan especiales?

2. ¿Qué vista histórica famosa puede visitar en Punta Perdiz?

3. Además de las hermosas playas ¿qué otra cosa puede disfrutar o descubrir y dónde?

El turismo rural, página 43

1. ¿Cuál es la principal característica del turismo rural?

2. ¿Cuáles son los dos tipos de alojamiento rural?

3. ¿Qué se recomienda como la mejor manera de encontrar información sobre este tipo de viaje en España?

San Miguel de Allende, página 44

1. ¿Muchos turistas de qué país van a San Miguel de Allende?

2. ¿Los estudiantes visitan San Miguel de Allende para estudiar qué?

Tulum, la ciudad sobre el mar, página 45

1. ¿Quiénes vivían en la ciudad sagrada y por qué?

Un pueblo sin tradición es un pueblo sin porvenir.

Alberto Lleras Camargo

Tradición

La quinceañera
MÉXICO

Cumplir 15 años es muy importante para las mujeres mexicanas. **Si bien** en otros países la transición de las adolescentes que **se convierten** en mujeres también se celebra a esta **edad**, en México tiene una **relevancia** y un **festejo** particular.

Se da por sentado que fueron los conquistadores españoles los que **trajeron** esta costumbre a México, **tomando** la tradición de la mujer azteca y **adaptándola** al cristianismo. Los aztecas celebraban la **llegada** de las niñas a la **madurez** con una ceremonia religiosa y un banquete. Los conquistadores tomaron la celebración pagana y la **convirtieron** a la Iglesia católica. Así, **hoy en día**, la chica que cumple 15 años **se adentra** en el mundo de la **adultez femenina** con una **misa de acción de gracias**, donde **agradece** y se prepara para los nuevos **retos** por vivir. **Posteriormente**, se celebra una gran fiesta con baile incluido, donde **comparte** su alegría con sus **seres queridos**.

La quinceañera, **vestida de gala** en colores pastel, con **ramo de flores**, **anillo** y **a veces** hasta **corona**, recibe la misa acompañada por familiares, amigos y sobre todo por 14 chicas (representando sus primeros 14 años) y sus **chambelanes** (acompañantes masculinos o **caballeros de honor**). La misa **culmina** con una **oración**, la bendición de los **dones** y la **entrega** del ramo de flores que hace la del cumpleaños a la Virgen María.

Después de la misa, la fiesta es pura **alegría**, baile, comida y **regalos**. Algunas hasta cuentan con la famosa piñata. El momento del **vals** también es **esperado** por todos. La quinceañera baila su primer vals con su padre y luego con todo el que quiera **acercarse a** la **pista de baile**. Así **sigue** la **diversión** y el festejo, entre más bailes y, **por supuesto**, el **pastel**, especialmente preparado para la ocasión.

---

cumplir 15 años: to turn 15 years old
si bien: although
se convierten/convertirse: they become/to turn into, to become
edad: age
relevancia: importance
festejo: celebration

se da por sentado: it is taken for granted
trajeron/traer: they brought/to bring
tomando/tomar: taking/to take
adaptándola/adaptar: adapting it/to adapt
llegada: arrival
madurez: maturity
convirtieron/convertir: they converted/to convert
hoy en día: nowadays
se adentra/adentrarse: she goes deep/to go deep
adultez femenina: feminine maturity, adulthood
misa de acción de gracias: Thanksgiving Mass
agradece/agradecer: she thanks/to thank
retos: challenges
posteriormente: later
comparte/compartir: she shares/to share
seres queridos: loved ones

vestida de gala: dressed up
ramo de flores: bouquet of flowers
anillo: ring
a veces: sometimes
corona: crown
chambelanes: formal escorts
caballeros de honor: men of honor
culmina/culminar: it culminates/to culminate, to finish
oración: prayer
dones: gifts, talents
entrega: hand over, deliver

alegría: joy
regalos: presents
vals: waltz
esperado/esperar: expected/to expect, to wait for
acercarse a: to approach
pista de baile: dance floor
sigue/seguir: it continues/to continue
diversión: fun
por supuesto: of course
pastel: cake

Chichicastenango
GUATEMALA

Guatemala, **ubicada** en el centro del continente americano, fue, **antes** de la conquista, **núcleo** del Imperio Maya (en **lengua** de los mayas, su nombre quiere decir "tierra de árboles"). Es **precisamente** por esta historia que **se caracteriza** por una gran **diversidad** étnica y cultural. Los grupos principales que hoy la **habitan** son: los indígenas, descendientes de los mayas, subdivididos a su vez en varios grupos que **forman** la familia maya-quiché; y los mestizos y europeos. **Afortunadamente**, estas culturas mantienen todavía sus costumbres celebrando en **casi todos** los pueblos su **propia** fiesta, con bailes y eventos sociales, culturales y deportivos, haciendo de Guatemala un **paraíso** de tradición y color.

Una de las celebraciones más importantes es la que conmemora el pueblo maya-quiché de Chichicastenango en honor a su patrón, Santo Tomás. En la catedral que lleva su nombre y que fue **construida** en 1540, los descendientes de este pueblo **elevan** sus **plegarias** entre **velas**, **pino** y flores, **esparcidas** en el **suelo**, y **queman** **copal**, un **incienso** típico del país. En la fiesta, que se celebra del 14 al 21 de diciembre, **se llevan a cabo** procesiones y se bailan danzas autóctonas acompañadas por la marimba, un instrumento tradicional y característico de Guatemala. Sin embargo, una de las actividades más curiosas en esta fiesta **gira en torno al** famoso "Palo Volador". En la plaza central, instalan un **palo** o poste muy alto, desde el que varios **jóvenes se lanzan** hacia el suelo, sostenidos por un **lazo** o **soga**, como si **volaran**. ¡Sólo para **valientes**!

Chichicastenango es **conocida**, también, por ser **cuna** de uno de los **legados culturales** más **preciados**: el manuscrito del Popol Vuh, el **libro sagrado** de los maya-quichés. Se dice que este manuscrito, escrito en el siglo XVI por un indígena maya **anónimo**, fue **reescrito** por un religioso de esta localidad **alrededor** del 1700. El Popol Vuh es una **obra literaria única** en la que **se cuenta** la historia y las **leyendas** de los que habitaron, y **aún** habitan, el área de Chichicastenango.

ubicada/ubicar: located/to locate
antes: before
núcleo: nucleus, core
lengua: language
precisamente: precisely
se caracteriza/caracterizarse: it characterizes/to characterize
diversidad: diversity
habitan/habitar: they live/to live
forman/formar: they form/to form
afortunadamente: fortunately
casi todos: almost all
propia: own
paraíso: paradise

construida/construir: built/to build
elevan/elevar: they raise/to raise
plegarias: prayers
velas: candles
pino: pine
esparcidas/esparcir: spread/to spread
suelo: ground
queman/quemar: they burn/to burn
copal: a typical incense of the country
incienso: incense
se llevan a cabo: they carry out
gira en torno al: revolve around
palo: pole, stick
jóvenes: young people
se lanzan/lanzar: they throw themselves, they jump/to jump
lazo: bow
soga: rope
volaran/volar: they fly/to fly
valientes: brave

conocida/conocer: known/to know
cuna: origin, birthplace
legados culturales: cultural legacy
preciados: prized, valued
libro sagrado: sacred book
anónimo: anonymous
reescrito/reescribir: re-written/ to re-write
alrededor: around
obra literaria única: unique literary work
se cuenta/contar: it is told/to tell
leyendas: legends
aún: still

tribu indígena: indigenous tribe
noreste: northeast
veneraban/venerar: they worship/to worship
la llamaban/llamar: they called her/to call
proviene/provenir: it comes from/to come from
ofrecían/ofrecer: they offered/to offer
le agradecían/agradecer: they thanked her/to thank
les daba/dar: she gave them/to give
engendraba/engendrar: it caused/to cause
daba vida/dar vida: it gave life/to give life

sigue/seguir: it keeps/to keep
andina: Andean
año tras año: year after year
se le rinde tributo a: they pay tribute to
naturaleza: nature
hace germinar: it makes germinate
semillas: seeds
madurar: to ripen
jóvenes: young people
viejos: old people
cumplen/cumplir: they keep/to keep
pidiendo/pedir: asking for/to ask for
fecundidad: fertility
terrenos: pieces of land
felicidad: happiness

festejo: celebration
ofrendas: presents, gifts
demanda/demandar: it requires/to require
mazorcas de maíz: corn cobs
habas: broad beans
hojas de coca: coca leaves
se junta/juntar: it is put together/to put together
alimentar: to feed
devolverle/devolver: giving her back/to give back
así: this way
se decoran/decorar: they are decorated/to decorate
globos: balloons
serpentinas: streamers
platos: dishes
a base: using
se degusta/degustar: it is sampled/to sample

La Pachamama
PERÚ

Los incas, **tribu indígena** de la zona de Perú, Bolivia y **noreste** argentino, **veneraban** a la Madre Tierra. **La llamaban** Pachamama, nombre que **proviene** de "pacha" (universo, mundo, tiempo, lugar) y de "mama" (madre). En su honor **ofrecían** una ceremonia en la que **le agradecían** por todo lo que **les daba**. Según ellos, la Pachamama producía, **engendraba** y **daba vida**.

Afortunadamente esta tradición **sigue** celebrándose entre la población **andina**, **año tras año**, cada 1 de agosto. **Se le rinde tributo a** la Madre Tierra, la **naturaleza** que **hace germinar** las **semillas** y **madurar** los frutos. **Jóvenes**, **viejos** y niños **cumplen** este homenaje **pidiendo** por la **fecundidad** de sus **terrenos** y la **felicidad** en sus vidas.

Para el **festejo** se preparan durante varias semanas, ya que buscar y preparar las **ofrendas demanda** un gran trabajo: **mazorcas de maíz, habas**, chicha (bebida que se prepara a base de harina de maíz), ciga-rrillos, **hojas de coca**, alcohol, cerveza y vino, todo **se junta** para **alimentar** a la tierra y **devolverle así** algo de lo que ella da. Las casas **se decoran** con **globos**, **serpentinas** y flores. Se preparan **platos** típicos y el *yerbiao*, una infusión **a base** de hierbas aromáticas, azúcar, yerba, agua y alcohol, que luego **se degusta** entre todos.

Cuando todo está listo se procede a la ceremonia que puede oficiarse en cualquier momento del día. Se cava un pozo en la tierra, se colocan brazos y sahumerios en su interior para sahumarla y se tapa con un poncho o manta.

Mientras tanto, la tierra que se saca se coloca a un costado y allí se depositan los cigarrillos encendidos por cada uno de los presentes. La tradición dice que de acuerdo a cómo la tierra vaya fumando, así será la suerte de cada uno en ese año.

Una vez sahumada, se destapa el pozo y se da de comer a la Tierra con las ofrendas preparadas: se entierran las hojas de coca, las bebidas y las comidas. También se coloca papel picado (que simboliza la alegría) y artesanías hechas con retazos de lana de oveja (que simbolizan los deseos e intenciones de cada asistente). Luego se tapa la boca de la tierra, se deja caer abundante papel picado y se coloca una piedra grande sobre todo.

Entonando lindas coplas, todos los presentes se preparan para degustar la comida, la bebida y el *yerbiao* hecho para la ocasión.

---

cuando todo está listo: when everything is ready
se procede/proceder: one proceeds/to proceed
se cava/cava: it is dug/to dig
pozo: deep hole
se colocan/colocar: they are placed/to place
brazos: branches
sahumerios: incense
sahumarla: to perfume/fumigate with scented smoke
se tapa/tapar: it is covered/to cover
manta: blanket

mientras tanto: in the meantime
se saca/sacar: it is taken out/to take out
a un costado: on the side
se depositan/depositar: they put/to put, to place
cigarrillos encendidos: lit cigarettes
por cada uno de los presentes: for each one present
de acuerdo: according
vaya fumando/fumar: it smokes/to smoke
así será la suerte de cada uno en ese año: that is the way luck will be for each one that year

se destapa/destapar: they uncover/to uncover
se da de comer/dar de comer: they feed/to feed
se entierran/enterrar: they bury/to bury
bebidas: drinks
papel picado: chopped paper, confetti
alegría: joy
artesanías: handicrafts
retazos de lana de oveja: pieces of sheep wool
deseos: wishes
asistente: attendee
luego: afterwards
se deja caer: they let fall
piedra: rock
sobre todo: on top of everything

entonando/entonar: singing/to sing
lindas coplas: beautiful verses
todos los presentes: everybody present
se preparan/preparse: they get ready/to get ready

en pleno: in the middle of
siglo XXI: 21st century
ciencia: science
muestra: sample
avances/avanzar: advances/to advance
calidad de vida: quality of life
corriente de volver: current of returning to
fuentes: origins, sources
auge: peak
si bien: although
trajeron aparejados: they brought with them
ventajas: advantages
separaron: separated
innata: innate
entender: to understand
crecimiento: growth

alguien: someone
dijo/decir: said/to say
alguna vez: once
sabia: wise
bastaría imitarla u observarla: it would be enough to imitate or observe her
mantenerse saludable: keep healthy
se ha vuelto popular: it became popular
pueden/poder: they can/can
comprobarse: verify, prove
té: tea
tinturas: tinctures
junto a: along with, together with
curar, calmar o relajar: to cure, to calm, or to relax

hoja abierta: open leaf
desinflama: to reduce inflamation
cicatriza: to heal
cualquier: any
quemadura: burn
hojas de tilo: lime tree leaves
manda a dormir: send to sleep
estresado: stressed
ansiedad: anxiety
hacer frente: to face, to confront
tisanas de hipérico: st.johns wort tea, infusion
hojas amarillas: yellow leaves
alargados: elongated
estrella: star
menta: mint
propiedades expectorantes: expectorant properties
carminativas: carminative

al alcance de la mano: within hand's reach
sanas: healthy

El uso de las plantas medicinales
ARGENTINA

En pleno siglo XXI, donde la tecnología, la **ciencia** y la medicina tradicional dan **muestra** de increíbles **avances** con el objetivo de mejorar la **calidad de vida**, una **corriente de volver** a las **fuentes** y a la naturaleza también está en **auge**. Porque, **si bien** los avances tecnológicos y la globalización **trajeron aparejados** enormes **ventajas**, también **separaron** al hombre de su sensibilidad **innata** y del contacto con la naturaleza: cuestiones fundamentales para **entender** y acompañar el **crecimiento** del ser humano y los ciclos de la vida.

Si, como **alguien dijo alguna vez**, la naturaleza es **sabia**, **bastaría imitarla u observarla** más detenidamente para volvernos, también, un poco más eruditos, inteligentes y seguramente más felices. En Argentina, el uso de las plantas medicinales como remedios naturales contra algunas afecciones o como ayuda preventiva para **mantenerse saludable se ha vuelto popular**, y sus enormes ventajas y benéficos efectos **pueden comprobarse** en poco tiempo. En forma de **té** o de **tinturas**, **junto a** cremas y lociones o simplemente con el contacto de ellas, todo es válido a la hora de **curar**, **calmar o relajar**.

Una **hoja abierta** de aloe vera, por ejemplo, **desinflama** y **cicatriza cualquier quemadura**; un té de **hojas de tilo** calma los nervios y una infusión de valeriana **manda a dormir** al insomnio más **estresado**. A las depresiones leves y la **ansiedad** se puede **hacer frente** con **tisanas de hipérico**, una planta de **hojas amarillas** con pétalos **alargados** en forma de **estrella**; y el aromático té de **menta**, además de ayudar a una buena digestión tiene **propiedades expectorantes** y **carminativas**.

Están **al alcance de la mano**. Y son mucho más económicas, **sanas** y naturales que los medicamentos tradicionales.

Una Navidad en Paraguay
PARAGUAY

En todos los países de Sudamérica, la **llegada** de la Navidad **coincide con** la llegada del **verano** y el tiempo cálido. Por eso, la mayoría de los niños **se preguntan** por qué Papa Noel está **vestido** con un **traje** tan **abrigado** y el **arbolito** está **lleno de nieve**.

Una de las tantas versiones que **circulan sobre** su origen **se basa en** las raíces de la **mitología nórdica**, según la cual existía un **dios** que **vivía** en una **estrella**, tenía una **larga barba blanca** y **cabalgaba** por el **cielo** llevando **regalos**.

En Paraguay, el **festejo** de la Navidad no es muy diferente a como se celebra en otros países del **Cono Sur**, ya que no sólo **comparten** proximidad sino también un **clima** similar. En Paraguay la **gente** es muy **creyente** de la religión católica. **En casi todos** los **hogares**, **además de armar** el arbolito, se arma un **pesebre** que **se adorna** con una **flor típica** del lugar: la flor del **cocotero**, cuyo perfume es muy dulce.

En la Nochebuena (24 de diciembre por la noche) las familias van a la Misa del Gallo y luego comparten en la mesa familiar la **cena preparada** con comidas y bebidas típicas: **no pueden faltar** la sopa paraguaya, que se prepara a base de harina de maíz y es más **espesa** que un caldo tradicional, o el **chipa guasu**, como la sopa paraguaya pero con **maíz fresco** en lugar de **harina**. Todo se acompaña con un **refrescante clericó**: bebida hecha con vino tinto o blanco, frutas de estación, un poco de azúcar y abundante hielo. Los niños visitan los pesebres de las casas **vecinas** del **barrio**, **cantan villancicos** y en **agradecimiento**, los **dueños** de las casas les dan **golosinas** y refrescos. El 25 al mediodía, esto **se repite** en la mayoría de las casas: las familias, amigos y vecinos comparten **almuerzos** y **estadías juntos**.

---

llegada: arrival
coincide con: coincides with
verano: summer
se preguntan: they ask themselves
vestido: dressed
traje: suit
abrigado: warm
arbolito/árbol: small tree/tree
lleno de: full of
nieve: snow

una de las tantas: one of many
circulan: circulate
sobre: about
se basa en: is based on
mitología nórdica: Nordic mythology
dios: god
vivía/vivir: lived/to live
estrella: star
larga barba blanca: long white beard
cabalgaba/cabalgar: he used to ride/ to ride
cielo: sky
regalos: presents

festejo: celebration
Cono Sur: South America (southern part)
comparten/compatir: they share/ to share
clima: weather
gente: people
creyente: believer
en casi todos: in almost all
hogares: homes
además de: besides
armar: to assemble, put together
pesebre: manger
se adorna/adornar: it is decorated/ to decorate
flor típica: typical flower
cocotero: coconut tree

cena: dinner
preparada/preparar: prepared/ to prepare
no pueden faltar: they cannot miss
espesa: thick
chipa guasu: typical Paraguayan dish
maíz fresco: fresh corn
harina: flour
refrescante: refreshing
clericó: a typical drink made with wine and fruits
vecinas: neighboring
barrio: neighborhood
cantan/cantar: they sing/to sing
villancicos: Christmas Carols
agradecimiento: gratitude
dueños: owners
golosinas: candies
se repite/repetir: it repeats/to repeat
almuerzos: lunch
estadías juntos: stays together

La gritería
NICARAGUA

Glossary	
viaje de vuelta: return trip	
estancia: stay	
tuvimos la oportunidad: we had the opportunity	
disfrutar: to enjoy	
mariano: relating to the virgin Mary	
vida cotidiana: daily life	

viaje de vuelta: return trip

estancia: stay

tuvimos la oportunidad: we had the opportunity

disfrutar: to enjoy

mariano: relating to the virgin Mary

vida cotidiana: daily life

está sufriendo/sufrir: it is suffering/to suffer

se olvidan/olvidarse: they forget/to forget

sufrimiento: suffering

se unen/unirse: they join/to join

van de casa en casa: they go from house to house

en punto: o'clock

cohetes: fireworks

revientan/reventar: they burst/to burst

por unos instantes: for a few moments

cielo: sky

brilla/brillar: it shines/to shine

fuegos artificiales: fireworks

se oyen/oír: they are heard/to hear

empieza/empezar: it begins/to begin

así: this way

únicamente: only, solely

nicaragüense: Nicaraguan

ningún: no (other country)

pólvora: gunpowder

anuncia/anunciar: it announces/to announce

comienzo: beginning

dura/durar: it lasts/to last

medianoche: midnight

incluyen/incluir: included/to include

gritando/gritar: shouting/to shout

se conoce/conocerse: it is known/to be known

¿Quién causa tanta alegría?: Who causes so much joy?

respuesta: answer

enfrente de: in front of

erigidos/erigir: erected, built/to build

inquilinos: tenants

Después de 19 años, decidimos hacer un **viaje de vuelta** a Nicaragua. Durante nuestra **estancia** allá, también **tuvimos la oportunidad** de **disfrutar** de una tradición propia de Nicaragua: la gritería. Este estado centroamericano es un país muy religioso y durante el mes de diciembre se celebra el fervor **mariano** en todos los aspectos de la **vida cotidiana**.

Nicaragua **está sufriendo** severos problemas económicos; sin embargo, el 7 de diciembre todos sus habitantes **se olvidan** de su **sufrimiento** y **se unen** a los diversos grupos que **van de casa en casa**. A las seis **en punto** de la tarde los **cohetes revientan** y, **por unos instantes**, el **cielo** del país **brilla**. Durante las próximas seis horas, los cohetes esporádicos y los **fuegos artificiales se oyen** por todas las calles de las ciudades de Nicaragua. **Empieza así** la gritería.

Esta tradición es **únicamente nicaragüense**. **Ningún** otro país celebra de esta manera la festividad de la Purísima. La **pólvora anuncia** el **comienzo** de la gritería a las seis de la tarde y **dura** hasta la **medianoche**. Los grupos que **incluyen** adultos y niños, van de casa en casa **gritando** lo que **se conoce** como "la gritería": **¿Quién causa tanta alegría?** " Y la **respuesta** es: "La concepción de María". Todo esto se hace **enfrente de** los altares a la virgen **erigidos** por los **inquilinos** de las casas.

Después los grupos **cantan canciones** a la Virgen María que van **leyendo** de unos **libritos** que se compran por dos o tres **córdobas** cada uno. Los inquilinos **regalan** a los cantantes productos típicos como **matracas**, **indios**, **cañas**, limones, **pitos** y otras **cositas**.

Según la tradición, la gritería tiene su origen en León, pueblo que **se caracteriza** por sus celebraciones religiosas, **siendo** la más **alegre** y **grandiosa** la gritería. El creador de la gritería fue monseñor Giordano Carranza en el año 1857, quien **tenía como propósito** tocar los corazones espirituales del pueblo nicaragüense, a quienes **animaba** a gritar a **la Purísima** y a **construir** altares con sus **propias manos**. **Posteriormente** esta tradición **se trasladó** a Masaya y a Granada para luego **iniciarse** en todos los **barrios** de Monimbó y otras ciudades del país hasta llegar a todos sus **rincones**.

En la casa en donde nosotros estábamos se hicieron hasta 900 regalos, es decir, que allí había más de 900 personas **reunidas**, gritando y cantando **delante del** altar. Yo nunca **había visto tanta** gente **como vi** esa noche. Era realmente un **espectáculo**. Muchos de esos altares fueron elaboradamente construidos y era evidente también que **se gastó** mucho dinero en comida y **chunches** para regalar. **Ni siquiera** la crisis económica que **atraviesa** el país **conseguirá menguar** la fiesta de la gritería.

cantan/cantar: they sing/to sing
canciones: songs
leyendo/leer: reading/to read
libritos: little books
córdobas: the Nicaraguan currency
regalan/regalar: they give as a present/to give as a present
matracas: rattles
indios: clay dolls
cañas: sugar canes
pitos: whistles
cositas: little things

se caracteriza/caracterizarse: is characterized/to be characterized
siendo/ser: being/to be
alegre: merry, lively
grandiosa: impressive
tenía como propósito: he had as his goal
animaba/animar: he encouraged/to encourage
la Purísima: the immaculate conception
construir: to build
propias manos: own hands
posteriormente: subsequently, later
se trasladó/trasladarse: it went/to go
iniciarse: to be started
barrios: neighborhoods
rincones: corners

reunidas: gathered
delante del: in front of
había visto/ver: I had seen/to see
tanta: so many
como vi/ver: as I saw/to see
espectáculo: show
se gastó/gastarse: was spent/to be spent
chunches: things (slang word referring to anything with no specific name)
ni siquiera: not even
atraviesa/atravesar: it crosses/to cross
conseguirá/conseguir: it will succeed/to succeed
menguar: to diminish

los tiempos: the times
abuelo: grandfather
me llevaba/llevar: he would take me/to take
recoger: to gather, pick up
pasto: grass
camellos: camels
íbamos/ir: we went/to go
ponía/poner: I would put/to put
hierba: grass
caja: box
nervios: excitement
no me dejaban/dejar: they would not let me/to let
se aseguraba/asegurar: she assured me/to assure
sobre todo: above all
no saliera/salir: I did not leave/ to leave
habitación: room

esperan/esperar: they wait/to wait
viejo gordo: fat old man
le decimos/decir: we call him/to say
aunque: although
madrugada: dawn
debajo: under
cama: bed
traen/traer: they take/to take
Tres Reyes Magos: Three Wise Men
lejanas: distant, far off
encuentran/encontrar: they find/ to find
tanta: so much
cariño: affection
obsequios: gifts
largo y ancho: long and wide

leerse/leer: they read/to read
cartas: letters
escritas: written
pidiendo/pedir: asking/to ask
juguete: toy
deseo: wish
verdaderos: true, real
Navidad boricua: Puerto Rican Christmas
remonta/remontar: goes back to/ to go back
nacimiento: birth
humilde: humble
pesebre: manger

Gaspar, Melchor y Baltasar
PUERTO RICO

Eran **los tiempos** en que mi **abuelo me llevaba** a **recoger pasto** para los **camellos**. **Íbamos** al patio y yo **ponía** toda la **hierba** en una **caja** grande. Los **nervios no me dejaban** dormir esa noche pero mi abuela **se aseguraba** de que, **sobre todo**, **no saliera** de mi **habitación**.

La noche del 24 de diciembre todos los niños puertorriqueños **esperan** a Santa Claus o al **viejo gordo** como también **le decimos** en la isla. Esta es una tradición adoptada de los Estados Unidos, **aunque** la celebración más importante de Puerto Rico tiene lugar en la **madrugada** del día 6 de enero. La noche del día 5 todos los pequeños salen a recoger hierba fresca que dejan en una caja **debajo** de la **cama** para los camellos que **traen** a los **Tres Reyes Magos** desde tierras **lejanas**. Hierba fresca y agua es lo que **encuentran** los reyes quienes, a cambio de **tanta** demostración de **cariño**, dejan **obsequios** a los niños a lo **largo y ancho** de todo el país.

Días antes pueden **leerse** miles de **cartas escritas** por los más pequeños **pidiendo** su **juguete** favorito, un **deseo** feliz para su familia o simplemente deseando que los reyes visiten su casa. Gaspar, Melchor y Baltasar son los **verdaderos** reyes de nuestra **Navidad boricua**. La historia de los Tres Reyes Magos se **remonta** al **nacimiento** del niño Jesús en un **humilde pesebre** en Belén.

Fueron ellos quienes, **guiados** por la **Estrella de Belén**, llegaron hasta el **recién nacido** para **ofrecerle oro**, mirra e incienso. Desde entonces, cada diciembre muchas personas miran al cielo por la noche buscando la estrella que guió a estos **entrañables personajes**. **Asimismo**, el día 5 de enero el **primer mandatario** del país **abre** las puertas de la Fortaleza y, entre música y comida típica, honra a todos los niños quienes con su inocencia **devuelven** la **esperanza** y **alegría**. Se trata de una fiesta familiar y de pueblo que se extiende hasta el **anochecer**.

En Puerto Rico el periodo navideño **comienza** después de la celebración del **Día de Acción de Gracias** y se extiende hasta la segunda semana de enero cuando nos **deleitamos** con las **octavitas**, los últimos ocho días de fiesta donde aún puede **sentirse** el aire festivo. Yo no escapo a esta tradición. **Lo mismo que hice** de niña lo **hago de adulta**. Todos los años **espero** a los Tres Reyes Magos **junto** a mis hijos con la misma emoción que sentía cuando era pequeña. Nuestras tradiciones **nunca deben morir**.

guiados: guided
Estrella de Belén: Star of Bethlehem
recién nacido: newborn
ofrecerle: to offer him
oro: gold
entrañables personajes: deeply important figures
asimismo: also, as well
primer mandatario: president
abre/abrir: it opens/to open
devuelven/devolver: they give back/ to give back
esperanza: hope
alegría: happiness
anochecer: dark, nightfall

comienza: begins, starts
Día de Acción de Gracias: Thanksgiving
deleitamos/deleitar: we enjoy ourselves/to enjoy oneself
octavitas: 8 day period of celebration after the Epiphany (little octaves)
sentirse/sentir: you can feel/to feel
lo mismo que hice: the same as I did
hago de adulta: I do it as an adult
espero/esperar: I wait/to wait
junto: together with
nunca deben morir: must never die

CULTURE NOTE

In Spain, Christmas Eve is known as *Nochebuena* or "the Good Night." Family members gather together to rejoice and feast around the Nativity scenes that are present in nearly every home. A traditional Christmas treat is *turrón*, an almond candy. The *Magi* are also revered in Spain. Children leave their shoes on the windowsills and fill them with straw, carrots, and barley for the horses of the Wise Men. Their favorite is *Baltasar*, who rides a donkey and is the one believed to leave the gifts.

The main Christmas celebration in Mexico is called *las posadas*, which refers to processions reenacting Joseph and Mary's search for a place to stay in Bethlehem. The pilgrims travel from house to house asking for shelter and are refused until they finally reach the house where an altar and nativity scene have been set up. Here they are admitted with great rejoicing, a traditional prayer is spoken, and the celebration begins. The holiday flower, the poinsettia, is native to Mexico. The enchanting legend of the poinsettia dates back several centuries to a Christmas Eve in Mexico when a small child had no gift to present to the Christ child. On the way to church the child gathered some branches found along the road. The legend tells that the branches were laid by the the altar and a miracle happened. The branches blossomed with brilliant red flowers. At that time they were called *Flores de Noche Buena;* today they are called poinsettias.

San Fermín: Pamplona's patron saint
sin duda: undoubtedly, without doubt
desenfreno: wild abandon, debauchery
inunda/inundar: it swamps/to flood
ríos de: floods of (literally: rivers of)
corren/correr: they run/to run
de boca en boca: to do the rounds
    (literally: from mouth to mouth)
canciones populares: folk songs
no dan tregua: they give no respite
descanso: rest, break
fajas y pañuelos: sashes and scarves
inmensos: enormous
toros bravos: fierce bulls
mostrando/mostrar: showing/to show
encoge el corazón: it makes their heart
    miss a beat
fama: fame
gozan/gozar: they enjoy/to enjoy
debe agradecerse: is due
en gran medida: to a great extent
ensalzaba/ensalzar: praised/to praise

no obstante: nevertheless
cuentan/contar: they tell/to tell
Sanfermines: popular name for the
    feast of San Fermín
surgieron/surgir: they appeared/to
    appear, to emerge
época de los romanos: Roman times
ferias comerciales: commercial show
taurinas: bullfighting (adjective)
ambas: both
se prolongaron/prolongarse: they
    went on/to go on
contaron/contar: they had/to have
pregón: local festival opening speech
torneo: tournament, competition
corrida de toros: bullfight
años sucesivos: consecutive years
mientras las fiestas crecían en días:
    while the feast grew in days
se fueron intercalando/intercalar:
    they were placed in/to put in
fuegos artificiales: fireworks

pistoletazo de salida: starting signal
chupinazo: fierce shot
cohete: rocket
se lanza/lanzar: it is launched/
    to launch
mediodía: midday, noon
balcón: balcony
ayuntamiento: city hall
se duchan/ducharse: they take a
    shower/to take a shower
vino tino: red wine

7 de julio San Fermín
ESPAÑA

La revolución llega a Pamplona cada 7 de julio. Ese día empiezan las fiestas de **San Fermín**, **sin duda**, una de las más famosas de España. Durante una semana, el **desenfreno inunda** las calles de la ciudad y **ríos de** vino **corren de boca en boca**, entre bailes y **canciones populares**, que **no dan tregua** al **descanso**.   Las imágenes de jóvenes vestidos de blanco con sus **fajas y pañuelos** rojos corriendo delante de **inmensos toros bravos** dan la vuelta al mundo cada año, **mostrando** así una tradición ancestral que **encoge el corazón** de los telespectadores. La **fama** internacional de que **gozan** estas fiestas pamplonesas **debe agradecerse**, **en gran medida**, al escritor norteamericano Ernest Hemingway, quien en su novela *The sun also rises* **ensalzaba** estas celebraciones.

TRADICIÓN ANCESTRAL

No obstante, las fiestas de San Fermín se celebran desde hace más de 400 años. **Cuentan** los historiadores que los **Sanfermines surgieron** de la unión de tres fiestas diferentes: las de carácter religioso en honor al santo y que existen desde la **época de los romanos**, las **ferias comerciales** y las **taurinas**, organizadas **ambas** a partir del siglo XIV. En 1591 nacieron los Sanfermines, que en su primera edición **se prolongaron** durante dos días y **contaron** con **pregón**, actuaciones musicales, **torneo**, teatro y **corrida de toros**. En **años sucesivos**, **mientras las fiestas crecían en días**, **se fueron intercalando** nuevas diversiones como los **fuegos artificiales** y las danzas.

Desde 1941 el **pistoletazo de salida** lo da el **chupinazo**, un **cohete** de gran potencia que **se lanza** el 6 de julio a las 12 del **mediodía** desde el **balcón** del **Ayuntamiento**. En ese momento los pamplonicas **se duchan**, literalmente, con litros y litros de **vino tinto**, bebida también preferida durante toda la semana.

En los bares y los **chiringuitos**, el alcohol se vende **en cantidades industriales** que ayudan a **mantener los ojos abiertos** durante tantos días. Las **sanfermineras**, con **letras mordaces** y divertidas, son escuchadas por todas las **esquinas**.

EL ENCIERRO

El encierro es el **momento estrella** de las fiestas de San Fermín. Antes de las ocho de la mañana, hora puntual del inicio, las bandas musicales **tocan** por las calles para despertar a los que quieran correr o ver el emocionante espectáculo. Aunque en televisión parecen **interminables**, los encierros son **carreras** muy cortas, de unos tres minutos de duración que se corren a gran velocidad a lo largo de unos 800 metros. Para este **reto** hay que estar preparado. **De hecho**, los auténticos **pamplonicas** que **se plantan delante de** las **bestias entrenan** durante todo el año para ser **capaces** de **aguantar** la velocidad y la resistencia necesarias para estar delante de seis toros, ocho **cabestros** y tres **mansos sueltos** que les persiguen. **Acabada la carrera**, los toros llegan a la plaza para morir en **apasionantes** corridas.

Por desgracia, cada año hay varios **heridos**, e incluso muertos en algunas ocasiones, **como resultado de** las heridas o contusiones que **sufren** durante los encierros. La **falta de sueño** y la **valentía inconsciente** que da el exceso de alcohol son **malos compañeros** para las decenas de jóvenes que se ponen a correr delante del toro por las **estrechas** calles del **casco antiguo** de Pamplona. Los **extranjeros** suelen ser los peor parados posiblemente porque la falta de información y el **desconocimiento** del español les hacen no prestar atención a las indicaciones y **advertencias** que los organizadores **transmiten** a **los asistentes**.

Y así, entre **cabezadas** en parques, plazas y **portales**, **borracheras** y mucha, mucha **juerga transcurren** los sanfermines hasta que el día 14, a las 12 de la **medianoche**, llegan oficialmente a su fin. Es el momento de cantar el **¡Pobre de mí!**, **quitarse** el pañuelo del cuello y **encender velas** en **señal de tristeza**, **no sin antes alegrarse de** que ya falta menos para las fiestas del **año que viene**.

---

chiringuitos: refreshment stands
en cantidades industriales: in huge amounts
mantener los ojos abiertos: to keep one's eyes open
sanfermineras: songs sung during the Sanfermines
letras mordaces: sharp, caustic lyrics
esquinas: corners

el encierro: the running of the bulls
momento estrella: star moment
tocan/tocar: they play/to play
interminables: never-ending
carreras: races
reto: challenge
de hecho: in fact
pamplonicas: noun to refer to the locals
se plantan: they plant themselves
delante de: in front of
bestias: beasts
entrenan/entrenar: they train/to train
capaces: capable, able
aguantar: to cope with, to stand
cabestros: leading-bull
mansos: tame
sueltos: loose
acabada la carrera: once the race is over
apasionantes: thrilling

por desgracia: unfortunately
heridos: wounded
como resultado de: as a result of
sufren/sufrir: they suffer/to suffer
falta de sueño: lack of sleep
valentía inconsciente: thoughtless courage
malos compañeros: bad partners
estrechas: narrow
casco antiguo: old quarter
extranjeros: foreigners
desconocimiento: ignorance
advertencias: warnings
transmiten/transmitir: they pass on/to pass on
los asistentes: those present

cabezadas: nods, dozes
portales: front door
borracheras: drunkenness
juerga: binge
transcurren/transcurrir: they pass/ to pass
medianoche: midnight
¡Pobre de mí!: Poor me!
quitarse: to take off
encender velas: to light candles
señal de tristeza: sign of sadness
no sin antes alegrarse de: not without being happy that
año que viene: next year

¡Viva el novio! ¡Viva la novia!
ESPAÑA

Hace pocos meses tuve la ocasión de **asistir** a la **boda** de mi **sobrina**. Aunque la costumbre española es celebrar la boda en la ciudad de la novia, mi sobrina **decidió casarase** en  Burgos, **a pesar de que** ella es de Madrid. ¿Por qué? La **razón** es muy **sencilla**: **sus padres se casaron** en esa **iglesia**. **Además**, es un **escenario** extraordinario, **debido al retablo** del **siglo** XVI. ¡Maravilloso!

Hablando de la celebración, **pocas cosas** han cambiado. En España, es tradición que la novia **llegue tarde** a la iglesia. Pero en esta boda, **tuvimos que esperar**...¡casi media hora! Mientras, el novio tiene que esperar, muy nervioso, **hasta que llegue el coche** con la novia y el **padrino** (normalmente el padre de la futura **esposa**).

Durante la celebración, la **misa sigue su curso normal**, **mientras que fuera de** la iglesia, los amigos de los novios **preparan una broma**. En este caso, cuando los novios **salieron** de la iglesia, **encontraron** su coche **lleno de globos**. Esta es una broma muy popular, pero hay bromas más originales, como por ejemplo, **alquilar** un **carro** y un **burro**, y **pasear a los novios** por el centro de la ciudad.

¡Viva!: Long live! Hurray!
novio: groom
novia: bride
hace pocos meses: few months ago
asistir: to attend
boda: wedding
sobrina: niece
decidió casarse: she decided to get married
a pesar de que: in spite of the fact that
razón: reason
sencilla: simple
sus padres se casaron: her parents got married
iglesia: church
además: also
escenario: scene
debido al retablo: due to the altarpiece
siglo: century

hablando/hablar: talking/to talk
pocas cosas: few things
llegue tarde: she is late
tuvimos que: we had to
esperar: wait
casi media hora: nearly half an hour
hasta que llegue el coche: until the car arrives
padrino: best man
esposa: wife

durante: during
misa: mass
sigue su curso normal: it takes its normal course
mientras que: whereas
fuera de: outside of
preparan una broma: they prepare a joke
salieron/salir: they went out/to go out
encontraron/encontrar: they found/ to find
lleno de globos: full of balloons
alquilar: to rent, to hire
carro: cart
burro: donkey
pasear a los novios: to take the bride and groom for a ride

Seguidamente, los novios van a **hacer las fotos**, mientras que los **invitados** vamos a "tomar algo", **como se dice usualmente**. "¿Tomar algo"? Sí, es simplemente ir a algún bar o cafetería cerca de la iglesia y **hacer tiempo hasta la hora de ir** al restaurante para comer o cenar.

En este caso, ya que la boda **se celebró** a las 5:30 de la tarde, todos los invitados **nos encontramos** en el hotel para cenar. Primero, un "lunch", y seguidamente fuimos al **comedor**. **Concretamente**, este hotel us un **antiguo convento rehabilitado**, y el comedor se encuentra en **el que antes era** el **claustro**. ¡Es **agradable** cenar **rodeado por** columnas con **tantos siglos** de historia!

Y finalmente, después de la cena...¡**fuimos a bailar**! Pero primero tienen que bailar los novios, y **por supuesto**, un **vals**. El baile **suele durar** unas 3 o 4 horas. **Poco a poco**, los invitados **nos iremos**, **deseando** a los **recién casados** mucha felicidad. ¡Y una preciosa **luna de miel**!

seguidamente: next	
hacer las fotos: take the pictures	
invitados: guests	
como se dice usualmente: as it is usually said	
hacer tiempo: to kill time	
hasta la hora de ir: until its time to go	
se celebró/celebrar: it was celebrated/ to celebrate	
nos encontramos/encontrarse: we met/to meet	
comedor: dining room	
concretamente: particularly	
antiguo convento rehabilitado: old restored convent	
el que antes era: what previously was	
claustro: cloister	
agradable: nice	
rodeado por: surrounded by	
tantos siglos: so many centuries	
fuimos a bailar: we went to dance	
por supuesto: of course	
vals: waltz	
suele durar: usually lasts	
poco a poco: little by little	
nos iremos: we will leave	
deseando/desear: wishing/to wish	
recién casados: newlyweds	
luna de miel: honeymoon	

CULTURE NOTE It has been a long-standing tradition for Spanish brides to carry orange blossoms in their bouquet. The orange blossom symbolizes chastity and purity; because the orange tree is an evergreen, it also represents everlasting love. It is also said that since the orange tree bears fruit and blossoms at the same time, its flowers represent happiness and fulfillment. Before getting married in Spain, the groom gives his bride a wedding present of thirteen coins. This gift is a symbol of his commitment to support her and a symbol of sharing everything together. The bride-to-be then carries these coins, in a small bag, to her wedding ceremony. After the wedding the bride tosses her bouquet into the air similar to American weddings. In addition the bride may have a basket of pins. The pins, often resembling lilies or orchids, are given to all the ladies at the reception. They wear them upside down while dancing. If the pin falls out, the girl will marry!

hay un lugar: there is a place
construir castillos en el aire: to build castles in the air
se trata de: it is about
desde hace más de dos siglos: since more than two centuries ago
se levantan/levantar: they built/ to build
torres humanas: human towers
las palabras no suelen hacer justicia: words don't usually do justice
espectáculo: show
suscita/suscitar: provokes/to provoke
en directo: live

parece ser que: it seems that
dio sus primeros pasos: it took its first steps
acababa elevando a algunos de sus bailarines: it ended up raising some of the dancers
ni mucho menos al nivel de: far from the level of
fue evolucionando: it evolved
hasta convertirse en: until they become

tambor: drum
gralla: oboe-like instrument
personas de diversas edades y sexos: people of different ages and genders
unas sobre de otras: one on top of the other
pies en los hombros: feet on the shoulders
que está debajo: that is underneath
que se van tocando: that are played
indican/indicar: they indicate/to indicate
de la base: of the base
qué altura lleva la torre: what is the height of the tower at that moment
puedan calcular: they can calculate
tendrán que resistir el peso: they will have to hold the weight
puede haber: there can be
y hasta: and up to
por piso: in each floor
dependiendo del tipo de "castell" que se levante: depending on the kind of "castell" that is being raised
se corona: it is crowned
altura maxima: maximum height
que se ha conseguido hasta ahora: that has been reached until now
que gira entre: that it is between
"caps de colla": expression to define the "casteller" that leads the "colla"
con base a: according to
reglas arquitectónicas: architectural rules
deciden/decidir: they decide/to decide
forman/formar: they form/to form
en función de: depending on
peso: weight
altura: height
fuerza: strength

Castillos en el aire
ESPAÑA

Hay un lugar en el mundo donde es posible **construir castillos en el aire**. **Se trata de** Cataluña, una región española en la que **desde hace más de dos siglos se levantan** "castells", unas **torres humanas** de más de 15 metros de altura. Esta es una de las tradiciones catalanas más difíciles de explicar ya que **las palabras no suelen hacer justicia** al **espectáculo** y a la emoción que una actuación de "castellers" **suscita en directo**.

Parece ser que esta tradición **dio sus primeros pasos** en Valencia en el siglo XVII, donde una de sus danzas tradicionales **acababa elevando a algunos de sus bailarines**, aunque **ni mucho menos al nivel de** los "castellers". Cuando este baile llegó a las tierras del sur de Cataluña **fue evolucionando hasta convertirse en** auténticas torres humanas.

A ritmo de **tambor** y "**gralla**", **personas de diversas edades y sexos** se levantan **unas sobre de otras** con los **pies en los hombros** del compañero **que está debajo**. Las diferentes notas musicales **que se van tocando indican** a los "castellers" **de la base qué altura lleva la torre**, para que **puedan calcular** con mejor precisión cuánto tiempo más **tendrán que resistir el peso**. **Puede haber** dos, tres, cuatro **y hasta** cinco personas **por piso, dependiendo del tipo de "castell" que se levante**, aunque siempre **se corona** con un niño o niña. La **altura máxima que se ha conseguido hasta ahora** es de 10 pisos, unos 15 metros aproximadamente, con un número de personas **que gira entre** 50 y 100. Los "**caps de colla**", **con base a reglas arquitectónicas**, **deciden** la distribución de los "castellers" que **forman** la torre **en función de** su **peso**, **altura**, agilidad y **fuerza**.

Una competición de "castellers", **con varias collas participando**, **puede durar** varias horas, aunque para **levantar** un "castell" no se necesita más de 10 minutos. Unas torres **suben**, otras **caen**, unas son más **anchas**, otras más **altas**, pero en todas se produce una unión intergeneracional perfecta entre abuelos, padres, hijos y nietos. **Los mayores** en la base, los más jóvenes en la **cima**, en una **clara metáfora de la vida misma. A pesar de** que los "castells" **desafían** la **ley de la gravedad** en cada una de sus **actuaciones, no llevan ningún tipo de protección. El atuendo** de un "casteller" se compone de unos **pantalones blancos ajustados**, una **faja alrededor del cuerpo** de color negro, una **camisa holgada** del color distintivo de la "colla" y un **pañuelo rojo en la cabeza**. Los **pies están descalzos** para que **se agarren** mejor **sin hacer daño** a los cuerpos de sus compañeros durante la **escalada**.

No es extraño ver caer una de las torres, como si de un **castillo de naipes** se tratara. La estructura empieza a tambalearse y la torre **acaba derrumbándose**. La **gran cantidad** de "castellers" que **se concentra** en la base, **a modo de tela de araña, hace que sean las propias personas** las que **amortigüen** las posibles **caídas**. La competitividad entre las diferentes "collas" de Cataluña está presente **en cada** "díada castellera" **por ver quién** levanta la torre más alta, **reuniendo** a **cientos** de personas en un **ambiente** incomparable. Quizás los "castells" sean la tradición que mejor define el carácter de los catalanes: **trabajo en equipo, esfuerzo**, la **capacidad de sufrimiento, afán de superación** y **cordura**.

con varias collas participando:	with several "collas" participating
puede durar:	can last
levantar:	to raise
suben/subir:	they go up/to go up
caen/caer:	they fall down/to fall down
anchas:	wide
altas:	tall
los mayores:	the oldest ones
cima:	on the top
clara metáfora de la vida misma:	clear, evident metaphor of life itself
a pesar de:	in spite of
desafían/desafiar:	they challenge/to challenge, to defy
ley de la gravedad:	the law of gravity
actuaciones:	performances
no llevan ningún tipo de protección:	they don't wear any kind of protection
el atuendo:	the attire
pantalones blancos ajustados:	tight white pants
faja:	sash
alrededor del cuerpo:	around their bodies
camisa holgada:	loose shirt
pañuelo rojo en la cabeza:	red handkerchief on the head
pies están descalzos:	feet are bare
se agarren:	they hold on tightly
sin hacer daño:	without causing harm
escalada:	climb
castillo de naipes:	house of cards
acaba derrumbándose:	it ends up collapsing
gran cantidad:	great amount
se concentra:	gathers
a modo de:	like
tela de araña:	spider web
hace que sean las propias personas:	it makes the people be
amortigüen:	they break
caídas:	fall
en cada:	on each
por ver quién:	to see who
reuniendo/reunir:	gathering/to gather
cientos:	hundreds
ambiente:	atmosphere
trabajo en equipo:	teamwork
esfuerzo:	effort
capacidad de sufrimiento:	suffering capacity
afán de superación:	desire for self-improvement
cordura:	good sense

La leyenda de la Colosuca

HONDURAS

Cuenta la leyenda que en **tiempos remotos** una **viuda** y madre de **diez hijos se encontraba desesperada**. **Sabiéndose** sola en el **mundo** y **único sostén** de sus hijos, **no sabía dónde encontrar** los **recursos** necesarios **para alimentar** y **dar cobijo** a sus niños.

La mujer **salió** desesperada al **bosque** y **buscó** durante **largos días** frutos y hierbas que **le sirvieran** de **alimento**. Sin embargo, **no pudo encontrar** nada y **sintiéndose acorralada** una noche **le pidió llorando** a su dios que no permitiera que sus hijos **murieran** de **hambre**. Esa noche, su **dios le habló** en sus **sueños** y **le indicó** cómo encontrar alimentos.

Al **día siguiente**, cuando la mujer despertó, **vio** a sus hijos **felices** y **jugando** en el bosque. Pero como **no confió** en su dios, **desoyó** las indicaciones que **le fueron dadas** en el sueño y **volvió otra vez** al bosque a buscar alimentos.

El espíritu divino **se enfureció al ver** que **ella pedía ayuda** y, al **recibirla**, **desoía** sus **palabras**. Su **enojo** fue tal que **decidió castigarla** y mientras la viuda buscaba alimentos, una gran tormenta **se desató** en el bosque. Un enorme **rayo la alcanzó** y la transformó en un **pájaro**. Su **cuerpo se cubrió** de **plumas** y sus **brazos** se transformaron en **alas**. Sólo su **rostro se mantuvo intacto**.

Desde ese día **se dice** que la colosuca es un **ave** con rostro de mujer que **sobrevuela** la región de los lenca, a quienes se considera como sus hijos.

---

cuenta/contar: tells/to tell, to narrate
tiempos remotos: remote times
viuda: widow
diez hijos: ten children
se encontraba desesperada: was desperate
sabiéndose: knowing herself to be
mundo: world
único sostén: only support
no sabía/saber: (she) didn't know/ to know
dónde encontrar: where to find
recursos: resources
para alimentar: to feed
dar cobijo: to give shelter

salió/salir: went out/to go out
bosque: forest
buscó/buscar: looked for/to look for
largos días: long days
le sirvieran: would serve her
alimento: food
no pudo encontrar: wasn't able to find
sintiéndose acorralada: feeling trapped
le pidió/pedir: (she) asked (him/her)/ to ask
llorando: crying
murieran/morir: to die/to die
hambre: hunger
dios: god
le habló/hablar: talked to her/to talk
sueños: dreams
le indicó/indicar: pointed out to her, indicated/to indicate

día siguiente: next day
vio/ver: saw/to see
felices: happy
jugando/jugar: playing/to play
no confió/confiar: didn't trust/to trust
desoyó/desoír: disregarded/ to disregard, to ignore
le fueron dadas: were given to her
volvió/volver: returned/to return
otra vez: again

se enfureció/enfurecerse: become furious/to become furious
al ver: seeing
ella pedía ayuda: she asked for help
recibirla: receiving it
desoía/desoír: disregarded/to disregard
palabras: word
enojo: anger
decidió castigarla: decided to punish her
se desató/desatarse: was unleashed/ to unleash
rayo: lightning bolt
la alcanzó: reached her
pájaro: bird
cuerpo: body
se cubrió/cubrir: was covered/to cover
plumas: feathers
brazos: arms
alas: wings
rostro: face
se mantuvo intacto: remained intact

se dice/decir: it is said/to say
ave: bird
sobrevuela/sobrevolar: flies over/ to fly over

Día Internacional del Libro

ESPAÑA

En 1995, la Conferencia General de la UNESCO reunida en París **dio su visto bueno** a la celebración del Día Internacional del Libro y de los **Derechos de Autor**, que **había sido propuesto** por la Unión Internacional de Editores. La **fecha** que **se escogió** fue el 23 de abril por una razón muy **sencilla**: en ese día de 1616 **murieron** dos grandes **escritores** de la literatura universal: William Shakespeare y Miguel de Cervantes. Gracias al Día del Libro **se fomenta** la **lectura** y también la defensa de la **propiedad intelectual**. Aunque fue oficialmente **instaurado** para todo el mundo en el año 1995, en España se celebra desde el 23 de abril de 1930. La tradición **se amplió posteriormente**, en el año 1964, a todos los países de **habla** castellana y portuguesa y por último, en el 1993, **fue adoptado** por la Unión Europea.

En España es un día muy especial. En la **calle**, la gente pasea y **se para** en los **puestos** que los **libreros instalan** en las zonas céntricas de cada localidad. Las librerías hacen **descuentos** en el **precio** de las publicaciones y, en las principales ciudades, escritores **de renombre promocionan** sus obras **firmando** los libros de quiénes las han comprado los **compradores** que **quieren** tener su autógrafo. Desde las últimas **novedades** en novela o poesía hasta libros de arte, decoración o fotografía, pasando por publicaciones dedicadas a la historia, a la **cocina** o a esos **antiguos** libros que los **coleccionistas** y **amantes** de la literatura **compran** con los **ojos cerrados**. Libros dedicados a diferentes aficiones como la **pintura**, el **dibujo**, las **manualidades** o el **ganchillo**.

Pero también hay una gran variedad de oferta literaria para los más pequeños de la casa. No sólo libros educativos sino también **tebeos** y libros de aventuras, pensados para fomentar la lectura entre los niños. Éste es uno de los **objetivos** fundamentales del Día Internacional del Libro, que siempre **recibe** un gran **apoyo** por parte de **entidades** públicas y privadas, los escritores, las **bibliotecas**, los libreros y los **medios de comunicación**.

---

dio su visto bueno/dar el visto bueno: it approved/ to approve
Derechos de Autor: Author's Copyrights
había sido propuesto/ser proponer: it had been proposed/to propose
fecha: date
se escogió/escoger: it was chosen/ to choose
sencilla: simple
murieron/morir: they died/to die
escritores: writers
se fomenta/fomentar: it is promoted/ to promote
lectura: reading
propiedad intelectual: intellectual property
instaurado/instaurar: established/ to establish
se amplió/ampliar: it was extended/ to extend
posteriormente: later
habla: language
fue adoptado/adoptar: it was adopted/to adopt

calle: street
se para/parar: (people) stop/to stop
puestos: stands
libreros: booksellers
instalan/instalar: they set up/to set up
descuentos: discounts
precio: price
de renombre: renowned, famous
promocionan/promocionar: they promote/to promote
firmando/firmar: signing/to sign
compradores: buyers
quieren/querer: they want/to want

novedades: novelties
cocina: cooking
antiguos: old
coleccionistas: collectors
amantes: lovers
compran/comprar: they buy/to buy
ojos cerrados: eyes closed
pintura: painting
dibujo: drawing
manualidades: handicrafts
ganchillo: crochet

tebeos: comics
objetivos: goals
recibe/recibir: it receives/to receive
apoyo: support
entidades: organizations, institutions
bibliotecas: libraries
medios de comunicación: mass media

a tan sólo: only
se encuentra/encontrarse: is/to be
riqueza: richness, wealth
parece/parecer: seems/to seem
estar dispuesta: to be willing
conservar: to preserve
aquellos: those
rasgos: characteristics
la distinguen: distinguish it
aunque: even though
claro está: of course
tarea: task
la circundan: surround it

se compone de/componerse de: is
  made up of/to be made up of
mestizos: *of mixed heritage, particularly
  of Indian and white parentage*
se suma/sumar: is added/to add
propia: own
hace que: makes, causes
se distinga/distinguirse: is
  characterized/to be characterized
se pueda establecer: it is possible
  to establish
entre: between
tanto... como: as... as
ambas: both

posee/poseer: has/to have
marcados: marked
se destacan/destacarse: stand out/
  to stand out, to distinguish
vida familiar: family life
se organiza/organizar: is organized/
  to organize
agrupadas: grouped
se trabaja/trabajar: one works/to work
de modo mancomunado: joining forces
regida por: ruled by
mediar: to mediate
gestionar: to manage
recursos: resources
tomar: to take
portavoz: spokeperson
debe reunirse: has to get together
vecinos: neighbours
líderes: leaders
se reúnen/reunirse: get together/
  to get together
se forma/formar: is formed/to form
cabildo: council
se tratan/tratar: are dealt with/
  to deal with
clave: key
mencionar: to mention
desarrollo: development
cosechas: harvests
apertura: opening
mantenimiento: maintenance
caminos: roads, ways, paths
de las que depende: from which
  ... depends
supervivencia de todos: everybody's
  survival

Otávalo
ECUADOR

En Ecuador, **a tan sólo** 110 kilómetros al norte de Quito, **se encuentra** Otávalo. En esta región, la **riqueza** de las culturas locales **parece estar dispuesta** a **conservar aquellos rasgos** que **la distinguen aunque**, **claro está**, esta **tarea** se encuentra en permanente diálogo con las regiones urbanas que **la circundan**.

La población de Otávalo **se compone de mestizos** y aborígenes. Esta heterogeneidad, a la que **se suma** además la **propi**a de los diferentes grupos indígenas, **hace que** la zona **se distinga** por su abundante producción y riqueza cultural. Aunque **se pueda establecer** una distinción **entre** áreas rurales y urbanas, **tanto** mestizos **como** indígenas se encuentran presentes en **ambas** zonas.

La comunidad indígena **posee** rasgos **marcados** entre los que **se destacan** su organización social, la **vida familiar** y comunitaria. La vida comunitaria de los indígenas **se organiza** en runas **agrupadas** en un mismo territorio. Allí **se trabaja de modo mancomunado**. La comunidad se encuentra **regida por** un grupo responsable de **mediar** en los conflictos, **gestionar recursos** y **tomar** decisiones importantes. Este grupo oficia de **portavoz** en aquellas oportunidades en que cada grupo **debe reunirse** con sus **vecinos**. Cuando los **líderes** de los diferentes grupos **se reúnen**, **se forma** un **cabildo** en el **se tratan** temas **clave**. Entre estos temas se puede **mencionar** el **desarrollo** de las **cosechas**, la **apertura** y **mantenimiento** de los **caminos**, la administración del agua y otras cuestiones **de las que depende** la **supervivencia de todos**.

El **jefe** supremo, quien es **elegido** entre los **varones** que representan a los diferentes grupos, ocupa el **lugar** de la **ley** y es el **hombre** que **posee** el mayor prestigio y **reconocimiento** social. Él es el **encargado** de **celebrar matrimonios** y es portavoz de todos.

La familia posee un **lugar central** para los grupos indígenas de Otávalo. **De hecho**, los aborígenes consideran "familia" hasta la cuarta generación. Esto significa que los **lazos comunitarios** resulten especialmente **estrechos** y marcados por el **devenir** de las relaciones familiares.

La celebración del matrimonio es un **acontecimiento que convoca no sólo** a las familias **involucradas sino también** a vecinos y **allegados**. **Durante** la ceremonia, el jefe supremo hace que las familias **intercambien** sus respectivos rosarios familiares y **habla** de la relación entre los **esposos**, los **hijos** y de **asuntos** relacionados a la convivencia familiar. **Luego de** que esta ceremonia comunitaria **se realiza**, los esposos **pueden contraer matrimonio** en el registro civil oficial.

Los ancianos ocupan un lugar de referencia **dentro de** la vida comunitaria y familiar. **Sin embargo**, en **épocas pasadas** esta situación era **aún más notoria** que en **estos días**. Esto **se debe** a que las migraciones de las generaciones más **jóvenes reorganizan** la dinámica social. Al **buscar nuevos horizontes**, los jóvenes se encuentran **obligados a establecer** relaciones con el **afuera** y a **aprender** nuevas **destrezas** y **habilidades** que **les permitan sobrevivir**. La educación bilingüe que las nuevas generaciones **reciben** es un factor clave que les permite establecer relaciones con las áreas urbanas y comunidades vecinas en las que **no se habla** el dialecto específico del grupo al **que pertenecen**.

jefe: chief
elegido: elected, chosen
varones: males
lugar: place
ley: law
hombre: man
posee/posser: has/to have
reconocimiento: recognition
encargado: in charge
celebrar: to perform
matrimonios: marriages

lugar central: central place
de hecho: in fact
lazos comunitarios: community ties
estrechos: tight
devenir: evolution

acontecimiento que convoca: event that summons
no sólo … sino también: not only... but also
involucradas: involved
allegados: close friends
durante: during
intercambien: exchange
habla/hablar: talks/to talk
esposos: husband and wife, spouses
hijos: children
asuntos: topics
luego de: after
se realiza/realizar: is done/to do
pueden contraer matrimonio: can marry

los ancianos: older people
ocupan/ocupar: occupy/to occupy
dentro de: within, in
sin embargo: however
épocas pasadas: the past
aún más notoria: even more evident
estos días: nowadays
se debe/deberse: is due to/to be due to
jóvenes: young people
reorganizan: reorganize
buscar: to look for
nuevos horizontes: new horizons
obligados a establecer: forced to establish
afuera: outside
aprender: to learn
destrezas: skills
habilidades: skills
les permitan: allow them
sobrevivir: to survive
reciben/recibir: receive/to receive
no se habla: is not spoken
que pertenecen: they belong to

Examina tu comprensión

Chichicastenango, página 57

1. ¿Qué santo es celebrado y honrado aquí?

2. ¿Cuál es el nombre de la actividad más curiosa en la celebración?

3. ¿Por qué manuscrito es famoso Chichicastenango?

La Pachamama, página 58

1. ¿Qué significa la palabra pachamama?

2. ¿Qué tipos de ofrendas se preparan?

3. Al final de la ceremonia se colocan ofrendas en la tierra. ¿Qué simbolizan esas ofrendas?

Una Navidad en Paraguay, página 61

1. En América del Sur, ¿en qué estación se celebra Navidad?

2. ¿Con qué se decora el pesebre?

La gritería, página 62

1. ¿A qué da comienzo esta celebración?

2. ¿Qué gritan los nicaragüenses? ¿Cuál es la respuesta?

Test your comprehension

Gaspar, Melchor y Baltasar, página 64

1. ¿Qué suelen dejar los niños puertorriqueños debajo de sus camas?

2. ¿Qué hace el presidente de Puerto Rico el 5 de enero?

7 de julio San Fermín, página 66

1. ¿A quién atribuyen los españoles esta tradición, tal cual se practica hoy en día? ¿Qué libro fue escrito acerca de esta tradición?

2. ¿Cuánto tiempo hace que se celebra esta tradición?

3. ¿Cuál fue el motivo original de esta tradición?

¡Viva el novio! ¡Viva la novia!, página 68

1. ¿Cuál era la broma que se le hacía al novio y la novia después de la boda?

2. ¿Qué tipo de edificio fue el hotel antes de la restauración?

3. ¿Qué tipo de baile bailaban los novios?

Castillos en el aire, página 70

1. ¿Qué son los castillos en el aire?

2. ¿Cómo es el torre una clara metáfora de la vida misma?

3. Describa la ropa de los castellars.

Algún día en cualquier parte, en cualquier lugar
indefectiblemente te encontrarás a ti mismo, y ésa, sólo ésa,
puede ser la más feliz o la más amarga de tus horas.

Pablo Neruda

Celebración

La Mamá Negra

ECUADOR

La Mamá Negra no es una mujer ni tiene la **piel oscura**. Es una gran fiesta local ecuatoriana que **se celebra** en la **localidad** de Latacunga, a poco más de 80 kilómetros de Quito y cuya máxima representación es un hombre disfrazado de mujer y con la **cara pintada** de negro. ¿Quieren saber más? **¡Pues sigan leyendo!** **Existen** varias versiones **acerca** del origen de la fiesta de la Mamá Negra pero la más popular es la que **sostiene** que es la celebración para **venerar** a la Virgen de la Merced o Santísima Tragedia. En 1742 la ciudad quedó **arrasada** por la erupción del Volcán Cotopaxi. Desde entonces su población **empezó a rendirle homenaje**, con la **esperanza** de que los **protegiera** de nuevas erupciones. Con esta celebración, los habitantes de la ciudad también **festejan** el aniversario de su independencia. Por el carácter pagano que tiene la tradición, algunos **sacerdotes** de la época **suspendieron** el festejo, pero las autoridades de Latacunga **se encargaron** de **promoverla** y **oficiarla nuevamente** en homenaje a la independencia de la ciudad. Por este motivo, hoy en día **se festeja por partida doble**: el 23 de septiembre, fecha que corresponde al día de la Virgen de la Merced, y el 8 de noviembre por la independencia.

Un mes antes de la fecha, el pueblo entero se prepara y **ensaya** los distintos **papeles** de los personajes que **intervendrán** en la danza y el **desfile**. La figura central es la Mamá Negra que, llevando una **muñeca** negra representando a su hija, **cabalga** durante la procesión hasta llegar a la **iglesia** de la Merced. Diferentes personajes la acompañan: su **esposo**, los **huacos**, seres que realizan exorcismos para **limpiar** las **almas** y que **marcan** la presencia de los **chamanes**; el ángel de la estrella que representa al ángel Gabriel; el **rey** moro que simboliza la llegada de los españoles a Ecuador; el capitán símbolo del ejército y muchos más, algunos de los cuales van **repartiendo tragos** a su **paso**. Este **cortejo recorre** las calles **bailando** y **cantando** al **compás** de las bandas que **deleitan incansanbles** con su música.

---

piel oscura: dark skin

se celebra/celebrarse: it is celebrated/ to celebrate

localidad: location, place

cara: face

pintada: painted

¡Pues sigan leyendo!: Then, keep on reading!

existen/existir: they exist/to exist

acerca: about

sostiene/sostener: it supports/to support

venerar: to adore, to worship

arrasada/arrasar: devastated/ to devastate

empezó/empezar: it began/to begin

rendirle homenaje: to pay homage to her

esperanza: hope

protegiera/proteger: it would protect/ to protect

festejan/festejar: they celebrate/ to celebrate

sacerdotes: priests

suspendieron/suspender: they cancelled/to cancel, to call off

se encargaron/encargarse: they look after/to look after

promoverla: to promote it

oficiarla: to celebrate it, to officiate it

nuevamente: again

se festeja por partida doble: two things at once are celebrated

ensaya/ensayar: they rehearse/ to rehearse, to practice

papeles: roles

intervendrán/intervenir: they will perform/to perform

desfile: parade

muñeca: doll

cabalga/cabalgar: it rides/to ride

iglesia: church

esposo: spouse

huacos: beings that conduct exorcisms

limpiar: to clean

almas: souls

marcan/marcar: they mark/to mark

chamanes: shamans

rey: king

repartiendo/repartir: distributing/ to distribute

tragos: drinks

paso: passing

cortejo: entourage

recorre/recorrer: goes through/ to go through

bailando/bailar: dancing/to dance

cantando/cantar: singing/to sing

compás: rhythm

deleitan/deleitar: they delight/to delight

incansables: tireless

El Salvador del Mundo

SAN SALVADOR

Cada año, cuando **comienza** el mes de agosto, los salvadoreños están de fiesta. Del 4 al 6 de ese mes **le rinden homenaje** a su patrono, San Salvador del Mundo, y las **festividades** que **se organizan** en su honor son unas de las más importantes del país.

Durante **toda la semana**, los habitantes **participan** de **desfiles**, procesiones y actos religiosos y culturales. Las actividades culturales y **recreativas** van desde los conciertos de **música folklórica** hasta **espectáculos de fuegos artificiales**. También se organiza una **feria** donde los presentes pueden **comprar recuerdos** de su patrono y otras **artesanías**. **Aunque se trata** de una celebración nacional, los habitantes de la capital son los que **cuentan** con la agenda más **abultada** ya que **casi todas** las actividades **se concentran** allí.

Los actos religiosos **se realizan** en la **Basílica del Sagrado Corazón** y la **atracción principal** es la tradicional "bajada" o **procesión del santo**, la cual hace un **recorrido** por las **calles principales** del centro de San Salvador **representando** la transfiguración de Jesucristo.

cada año: each year
comienza/comenzar: it starts/to start
le rinden homenaje: they pay homage
festividades: festivitites
se organizan/organizarse: they are organized/to organize

toda la semana: all week
participan/participar: they participate/to participate
desfiles: parades
recreativas: recreational
música folklórica: folk music
espectáculos de fuegos artificiales: fireworks show
feria: fair
comprar: to buy
recuerdos: keepsakes, souvenirs
artesanías: crafts
aunque: although
se trata/tratarse: it is about/ to be about
cuentan/contar: they have/to have
abultada: big
casi todas: almost all
se concentran/concentrarse: they concentrate/to concentrate

se realizan/realizarse: are carried out/ to carry out
Basílica del Sagrado Corazón: Basilica of the Sacred Heart
atracción principal: main attraction
procesión del santo: procession of the saint
recorrido: round
calles principales: main streets
representando: representing

CULTURE NOTE

Because Spanish was introduced so long ago to Central America, the Spanish spoken in this region has variants and idioms, some regional and others particular to each country. Many *Nahuatl* words are used in El Salvador. Salvadoran Spanish is also more formal than in other countries. People will often address you with a title such as *señor* or *señora* before speaking your name. When entering a shop or café, Salvadorans frequently speak a brief yet polite greeting to everyone in the room. Watching a group of Salvadorans interact is a delight! Gestures, loud voices, and enthusiasm give life to their communication. Greeting by shaking hands and saying *buenos días* or *buenas tardes* is customary. Salvadorans are also very social. Getting together with family and friends is a favorite activity. Dropping in without making prior arrangements is considered acceptable and welcomed.

El Día de los Muertos
MÉXICO

muerte: death
destino: destiny
inexorable: inexorable
vida humana: human life
asusta/asustar: it scares/to scare
angustia: anguish
imitar: to imitate
vivirla: to live it
alegría: joy
reconciliarnos: become reconciled
enfrentar: to confront
miedo: fear
burla: joke
festejar: to celebrate
llorar: to cry

espejo: mirror
refleja/reflejar: it reflects/to reflect
ha vivido: has lived/to live
ilumina/iluminar: it illuminates/
  to illuminate
carece de sentido: it lacks sense
tampoco: neither

hecho de morir: the fact of dying
desconocido: unknown
comienzo: beginning
algo nuevo: something new

luto: mourning
diversión: fun
tristeza: sadness
frente: towards
burlándose: mocking
jugando/jugar: playing/to play
conviviendo: living together
irónicamente: ironically
calaca: death
huesuda: "the bony one"
flaca: "the thin one"
parca: death

se recuerda/recordarse: it is
  remembered/to remember
se llenan/llenarse: they get full of/
  to get full of
ansiosa: eager
compartir: to share
fecha: date
difuntos: the dead
tumba: grave, tomb
compañía: company

La **muerte** es el **destino inexorable** de toda **vida humana**. A muchos su sola idea **asusta** y **angustia**. Pero ¿por qué no **imitar** al pueblo mexicano y **vivirla** con **alegría**? Si es inevitable, ¿por qué no **reconciliarnos** con ella? ¿Por qué no **enfrentar** nuestro **miedo** con la **burla**? ¿Por qué no **festejar** en lugar de **llorar**?

Para los mexicanos la muerte es como un **espejo** que **refleja** la forma en que uno **ha vivido**. Cuando la muerte llega, **ilumina** la vida de uno. Para ellos, si la muerte **carece de sentido**, **tampoco** lo tuvo la vida.

Más que el **hecho de morir,** importa lo que sigue al morir. Ese otro mundo **desconocido** y **comienzo** de **algo nuevo**.

Luto y alegría, **diversión** y **tristeza**, son los sentimientos del pueblo mexicano **frente** a la muerte: ellos también le tienen miedo pero a diferencia de otros, lo reflejan **burlándose, jugando** y **conviviendo** con ella. **Irónicamente**, la llaman "**calaca**", la "**huesuda**", la "**flaca**", la "**parca**".

El 2 de noviembre **se recuerda** no sólo a los muertos sino a la continuidad de la vida: los cementerios del país **se llenan** de gente **ansiosa** por **compartir** esta **fecha** con sus **difuntos**. Familiares y amigos llegan a la **tumba** de su ser querido, con flores, comida y música para disfrutar en su **compañía**.

En la mayoría de los **casos** la fiesta continúa en la casa de alguno, haciendo honor al célebre **dicho popular**: "El muerto al **cajón** y el **vivo al fiestón**".

En las casas **se improvisan** los famosos altares: **sobre** una mesa **cubierta** con un mantel, **se coloca** una fotografía de la persona **fallecida** y allí se hacen las ofrendas.

El rito de la ofrenda es respetado por toda la familia; todos participan **recordando** a los que se **han ido**, y quienes, según **se cree**, **regresan** este día para **gozar** lo que en vida más **disfrutaban**. Se colocan **velas**, flores, guirnaldas y los objetos personales preferidos del **difunto**. También **se disponen** platos tradicionales de la cocina mexicana y todo **se adorna** con calaveritas de azúcar. Entre las ofrendas más importantes está el "pan de muerto": un **pan dulce** preparado especialmente para la ocasión y el cual se adorna con formas de **huesos** hechos de la **misma masa**.

El aire de la casa **se impregna** con el aroma del **copal** que **se quema** en **sahumadores**, según la **creencia** de que los aromas **atraen** al **alma** que **vaga**.

Con todo esto, **no digo** que uno quiera **morirse** pero finalmente, **¿no estaría tan mal, no?**

casos: cases
dicho popular: popular saying
cajón: big box
vivo al fiestón: the living to the big party

se improvisan/improvisarse: they are improvised/to improvise
sobre: on top of
cubierta: covered
se coloca/colocarse: it is placed/ to place
fallecida: passed away

recordando/recordar: remembering/ to remember
han ido/irse: are gone/to be gone
se cree/creerse: it is believed/to believe
regresan/regresar: they return/ to return
gozar: to enjoy
disfrutaban/disfrutar: they enjoyed/ to enjoy
velas: candles
difunto: deceased
se disponen/disponer: are arranged/ to arrange
se adorna/adornar: it is decorated/ to decorate
calaveritas de azúcar: little skulls made out of sugar
pan dulce: sweet bread
huesos: bones
misma masa: same dough

se impregna/impregnarse: it is infused or filled/to infuse or fill
copal: incense
se quema/quemar: it is burned/ to burn
sahumadores: where you put the incense to burn
creencia: belief
atraen/atraer: they attract/to attract
alma: soul
vaga/vagar: it wanders/to wander

no digo/decir: I'm not saying/to say
morirse: to die
¿no estaría tan mal, no?: It wouldn't be that bad, would it?

Festeja su independencia
CHILE

bastón: baton

disponed/disponer: make use of/ to make use of

mando: command

palabras: words

Gobernador: Governor

acudieron/acudir: they came/ to come

vecinos: neighbors

paso: step

unidos: united

tenían/tener: they had/to have

proclamaban/proclamar: they proclaimed/to proclaim

aunque: although

tendrían/tener: they would have/ to have

luchar: to fight

lograr: to obtain

se concretó: it became definite

después: after

conmemora/conmemorar: it commemorates/to commemorate

nuevo: new

llamadas: so-called

festejan/festejar: they celebrate/ to celebrate

nacimiento: birth

libre: free

identidad propia: own identity

duran/durar: they last/to last

toda una semana: all week

feriados: holidays

disfrutan/disfrutar: they enjoy/ to enjoy

desfiles: parades

comidas típicas: typical food

orgullo nacional: national pride

campesinos a caballo: peasants on horseback

ataviados: dressed up

vestimentas de gala: festive clothing

participan/participar: they participate/to participate

se organizan/organizarse: they are organized/to be organized

"Aquí está el **bastón**, **disponed** de él y del **mando**". Con estas **palabras** inició Mateo de Toro y Zambrano, **Gobernador** de Chile en ese momento, la sesión de Cabildo Abierto a la que **acudieron** los máximos representantes de la ciudad y **vecinos** más importantes. Esta reunión, el 18 de septiembre de 1810, era el primer **paso** hacia la Independencia de su país: los chilenos **unidos** por el amor que **tenían** hacia su tierra, **proclamaban** su independencia de España, **aunque tendrían** que **luchar** un tiempo más para **lograr** su libertad total, ya que ésta **se concretó** 8 años **después** (el 12 de febrero de 1818, luego de la Batalla de Maipú. Cada 18 de septiembre el pueblo chileno **conmemora** un **nuevo** aniversario de la Independencia nacional en las **llamadas** Fiestas Patrias. Cada 18 de septiembre **festejan** el **nacimiento** de Chile como una nación independiente, **libre** y con **identidad propia**.

¡A pura fiesta! Las Fiestas Patrias **duran toda una semana**, comenzando el 18. Estos días en general son **feriados** y los chilenos **disfrutan** de **desfiles**, bailes, juegos, música, **comidas típicas** y otras exhibiciones de **orgullo nacional**. En los desfiles, los "huasos" (**campesinos a caballo**), **ataviados** con sus **vestimentas de gala**, **participan** de los rodeos que **se organizan** para la ocasión.

Muchas de las celebraciones se organizan en "**ramadas**" o "**fondas**" cuyo origen data de **aquella época**: estos eran los lugares de entretenimiento del pueblo, que **se establecían** en **terrenos abiertos** y donde **se reunían** a bailar, comer y **distenderse**.

Los músicos **se instalaban** en carros generalmente **techados** con **caña o paja**, y **tocaban** sus instrumentos para **atraer compradores** a las mesas **cubiertas con tortas**, licores y otras delicias. Hoy en día, **rescatando** la tradición e **imitando** las de entonces, las ramadas **se arman** temporalmente en **fincas**, **predios** o **edificios** abiertos con las terrazas cubiertas con paja y **ramas de árboles** y adornados con **guirnaldas**. Allí **se ubican sillas** y mesas dejando un lugar amplio para el baile: entre **cumbias**, **polcas y cuecas**, se ofrece una gran variedad de comidas típicas que incluye el **asado**, las empanadas y la **chicha**.

¡A jugar! Una de las características de estas fiestas es la **cantidad** de juegos tradicionales que se practican. Para nombrar sólo algunos, "el palo ensebado" es uno de los preferidos: consiste en un **palo de madera** de 5 a 6 metros de alto **enterrado** en la tierra, que **se unta** con grasa y que debe ser **trepado** por los competidores que, resbalando una y otra vez, luchan por **alcanzar** el premio que está en la **cima**. Otro de los juegos tradicionales es la "**carrera de sacos**": los competidores corren **metidos** en bolsas o **sacos de arpillera**.

Otros como el **trompo**, la **rayuela**, la **pallana** y las **bolitas**, también **convocan** a grandes y chicos. Y los juegos no sólo están en la tierra sin también más arriba: durante toda esta semana patria, el **cielo chileno se cubre** de formas y colores en continuo movimiento. Es el **reinado** del "**volantín**" o **barrilete**, una de las actividades más populares.

---

ramadas: festival stall
fondas: refreshment stall
aquella época: that time
se establecían/establecerse: they were set up/to set up
terrenos abiertos: open terrain
se reunían/reunirse: they met/to meet
distenderse: to relax

se instalaban/instalarse: they located themselves/to locate oneself
techados: roofed
caña o paja: cane or staw
tocaban/tocar: they played/to play
atraer: to attract
compradores: purchasers, buyers
cubiertas con tortas: covered with cakes
rescatando/rescatar: rescuing/to rescue
imitando/imitar: imitating/to imitate
se arman/armarse: they are set up/ to be set up
fincas: properties
predios: premises
edificios: buildings
ramas de árboles: tree branches
guirnaldas: garlands
se ubican/ubicarse: they are located/ to be located
sillas: chairs
cumbias, polcas y cuecas: dance music
asado: barbecue
chicha: type of alcoholic beverage

cantidad: quantity
palo de madera: wood pole
enterrado/enterrar: buried/to bury
se unta/untar: it is smeared/to smear
trepado: climbed
alcanzar: to reach
cima: top
carrera de sacos: sack race
metidos/meter: put in/to put
sacos de arpillera: cloth sacks

trompo: top, spinning top
rayuela: hopscotch
pallana: game played with little stones
bolitas: marbles
convocan/convocar: they summon/ to summon
cielo chileno: Chilean sky
se cubre/cubrirse: it is covered/ to cover
reinado: reign
volantín: kite
barrilete: kite

¡Menudo tomate!
ESPAÑA

Ríos de **salsa roja fluyen** por las calles de Buñol (Valencia) **como si** de lava de un **volcán** en **erupción** se tratara. La imagen de miles de personas **protagonizando** una **guerra** "**pacífica**" de tomates lleva años **dando la vuelta al mundo** y es que "La Tomatina" es una de las fiestas españolas más conocidas **allende las fronteras** del país.

Como ocurre con muchas otras celebraciones populares, esta tradición **surgió de forma casual**. En agosto de 1945 un grupo de jóvenes **se enzarzó** en una **pelea** en la plaza del pueblo **a la que cada vez se fue sumando** más gente. El **destino quiso** que hubiera cerca un **puesto de verduras y frutas en los alrededores** con las **cajas expuestas** en la calle **para su venta, por lo que** los **implicados** en la **tangana** cogieron tomates y empezaron a **tirárselos unos a otros**, empezando una auténtica **batalla campal**. La policía tuvo que **mediar** en el **asunto** y los responsables del **altercado pagar** todos los **destrozos**.

El **tremendo alboroto no se olvidó** y al año siguiente, **al llegar el mismo miércoles** de agosto, los jóvenes de Buñol volvieron a reunirse en la plaza, **llevando** esta vez ellos los tomates. **Desde entonces y hasta hoy**, cada último miércoles del mes de agosto se celebra La Tomatina.

---

ríos: rivers
salsa roja: red sauce
fluyen/fluir: they flow/to flow
como si: as if
volcán: volcano
erupción: eruption
protagonizando/protagonizar: starring/to star
guerra pacífica: pacific war
dando la vuelta al mundo: going around the world
allende las fronteras: beyond the borders

como ocurre: as it happens
surgió/surgir: it appeared/to appear
de forma casual: in a spontaneous way
se enzarzó/enzarzarse: they got involved/to get involved
pelea: fight
a la que cada vez: to which more and more
se fue sumando/sumarse: they started to join/to join
destino: destiny
quiso: it wanted/to want
puesto de verduras y frutas: fruit and vegetable stand
en los alrededores: in the surrounding areas
cajas: boxes
expuestas: displayed
para su venta: for sale
por lo que: and consequently
implicados: the people involved
tangana: fight, fuss
tirárselos unos a otros: to throw them at one another
batalla campal: pitched battle
mediar: to intercede
asunto: matter, subject
altercado: argument, altercation
pagar: to pay
destrozos: damage, havoc

tremendo alboroto: tremendous uproar
no se olvidó/olividar: it wasn't forgotten/to forget
al llegar el mismo miércoles: when the same Wednesday arrived
llevando/llevar: carrying/to carry
desde entonces y hasta hoy: from then until now

A pesar de la oposición de las autoridades locales durante los primeros años, **lo cierto es que** el **Ayuntamiento** es quien organiza la fiesta y quien compra las más de 120 **toneladas** de tomates que se **lanzan en poco más de** una hora.

El ritual de La Tomatina empieza con la empalmá, que es una **larguísima** noche de fiesta que se "**empalma**" con la mañana. Así, antes del gran momento, los habitantes de Buñol **se reúnen** para **tomar** juntos un gran **desayuno** y **coger fuerzas** para la **lucha**.

Al punto del mediodía, cinco grandes **camiones llenos de tomates hasta arriba descargan** su **mercancía** en la plaza del pueblo para **abastecer** las manos de las más de 25.000 personas que cada año **se congregan** en este pueblo valenciano.

El secreto **para que ésta sea una batalla** sin **heridos consiste en aplastar** las **hortalizas** antes de lanzarlas. En los últimos momentos de esta guerra **sin igual**, los tomates están tan **chafados** que pierden su consistencia por lo que a los **combatientes** sólo les queda **restregarlos** contra el vecino o **bañarse** en su salsa.

Calzadas, **paredes**, **farolas**, coches y árboles **quedan teñidos** de un rojo intenso. Sin embargo, los participantes en la **contienda se ponen manos a la obra** para **limpiarlo** todo y hacer que, en menos de dos horas, no quede **ni rastro** de La Tomatina.

Exhaustos por la batalla, los buñolenses **se retiran** a sus casas para **iniciar** una "siesta popular", una tradición **casi tan antigua** como esta guerra de tomates única en el mundo.

lo cierto es que: the truth is that
Ayuntamiento: Town Hall
toneladas: tons
lanzan/lanzar: they throw/to throw
en poco más de: in a little more than

larguísima: very long
empalma/empalmar: to join the night with the morning (expression used when someone stays out all night)
se reúnen/reunirse: they gather/to gather
tomar: to have
desayuno: breakfast
coger fuerzas: to get strength
lucha: fight, struggle

al punto del mediodía: at 12 pm
camiones: trucks
llenos de tomates hasta arriba: filled to the top with tomatoes
descargan/descargar: they unload/ to unload
mercancía: goods
abastecer: to supply
se congregan/congregarse: they gather/to gather, to concentrate

para que ésta sea una batalla: for this one to be a battle
heridos: injured people, casualties
consiste en/consistir en: it consists of/to consist of
aplastar: to smash, to squeeze
hortalizas: vegetables
sin igual: unrivaled
chafados: mashed, crushed
combatientes: combatants
restregarlos/restregar: rub them/ to rub
bañarse: to take a bath

calzadas: roads
paredes: walls
farolas: street lights
quedan teñidos: end up dyed
contienda: contest, struggle
se ponen manos a la obra: they put their hands to work
limpiarlo/limpiar: clean it/to clean it
ni rastro: without a trace

exhaustos: exhausted
se retiran/retirarse: they go back/ to go back
iniciar: to begin
casi tan antigua: almost as old

El baile del palo de mayo
NICARAGUA

"Tulululu pasa, tulululu, pasa..." empiezan a **cantar** en **misquito**, una **mezcla** entre el español y el inglés. Empiezan a bailar **alrededor** de un "Palo" con un ritmo africano y una fusión étnica **que le hacen a uno menearse**. Esta danza **originaria de** la Costa Atlántica de Nicaragua por **los indios misquitos se ha popularizado** por todo el país de Nicaragua.

El baile que tiene su **apogeo a comienzos del** mes de mayo **se ha difundido** por grupos como la Dimensión Costeña. Este **conjunto conmueve** al pueblo nicaragüense con su música **al tocar** sus canciones del Palo de Mayo. **Enfrente del** grupo, **bailan dos mujeres** con **movimientos y meneos** que **jamás se han visto** y uno **no puede quitarse los ojos de ellas** mientras que bailan durante cada **canción cadenciosa**.

Desde el siglo XIX, La Gran Bretaña **había puesto su codiciosa mirada sobre** la Costa Atlántica. **Súbditos ingleses se establecieron** en la región y empezaron a **ubicarse** con los indios. La cultura costeña es el resultado de una confluencia de variadas culturas. Esta convergencia **se llevó a cabo** principalmente en el siglo del romanticismo. A lo largo de los años, por la Costa Atlántica, como en la región de Bluefields, **acudieron** numerosos personas **oriundas de** Las Islas Antillanas, principalmente de Jamaica. **En aquellos tiempos**, los jóvenes de ambos sexos **salían a coger** flores y **aportaban** un poste que llamaban "el palo de mayo" adornado con frutas y flores en el centro del lugar donde se celebraban las fiestas de ese día. **Lo que se produjo** era una música energética y cultural de los países caribes.

Algunos **lo han llamado el baile prohibido** por sus tonos sexuales, pero como la marimba de Nicaragua, la samba de Brasil o la cumbia de Colombia, el palo de mayo **se ha vuelto** como parte del folklore nicaragüense.

empiezan a/empezar: they start to/ to start

cantar: to sing

misquito: language spoken by the Miskito Indians

mezcla: mixture

alrededor: around

que le hacen a uno menearse: that makes one shake

originaria de: originating from

los indios misquitos: the Miskito Indians

se ha popularizado: has been popularized

apogeo: peak

a comienzos del: in the beginning of

se ha difundido/difundir: has been spread/to spread

conjunto: group, band

conmueve/conmover: move/to move

al tocar: upon playing

enfrente del: in front of the

bailan dos mujeres: two women dance

movimientos y meneos: movements and swinging

jamás se han visto: have never been seen before

no puede quitarse los ojos de ellas: cannot take their eyes off them

canción cadenciosa: rhythmical song

había puesto/poner: had placed/to put

su codiciosa mirada sobre: their covetous look upon

súbditos ingleses: English subjects

se establecieron: established themselves

ubicarse: to situate or locate

se llevó a cabo: was carried out

acudieron/acudir: came/to come

oriundas de: indigenous to, native to

en aquellos tiempos: in those days

salían/salir: would leave/to leave

a coger: to pick

aportaban/aportar: carried/to carry

lo que se produjo: what was produced

lo han llamado/llamar: have called it/ to call

el baile prohibido: the forbidden dance

se ha vuelto: has become

Celebración del mercado medieval
ESPAÑA

Los **pasados** días 30 y 31 de mayo, y el 1 de Junio, los **ciudadanos** de Burgos tuvimos la posibilidad de visitar el **Mercado Medieval**, situado cerca de la Catedral. Este **acontecimiento** se celebra cada año, y su **principal aliciente** es el maravilloso **ambiente** y la **exposición** de los **oficios** más característicos del Medioevo en Castilla y León, comunidad autónoma española **en la que está incluida** Burgos.

En realidad, es **la segunda vez** que **visito** este Mercado, y la experiencia es realmente interesante. **Nosotros llegamos** el día de la inauguración, y aunque **al principio no había mucha gente**, en menos de una hora era difícil **andar entre la multitud**.

Para empezar, **compramos** unos **rollos de anís** y otros de chocolate. **Hay que decir** que todos los **alimentos a la venta** eran **artesanales**, al igual que los demás productos: **cestas**, **vidrios**, **collares**, **anillos**. Pudimos ver **cómo se hacía entonces** el pan, el **hojaldre** en **verdaderos hornos**, **al aire libre**. Verdaderos **panaderos cocinaban** sus productos y **cualquier visitante** podía comprarlos **recién hechos**.

También vimos a un **escriba**, a un **artesano del vidrio**, a personas **tejiendo** cestos de **mimbre** e incluso a **cetreros**, haciendo exhibiciones. ¡Las aves **volaban sobre nuestras cabezas**! Y, **por supuesto**, entre la gente estaban los **bufones**, **divirtiendo** al público.

Todo esto, en un **entorno** tan apropiado como las dos plazas de la catedral de Burgos. Al terminar la visita, y **pasar bajo** el Arco de Santa María, **fue como si hubiéramos hecho** un viaje en el tiempo, y **de repente volviéramos** al año 2005.

¡Una experiencia **inolvidable**!

---

pasados: last
ciudadanos: citizens
Mercado Medieval: Medieval Market
acontecimiento: event
principal aliciente: main incentive
ambiente: atmosphere
exposición: exhibition
oficios: professions
en la que está incluida/incluir: in which is included/to include

en realidad: actually
la segunda vez: the second time
visito/visitar: I visit/to visit
nosotros llegamos/llegar: we arrived/ to arrive
al principio: at the beginning
no había mucha gente: there were not many people
andar entre la multitud: to walk among the crowd

para empezar: to begin
compramos/comprar: we bought/ to buy
rollos de anís: anise rolls
hay que decir: it is necessary to say
alimentos a la venta: food on sale
artesanales: traditional, handcrafted
cestas: baskets
vidrios: glass
collares: necklaces
anillos: rings
cómo se hacía entonces: how it was made at that time
hojaldre: puff pastry
verdaderos hornos: real ovens
al aire libre: in the open air
panaderos: bakers
cocinaban/cocinar: they cooked/ to cook
cualquier visitante: any visitor
recién hechos: freshly made

escriba: scribe
artesano del vidrio: glass artisan
tejiendo/tejer: weaving/to weave
mimbre: wicker
cetreros: people who train falcons
volaban sobre nuestras cabezas: they flew over our heads
por supuesto: of course
bufones: jesters
divirtiendo: entertaining

entorno: scene
pasar bajo: to go under
fue como si hubiéramos hecho: it was as if we had taken
de repente: suddenly
volviéramos/volver: we came back/ to return, to come back

inolvidable: unforgettable

La Virgen de la Candelaria
PERÚ

En Puno, en **pleno altiplano peruano** y **cerca** del **lago** Titicaca, existe una gran celebración donde la **alegría**, la **música andina**, las **danzas incaicas** y la **fe se unen** para **dar honores** a la Virgen de la Candelaria y a la **Madre Tierra**.

La devoción a la **imagen** de esta virgen **se halla** muy **extendida** en Latinoamérica, **ya que se venera** en **casi todos** los países de América donde España **impuso** su religión. La figura de esta **santa madre fue traída** desde España a Puno el 2 de febrero de 1583, momento en el que los **indígenas autóctonos iniciaron** su conversión al catolicismo.

La festividad, que **se desarrolla** en el mes de febrero, es una de las más grandes celebraciones de Sudamérica **junto con** el Carnaval de Río de Janeiro en el Brasil y el Carnaval de Oruro, en Bolivia.

Esta fiesta del altiplano andino está **llena de** símbolos y **manifestaciones artístico-culturales** de la cultura quechua, aymara y mestiza. Es por este **motivo** que, en noviembre de 1985, el **gobierno** del Perú **designó** a Puno Capital del Folklore Peruano. La actividad en honor a la Virgen de la Candelaria **se inicia** el 2 de febrero y **se prolonga** durante 15 días.

Es en la **primera semana** donde la fiesta **llega** a su **apogeo**. A la **misa** de la **iglesia** San Juan Bautista y la procesión a la Plaza de Armas, le **sigue** un **desfile** de grupos folklóricos en dirección al **estadio** Enrique Torres Bellón.

---

pleno: full
altiplano peruano: Peruvian high plains
cerca: near
lago: lake
alegría: happiness, joy
música andina: Andean music
danzas incaicas: Incan dances
fe: faith
se unen/unirse: unites, joins/ to unite, to join
dar honores: to give honors
Madre Tierra: Mother Earth

imagen: image
se halla/hallar: is found/to find
extendida: widespread, spread out
ya que: since
se venera/venerar: is worshipped/to worship
casi todos: almost all
impuso/imponer: imposed/to impose
santa madre: holy mother
fue traída/traer: was brought/to bring
indígenas autóctonos: indigenous natives
iniciaron/iniciar: they began/to begin

se desarrolla/desarrollar: is developed/ to develop
junto con: together with

llena de: full of
manifestaciones artístico-culturales: artistic cultural displays
motivo: reason
gobierno: government
designó/designar: designated/ to designate
se inicia/iniciar: begins/to begin
se prolonga/prolongar: it extends/ to extend

primera semana: first week
llega/llegar: it arrives/to arrive
apogeo: its height
misa: mass
iglesia: church
sigue/seguir: follows/to follow
desfile: parade
estadio: stadium

En este **lugar deportivo se congregan** unas 70 bandas musicales, **algunas conformadas** por 300 personas, entre músicos y **bailarines**. Todas estas **agrupaciones esperan ganar** el **concurso** de danzas folklóricas. La música y la danza son **variadas**, **dependiendo** de la región del Perú de donde **provengan** los danzarines. Los ritmos del huayno y de la saya **colorean** el **ambiente** del **recinto deportivo**. Las bombardas por todo lo alto hacen **vibrar** al **expectante** pueblo puneño.

Centenares de **visitantes locales** y **extranjeros** llenan las calles y las **graderías** del estadio, en una **magna** fiesta en la que todos **se contagian**. Música andina, máscaras, **disfraces** de ángeles y demonios **se mezclan** con un **único** objetivo: dar honores a la **querida** imagen de la Virgen de la Candelaria. **Bastarán** sólo ocho minutos de coreografías para que los **jueces** decidan qué **banda artística** ganará el **título del año**. Bastarán sólo ocho minutos para **escoger** como ganadora a una banda que **destaque** entre las demás por el ritmo, color, **fuerza** y **sentimiento**.

La tradición incaica y aymara llega a su **plenitud** en esta **festividad**. **No cabe duda** que Puno es la **capital folklórica** del continente.

lugar deportivo: sports place
se congregan/congregar: they congregate/to congregate
algunas: some
conformadas: made
bailarines: dancers
agrupaciones: associations
esperan/esperar: they wait/to wait
ganar: to win
concurso: competition, contest
variadas: varied, assorted
dependiendo/depender: depending/to depend
provengan/provenir: they come from/to come from
colorean/colorear: they color/to color
ambiente: atmosphere, environment
recinto deportivo: sports precinct
vibrar: to vibrate
expectante: expectant

centenares: hundreds
visitantes locales: local visitors
extranjeros: foreign
graderías: stands
magna: great
se contagian/contagiarse: they spread/to spread
disfraces: disguises, costumes
se mezclan/mezclar they get mixed/to mix
único: unique
querida: dear, beloved
bastarán/bastar: will be enough/to be enough, to suffice
jueces: judges
banda artística: artistic band
título del año: title of the year
escoger: to chose
destaque/destacar: emphasizes/to emphasize, stress
fuerza: strength
sentimiento: feeling

plenitud: fullness
festividad: festivity
no cabe duda: there is no doubt
capital folklórica: folklore capital

La Pascua y Semana Santa
ARGENTINA

La Semana Santa **conmemora los últimos días** de la **vida de Cristo**. **La Pascua** es el **recordatorio** de la **muerte** y la resurrección de Cristo.

De hecho, la palabra "pascua" significa **"paso"** de la muerte a la vida. En Argentina, todos los **Jueves Santos** al mediodía se celebra una **misa** en la **catedral** o en las **iglesias**. Por la tarde, se oficia una misa de **la cena** del **Señor** en donde se **rememora** la **última** cena de Cristo con los **doce apóstoles**.

El Viernes Santo se rememora la crucifixión; en algunas casas católicas se practica el **ayuno**. Algunos también lo **consideran** un día de **silencio** y reflexión. En muchas ciudades, se celebra con **peregrinaciones** que **evocan** el sacrificio de Cristo y también **pasajes bíblicos**.

El sábado está **dedicado** al **lamento** por la muerte de Cristo **mientras que** el "**Domingo de Pascua**" es un día de celebración familiar. Se celebra la **fiesta** de la **Cristiandad**, que es la creencia en la resurrección.

Uno de los **símbolos** que **se utiliza** en la Pascua son los **huevos de Pascua**, que se asocian a la fiesta de Pascua aunque tengan un **origen pagano, para que los chicos se diviertan**. Muchas familias **acostumbran** hacer una **búsqueda de huevos.** El huevo de Pascua es de chocolate y está **relleno** de **confites** y **sorpresas** que generalmente **consisten de** pequeños **juguetes de plástico**. Los huevos de Pascua tienen diferentes **tamaños**. ¡Los hay **hasta** de dos **kilos**!

---

la Semana Santa: Holy Week
conmemora los últimos días: commemorates the last days
vida de Cristo: life of Christ
La Pascua: Easter
recordatorio: remembrance
muerte: death

de hecho: in fact
paso: way, path
Jueves Santos: Holy Thursdays
misa: mass
catedral: cathedral
iglesias: churches
la cena: supper
Señor: Christ
rememora/rememorar: remembers/ to remember
última: last
doce apóstoles: twelve apostles

El Viernes Santo: Good Friday
ayuno: fasting day
consideran: consider
silencio: silence
peregrinaciones: pilgrimages
evocan/evocar: they evoke/to evoke
pasajes bíblicos: Bible passages

dedicado/dedicar: dedicated/ to dedicate
lamento: lament
mientras que: while
Domingo de Pascua: Easter Sunday
fiesta: celebration
Cristianidad: Christendom

símbolos: symbol
se utiliza/utlizar: it is used/to use
huevos de Pascua: Easter eggs
origen pagano: pagan origin
para que los chicos se diviertan: so that the kids have fun
acostumbran: (some families) are used to, have a customary practice
búsqueda de huevos: an egg hunt
relleno: filling
confites: confetti, candy
sorpresas: surprise
consisten de: consist of
juguetes de plástico: plastic toys
tamaños: sizes
hasta: even
kilos: pounds

Un lento retorno
CUBA

En Semana Santa todos **los fieles católicos** del mundo **recuerdan** el **calvario**, la crucifixión, la **muerte** y la resurrección de Cristo. **Y si bien** en todos los países no **se celebra** de la **misma** forma **ni** con el mismo fervor, este tipo de tradiciones católicas son, casi en su **mayoría**, **comunes** con las tradiciones de los pueblos de matriz ibérica y **poseen** características similares a las de estos pueblos. Las celebraciones **incluyen** procesiones y ceremonias religiosas.

En Cuba, este es **apenas** el **octavo** año que **se festeja** la Semana Santa desde que Fidel Castro **asumió** el **poder**, en 1959. El actual **gobierno socialista** había **suprimido** todos los actos en los que **se mezclaba** lo religioso con la fiesta popular, y **se restauraron tras** la visita del Papa Juan Pablo II, en 1998.

Hoy en día, en las iglesias se celebran los actos religiosos y en los parques o en **algunas** plazas **se levantan tiendas** que **venden** comidas y bebidas, y se **oye** música y **suele** haber bailes. **Aunque** las procesiones y todos los actos religiosos se organizan todavía **tímidamente ya que** todo necesita contar con las **debidas autorizaciones** del gobierno.

Luego de tantos años de **enfrentamientos** entre la Iglesia y el régimen, estos permisos oficiales son vistos como una **señal de apertura**, pero tras varias décadas de **poca enseñanza católica**, son pocos los **jóvenes** que **conocen ritos**, **cánticos** o el **significado real** de las ceremonias.

---

los fieles católicos: catholic congregation
recuerdan/recordar: they remember/ to remember
calvario: Calvary
muerte: death
y si bien: and even if
se celebra/celebrar: it is celebrated/ to celebrate
misma: same
ni: nor
mayoría: majority
comunes: common
poseen/poseer: they have/to have
incluyen/incluir: they include/ to include

apenas: just
octavo: eighth
se festeja/festejar: it is celebrated/ to celebrate
asumió/asumir: he took over/to take over
poder: power, authority
gobierno socialista: socialist government
suprimido/suprimir: suppressed/ to suppress
se mezclaba/mezclar: it mixed/to mix
se restauraron tras/restaurar: they were reinstated after/to be reinstated

hoy en día: nowadays
algunas: some
se levantan/levantar: they stand up/ to stand up
tiendas: stores
venden/vender: they sell/to sell
oye: listen
suele/soler: it is usual/to be usual
aunque: even though
tímidamente: timidly
ya que: given that
debidas: pertinent
autorizaciones: authorizations

luego de tantos: after so many
enfrentamientos: confrontations
señal de apertura: sign of opening
poca enseñanza católica: little catholic education
jóvenes: young people
conocen/conocer: they know/ to know
ritos: rites
cánticos: canticles (a hymn derived from the bible)
significado real: real meaning

La fiesta con más Gracia

ESPAÑA

Visitar el **barrio** de Gracia en Barcelona durante su fiesta mayor es **trasladarse** a un mundo **mágico**. En un **paseo de poco más de una hora** se puede **pasar de cielo** al **infierno**, viajar de la China al **Lejano Oeste** o "nadar" en el **fondo del mar**. **Y todo gracias a** la imaginación de sus **vecinos**.

La tradición de decorar las calles **se remonta** al siglo XVIII, cuando Gracia todavía era un pueblo a las **afueras** de la ciudad de Barcelona (**se unió** definitivamente en 1850). La preparación **dura** casi 12 meses pero el resultado final **justifica** los **centenares** de horas **empleadas**. A los pocos días de finalizar las fiestas, los vecinos **empiezan ya** a **generar** ideas para la **ornamentación** de las calles del próximo año.

Una vez escogido el tema para la **escenografía**, los **improvisados artistas deberán** pensar cómo van a **llevar a cabo** su idea y qué materiales necesitan **recolectar** para **diseñar** las diversas formas y texturas.

Desde hace varios años la mayoría de vecinos **reciclan** objetos y **envases** de la **vida cotidiana** para **elaborar** sus creaciones: **periódicos**, **botellas de plástico**, **vasos de yogur**, **alambres**, **cajas de cartón** o **hueveras**. **Resulta** realmente **asombroso** ver el **espectáculo** que con cosas tan simples **se consigue**.

Una veintena de calles, **vestidas con sus mejores galas**, **acoge** conciertos, espectáculos con **magos** y **orquestas populares** cada noche.

---

barrio: neighborbood
trasladarse: to move
mágico: magic
paseo: walk, stroll
de poco más de una hora: a little more than an hour
pasar de: to go from
cielo: heaven
infierno: hell
Lejano Oeste: Far West
fondo del mar: bottom of the sea
y todo gracias a: and all this thanks to
vecinos: neighbors

se remonta/remontarse: it goes back to/ to go back to
afueras: outskirts
se unió/unirse: it joined/to join
dura/durar: it lasts/to last
justifica/justificar: it accounts for it/to account for, to justify
centenares: hundreds
empleadas: used
empiezan ya: they start already
generar: to create, to generate
ornamentación: ornaments

una vez: once
escogido/escoger: chosen/to choose
escenografía: stage design
improvisados artistas: improvised artists
deberán/deber: they will have to/ to have to
llevar a cabo: to carry out
recolectar: to collect
diseñar: design

reciclan/reciclar: they recycle/ to recycle
envases: containers
vida cotidiana: everyday life
elaborar: to produce, to make
periódicos: newspapers
botellas de plástico: plastic bottles
vasos de yogur: yogurt cups
alambres: wire
cajas de cartón: cardboard boxes
hueveras: egg boxes
resulta: it turns out
asombroso: amazing, astonishing
espectáculo: show
se consigue/conseguir: it is obtained/ to obtain
una veintena: about twenty
vestidas con sus mejores galas: showing their best face, best dress
acoge/acoger: it holds/to hold
magos: magicians
orquestas populares: popular dance bands

A lo largo de sus **aceras** tienen **barras** en las que **los propios vecinos sirven copas** a los visitantes, que bailan y beben **hasta bien entrada la noche**. **De esta manera**, los organizadores de las calles **consiguen** dinero para pagar los costes de la elaboración de los **decorados**.

Tanto **esfuerzo** vecinal **se ve recompensado** el primer día de fiesta mayor cuando un **jurado popular entrega** diversos **premios** a las mejores calles: a la más original, la mejor **iluminada**, la que más ecológica y la más bella. La curiosidad de los que **se acercan** hasta Gracia por conocer a las calles **agraciadas** hace que sean estas vías las más visitadas y, **en consecuencia**, las que más bebidas venden y dinero **recaudan**.

Además de estas fantásticas calles decoradas, en las fiestas de Gracia se celebran **clases de baile**, exhibiciones de castellers, **desfiles de gigantes y cabezudos**, **chocolatadas** populares, **carreras**, **exposiciones** y mucha, mucha música **forman parte de** la **oferta festiva** de estos **cálidos días de verano** en Barcelona aunque, sin duda, lo que las hace especiales es la decoración de sus calles.

A pesar de que en agosto la ciudad **suele quedarse con la mitad de sus ciudadanos puesto que** es el **mes preferido** por los españoles para sus vacaciones de verano, Gracia **atrae** cada mes de agosto (en su **tercera semana**) a más de **un millón y medio** de visitantes… y es que **perderse** estas fiestas estando en Barcelona **sería** un **pecado**.

---

a lo largo de: all along
aceras: sidewalks
barras: bars
los propios vecinos: the neighbors themselves
sirven/servir: they serve/to serve
copas: drinks
hasta bien entrada la noche: until well into the night
de este manera: in this way
consiguen/conseguir: they get (the money)/to get
decorados: set, scenery

esfuerzo: effort
se ve recompensado/recompensar: it is rewarded/to reward
jurado popular: popular panel of judges
entrega/entregar: it presents/ to present, to give
premios: prizes
iluminada: lit up
se acercan/acercarse: they go over/ to go over
agraciadas: the lucky ones, the winner
en consecuencia: consequently
recaudan/recaudar: they collect/ to collect

clases de baile: dance classes
desfiles: parades
gigantes y cabezudos: giant figures made from paper and wood
chocolatadas: popular meetings where people eat hot chocolate and churros
carreras: races
exposiciones: exhibitions
forman parte de/formar parte de: they are part of/to be part of
oferta festiva: festive offer
cálidos días de verano: hot days of summer

a pesar de que: despite the fact that
suele quedarse con la mitad de sus ciudadanos: half of the citizens remain, stay
puesto que: since, as
mes preferido: favorite month
atrae/atraer: it attracts/to attract
tercera semana: third week
un millón y medio: a million and a half
perderse/perder: miss/to miss
sería/ser: it would be/to be
pecado: sin

El carnaval de Cádiz
ESPAÑA

oír: to hear
todo el mundo: everyone, all over the world
piensa/pensar: (they) think/to think
encanto propio: their own charm
lugares: places
tiene lugar/tener lugar: it takes place/to take place
fecha: date
Martes de Carnaval: Shrove Tuesday
para saber: in order to know
hay que tener en cuenta: one must take into account
Cuaresma: Lent
mantenida/mantener: maintained/to maintain
en cualquier lugar: anywhere

se remontan/remontarse: they go back/to go back (in time), to date from
siglo XVI: 16th century
puertos marítimos: seaports
entonces: then
gaditanos: people from Cádiz
copiaron/copiar: they copy/to copy
con el tiempo: with time, eventually
lo adaptaron/adaptar: they adapted it/to adapt
propias costumbres: own customs

hecho: fact
bastante: pretty
gente: people
no se reúne/reunirse: they do not gather/to gather
ocurre/ocurrir: it happens/to happen
calles: streets
se llenan de/llenarse: they get full of/to get full of
disfraces: costumes
verdaderamente: truly
cantando/cantar: singing/to sing
disfrutando/disfrutar: enjoying/to enjoy
olvidar: to forget
marcadas: marked

Al **oír** la palabra "carnaval" **todo el mundo piensa** en Brasil, pero hay una ciudad en España, llamada Cádiz, cuyos carnavales tienen un **encanto propio**. Como en el resto de los **lugares** que celebran estas fiestas, el carnaval de Cádiz **tiene lugar** durante el mes de febrero. Su **fecha** central es el **Martes de Carnaval**. **Para saber** la fecha aproximada de la celebración de los carnavales, **hay que tener en cuenta** que tienen lugar 40 días antes de **Cuaresma**, costumbre **mantenida en cualquier lugar** con tradición católica.

Los orígenes del carnaval de Cádiz **se remontan** al **siglo XVI**, cuando la ciudad tenía uno de los **puertos marítimos** más importantes del mundo. Fue **entonces** cuando los **gaditanos copiaron** el carnaval de Venecia y **con el tiempo**, **lo adaptaron** a sus **propias costumbres**.

Un **hecho bastante** curioso es que durante esta fiesta, la **gente no se reúne** en un lugar específico como **ocurre** en muchas ciudades, sino que todas las **calles** de Cádiz **se llenan de** gente con **disfraces verdaderamente** originales, **cantando** y **disfrutando** de unos días dedicados a **olvidar** las prohibiciones y restricciones **marcadas** por la religión.

Durante **la Guerra Civil** y los 40 años de dictadura franquista, los carnavales **fueron prohibidos** en todo el territorio español. **Sin embargo**, Cádiz **se opuso** a esta norma y **continuó celebrándolos**.

Los principales **acontecimientos** celebrados durante los carnavales de Cádiz son la **coronación** de la Diosa del carnaval y la **lectura** del **pregón**. También **destacan** los **desfiles** que **discurren** por toda la ciudad, los **pasacalles**, las **fiestas infantiles** y los **bailes de disfraces**. Pero sin duda, lo que hace a este carnaval uno de los más famosos de España son las **canciones** de las **comparsas**, que destacan por su sátira y comicidad.

En el Gran Teatro de la Falla se celebra el **concurso** oficial de canciones and baile, donde **se escogerá** a la mejor composición. **Existen** varios grupos de amigos, llamados comparsas o agrupaciones carnavalescas que **cantan coplas** o canciones, **satirizando** a **personajes** o hechos importantes de la **actualidad**. Sus canciones son verdaderamente originales y es imposible no **sonreír** (¡o **reír a carcajadas**!) mientras **se escuchan**.

¡Son un verdadero espectáculo!

---

la Guerra Civil: The Civil War
fueron prohibidos/prohibir: they were banned/to ban
sin embargo: however
se opuso/oponer: opposed/to oppose
continuó/continuar: it continued/to continue
celebrándolos/celebrar: celebrating them/to celebrate

acontecimientos: events
coronación: crowning, coronation
lectura: reading
pregón: street cry
destacan/destacar: they stand out/ to stand out
desfiles: parades
discurren/discurrir: they flow/to flow
pasacalles: a type of "unofficial" parade usually early in the morning, with bands playing typical songs, and they aim to wake up people to go on with the carnival
fiestas infantiles: parties for children
bailes de disfraces: costume balls
canciones: songs
comparsas: teams of singers who write and sing their own songs

concurso: contest
se escogerá/escoger: will be chosen/to choose
existen/existir: exist/to exist
cantan/cantar: they sing/to sing
coplas: popular songs from Andalucía
satirizando/satirizar: satirizing/to satirize
personajes: celebrities, characters
actualidad: current affairs
sonreír: smile
reír a carcajadas: to roar with laughter
se escuchan/escuchar: they listen to them/to listen

¡Son un verdadero espectáculo!: They are an amazing show!

Celebración de Navidad
COLOMBIA

Navidad, **época** en la que los cristianos **conmemoran** el **nacimiento** de Jesús, pero al margen del **significado religioso,** la **gente** en Colombia **aprovecha** la ocasión **para reunirse con** los **seres queridos** y **manifestarles,** con **regalos y comida,** su **cariño y amor.** En Colombia, diciembre es época de **aguinaldos** y fiestas; también es un mes **propicio** para el **descanso** y las vacaciones. Los niños **esperan con ansiedad** la Navidad, la cual transforma los paisajes tradicionales con **luces multicolores** en **árboles, pesebres, calles,** establecimientos públicos y en la mayoría de **hogares.**

CELEBRACIÓN NAVIDEÑA COLOMBIANA

Hay cuatro días que son especiales. Los más importantes son el 24 y 31 de diciembre. Le **siguen** en importancia el 8 de diciembre y en **menor proporción** el 28 de diciembre.

El 8 de diciembre es **el día de las velitas.** Ese día se celebra la anunciación del arcángel a María, aunque realmente **muy pocos** colombianos **lo saben.** Este día, y algunas veces también el 7 de diciembre, celebramos en Colombia "El día de las velitas" o **"El alumbrado"** en el cual todas las familias colombianas

encienden centenares de velas en los andenes de las calles y **ventanas de sus casas,** convirtiendo las ciudades y los campos en una **hermosa tierra alumbrada** por miles y miles de pequeñas lucecitas. Los niños felices **prenden** sus **chispitas mariposas** y los **juegos pirotécnicos adornan** cada calle.

época: period
conmemoran/conmemorar: they commemorate/to commemorate
nacimiento: birth
significado religioso: religious meaning
gente: people
aprovecha/aprovechar: take advantage/to take advantage
para reunirse con: to get together with
seres queridos: loved ones
manifestarles: to demonstrate, show them
regalos y comida: gifts and food
cariño y amor: fondness and love
aguinaldos: a word used to describe the gifts of Christmas Eve
propicio: ideal, favorable
descanso: rest
esperan con ansiedad/esperar: they wait anxiously/to wait
luces multicolores: multicolored lights
árboles: trees
pesebres: mangers, nativity scenes
calles: streets
hogares: homes

siguen/seguir: they follow/to follow
menor proporción: less important

el día de las velitas: the day of the little candles
muy pocos: very few
lo saben/saber: they know it/to know
el alumbrado: the lighting
encienden/encender: they light/to light
centenares: hundreds
ventanas de sus casas: windows of their houses
hermosa tierra: beautiful land
alumbrada: lit
prenden/prender: they catch/to catch
chispitas mariposas: little sparkles of light called butterflies
juegos pirotécnicos: fireworks
adornan/adornar: they adorn/to adorn

El 24 de diciembre es la Navidad. Durante los nueve días anteriores a la navidad **se reza** la novena de aguinaldos, la cual comienza a las seis de la tarde. Los **vecinos** van de **casa en casa cantando villancicos**, y **con el interés de recibir dulces y postres** al final de cada novena.

La noche es una fiesta, todos **bailan** al ritmo de salsa. **Canciones** especiales de estas fechas **suenan y resuenan una y otra vez**. A las 12 de la noche **se reparten** los aguinaldos. Después la fiesta **continúa hasta el amanecer**. La mañana del 25 es la fecha en la que los niños encuentran los regalos que les envía "el niño Dios", quien es el **encargado de traer** los regalos en Colombia.

El 28 de diciembre es el **Día de los Santos Inocentes**. Este día es el equivalente al April Fool's Day americano. Está **permitido** hacer **bromas** a los amigos y **familiares**. Durante este día **se debe andar** con **mucho cuidado** y con los **ojos bien abiertos** para **no caer** en alguna "**inocentada**".

El 31 de diciembre es la fiesta de fin de año. Muchas veces es una fiesta mucho mayor que la del 24. Las mamás y las abuelas **expresan** su amor con la **cena** que preparan para la medianoche. En muchas regiones del país, **se acostumbra** hacer un **muñeco con ropa vieja**, **relleno de guasca de plátano** y de **pólvora**. A las 12 de la noche en punto, mientras todos **se abrazan** y **se desean** un feliz año, el muñeco es **incinerado** ante la vista de todos en **señal** de que el año **ha muerto** y como bienvenida al nuevo año. También es muy común la creencia en los **agüeros** de fin de año, como por ejemplo ponerse **ropa interior amarilla**; **correr con las maletas en las manos** dándole la vuelta a la casa **para poder viajar** el año **siguiente**; **comer doce uvas** al ritmo de las doce **campanadas**, y mucho más.

se reza/rezar: it is recited/to recite
vecinos: neighbors
casa en casa: house to house
cantando/cantar: singing/to sing
villancicos: Christmas carols
con el interés de: with the interest of
recibir: to receive
dulces y postres: sweets and desserts

bailan/bailar: they dance/to dance
canciones: songs
suenan y resuenan una y otra vez: sound and resound again and again
se reparten/repartir: they are distributed, given out/to give out
continúa/continuar: it continues/ to continue
hasta el amanecer: until dawn
encargardo de: in charge of
traer: to bring

Día de los Santos Inocentes: Innocent Saints Day
permitido/permitir: allowed/to allow
bromas: jokes
familiares: relatives
se debe andar: one must walk
mucho cuidado: very carefully
ojos bien abiertos: eyes wide open
no caer: do not fall
inocentada: practical joke

expresan/expresar: they express/to express
cena: dinner
se acostumbra: it is customary
muñeco con ropa vieja: doll made with old clothes
relleno de guasca de plátano: full of bark from the plantain tree
pólvora: gunpowder
se abrazan: they hug each other
se desean: they wish each other
incinerado/incinerar: incinerated/ to incinerate
señal: sign, signal
ha muerto: has died
agüeros: omens, superstitions
ropa interior amarilla: yellow underwear
correr con las maletas en las manos: to run with suitcases in hand
para poder viajar: to be able to travel
siguiente: following
comer doce uvas: eat twelve grapes
campanadas: bells (of midnight)

lugar: place	
ubicada case: located almost	
isla griega: Greek island	
de ... deriva: comes from	
conocida como: known as	
luz: light	
cuna: cradle	
escritores: writers	
iluminaron: illuminated	
pueblo: people	
algunos: some	
llaman/llamar: call/to call	
desde donde: from where	
salieron/salir: left/to leave	
fundadores: founders	
poblaciones vecinas: neighboring villages	
muestra: sample	
estilo: style	
casas típicas: typical houses	
tejas de barro: clay tiles	
vistosos: eye-catching	
balcones: balconies	
adornados con: decorated with	
alegres flores: joyful flowers	
mezclados: mixed	
último mes: last month	
propone/proponer: proposes/ to propose	
razón extra: extra reason	
se lleva a cabo: is carried out	
llena de: full of	
noche del fuego: night of the fire	
se conmemora: is commemorated	
tomó vuelo propio: itself took off	
cada vez: each time	
más gente: more people	
se acerca a disfrutar: comes to enjoy	
se suspende/suspender: is cancelled/ to cancel	
alumbrado público: street lighting	
se apaga/apagar: is turned off/ to turn off	
cerca de: close to	
faroles: streetlights	
velitas: little candles	
se encienden/encender: are lightened/ to lighten	
a lo largo y a lo ancho: throughout, across the length and the width	
piso: floor	
sobre: on	
calles: streets	
puertas: doors	
zaguanes: halls	
colgando de: hanging from	
ventanas: windows	
bailan/bailar: dance/to dance	
penumbra: twilight, semidarkness	
escenario: stage, scene, setting	
de fondo: background	
espectáculos: show	
en vivo: live	
fuegos artificiales: fireworks	
brilla/brillar: shines/to shine	
a la luz de las velas: at candlelight	

Noche del fuego en Salamina
COLOMBIA

El **lugar** – Salamina es una ciudad **ubicada casi** en el centro de Colombia. También es una **isla griega** y de allí **deriva** el nombre de la primera.

Esta ciudad colombiana del departamento de Caldas es **conocida como** la "Ciudad **Luz**" porque fue **cuna** de poetas, músicos, actores, **escritores** y artistas que "**iluminaron**" la cultura de su **pueblo**. **Algunos** la **llaman** también "Madre de Pueblos" por ser uno de los epicentros **desde donde salieron** los **fundadores** y primeros habitantes de algunas **poblaciones vecinas**.

Salamina fue declarada Patrimonio Histórico de la Humanidad en 1982. Su centro histórico es una **muestra** arquitectónica del **estilo** antioqueño con **casas típicas** con **tejas de barro**, **vistosos balcones adornados con alegres flores** y en los patios interiores, los colores de la naturaleza **mezclados** con la arquitectura.

El festival – El **último mes** del año **propone** una **razón extra** para visitar Salamina. Desde el 2002, cada 7 de diciembre, **se lleva a cabo** una tradicional celebración **llena de** luz y cultura: la **noche del fuego**. Su origen es religioso, **se conmemora** a la Virgen de la Inmaculada Concepción, pero la fiesta ya **tomó vuelo propio** y **cada vez más gente se acerca a disfrutar** de este evento. Esa noche **se suspende** el **alumbrado público**, toda la ciudad **se apaga** y **cerca de** 45 mil **faroles** con **velitas se encienden a lo largo y a lo ancho** del centro histórico: en el **piso**, **sobre** las **calles**, las **puertas**, los **zaguanes**, los patios y también **colgando de** balcones y **ventanas**. Todo se llena de pequeñas lucecitas de fuego que **bailan** en la **penumbra**. Con este **escenario de fondo** la noche propone una programación variada: **espectáculos** de danzas, representaciones teatrales, música **en vivo** y como colofón un show de **fuegos artificiales**. Locales y turistas disfrutan de esta fiesta románticamente iluminada. Salamina **brilla a la luz de las velas**.

San Pedro de Macorís y su carnaval
REPÚBLICA DOMINICANA

San Pedro de Macorís es la provincia de la República Dominicana donde **se encuentra** la playa Juan Dolio. Desde sus orígenes, el motor económico de la provincia fue la agricultura y, en especial, el **cultivo** y la **cosecha** de la **caña de azúcar**. **De hecho**, San Pedro de Macorís es la provincia con **mayor cantidad de ingenios azucareros** del **país**. **Antiguamente** la playa era utilizada fundamentalmente como **puerto pesquero** y como punto de comercio de productos agrícolas.

A partir de la segunda **mitad** del siglo XX, el turismo **comenzó a desarrollarse** y **recién** en los **últimos veinte años experimentó** un **verdadero auge** con la **llegada** de turistas **extranjeros**. **Sin embargo**, el **desarrollo** de la agricultura fue **el que impulsó** movimientos migratorios desde provincias dominicanas **vecinas** e **islas inglesas** del Caribe, y también desde Cuba y Puerto Rico. Estas migraciones **hicieron que** San Pedro de Macorís **sea** uno de los **lugares** con mayor diversidad cultural de la República Dominicana.

Un evento cultural que **convoca todos los años** a los locales y **atrae** la curiosidad de los **visitantes** es el carnaval. En esta celebración los "Guloyas" **se llevan todas las miradas** y son los **verdaderos** protagonistas. Se llama Guloyas a quienes **se disfrazan de diablo** y **visten trajes** de **llamativos colores**, **adornados** con **pequeños espejos** y **capas amarillas y rojas**.

El carnaval de San Pedro de Macorís es realmente interesante por la fusión cultural que **se observa** en la zona. Los *cocolos*, migrantes de las islas **angloparlantes** vecinas, **aportaron** sus costumbres, **creencias** y tradiciones a la cultura y al carnaval locales. Todo el color y **ritmo** de estas culturas **late** en el **corazón** del carnaval de San Pedro de Macorís. Por eso, si alguna vez tiene la oportunidad de visitarlo, **no dude en hacerlo**.

se encuentra/encontrarse: is (located)/to be (located)
cultivo: growing, cultivation
cosecha: harvesting
caña de azúcar: sugar cane
de hecho: in fact
mayor cantidad de: the most, the greatest number of
ingenios azucareros: sugar mills
país: country
antiguamente: in the past, long ago
puerto pesquero: fishing harbor

a partir de … : from … on
mitad: half
comenzó a desarrollarse: began to develop
recién: only, just
últimos veinte años: last twenty years
experimentó/experimentar: experienced/to experience
verdadero auge: real boom
llegada: arrival
extranjeros: foreign
sin embargo: however
desarrollo: development
el que impulsó/impulsar: what drove/to drive
vecinas: neighboring
islas inglesas: English islands
hicieron que … sea: made of …
lugares: places

convoca/convocar: brings together/ to bring together
todos los años: every year
atrae/atraer: attracts/to attract
visitantes: visitors
se llevan todas las miradas: catch all the eyes
miradas: looks, gazes
verdaderos: true
se disfrazan de diablo: dress up as the devil
visten/vestir: wear/to wear
trajes: costumes
llamativos colores: bright colors
adornados: decorated
pequeños espejos: small mirrors
capas: capes, cloaks
amarillas y rojas: yellow and red

se observa/observar: can be observed/ to observe
angloparlantes: English-speaking
aportaron/aportar: contributed/ to contribute
creencias: beliefs
ritmo: rhythm
late/latir: beats/to beat
corazón: heart
no dude en hacerlo: do not hesitate to do it

Examina tu comprensión

La Mamá Negra, página 80

1. La Mamá Negra es la celebración ¿de qué dos eventos?

2. ¿Cómo se representa a la Mamá Negra en el desfile?

3. ¿Qué son los Huacos?

4. Durante esta celebración, ¿qué simbolizan los siguientes personajes: el ángel de la estrella, el Rey Moro, el capitán?

El Día de los Muertos, página 82

1. Para los mexicanos la muerte, ¿qué refleja?

2. Cuando comienza la fiesta, ¿qué dicho es popular?

3. ¿Con qué se adorna el pan dulce?

Festeja su independencia, página 84

1. ¿Cuál es el nombre del Día Nacional de la Independencia que se celebra en Chile?

2. ¿Cuánto dura esta celebración?

3. Describa qué entretenimiento y qué vendedores callejeros hay.

4. Describa el juego más popular durante ese tiempo.

¡Menudo tomate!, página 86

1. ¿Cómo comenzó la fiesta de La Tomatina?

2. Durante la primera celebración ¿cuántos tomates compró el ayuntamiento y cuánto tiempo les tomó a los ciudadanos lanzarlos?

3. ¿Qué hacen las personas para prepararse para la batalla?

Test your comprehension

La Virgen de la Candelaria, página 90

1. ¿Cuándo se realiza este evento y qué celebra?

2. Puno fue designada la capital ¿de qué? ¿Por qué?

3. Las festividades culminan ¿en qué estadio y qué pasa allí?

La Pascua y Semana Santa, página 92

1. ¿Qué ocurre durante el Viernes Santo?

2. ¿A qué se dedica el sábado?

La fiesta con más Gracia, página 94

1. ¿Quién dirige este evento? ¿Qué materiales se usan para decorar las calles?

2. ¿Qué criterios se utilizan para juzgar las calles? ¿Qué recompensa reciben los ganadores?

El carnaval de Cádiz, página 96

1. ¿En qué mes se festeja el carnaval de Cádiz?

2. ¿Cuál es el origen de la celebración?

3. ¿Qué evento se lleva a cabo en el Gran Teatro de la Falla?

Cuando hay gente unida que cree en algo firmemente,
ya religión, política o sindicato, algo sucede.

César Chávez

Personas

conocí/conocer: I met/to meet
por primera vez: for the first time
fue entonces: it was then
narración corta: short narrative
se convirtió: became
se abriría/abrir: would open/to open
descubrir: to discover
el mundo mágico: the magical world
el mejor escritor: the best writer
ha sido/ser: has been/to be
novela de suspenso: suspense novel
he leído alguna vez: I have ever read
obra maestra: masterpiece
libro más leído: most read book
tesis de maestría: masters thesis

célebre escritor: famous writer
primeros ocho años: first eight years
cuando vivió/vivir: when he lived/to live
abuelos maternos: grandparents on
   his mother's side
en algún momento: at some point
pensó/pensar: he thought/to think
derecho: law
según él: according to him
me aburría a morir esa carrera: I was
   bored to death with that career
se adentró/adentarse: it went deep/
   to go deep
el mundo de las palabras: the world
   of words
periodismo: journalism

carrera periodística: journalism career
lo lleva/llevar: takes him/to take
más tarde: later
viajó: traveled
escritores favoritos: favorite writers
junto a su esposa: along with his wife
pueden encontrarse: can be found
personajes: characters
desde muy joven: since I was very
   young
me sentí atraída: I felt attracted
hacia: towards
quizás sean: maybe it is
años felices de infancia: happy
   childhood years
compartir: share
**abuela enérgica que adivinaba el
futuro:** a grandmother full of energy
   who was able to tell the future
haber conocido: had known
el sur estadounidense: the south of
   the United States
no necesita magia: he does not need
   magic
transformada/transformar:
   transformed/to transform

La magia de García Márquez
COLOMBIA

Conocí a Gabriel García Márquez **por primera vez** cuando tenía diecisiete años. **Fue entonces** cuando leí *El coronel no tiene quien le escriba*. Esta **narración corta se convirtió** en la puerta que **se abriría** para **descubrir el mundo mágico** de quien para mí es y seguirá siendo **el mejor escritor** latinoamericano. *Crónica de una muerte anunciada* **ha sido** la única **novela de suspenso** que **he leído alguna vez** y, su **obra maestra**, *Cien años de soledad*, se convirtió en mi **libro más leído** y base fundamental de mi **tesis de maestría**.

Este **célebre escritor** nació en Aracataca, Colombia, un 6 de marzo de 1928. **Sus primeros ocho años** de vida fueron los más importantes de su vida, años **cuando vivió** con sus **abuelos maternos**, Nicolás Márquez y Tranquilina Iguarán. **En algún momento** de su vida **pensó** estudiar **derecho** pero, **según él**, "**me aburría a morir esa carrera**". Así **se adentró** en **el mundo de las palabras** y las páginas blancas. Comienza en el **periodismo** trabajando en "El Heraldo", mientras empieza a trabajar en su primera novela *La Hojarasca*.

Su **carrera periodística lo lleva** a conocer Europa y **más tarde** los Estados Unidos, donde **viajó** por los caminos de sus **escritores favoritos**: Kafka, Faulkner, Virginia Wolf y Hemingway. En los últimos años, García Márquez ha vivido en México **junto a su esposa**, Mercedes Barcha. Su libro más reciente, *Vivir para contarla*, es su autobiografía donde **pueden encontrarse** muchos de los **personajes** de sus libros. **Desde muy joven me sentí atraída hacia** el escritor y sus palabras. **Quizás sean** nuestros **años felices de infancia**, el **compartir** esa **abuela enérgica que adivinaba el futuro**, nuestro gusto por Hemingway o el **haber conocido el sur estadounidense**. Gabriel García Márquez **no necesita magia** para escribir. Él es la magia **transformada** en palabras.

Las hazañas de Rita Moreno
PUERTO RICO

Muchos la **recuerdan** como la Anita de la película *West Side Story*. Para los puertorriqueños, Rosita Dolores Alverio representa uno de **nuestros orgullos** más importantes. Esta **dama** del **cine** y la televisión nació el 11 de diciembre de 1931 en el **pequeño pueblo** de Humacao. Aquí vivían sus padres, **trabajadores** y **amantes de la tierra**.

La Depresión de los años 30 los llevó a abandonar la isla **para probar suerte** en las **frías calles** de Nueva York. **Aunque el cambio fue drástico** y existía la **barrera del lenguaje**, Rita **demostró** desde pequeña su inmenso talento.

Mucho tiempo ha pasado desde *West Side Story*, la historia moderna de Romeo y Julieta. Desde entonces ha trabajado en más de 70 películas **a lo largo de** su **exitosa carrera**. *King of the Corner* **ha sido** su más reciente **aparición** y muchos la **podrán** recordar como Juana en *American Family*, donde también **se destacan** otros hispanos **notables**.

Rita Moreno ha sido la **única** hispana que ha ganado los **premios** Oscar, Tony, Emma y Grammy. Por su hazaña, aparece en el *Libro Guinness de Récords*. En 2004, el presidente George Bush **le otorgó** la **Medalla Presidencial de la Libertad** en honor a todos sus **logros** y **labor cívica**.

Rita Moreno, siempre **orgullosa** de su origen y su **herencia**, **pasará a la posteridad** como una de las artistas más famosas y **queridas** de la historia.

hazañas: outstanding achievements
recuerdan/recordar: they remember/ to remember
nuestros orgullos: our pride
dama: lady
cine: cinema
pequeño pueblo: small village, town
trabajadores: hard workers
amantes de la tierra: lovers of the land

para probar suerte: to try one's luck
frías calles: cold streets
aunque el cambio fue drástico: although the change was drastic
barrera del lenguaje: language barrier
demostró/demostrar: she showed/ to show

mucho tiempo ha pasado: a long time has gone by
a lo largo de: throughout
exitosa carrera: successful career
ha sido/ser: it has been/to be
aparición: appearance
podrán/poder: they will be able to/can, to be able to
se destacan/destacar: stand out/ to stand out
notables: outstanding

única: only one
premios: awards
le otorgó/otorgar: he awarded/ to award, to grant
Medalla Presidencial de la Libertad: Presidential Medal of Freedom
logros: achievements
labor cívica: civil work

orgullosa: proud
herencia: heritage
pasará a la posteridad: she will go down in posterity, history
queridas: beloved

primera vez: first time
supe de/saber: I heard about, I found out about/to know
acercamiento: approach
amada: sweetheart
pensarlos: to think about them
separados: far from each other
tuvieron/tener: they had/to have
dolorosa: painful
amorosa: loving
pareja: couple
sea/ser: it is/to be
recordadas/recordar: remembered/to remember
época: age
además: besides
del amor que se tenían el uno al otro: the love they felt for each other
unió/unir: it united/to unite
pintura: painting
política: politics
se admiraron/admirar: they admired each other/to admire
mutuamente: mutually
se amaron/amar: they loved each other/to love
se odiaron/odiar: they hated each other/to hate

mujeriego: womanizer
imponente: imposing, impressive
escandaloso: scandalous
feo: ugly, nasty
encantador: charming
si no el mayor: if not the greatest
aunque: although
pintor de caballete: easel painter
dibujante: draftsman
aporte: contribution

buscó/buscar: he sought/to seek
gran contenido social: great social content
gente: people
techos: ceilings
paredes: walls
edificios públicos: public buildings
debía/deber: it should/must
clase trabajadora: working class
a su alcance: within its reach

Diego Rivera
MÉXICO

La **primera vez** que **supe de** Diego Rivera fue por mi **acercamiento** y admiración hacia Frida Kahlo, su **amada**, pero también una gran artista. Es difícil **pensarlos separados** y la relación que **tuvieron** tan tormentosa, **dolorosa, amorosa** y pasional hace que esta **pareja sea** una de las más **recordadas** de su **época. Además del amor que se tenían el uno al otro**, les **unió** también su amor por la **pintura** y la **política. Se admiraron mutuamente** y **se amaron**, pero también **se odiaron**.

Diego Rivera nació en 1886 en Guanajuato (México) y fue uno de los pintores más famosos e importantes del mundo. **Mujeriego, imponente, escandaloso, feo** y **encantador**, Rivera fue uno de los máximos representantes, **si no el mayor**, del muralismo mexicano, **aunque** su obra también incluye trabajos como **pintor de caballete, dibujante** e ilustrador. Su **aporte** al mundo del arte moderno fue decisivo.

Diego Rivera fue un pintor revolucionario que siempre **buscó** llevar su arte, de **gran contenido social**, a la **gente**, a las calles, a los **techos** y **paredes** de **edificios públicos** ya que consideraba que el arte **debía** servir a la **clase trabajadora** y estar **a su alcance**.

Estudió Bellas Artes en México y luego en Europa, donde vivió varios años, **se enriqueció** con los distintos movimientos culturales y pictóricos. También visitó la Unión Soviética, **cuna** de sus ideales políticos. **De regreso** a México en 1921, **fundó** el Partido Comunista Mexicano y **se casó con** la pintora Frida Kahlo. Ambos **combinaron** su trabajo artístico con una **agitada** actividad política. En Rivera estaban tan **mezcladas** ambas expresiones que en la mayoría de sus murales **se ven reflejados** sus ideales: revolución social mexicana, resistencia a la opresión **extranjera**, la **valoración del indígena**, sus raíces, el **pasado** y el futuro de su país.

Su fama le llevó también a vivir y exponer su obra en Estados Unidos, aunque en su **país natal** es donde **se encuentra** su **legado** más importante. **Decoró** muchos edificios y ministerios públicos; dos de los más conocidos e importantes son *La Tierra Fecunda* en la Escuela Nacional de Agricultura de Chapingo y el mural con su **propia interpretación** sobre la historia de México, en el Palacio Nacional de la capital.

Murió el 24 de noviembre de 1957 en su casa de San Ángel de la ciudad de México.

*"Era un hombre adorable que **no sabía dar la cara** en su vida personal pero que en su vida pública era un **luchador**. Era muy **capaz de pararse** en público y **demoler**, por ejemplo, a los Rockefeller en 10 minutos".* Louise Nevelson

*"**Vuelvo a verte** con tu estatura monumental, tu **vientre** siempre adelantándosete, tus **zapatos sucios**, tu viejo sombrero alabeado, tu **pantalón arrugado**, y pienso que nadie **podría** llevar con tanta **nobleza** cosas tan **estropeadas".* Elena Poniatowska

---

se enrieció/enriquecer: he became enriched/to enrich
cuna: cradle
de regreso: back from
fundó/fundar: he founded/ to found
se casó con: he married
combinaron/combinar: they combined/to combine
agitada/agitar: agitated/to agitate
mezcladas/mezclar: mixed/ to mix
se ven reflejados/reflejar: they are seen reflected/to reflect
extranjera: foreign
valoración del indígena: valuation of indigenous people
pasado: past

país natal: country of origin
se encuentra/encontrarse: it is found/to find
legado: legacy
decoró/decorar: he decorated/ to decorate
propia interpretación: own interpretation

murió/morir: he died/to die

no sabía: he wasn't able (literally: he didn't know)
dar la cara: to face the consequences of one's acts
luchador: fighter
capaz de pararse: to be able to stand up
demoler: to demolish

vuelvo a verte/volver: I see you again/to see
vientre: abdomen, stomach
zapatos: shoes
sucios: dirty
pantalón: pants
arrugado: wrinkled
podría/poder: nobody could/can
nobleza: nobility
estropeadas: damaged

Frida Kahlo
MÉXICO

"La pintura **llenó** mi **vida**. **Perdí** tres hijos y **otra serie de cosas** que **hubieran podido** llenar mi horrible vida. Todo eso lo **reemplazó** la pintura". "Para estar **desesperada**, **más vale** ser productiva. Siempre es algo que **le robamos** a la pura y simple autodestrucción…"

Estas palabras son de Frida Kahlo y dejan **vislumbrar** algo de lo que fue su vida. Una vida llena de **dolor**, **tristeza**, desesperación pero también de **luz**, pasión, amor, **fuerza** y resistencia. Una vida corta pero intensa. ¿Por qué será que la mayoría de los que viven una vida tan intensa, viven pocos años? **Quizás** porque de otro **modo no la aguantarían**.

Nació en México en 1907. En la adolescencia tuvo un terrible accidente que **le cambió** la existencia para siempre. Como consecuencia, no sólo **no pudo** tener **hijos**, sino que el **dolor físico** la acompañó en todo momento: la operaron más de siete veces de la **columna**, tres de una **pierna** (que al final terminó perdiendo), y todo su **cuerpo** fue un constante sufrir. **Comenzó** a pintar "**sin prestar mucha atención**", casi por casualidad, **postrada** en una cama y para **mitigar** su soledad y sus **largas horas** de convalecencia. **A través de** su obra **se expresaba** y **se liberaba**: "La fuerza de lo que no se expresa es **implosiva**, **arrasadora**, autodestructiva. Expresar es **liberarse**", aseguraba.

Sus **cuadros** están llenos de símbolos. Todos representan su realidad, su vida y la de sus **seres queridos**. Cuando **le preguntaban** por qué pintaba tantos **autorretratos**, ella contestaba que **se retrataba** a sí misma porque pasaba mucho tiempo sola y porque era el motivo que mejor **conocía**. Sus cuadros son **femeninos**, sinceros, sensibles y **feroces**.

---

llenó:/llenar: it fulfilled/to fulfill
vida: life
perdí/perder: I lost/to lose
otra serie de cosas: many other things
hubieran podido: could have
reemplazó/reemplazar: replaced/ to replace
desesperada: desperate, hopeless
más vale: it is better
le robamos/robar: we steal/to steal

vislumbrar: to glimpse
dolor: pain
tristeza: sadness
luz: light
fuerza: strength
quizás: perhaps
modo: way, manner
no la aguantarían/aguantar: they wouldn't tolerate/to tolerate

le cambió/cambiar: it changed her/ to change
no pudo/poder: she wasn't able/ can, to be able to
hijos: children
dolor físico: physical pain
columna: spinal column
pierna: leg
cuerpo: body
comenzó/comenzar: she started/to start
sin prestar mucha atención: without paying much attention
postrada/postrarse: prostrated/to prostrate oneself, kneel down
mitigar: to mitigate
largas horas: long hours
a través de: through
se expresaba/expresarse: she expressed herself/to express
se liberaba/liberarse: she liberated herself/to liberate
implosiva: implosive
arrasadora/arrasar: devastating/ to devastate, to destroy
liberarse: to go free
aseguraba/asegurar: she assured/ to assure

cuadros: paintings
seres queridos: loved ones
le preguntaban/preguntar: she was asked/to ask
autorretratos: self portraits
se retrataba: she painted a self-portrait
conocía/conocer: she knew/to know
femeninos: feminine
feroces: ferocious

Se **casó con** Diego Rivera, famoso muralista mexicano. Su amor por él fue inmenso, **inagotable**, incondicional. **Juntos participaron** políticamente en el partido nacional-socialista y **viajaron** por Europa y Estados Unidos, donde Frida exhibió por primera vez, en Nueva York, su obra individualmente.

Fue una relación tormentosa que **superó** las infidelidades de él, los **amoríos** de ella, las obligaciones de trabajo de Diego, los problemas de salud de Frida, varios abortos, el divorcio y otra vez el matrimonio. La pasión que los **unió** los **acompañó** hasta sus últimos días.

Frida murió en 1954. Su último cuadro, una naturaleza muerta en el que **se ven** unas **sandías abiertas**, se titula *Viva la vida*. Sus últimas frases escritas en su diario íntimo, "**Espero alegre** la **salida**… y espero no **volver** más", **resumen su paso** por esta vida.

se casó con/casarse: she married/ to marry
inagotable: inexhaustible, tireless
juntos: together
participaron/participar: they were involved/to be involved
viajaron/viajar: they traveled/to travel

superó/superar: she overcame/ to overcome
amoríos: love affairs
unió/unir: it joined/to join
acompañó/acompañar: it accompanied/to accompany

se ven/ver: they are shown/to show
sandías abiertas: open watermelons
espero/esperar: I hope/to hope
alegre: happy
salida: exit
volver: to return
resumen/resumir: they summarize/ to summarize
su paso: her route, her way

CULTURE NOTE

People often ask if Castilian Spanish, as it is spoken in Spain, is different from the Spanish of Latin America. In addition to a different accent, there are some differences in grammar, vocabulary, and at times, pronunciation. Two of the greatest differences are the *leísmo* of Spain and the use of the pronoun *vosotros* instead of *tú*. Another major difference is that *vosotros* is often used as the plural of *tú* (the singular familiar "you") in Spain, while in Latin America *ustedes* is usually used. Another difference is that many Spaniards often pronounce the "z" and the "c" before "i" or "e" like the "th" in thin, while many Latin Americans pronounce it the same as the "s". Speakers in some areas (Argentina in particular) often pronounce the "ll" and "y" like the "s" in *measure*. In some areas, you will hear speakers drop "s" sounds, so *está* sounds like *etá*. In some areas, the "j" sounds like the "ch" in *loch* (difficult for many native English speakers to master), while in others it sounds like the English "h". In some areas, the "l" and the "r" at the end of a word sound alike. Over time you may be able to tell where someone is from based on their accent. Rest assured, regardless of where you study, whether your accent is Castilian or Mexican or Bolivian, with good pronunciation you will be understood most anywhere in the Spanish-speaking world.

Celia Cruz

CUBA

Celia Cruz **nació** el 21 de octubre de 1925 en La Habana, Cuba. Su vocación era la música pero **aparte de** su talento, Celia con moral e integridad **alcanzó** su misión de **entusiasmar al mundo**. **Puesto que** ella **no pudo** tener niños, **adoptó** a **centenares** de **ahijados** y **demostró** respeto **hacia** su audiencia con positivismo y **fe**.

En el año 1961, Celia y Pedro Knight hicieron de Manhattan su **hogar**. **Al lado** de Tito Puente, Celia alcanzó una **meta** importante: ser la primera mujer hispana en el Carnagie Hall. En 1974 la vida de Celia **comenzó** con músicos como Héctor Lavoe, Cheo Feliciano, Johnny Pacheco, Rubén Blades y Willie Colón, entre muchos otros. Celia, la **fiel dama sonriente** y devota de la Virgen de la Caridad del Cobre, fue **siempre humilde**, pero **obtuvo frutos** como ser nominada 12 **veces** al Grammy **ganándolo** por primera vez en 1989. **Cantó** con Pavarotti y Liza Minelli entre otros artistas. **Recibió doctorados** de la Universidad de Yale, la Universidad Internacional de la Florida y la Universidad de Miami. **Participó** en varias **películas y telenovelas**. Sus manos están en el Paseo de la Fama en Hollywood, en Miami, e **incluso** muchas ciudades tienen calles que **llevan** su nombre. Celia Cruz obtuvo también la Medalla Presidencial de las Artes de las **manos** del presidente Bill Clinton. A los 77 años, el 16 de Julio del 2003 Celia Cruz abandonó esta tierra luego de sufrir un **tumor cerebral**. En su **velorio**, que **duró** días, cantó Patti LaBelle, y asistió gente de todas partes del mundo, entre ellos sus amigos íntimos y su **amado** Pedro, con quien un par de días antes Celia cumplió 41 años de unión. Su cuerpo fue enterrado en Nueva York **junto a** un **puño de tierra** que **trajo** desde Guantánamo años antes, cuando **supo** que no podría **volver** a su isla. Su música **sigue sonando** en los **rincones más remotos** del mundo y su legado **no tendrá fin** pues fue una dama que **convirtió** su vida en la **fuerza** de su canción.

---

nació/nacer: was born/to be born
aparte de: apart from
alcanzó/alcanzar: it reached/to reach
entusiasmar al mundo: to delight the world
puesto que: since
no pudo: she was not able to
adoptó/adoptar: she adopted/ to adopt
centenares: hundreds
ahijados: godchildren
demostró/demostrar: she showed/ to show
hacia: towards
fe: faith

hogar: home
al lado: beside
meta: goal, objective
comenzó/comenzar: began/to begin
fiel: faithful
dama: lady
sonriente/sonreír: smiling/to smile
siempre: always
humilde: humble, modest
obtuvo/obtener: obtained/to obtain
frutos: profits
veces: times
ganándolo: winning it/to win
cantó/cantar: she sang/to sing
recibió/recibir: she received/to receive
doctorados: doctorates
participó: she participated/ to participate
películas y telenovelas: films and soap operas
incluso: even
llevan/llevar: take/to take
manos: hands
tumor cerebral: brain tumor
velorio: wake
duró/durar: it lasted/to last
amado: beloved
junto a: next to
puño de tierra: handful of earth
trajo/traer: she brought/to bring
supo/saber: she knew/to know
volver: to return
sigue sonando: it keeps on sounding
rincones más remotos: outermost corners
no tendrá fin: will not end
convirtió/convertir: changed/ to change
fuerza: strength

Rubén Darío
NICARAGUA

Pensar en Nicaragua es **acordarse inevitablemente** de Rubén Darío y de esos poemas que a uno **le enseñaron** en el **colegio secundario** y que **hacían**, y hacen, **suspirar**.

La poesía es una de las artes más **queridas** de este país gracias a su gran poeta y escritor, uno de los mayores **exponentes** de todo Centroamérica. Desde su **infancia** fue un **niño prodigio**, **aprendió** a **leer** cuando **apenas** tenía tres años y **antes** de **cumplir los trece**, ya **había escrito** su primer poema.

Tuvo una vida **agitada**, **gozó** con exceso de todos los **placeres mundanos**. Fue **hombre de amores tempestuosos**, temperamental y sensual.

El **afán** de perfección fue una de sus características más **destacadas**. El ritmo, las nuevas combinaciones **métricas** y la armonía en sus composiciones **aportaron innovaciones** fundamentales en toda la literatura de **lengua** castellana. Fue el gran **inspirador** y máximo representante del Modernismo, **corriente** literaria que **se destacó** por la renovación radical en los conceptos básicos de la poesía, **otorgándole riqueza** y musicalidad.

Combinó su pasión por la escritura con **trabajos periodísticos** y diplomáticos que **le permitieron** viajar por algunos países. La poesía de Rubén Darío no sólo **se lee**, sino que **se escucha** como una **melodía cautivante**, como una canción que emociona y **llega** al **alma**.

pensar: to think
acordarse: to remember
inevitablemente: inevitably
le enseñaron/enseñar: one was taught/ to teach
colegio secundario: secondary school
hacían/hacer: they made/to make
suspirar: to sigh

queridas: beloved
exponentes: exponents
infancia: childhood
niño prodigio: child prodigy
aprendió/aprender: he learned/ to learn
leer: to read
apenas: hardly
antes: before
cumplir los trece: reaching 13
había escrito/escribir: he had written/ to write

tuvo/tener: he had/to have
agitada: agitated
gozó/gozar: he enjoyed/to enjoy
placeres mundanos: material pleasures
hombre de amores tempestuosos: man of tempestuous loves (love affairs)

afán: effort
destacadas: outstanding
métricas: metrics
aportaron/aportar: they contributed/ to contribute
innovaciones: innovations
lengua: language
inspirador: inspiring
corriente: tendency
se destacó/destacarse: he stood out/ to stand out
otorgándole/otorgar: bestowing upon it/to bestow
riqueza: wealth

combinó/combinar: he combined/ to combine
trabajos periodísticos: journalistic work
le permitieron/permitir: they allowed him/to allow
se lee/leer: it is read/to read
se escucha/escuchar: it is listened/ to listen
melodía cautivante: gripping melody
llega/llegar: it reaches/to reach
alma: soul

con el paso de los años: as years went by

se transformó/transformarse: became/ to become

lucha: struggle

pobres: poor

mirada desafiante: defiant look

morir: to die

dispara/disparar: shoot/to shoot

cobarde: coward

estás matando/matar: you are killing/ to kill

inventadas/inventar: made up/to invent

contribuyeron/contribuir: they contributed/to contribute

construcción: building

guerrero: warrior

implacable: relentless, implacable

pocos: few

saben/saber: they know/to know

con exactitud: precisely, exactly

pormenores: details

como sucede: as it happens

se convierten/convertir: they become/ to become

justamente: precisely

supera/superar: it exceeds/to exceed

desvirtúa: it distorts

de carne y hueso: real, only human

nació/nacer: he was born/to be born

chiquito: child

sufrió/sufrir: he suffered/to suffer

hacer la educación: took his education

hogar: home

no le impidió/impidió: it didn't prevent him from/to prevent from

sobresalir: to stand out

entre los demás: among the rest

doctorarse: to get one's doctorate

realizó/realizar: he made/to make

descubriendo/descubrir: discovering/ to discover

miseria: extreme poverty

masas: masses, people

se formó: he was educated

conoció/conocer: he met/to meet

se vinculó: he joined

médico: doctor

sindicatos: labor unions

participó/participar: he participated/ to participate

posteriormente: later

partió/partir: he left/to leave

encuentro: gathering

integrante: member

luchaba/luchar: he fought/to fight

El Che Guevara
ARGENTINA

Con el paso de los años, el Che Guevara **se transformó** en icono de la revolución, la **lucha** y la defensa de los **pobres**. Su **mirada desafiante** en la fotografía que lo inmortalizó en posters, y sus últimas palabras antes de **morir**, "**Dispara, cobarde**, sólo **estás matando** a un hombre", **inventadas** o reales, **contribuyeron** a la **construcción** de esta imagen de **guerrero implacable**. En realidad, **pocos saben con exactitud** quién fue Ernesto Guevara, cuáles fueron sus ideales y los **pormenores** de su vida privada y de combate. **Como sucede** con la mayoría de las personas famosas que **se convierten** en mito, es **justamente** esa imagen mítica la que **supera**, y a veces también **desvirtúa**, al hombre real, al **de carne y hueso**.

Ernesto Guevara de la Serna **nació** en Rosario (Argentina) el 14 de junio de 1928. Desde **chiquito sufrió** de asma, por lo que tuvo que **hacer la educación** primaria en su **hogar**, pero esto **no le impidió sobresalir entre los demás**.

En 1953, tras **doctorarse** en Medicina en la Universidad de Buenos Aires, **realizó** su segundo viaje por Centroamérica y Sudamérica gracias al que, **descubriendo** la **miseria** dominante entre las **masas** y la omnipresencia del imperialismo, **se formó** políticamente con inclinación a la ideología marxista. Durante este viaje **conoció** también a varios revolucionarios cubanos, guatemaltecos y de otros países del continente (entre ellos a quien sería su futura esposa, Hilda Gadea Ontalia, economista exiliada peruana). **Se vinculó** al Partido Guatemalteco del Trabajo, trabajó como **médico** en los **sindicatos** y **participó** activamente en la política interna del país.

Posteriormente partió a México donde conoció a los hermanos Castro, Fidel y Raúl. Después de este **encuentro**, el Che se convirtió en un **integrante** del grupo de revolución cubana que **luchaba** contra el dictador Fulgencio Batista, presidente de Cuba en ese momento.

En 1955 **se casó** con Hilda Gadea, con quien tuvo una **hija**. **Sin embargo**, este **nacimiento no logró mantener** a la **pareja** unida y se divorciaron al poco tiempo. Tres años después, el Che se casaría **de nuevo** con Aleida March Torres, una joven cubana de 22 años, con la que tuvo cuatro **hijos**. A finales de 1956, en el **yate** Granma, el Che y una **superpoblación** de **tripulantes desembarcaron** en el este de Cuba para **dar comienzo** a la guerrilla revolucionaria. Desde entonces, participó activamente en varios **combates** y **batallas** hasta que, en enero de 1959, Cuba fue liberada y Batista tuvo que partir al **exilio**. En honor a los **servicios prestados** al país, Ernesto Guevara fue declarado ciudadano cubano por el **Consejo de Ministros**.

Durante varios años **cumplió funciones** oficiales dentro del **gobierno** cubano, tuvo responsabilidades de carácter militar y económico (una de sus funciones fue la de Presidente del Banco Nacional de Cuba) y viajó por Egipto, Sudán, Pakistán, India, Indonesia y Ceilán, entre otros países. En octubre de 1960, Estados Unidos **decretó** el embargo **comercial** a Cuba y al año siguiente **rompieron** relaciones diplomáticas. Desde varios puestos políticos y militares, el Che **siguió** su lucha revolucionaria **sin descanso** durante años, además de escribir **numerosos** artículos y varios libros donde **volcó** sus ideas y **pensamientos**. Su **carrera** y funciones políticas **le llevaron** a viajar **por todo el mundo**. Para poder **seguir adelante** con sus ideales progresistas, **solicitó** a la Dirección de la Revolución Cubana su **liberación** en las responsabilidades que tenía con ese país para **reiniciar** la **lucha armada** en solidaridad con los pueblos del mundo.

A finales de 1966 entró clandestinamente a Bolivia para **unirse** inmediatamente a un pequeño grupo de combatientes bolivianos, cubanos y de otras nacionalidades. Así, **fundó** el Ejército de Liberación de Bolivia, instalando una guerrilla que **pudiera irradiar** su influencia hacia Argentina, Chile, Perú, Brasil y Paraguay. El 8 de octubre de 1967, a los 39 años de edad, después de **ser apresado** y **ser seriamente herido**, el Che fue ejecutado por soldados bolivianos. En La Habana, en la Plaza de la Revolución, Fidel Castro informó a medio millón de **acongojados** cubanos, la **triste noticia** de la muerte del Comandante Ernesto Che Guevara.

se casó/casarse: he got married/to get married
hija: daughter
sin embargo: however
nacimiento: birth
no logró/lograr: it didn't succeed in/to succeed in
mantener: to keep
pareja: couple
de nuevo: again
hijos: children
yate: yacht
superpoblación: overpopulation
tripulantes: crew members
desembarcaron/desembarcar: they disembarked/to disembark
dar comienzo: to begin, to start
combates: combat
batallas: battles
exilio: exile
servicios prestados: services given
Consejo de Ministros: cabinet meeting

cumplió funciones: he worked as
gobierno: government
decretó/decretar: it decreed/to decree
comercial: trade
rompieron/romper: they broke/to break
siguió/seguir: he continued/to continue
sin descanso: without having a rest
numerosos: several
volcó/volcar: he dumped/to dump, to empty out
pensamientos: thoughts
carrera: career
le llevaron: they made him
por todo el mundo: around the world
seguir adelante: to keep going
solicitó/solicitar: he asked/to ask
liberación: freeing, liberation
reiniciar: restart
lucha armada: armed struggle

unirse: to join
fundó/fundar: he founded/to found
pudiera/poder: it could/can
irradiar: to radiate
ser apresado/apresar: to be captured/to catch
ser seriamente herido: to be seriously injured
acongojado: distressed
triste: sad
noticia: news

eterno: eternal	
escritor: writer	
nació/nacer: he was born/to be born	
sin embargo: nevertheless	
no fue/ser: it was not/to be	
conocí/conocer: I knew about/ to know about	
donde hoy descansa su cuerpo: where his body lies today	
podía/poder: I was able to/ can, to be able to	
sepultura: grave	
contrajo matrimonio/contraer matrimonio: he got married/to get married	
recuerdos: memories	
en torno: revolved around	
rector: dean	
despojaron/despojar: they stripped/to strip, to take away from	
cargo: position	
mismas afliaciones: same affiliations	
deportado/deportar: deported/ to deport	
para morir: to die	
de manera extraña: in a strange way	
Año Viejo: New Year's Eve	
escuela superior: university, college	
sufrí /sufrir: I suffered/to suffer	
a través de: through	
estadía: stay	
Niebla: *Fog* (Unamuno's novel)	
obra maestra: masterpiece	
ser humano: human being	
demonios: demons	
batallamos/batallar: we battle/ to battle	
después de todo: after all	

Unamuno, el eterno poeta
ESPAÑA

Este **escritor** inmortal **nació** en Bilbao, España, en 1864. **Sin embargo**, **no fue** allí donde **conocí** su historia sino en la ciudad donde vivió gran parte de su vida y **donde hoy descansa su cuerpo**, Salamanca. Desde mi habitación **podía** ver su **sepultura** y en muchas ocasiones tuve conversaciones imaginarias con él.

En 1891, llegó a esta ciudad donde también **contrajo matrimonio** con Concepción Lizarraga. En su *Diario Intimo* quedan los **recuerdos** de su amor y sus crisis personales **en torno** a la religión.

En 1900 fue nombrado **rector** de la famosa y antigua Universidad de Salamanca, aunque sus ideas políticas lo **despojaron** del **cargo** 14 años más tarde. Estas **mismas afiliaciones** con el Partido Socialista le llevaron a ser **deportado** a la isla de Fuerteventura, luego a Hendaya y finalmente a París.

Regresó a Salamanca en 1931 **para morir** allí **de manera extraña** el 31 de diciembre de ese mismo año. Su cuerpo y su genio se fueron con el **Año Viejo**.

Cuando estaba en la **escuela superior**, **sufrí** sus agonías **a través de** *San Manuel Bueno, Mártir*. Durante mi **estadía** en Salamanca, descubrí al otro hombre, a quien muchos llamaron loco. Para mí, *Niebla* representa su **obra maestra**. En ella presenta la tragedia realista del **ser humano** y todos los **demonios** y ángeles con los que **batallamos**.

Después de todo, todos tenemos algo de locos, ¿no?

Hispanos para la historia
MÉXICO

Anthony Quinn fue un hispano famoso. **Nació** Antonio Rodolfo Oaxaca Quinn el 21 de abril de 1915 en Chihuahua, México de padre **irlandés** y madre mexicana. **Se movió** a los Estados Unidos **siendo** aun muy pequeño. **En las calles del barrio** al este de Los Ángeles, **vende periódicos** y **lustra zapatos** para **ayudar** a su familia **antes de convertirse** en uno de los actores más importantes de la nación americana.

Entre sus películas mas destacadas están: *Caminando en las nubes (A Walk in the Clouds)* 1995, *Ángelo vengador (Avenging Angelo)* 2002, *El viejo y el mar (The Old Man and the Sea)* 1990 y *Onassis* 1998. Hizo un total de 158 películas. También fue productor, director de cine y **ganador** del **premio** Oscar en **varias ocasiones**. Anthony Quinn **murió** el 3 de junio del 2001 **a causa de complicaciones respiratorias**.

Una de sus **citas** famosas **se refiere** a sus **comienzos de su carrera** cuando "*Todos decían que para lo único que servía era para hacer papeles de indio*".

Este hispano **demostró** que era **mucho más grande** y **se convirtió en un inmortal del cine**.

---

nació/nacer: was born/to be born
irlandés: Irish
se movió/mover: he moved/to move
siendo: when he still was
en las calles del barrio: the streets of the neighborhood
vende periódicos/vender: sells newspapers/to sell
lustra zapatos/lustrar: shines shoes/ to shine, to polish
ayudar: to help
antes de convertirse: before becoming

entre sus películas mas destacadas: among his most outstanding movies
ganador: winner
premio: award
varias ocasiones: various occasions
murió/morir: he died/to die
a causa de complicaciones respiratorias: caused by respiratory complications

citas: quotations
se refiere/referir: refers/to refer
comienzos de su carrera: beginning of his career
Todos decían que para lo único que servía era para hacer papeles de indio: Everybody used to say that I was only good to play the indian.

demostró/demostrar: showed/to show
mucho más grande: a lot bigger
se convirtió en un inmortal del cine: he became immortal on the big screen

está considerado/estar considerado:
  he is considered/to be considered
eruditos: scholars
esfuerzos: efforts
del plebeyo: of the peasants

búsqueda: quest, search
se inició/iniciar: he started/to start
temprana edad: early age
tío: uncle
le cantaba/cantar: sang/to sing
fingía/fingir: pretended/to pretend
rasguear: to strum
luthier: brand name of a guitar
cercano: close by, near
entonces: then
le acompañó/acompañar: it went
  with/to go with, to accompany
desalentó/desalentar: it discouraged/
  to discourage
debería haber tocado/tocar: he
  should have played/to play
verdadero: real
se propuso como meta: he was
  determined to set a new goal
llevar: to take, taking
consiguió/conseguir: he reached/to
  reach, to get
buscaba/buscar: he was looking for/to
  look for

incluyó /incluir: included/to include
supuestamente serios: so-called
  serious
público: audience
se reiría/reirse: it would laugh/
  to laugh
tendría/tener: it would have/to have
salir: to leave
creían/creer: they believed/to believe
asombró/asombrar: he amazed/
  to amaze, to surprise
los asistentes: those present
se encontró/encontrarse: he found/
  to find
no podía/poder: it wasn't able/
  can, to be able
producir: to produce
suficiente sonido: enough sound
llenar: to fill
salón: hall

Andrés Segovia
ESPAÑA

Andrés Segovia **está considerado** como el padre del movimiento clásico moderno de la guitarra por la mayoría de los **eruditos** modernos. Muchos piensan que sin sus **esfuerzos**, la guitarra clásica todavía se consideraría como un instrumento humilde **del plebeyo**.

La **búsqueda** de Segovia para elevar la guitarra a una posición prominente en el mundo de la música **se inició** a la **temprana edad** de cuatro años. Su **tío le cantaba** canciones en su regazo mientras él **fingía rasguear** una guitarra imaginaria. Afortunadamente había un **luthier cercano** y **entonces** la guitarra **le acompañó** siempre. Aunque su familia lo **desalentó** (según ellos, **debería haber tocado** un instrumento **verdadero**), él continuó persiguiendo su sueño. Segovia **se propuso como meta llevar** los estudios de guitarra a todas las universidades del mundo. Y así fue. Segovia **consiguió** lo que **buscaba**.

Este guitarrista universal dio su primer concierto en España a los 16 años, aunque su debut profesional no llegó hasta los 20. Su programa original **incluyó** transcripciones de Tárrega, así como sus propias transcripciones de Bach y de otros maestros. Muchos músicos **supuestamente serios** creyeron que el **público se reiría** tanto de Segovia, que **tendría** que **salir** del escenario porque **creían** que no se podía tocar música clásica con una guitarra. Sin embargo, Segovia **asombró** a **los asistentes** con su arte. El único problema con el que **se encontró** fue que la guitarra **no podía producir suficiente sonido** como para **llenar** el **salón**.

Con el paso de los años, Segovia **perfeccionó** su técnica experimentando con **maderas** y **diseños** nuevos, para **aumentar** la amplificación natural de la guitarra. **Más adelante**, con la **llegada** de las **cuerdas de nylon**, las guitarras empezaron a producir **tonos más constantes**, **a la vez** que proyectaban el sonido **más lejos**.

La búsqueda de Segovia le **llevó** a Norteamérica en 1928 para ofrecer su primer concierto en Nueva York. Una vez más, su público **quedó abrumado** con la técnica de su guitarra y la **maestría** de sus manos, **consiguiendo** así que sus disidentes empezaran a apreciar la guitarra clásica. Su **éxito** en la ciudad de los **rascacielos** le **condujo** a otras ofertas para más presentaciones en América y Europa e, incluso, un viaje a Oriente en 1929. Segovia y la guitarra clásica **habían llegado**.

Mientras **viajaba** por el mundo, el músico español y su guitarra **se hicieron** más y más populares. **A partir de entonces**, compositores de todo el mundo **empezaron** a **crear piezas originales** específicas para guitarra.

Asimismo, Segovia **adaptó obras maestras** a la guitarra. De hecho, su transcripción del Chaconne de Bach es una de las piezas más famosas y difíciles de **dominar**. Al escuchar la realizada por el maestro español, **parece** como si la intención de Bach **hubiera sido componerla** originalmente para guitarra en vez de para violín.

Además de crear un **amplio repertorio** y de mejorar la **calidad sonora** de la guitarra, Segovia consiguió **pasar** su **legado** de **conocimientos** a una nueva generación. El compositor español tuvo muchos **alumnos** a lo largo de su carrera. Entre los más famosos se encuentran Christopher Parkening, John Williams, Elliot Fisk y Oscar Ghiglia. Estos discípulos, entre muchos otros, continúan hoy la tradición de Segovia, a la vez que **extienden** la presencia, el repertorio y los límites musicales de la guitarra clásica.

con el paso de los años: as years went by
perfeccionó/perfeccionar: he improved/to improve, to perfect
maderas: woods, timbers
diseños: designs
aumentar: to increase
más adelante: later
llegada: arrival
cuerdas de nylon: nylon strings
tonos más constantes: more consistent tones
a la vez: at the same time
más lejos: further

llevó/ llevar: it took/to take
quedó: was
abrumado/abrumar: overwhelmed/ to overwhelm
maestría: expertise, skill
consiguiendo: obtaining, reaching
éxito: success
rascacielos: skyscrapers
condujo/conducir: it led him/to lead
habían llegado/llegar: they had arrived/to arrive

viajaba/viajar: he traveled/to travel
se hicieron/ hacerse: they became/ to become
a partir de entonces: from then on
empezaron/empezar: they started/ to start
crear: to create
piezas originales: original pieces

asimismo: also, as well
adaptó/adaptar: he adapted/to adapt
obras maestras: masterpieces
dominar: to master
parece/parecer: it seems/to seem
hubiera sido componerla: it would have been to compose it

amplio/ampliar: expanded/to expand
repertorio: repertoire
calidad sonora: sound quality
pasar: to go to
legado: legacy
conocimientos: knowledge
alumnos: students
extienden/extender: they spread/ to spread

Galeano, un uruguayo comprometido
URUGUAY

Es curioso como a veces **uno no valora** lo que tiene **cerca** hasta el momento en que **se encuentra** ya **demasiado lejos**. **A pesar de haber nacido** y **crecido** en Uruguay, mi primer contacto con la obra del escritor uruguayo Eduardo Galeano fue **recién cumplidos los 18 años**, durante una **estadía** en Alemania, y gracias a un amigo venezolano que **me prestó** uno de sus libros.

La introducción a Galeano fue nada más y nada menos que con su famosa **obra** *Memorias del fuego*. En esta trilogía el autor describe la historia de América **a través** de pequeñas historias y **personajes**, muchos reales y otros **míticos**. En el primer **tomo incluye mitos y leyendas** indígenas, memorias previas a la **llegada** de los europeos. El segundo tomo **comprende** la historia de las Américas durante el período que va desde la llegada de los españoles hasta **finales** del **siglo** XIX.

Por último, en el tercer tomo, **cubre en detalle** los **acontecimientos** del siglo XX. Esta obra **le valió** el **Premio del Libro Americano** en 1989, y para mí, representó el **redescubrimiento** de América Latina.

Este **escritor, periodista** y poeta uruguayo **saltó a la fama mundial** con su **obra periodística** *Las venas abiertas de América Latina*. En ese gran **trabajo de investigación**, el autor describe lo que años de colonización **dejaron** como **legado** al continente americano. Una de las imágenes **más poderosas** que **utiliza** y que **se ha quedado conmigo** a través de los años **es aquella que** compara a países latinoamericanos con una mano abierta, donde por sus venas las vías de comunicación que los **colonizadores abrieron se drena** al continente de sus riquezas.

---

es curioso: it is funny, it is curious
uno no valora/valorar: one does not appreciate/to appreciate
cerca: close
se encuentra/encontrarse: it is/to be
demasiado lejos: too far away
a pesar de: in spite of
haber nacido/nacer: having been born/to be born
crecido/crecer: grown/to grow
recién cumplidos los 18 años: right after my 18th birthday
estadía: stay
me prestó/prestar: lent me/to lend

obra: work
fuego: fire
a través: throughout
personajes: characters
míticos: mythical
tomo: volume
incluye/incluir: it includes/to include
mitos y leyendas: myths and legends
llegada: arrival
comprende/comprender: it includes/ to comprise, to include
finales: end
siglo: century

cubre/cubrir: it covers/to cover
en detalle: in detail
acontecimientos: events
le valió/valer: won him/to win
Premio del Libro Americano: American Book Award
redescubrimiento: rediscovery
escritor: writer
periodista: journalist
saltó a la fama mundial: he became famous all around the world
obra periodística: journalistic work
venas: veins
trabajo de investigación: investigative work
dejaron/dejar: they left/to leave
legado: legacy
más poderosas: most powerful
utiliza/utilizar: it uses/to use
se ha quedado/quedarse: it has stayed/to stay
conmigo: with me
es aquella que: it is the one that
colonizadores: colonists, settlers
abrieron/abrir: they opened/to open
se drena/drenar: is drained/to drain

Fuerte crítico social y activista, Galeano, que **ha sido traducido** a casi 20 idiomas, es un viejo **defensor** de los **grupos menos privilegiados** de la sociedad. Entre sus trabajos **más conocidos se encuentran** *Días y noches de amor y de **guerra**, Nosotros decimos no, El libro de los **abrazos*** y Las ***palabras andantes.***

Sus intereses son muy **amplios, como lo demuestra su libro** *El fútbol a sol y **sombra**,* donde habla sobre su **deporte** favorito, o el libro ***Patas arriba**: la escuela del mundo **al revés**,* donde **cuestiona** varios aspectos de la vida moderna. Su libro más reciente **se titula** *Bocas del tiempo* y **abarca** temas tan diversos como el agua, la música y la guerra.

Es imposible estar al día con la obra de un autor tan **prolífico**. Con esa forma tan rica y poética que lo caracteriza, Galeano escribe constantemente. Con innumerables **ensayos** y artículos periodísticos, **nos brinda** su opinión y **mirada crítica acerca** de los diferentes acontecimientos mundiales. A través de sus **preguntas nos lleva a reflexionar**, a pensar; a veces **nos hace reír**, otras, **nos saca una lágrima**.

Exiliado durante la dictadura militar de los años 70 y 80, Galeano **se encuentra instalado actualmente** en su **ciudad natal**, Montevideo. Su casa, **ubicada** en el **barrio** de Malvín, es **fácilmente** identificable por las **pinturas** en rojo que decoran la **fachada** y que son obra del **propio escritor**. Viviendo a tan pocas **cuadras** del Río de la Plata, a Galeano **se le puede ver a menudo caminando a lo largo** de la **rambla**, disfrutando del aire y del **mar**. O **se le puede encontrar** en uno de los **tantos** cafés que **pueblan** las **esquinas** de la ciudad y que, **como él bien dice**, **invitan** a la **charla** y la confesión.

---

fuerte: strong
ha sido traducido/tranducir: (his work) has been translated/to translate
defensor: defender
grupos menos privilegiados: least privileged groups
más conocidos: famous, more known
se encuentran/encontrarse: they are/ to be
guerra: war
abrazos: hugs
palabras andantes: walking words

amplios: broad
como lo demuestra su libro: as it is shown in his book
sombra: shade
deporte: sport
patas arriba: in a mess
al revés: upside down
cuestiona/cuestionar: he questions/ to question
se titula/titularse: it is entitled/ to be entitled
abarca/abarcar: it covers/to cover

prolífico: prolific, productive
ensayos: essay
nos brinda/brindar: it provides us/ to provide, to offer
mirada crítica: critical look
acerca: about
preguntas: questions
nos lleva a reflexionar: he makes us reflect
nos hace reír: he makes us laugh
nos saca una lágrima: he makes us cry

exiliado: exiled
se encuentra instalado: he lives
actualmente: these days
ciudad natal: home town
ubicada: located
barrio: neighborhood
fácilmente: easily
pinturas: paintings
fachada: facade
propio escritor: the writer himself
cuadras: blocks
se le puede ver: (Galeano) can be seen
a menudo: often
caminando/caminar: walking/to walk
a lo largo: along
rambla: boulevard
mar: sea
se le puede encontrar: he can be found
tantos: many
pueblan/poblar: they populate/ to populate
esquinas: corners
como él bien dice: as he well says
invitan/invitar: they invite/to invite
charla: chat

María Félix

MÉXICO

"**Acuérdate de** Acapulco, de **aquellas noches**, María Bonita, María del **alma**…". ¿**Quién no ha escuchado alguna vez de boca de** Agustín Lara, o de algún otro **cantante**, esta famosa **letra acompañada de** su romántica melodía? ¿**Quién no ha soñado**, por **haberla escuchado**, con **visitar tierras mexicanas** y **encontrar** su María bonita? Para los que **se preguntaban** quién era esa María de la **canción**, aquí **les desvelamos** el misterio.

"María Bonita" era María Félix. Y María Félix, María de los Ángeles Güereña. No, no es un **rompecabezas** ni una **adivinanza**. Es que María Félix **nació** en 1914 con el nombre de María de los Ángeles pero luego, para su **carrera artística**, **cambió** de nombre.

Fue una de las **principales** actrices del **cine** mexicano de los **años** 40 y 50 y un icono de este arte. María **puso en alto** la imagen de la mujer mexicana en el **mundo**, **pese a que** en su **vida privada** era lo **opuesto** de la realidad femenina que **se vivía** en México en esa **época**.

Nació en el rancho del Quiriego, en el **estado** de Sonora, un **lugar seco** y **duro** que fue escenario de la revolución mexicana. Tenía 11 **hermanos** y su amilia **estaba regida** por los principios morales tradicionales, en los que la **figura paterna** era la autoridad máxima.

Se fue de casa cuando **se casó** por primera vez a los 16 años. A este primer matrimonio **le siguieron** varios, algunos con artistas como el cantante Agustín Lara, de quien **estaba locamente enamorada**, pero cuya unión **duró** muy poco **debido a** los **celos** de él. También se casó con el actor Jorge Negrete, con quién **compartió protagonismo** en su primera **película**, *El peñón de las ánimas*, en 1942.

En la filmografía de su época, las actrices que **destacaban representaban** a la mujer mexicana urbana y **campesina**, a la dignidad y al sacrificio, a la **amargura** y al **abandono**. "La **Doña**" (como **la llamaron** algunos luego de la película Doña Bárbara), con su voz **grave** y **rostro** angelical, **rompió** con los estereotipos de la **mansedumbr**e femenina. La sociedad **tembló** ante el fenómeno social de la mujer que **fumaba** y **bebía e**n público, que se había divorciado y que **se vestía** de hombre.

Los contratos **se multiplicaron dentro y fuera** del **país**. En total **filmó** 47 películas, además de en México, en diferentes países de Sudamérica y Europa, donde la llamaban "La Mexicana"· María Félix fue una diva, con **estilo propio**, inteligencia y carácter. **Falleció mientras dormía**, el 8 de abril de 2002, el mismo día de su cumpleaños número 88, en México.

---

estado: state
lugar: place
seco: dry
duro: harsh
hermanos: siblings
estaba regida/regir: it was governed/ to govern
figura paterna: paternal figure

se fue de casa: she left home
se casó/casarse: she got married/ to get married
le siguieron/seguir: they followed/ to follow
estaba locamente enamorada: she was madly in love
duró/durar: it lasted/to last
debido a: due to
celos: jealousy
compartió protagonismo: she shared the main role
película: film
El peñón de las ánimas: The rock of the souls

destacaban/destacar: they stood out/ to stand out
representaban/representar: they represent/to represent
campesina: peasant-like, rural
amargura: bitterness
abandono: abandonment, desertion
doña: madam, lady
la llamaron/llamar: they called her/ to call her
grave: deep
rostro: face
rompió/romper: she broke/to break
mansedumbre: meekness
tembló/temblar: it trembled/to tremble
fumaba/fumar: she smoked/to smoke
bebía/beber: she drank/to drink
se vestía/vestir: she dressed/to dress

se multiplicaron/multipicar: are multiplied/to multiply
dentro y fuera: inside and outside
país: country
filmó/filmar: she filmed/to film
estilo propio: own style
falleció/fallecer: she died/to die
mientras dormía: while she was sleeping
mismo día: same day

Examina tu comprensión

La magia de García Márquez, página 106

1. ¿A qué carrera se dedicó García Márquez antes de comenzar a escribir?

2. ¿A qué género pertenecen sus libros?

3. ¿En qué otra carrera trabajó García Márquez?

4. ¿Quiénes son los escritores favoritos admirados por García Márquez?

Diego Rivera, página 108

1. ¿Qué mujer ayudó a Rivera con sus pinturas políticas?

2. Rivera tenía un estilo característico de pintar ¿en qué local?

3. Su mural en el Palacio Nacional fue su interpretación ¿de qué cosa?

4. ¿Qué ideales se reflejan en la pintura mural de Diego?

Frida Kahlo, página 110

1. Cuando era joven, Kahlo tuvo un accidente que cambió su vida. ¿Cuáles fueron las consecuencias de su accidente?

2. ¿Cuál fue su primer pintura?

3. ¿Con quién se casó Kahlo y donde exhibió Frida por primera vez?

Celia Cruz, página 112

1. Cruz tuvo una vocación en la música, pero una misión ¿para qué?

2. Cruz tiene el honor de ser la primera mujer hispana en hacer ¿qué cosa?

3. ¿De qué enfermedad murió Cruz?

Test your comprehension

Rubén Darío, página 113

1. Darío era un niño prodigio que es conocido ¿como qué?

El Che Guevara, página 114

1. Durante sus estudios de medicina, ¿qué descubrió Che Guevara?

2. ¿Cómo y dónde murió Che Guevara?

Unamuno, el eterno poeta, página 116

1. ¿Por qué se terminó su trabajo en la Universidad de Salamanca?

2. ¿Qué contenía el Diario Íntimo?

Andrés Segovia, página 118

1. ¿A qué edad comenzó el amor de Segovia por la música y la guitarra? ¿Cuándo fue su primer concierto?

2. Segovia encontró un problema particular con su guitarra. ¿Cuál fue el problema y cómo lo arregló?

3. Segovia adaptó otras obras maestras a la guitarra. ¿Cuál de ellas es considerada la más famosa y difícil?

Galeano, página 120

1. En la trilogía *Memorias del Fuego*, ¿qué es lo que se discute y describe en cada sección?

2. ¿Dónde vive Galeano y qué podría uno verlo haciendo allí?

Dime cómo te diviertes y te diré quién eres.

José Ortega y Gasset

Deportes

El arte de imitar a los pájaros

ARGENTINA

enclavado: located
corazón: heart
se encuentra/encontrar: it is located/
 to be located
más lindos: most beautiful
altura: height
sobre el nivel del mar: above sea level
zona serrana: mountain region
se destaca/destacar: it stands out/
 to stand out
no sólo...sino también: not only ...
 but also
paisajes de cuento: fairy tale
 landscapes
abanico: range
actividades recreativas: recreational
 activities
sin duda: without a doubt
estrella: star
vuelo libre: free flight
aladeltas: hang gliders
parapentes: paragliders
planeadores: gliders
intentar: to try
aves: birds
y lo mejor: and the best part
no hay que hacer ningún curso especial: there is no need to take a special
 course
primer vuelo: first flight
animarse: to dare to do it

contactar: to contact
pilotos biplaza: two seat pilot
se encuentran/encontrarse:
 there is/to be
mirador: viewpoint
sagrado: sacred
rampa de despegue: takeoff ramp
proporciona/proporcionar:
 it provides/to provide
casco: helmet
detalla/detallar: details/to give the
 details of, to list
travesía: flight
una vez: once
sentidos: senses
se exacerban/exacerbar: they are
 exacerbated/to exacerbate
mente: mind
se pone en blanco: it goes blank
disfrute: enjoyment
lo invade/invadir: it invades/to invade
flotar: to float
pluma: feather
no sería/ser: it would not be/to be
cruzarse: to pass somebody
mitad del vuelo: middle of the flight

aterrizaje: landing
justo al lado: right beside
si hace calor: if it is hot
refrescarse: to cool down
cálidas aguas: warm waters

A sólo 90 kilómetros de Córdoba capital, **enclavado** en el **corazón** del Valle de Punilla, **se encuentra** uno de los pueblos **más lindos** de esta región: La Cumbre. A 1.100 metros de **altura** **sobre** **el nivel del mar**, esta **zona serrana se destaca no sólo** por sus incomparables **paisajes de cuento sino también** por su enorme **abanico** de posibilidades para realizar **actividades recreativas** y de turismo aventura. **Sin duda**, la **estrella** en este tema es el **vuelo libre**. Desde **aladeltas** a **parapentes**, pasando por **planeadores**, todo es válido a la hora de **intentar** imitar a las **aves**. **Y lo mejor**: **no hay que hacer ningún curso especial** para el **primer vuelo**, sólo **animarse**.

Para volar en parapente, lo primero es **contactar** con alguno de los **pilotos biplaza** o ir directamente a Cuchi Corral, donde **se encuentran** el antiguo **mirador sagrado** y la **rampa de despegue**. Allí, el instructor **proporciona casco** y **detalla** las cuestiones mínimas a tener en cuenta durante la **travesía**. **Una vez** en el aire, los **sentidos se exacerban**, la **mente se pone en blanco** y el **disfrute lo invade** todo. Volar es **flotar**, flotar en el aire. Como una **pluma**, como un pájaro. O como un cóndor, al que por otra parte **no sería** raro **cruzarse** en **mitad del vuelo**.

El **aterrizaje** es suave, **justo al lado** del Río Pintos. Y **si hace calor**, y uno puede **refrescarse** en sus **cálidas aguas**, la gloria es completa.

Acampando en San Felipe
MÉXICO

No hay nada como acampar al **aire libre** bajo las **estrellas**, **fuera** de la ciudad y **gozando** de la **naturaleza**. Uno de los mejores lugares para acampar en México es en las **playas** de San Felipe, **situadas** al norte del estado de Baja California, cerca de Mexicali (México). Con sus playas **calientes**, San Felipe **atrae** a mucha gente que quiere **escapar** de la vida de las **ciudades**. Este lugar es uno de los favoritos para **jugar** en la **arena** y el **mar**.

San Felipe es árido y caliente, y el **terreno** que **lo rodea** es extremadamente desértico, **aunque** este **ambiente solitario** es lo que muchas personas encuentran **relajante**. Aquí **reinan** la **paz** y la **tranquilidad**. El **reloj parece caminar** más **despacio** y uno **se siente** como transportado a otro tiempo, a otro lugar, **alejado** de cualquier preocupación.

Situado al lado del Golfo de Baja California, San Felipe **proporciona** una experiencia **encantadora** a aquellos que **disfrutan** del calor. Las aguas del golfo son **tibias** a todas horas del día. Uno puede **nadar** por la noche y **sentir** el agua caliente, o **estirarse** en la arena y **mirar** al **cielo lleno de** estrellas. San Felipe es uno de los mejores lugares para observar las **maravillas** celestiales. No hay muchas **luces** fuera de la ciudad, y el cielo es tan **claro** y lleno de estrellas **brillantes** que en las noches en que no hay **luna**, las mismas estrellas **dan** suficiente luz como para **alumbrar** las playas. Es tan increíble que es difícil de **creer incluso estando allí**.

no hay nada como: there is nothing better than
acampar: to camp
aire libre: outdoors
estrellas: stars
fuera: out
gozando/gozar: enjoying/to enjoy
naturaleza: nature
playas: beaches
situadas: located
calientes: hot
atrae/atraer: it attracts/to attract
escapar: to get away
ciudades: cities
jugar: to play
arena: sand
mar: sea

terreno: land
lo rodea/rodear: it surrounds it/ to surround
aunque: even though
ambiente: atmosphere
solitario: solitary
relajante: relaxing
reinan/reinar: they reign/to reign
paz: peace
tranquilidad: calmness, tranquility
reloj: clock
parece/parecer: it seems/to seem
caminar: to walk
despacio: slow
se siente/sentirse: one feels/to feel
alejado: far away

proporciona/proporcionar: it provides/to provide
encantadora: charming
disfrutan/disfrutar: they enjoy/ to enjoy
tibias: tepid
nadar: to swim
sentir: to feel
estirarse: to stretch
mirar: to look
cielo: sky
lleno de: plenty of
maravillas: wonders
luces: lights
claro: light
brillantes: gleaming
luna: moon
dan/dar: they give/to give
alumbrar: to light, to illuminate
creer: to believe
incluso: even
estando allí/estar: being there/ to be

Surfing en Costa Rica
COSTA RICA

Miles de personas **visitan** Costa Rica **buscando** las mejores zonas para practicar el surf. Y Costa Rica reúne **en verdad** las **condiciones ideales** para la práctica de este deporte: **aguas cálidas, unas 700 millas** de costa, **gente amable** y unos **precios razonables**. Las zonas para practicar el surf en Costa Rica están definidas por su localización y **la estación del año**. Podemos distinguir cuatro zonas: La Costa Pacífica Norte, con playas como Tamarindo o Playa Negra, **algunas de ellas especialmente acondicionadas** para los surfeadores que prefieren una **estancia tranquila, sin vida nocturna**. Esta zona es **por lo general** el destino **más apropiado desde** diciembre **hasta** abril.

Por otra parte, **si queremos** practicar el surf entre los meses de mayo y noviembre, será preferible **dirigirnos tanto** a la Costa Pacífica Sur (Playas de Matapalo o Pavones) **como** a la Costa Pacífica Central (Playa Hermosa, Dominical). **En cambio**, la Costa del Caribe **estará en pleno auge** entre noviembre y marzo. **Teniendo en cuenta** estas características, podemos **planear** nuestras vacaciones, aunque **siempre hay que pensar** que estas diferencias son generales. Una buena idea para disfrutar de nuestro viaje a Costa Rica y practicar el surfing es **elegir** una ciudad, y desde ésta hacer **excursiones diarias** a otras ciudades en **coche de alquiler**. La distancia **entre ciudades** varía entre una hora y diez minutos. Así, **pasaremos más tiempo** en el agua y menos en la **carretera**.

Costa Rica es uno de los países con más turismo, **debido principalmente a** su **seguridad** en prácticamente **cualquier lugar del país**. Sus **índices de criminalidad** son bastantes bajos. Pero no seamos **confiados**, aunque en los hoteles los robos son **muy poco frecuentes**. ¡No es una buena idea guardar en el **salpicadero** del auto nuestro **reloj**, pasaporte u otros objetos valiosos **antes de ir** al agua!

---

miles: thousands
visitan/visitar: they visit/to visit
buscando/buscar: searching/to search
en verdad: really
condiciones ideales: ideal conditions
aguas cálidas: warm waters
unas 700 millas: some 700 miles
gente amable: nice people
precios razonables: reasonable prices
la estación del año: season of the year
algunas de ellas: some of them
especialmente acondicionadas: specially prepared, equipped
estancia tranquila: calm stay
sin vida nocturna: without nightlife
por lo general: generally
más apropiado: more appropriate
desde...hasta: from ... to

por otra parte: on the other hand
si queremos/querer: if we want/to want
dirigirnos/dirigir: to direct us to/to direct
tanto...como: both ... and
en cambio: on the other hand
estará en pleno auge: it will be at its very peak
teniendo en cuenta: taking into account
planear: to plan
siempre hay que pensar: it is always necessary to think
elegir: to choose
excursiones diarias: daily tours
coche de alquiler: rental car
entre ciudades: among cities
pasaremos más tiempo/pasar: we'll spend more time/to spend
carretera: road

debido principalmente a: mainly due to
seguridad: security
cualquier lugar del país: any place in the country
índices de criminalidad: crime rates
confiados: confident
muy poco frecuentes: very infrequent
salpicadero: dashboard
reloj: watch
antes de ir: before going

Escalando el Nevado Sajama

BOLIVIA

¿**Quién no pensó alguna vez** en tocar el **cielo** con las **manos**? **Escalar** el Nevado Sajama y llegar a la **cima** es una forma de **sentir algo parecido**. Nevado Sajama es el **pico** más alto del Bolivia. Son 6542 metros de **roca maciza** que se elevan en la provincia de Oruro.

Aunque esta aventura **no es fácil** ni es para cualquiera, el que **se proponga** realizarla y se prepare con varios días de **entrenamiento** y un **buen guía de montaña.** La preparación consiste básicamente en **ejercicios físicos** de aclimatación a la **altura** y una **alimentación adecuada**. Los **entendidos recomiendan pasar** varios días en la base del cerro, y hacer **ascensos** y **descensos** a montañas cercanas **combinándolos** con **días de descanso** y un plan **alimentario energético**. En estas altitudes el clima es riguroso y muchas veces hostil por lo que es muy importante **contar con indumentaria** especial y por supuesto el equipo básico: **arnés de cintura**, **mosquetones de seguridad** y **calzado de gran adherencia**.

La escalada es un deporte considerado de **alto riesgo**, en el que no sólo se utiliza la **fortaleza física** de **brazos** y **piernas** sino también **destreza técnica** y claridad mental para tomar las decisiones **adecuadas** a cada paso. Es una experiencia fascinante y **única** en la que **se templa** el espíritu, **se construye** una fuerza de **voluntad de acero** y el compañerismo juega un **papel** fundamental.

quién no pensó/pensar: who does not think/to think
alguna vez: sometimes
cielo: sky
manos: hands
escalar: to climb
cima: top
sentir: to feel
algo parecido: something similar
pico: peak
roca maciza: massive rock

no es fácil: it is not easy
se proponga/proponer: one suggests/ to suggest
entrenamiento: training
buen guía de montaña: good mountain guide
ejercicios físicos: physical exercise
altura: height
alimentación adecuada: appropriate diet, nutrition
entendidos: experts
recomiendan/recomendar: they recommend/to recommend
pasar: to spend
ascensos: ascents
descensos: descents
combinándolos/combinar: combining them/to combine
días de descanso: days of rest
alimentario energético: energy giving food
contar con: to count on
indumentaria: clothing
arnés de cintura: waist harness
mosquetones de seguridad: carabiners (security clamps)
calzado de gran adherencia: footwear with good grip, traction

alto riesgo: high risk
fortaleza física: physical strength
brazos: arms
piernas: legs
destreza técnica: technical skill
adecuadas: appropriate
única: unique
se templa/templar: it warms up/ to warm up
se construye/construir: it builds/ to build
voluntad de acero: iron will
papel: role

será/ser: it will be/to be
chiquitos: boys, male children
varones: males
cumpleaños: birthdays
regalan/regalar: they give/to give
  (as a gift)
pelota de fútbol: soccer ball
camiseta: t-shirt
equipo: team
intuye/intuir: he suspects/to suspect
temprana edad: early age
ciertas: certain
habilidades: skills
hará planes: they make plans
proyectará/proyectar: they project/
  to project
soñará/soñar: he will dream/to dream
verlo: to see him
preferido: favorite

siempre: always
hay tiempo: there is time
picadito: game without a serious
  rivalry, usually between friends
ida al campo: trip to the countryside
juntarse: to get together
acompañado: accompanied
asado: roast
no hay mejor: there is not a better
siguiente: following
se comentarán/comentar: they
  comment/to comment
hazañas: deeds, exploits
desaciertos: mistakes, errors
jugador: player
desmesurada: excessive
como si: as if
valores: values
decisivos: decisive
piel de gallina: goose bumps (literally:
  chicken skin)
aficionados: fans, enthusiasts
genera/generar: it generates/
  to generate
amargura: bitterness
llanto: crying
gritos: shouts
seguidores: fans

El fútbol
ARGENTINA

¿Por qué **será** que de **chiquitos**, a los **varones** argentinos, en alguno de sus **cumpleaños** les **regalan** una **pelota de fútbol** o la **camiseta** de algún **equipo**? Si algún padre **intuye** que su hijo desde **temprana edad** tiene **ciertas habilidades** con ese deporte, **hará planes**, **proyectará** ilusiones y **soñará** con **verlo** jugar en su equipo **preferido**.

Los domingos **siempre hay tiempo** para un **picadito** con los amigos, para una **ida al campo** en grupo o, simplemente, para **juntarse** a ver por televisión al equipo de sus sueños. Si todo esto viene luego **acompañado** de un **asado**, **no hay mejor** domingo. Al día **siguiente se comentarán** las **hazañas** o **desaciertos** de cada **jugador** con una pasión **desmesurada**, **como si** en cada relato se jugaran **valores** e ideales importantísimos y **decisivos**. El fútbol en Argentina es pura pasión y emoción, un deporte que pone la **piel de gallina** a sus **aficionados** y que **genera** tensión, alegría, **amargura**, **llanto** y **gritos** entre sus **seguidores**.

Gran parte del fenómeno en que el fútbol **se ha convertido** en Argentina **se lo debemos** a su máximo ídolo, Diego Armando Maradona. "El Pelusa", como **se le conoce mundialmente, ha dejado** un **legado sin igual** así como miles de niños que quieren **imitarlo**. Verlo en el campo era ver jugar al mejor. Maradona **mostraba** una habilidad superior con el balón, una **gracia digna de dioses**, una magia de otra dimensión. **Se desplazaba** como quien lo hace suspendido a unos centímetros **del suelo**. El campo era su **hogar**, la pelota una extensión de su **cuerpo**, sus compañeros de equipo un apoyo y sus rivales, obstáculos necesarios, pero **fáciles de sortear**, hasta llegar al gol. El número 10 que llevaba a su **espalda** coincidía, **sin duda**, con la **calidad** de sus habilidades como futbolista.

se ha convertido/convertir: it has become/to become
se lo debemos/deber: we owe it/to owe
se le conoce/conocer: he is known/to know
mundialmente: worldwide
ha dejado/dejar: he has left/to leave
legado sin igual: unrivaled legacy
imitarlo/imitar: imitate him/to imitate
mostraba/mostrar: he showed/to show
gracia digna de dioses: grace worthy of gods
se desplazaba/desplazar: he moved/to move
del suelo: from the ground
hogar: home
cuerpo: body
fáciles de sortear: easy to avoid, easy to get around
espalda: back
sin duda: without a doubt
calidad: quality

CULTURE NOTE

The name "Argentina" comes from a Latin word which means "silver." The origin of the name goes back to the first Spanish conquistadors' voyage to the *Río de la Plata*. The shipwrecked survivors of the expedition were greeted by Indians who presented them with silver objects. The news about the legendary *Sierra del Plata*, a mountain rich in silver, reached Spain around 1524. Since 1860 the official name of the country has been *República Argentina*.

When listening to Spanish in Argentina you will notice the the unmistakable *Porteño* accent, a seductive blend of an expressive, almost drawling intonation combined with colorful colloquialisms. In Buenos Aires, in particular, you will notice the strong pronunciation of "y" and "ll" as in *yo* and *calle*, a completely different sound to the weaker vowel-like sound used in Spain and much of Latin America. Another prominent difference is the use of *vos* as the second-person pronoun in place of *tú*. Something else you will notice in the Argentinian vocabulary is the use of *che* (it loosely approximates "hey" in English, used at the beginning of a phrase: *¿che, que decis?* "hey, how's it going?"). It is so much identified with Argentina that some Latin Americans refer to Argentineans as *"Los che."* The word was most famously applied as a nickname to Ernesto Guevara, popularly known as Che Guevara.

Comunidad Autónoma: Autonomous Region
País Vasco: Basque country
hace varios siglos: several centuries ago
en la actualidad: nowadays
no sólo...sino también: not only ...but also
concretamente: in particular
apuestas: betting
permitidas: allowed
es más: furthermore
ha llegado/llegar: it arrived/to arrive

fiesta alegre: joyful party
se practicaba/practicar: it was played/to play
en realidad: in fact
hacía referencia: it referenced
frontón: arena for Jai Alai
en sí: by itself
pelota: ball
posteriormente: afterwards
empezó a utilizarce: it started to be used
quizás: perhaps
bases y reglas: rules and basis
a pesar de: in spite of
no todo el mundo: not everybody
con detalle: in depth
no ha sufrido variaciones: it didn't change
acción: action
velocidad: speed

cancha: court
paredes: walls
aunque: though
se mencionó/mencionar: it was mentioned/to mention
anteriormente: before
hecha de granito: made of granite
suficientemente sólido: strong enough
soportar: to support, to hold up
golpes: hits
por último: finally
pantalla de seguridad: security screen
alambre: wire

El jai alai
ESPAÑA

Este deporte, nacido en la **Comunidad Autónoma** del **País Vasco hace varios siglos**, es **en la actualidad** muy popular **no sólo** en esta región española, **sino también** Latinoamérica y Estados Unidos, **concretamente** en los estados de Florida o Connecticut, donde las **apuestas** están **permitidas**. **Es más**, incluso **ha llegado** a países como China y Egipto.

El término "Jai Alai" es una palabra de origen vasco que significa "**fiesta alegre**", pues este juego **se practicaba** normalmente durante las fiestas anuales. **En realidad**, Jai Alai **hacía referencia**, originariamente, al **frontón**. El juego **en sí** se llama "**pelota**" o "Pelota vasca". **Posteriormente** el nombre "Jai Alai" **empezó a utilizarse** también para hacer referencia al juego. **Quizás** resulte interesante describir las **bases y reglas** de este juego, pues, **a pesar de** su popularidad, **no todo el mundo** lo conoce **con detalle**. Desde el nacimiento de este juego, hace más de 500 años, **no ha sufrido** muchas variaciones, y sus principales características siguen siendo la **acción** y la **velocidad**.

Jai Alai, o pelota vasca, se juega en una **cancha** con tres **paredes**, también llamada frontón (**aunque** su nombre original es Jai Alai, como **se mencionó anteriormente**). La pared principal de la cancha está **hecha de granito** ya que es un material **suficientemente sólido** para **soportar** los **golpes** de la pelota y las otras dos paredes están hechas de cemento. **Por último**, hay una **pantalla de seguridad** hecha de **alambre**, situada en la parte de la cancha sin pared, para proteger a los espectadores.

Los pelotaris, o **jugadores**, tienen que **lanzar** la pelota contra la pared principal **usando** una **cesta de mimbre atada al brazo** del jugador.

El **propósito** de este juego es lanzar la pelota contra la pared **de forma que** el jugador contrario **no pueda golpearla a su regreso**. La pelota, que está hecha de **caucho** y que puede **alcanzar** una velocidad de 230 kilómetros por hora, puede golpear la pared lateral o la posterior, pero nunca la zona de los espectadores. Un **dato muy significativo** es que estas pelotas tienen una vida de **tan sólo** 20 minutos. Con esto, podemos **hacernos una idea** de la fuerza y la velocidad con que se lanzan las pelotas contra el frontón.

Las reglas de juego son **bastante parecidas** a las del tenis. El jugador debe lanzar la pelota **por encima** de la línea de servicio y debe **rebotar** entre las líneas 4 y 7 del frontón. **Si no lo consigue**, el equipo contrario ganará un punto. **La mayoría de** las variantes de Jai Alai se juega a siete puntos, que **se doblan después de la primera vuelta**. Es un **juego de rotación** con ocho jugadores/equipos. Estos equipos también pueden ser dobles, **es decir, formados** por dos jugadores, uno en la parte **delantera**, y otro en la parte **trasera**. El juego es eliminatorio: el equipo ganador jugará **con el siguiente**, y así sucesivamente **hasta que haya un solo ganador**.

Esta es una descripción básica, pues **existen** muchas variantes del juego en todo el mundo, **desde** la forma inicial de juego, en el norte de España, **hasta** las reglas **fijadas** en países donde este juego **llegó gracias a** los emigrantes vascos.

jugadores: players
lanzar: to throw
usando/usar: using/to use
cesta de mimbre: wicker basket
atada al brazo: attached to the arm

propósito: purpose
de forma que: so that
no pueda golpearla: he cannot hit it
a su regreso: when it comes back
caucho: rubber
alcanzar: to reach
dato muy significativo: very significant data
tan sólo: only
hacernos una idea: we can get an idea

bastante parecidas: much like
por encima: over
rebotar: to bounce
si no lo consigue: if he cannot make it
la mayoría de: most of
se doblan/doblar: they are doubled/to double
después de la primera vuelta: after the first round
juego de rotación: rotation play
es decir: that is to say
formados: formed
delantera: front
trasera: back
con el siguiente: with the next one
hasta que haya un solo ganador: there is a single winner

existen/existir: they exist/to exist
desde...hasta: from ... to
fijadas: fixed
llegó/llegar: it arrived/to arrive
gracias a: thanks to

estación de esquí: ski resort	
se encuentra situada/encontrarse: it is located/to be located	
tan sólo: only	
gracias a: thanks to	
disfrutar: to enjoy	
nieve: snow	
invierno: winter	
primavera: spring	
a veces: sometimes	
posibilidad: chance	
no sólo…sino también: not only… but also	
parapente: paragliding	
patinaje sobre hielo: ice skating	
un sinfín de: a great many	
de hecho: in fact	
cuentan con: they have	
pistas: trails	
cañones de nieve: snow machines	

posee/poseer: it has/to have
instalaciones: facilities
alta calidad: high quality
cabinas remontadoras: lift cabins
con cabida: with enough room
pistas: trails
anchas: wide
señalización: signs
todo el mundo: all the world
tanto...como: both ... and
largas: long
pendiente: slope
esquiadores: skiers
sin olvidar: without forgetting
niveles: levels
cómodas: comfortable
acogieron/acoger: they host/to host

sin embargo: however
naturaleza: nature
montar a caballo: to ride a horse
bicicleta de montaña: mountain bike
emplazamiento: location
nos encontramos/encontrarse: we are/to be
se extiende/extenderse: it spreads out/to spread out
amplia: large, roomy
paisajes: landscapes
climas: climates

Sierra Nevada, el paraíso blanco
ESPAÑA

Sierra Nevada es la principal **estación de esquí** del sur de Europa y **se encuentra situada** a **tan sólo** 30 kilómetros de la ciudad de Granada, en Andalucía. **Gracias a** su altitud (entre 2.000 y 3.300 metros), se puede **disfrutar** de la **nieve** durante todo el **invierno** y hasta bien entrada la **primavera**, **a veces** incluso hasta el mes de mayo. Hay **posibilidad** de practicar **no sólo** el esquí **sino también** el *snowboard*, el esquí **parapente**, el **patinaje sobre hielo** y **un sinfín de** actividades más. **De hecho**, estas instalaciones **cuentan con** 53 **pistas**, un *snowpark*, 338 **cañones de nieve** y varios restaurantes.

Sierra Nevada **posee instalaciones** de **alta calidad**, con unas **cabinas remontadoras con cabida** para 14 personas. Las **pistas** son **anchas** y con una buena **señalización**, y hay para **todo el mundo**, **tanto** si los visitantes son principiantes (pistas **largas** y con poca **pendiente**) **como** si son expertos **esquiadores** (pistas rojas y negras), **sin olvidar** los **niveles** intermedios: las pistas azules, también largas y **cómodas**. En la década de los 90, estas pistas **acogieron** la final de la Copa de Europa de Esquí Alpino y los Campeonatos del Mundo.

Sin embargo, en Sierra Nevada no sólo se practican deportes de nieve. Para aquellos que quieran algo diferente y que quieran disfrutar de la **naturaleza**, existen actividades variadas como **montar a caballo** o hacer rutas en **bicicleta de montaña**. El **emplazamiento** es ideal, pues **nos encontramos** en el Parque Natural de Sierra Nevada, declarado Reserva de la Biosfera por la UNESCO en 1986. El parque tiene una superficie aproximada de 83.000 hectáreas y **se extiende** por las provincias de Granada y Almería. Posee una **amplia** variedad de **paisajes** y **climas** con una de las diversidades botánicas más importantes de Europa.

Conociendo Guatemala a caballo
GUATEMALA

Una forma diferente de conocer este **hermoso país** es, **sin duda**, **haciendo** una excursión a caballo. Es realmente la forma ideal de combinar el turismo activo con **experiencias únicas**. **No importa si** usted **nunca** ha **montado a caballo** o es un experto.

Los **recorridos** de estas excursiones son muy variados y **se puede** disfrutar de la **belleza** de los **paisajes** y recorrer zonas **no frecuentadas** por el **turismo masivo**. Las posibilidades son innumerables, entre las cuales se puede **citar** las **visitas** a **granjas**, pasar por **pueblos indígenas aislados**, por ruinas coloniales y por **bosques tropicales** y volcanes, o también disfrutar de las espectaculares vistas desde **diversos miradores**, explorar **cuevas** y **dormir bajo las estrellas**.

Actualmente existen diversas ofertas en el **mercado**. Algunas de ellas proporcionan **no sólo** excursiones a caballo, **sino también** diversos itinerarios utilizando **vehículos "todo terreno"**, sin olvidar la oportunidad de **navegar** los **ríos guatemaltecos** en **barca** y visitar interesantes sitios mayas, como Topoxté o Ixtinto. **Recuerde** que siempre será preferible si en la excursión les acompañan **guías bilingües** y en caso de tratarse de una excursión a caballo, es importante que éstos estén bien **alimentados** y **entrenados**. Una excursión a caballo es la forma perfecta de conocer y **amar** la biodiversidad de las tierras y la cultura de Guatemala.

Finalmente, unos **consejos prácticos**: es conveniente llevar **botas de equitación**, **pantalones largos**, protector solar, **gafas de sol**, **prismáticos**, **ropa para lluvia** y **sobre todo**, lo más importante, **deseo de disfrutar** de un **viaje relajado**, en unos **parajes inolvidables**.

---

hermoso país: beautiful country
sin duda: without doubt
haciendo/hacer: making/to make
experiencias únicas: unique experience
no importa si: it doesn't matter if
nunca: never
montado a caballo: rode a horse

recorridos: routes
se puede/poder: you can/can
belleza: beauty
paisajes: landscapes
no frecuentadas/to frequent: not frequented/to frequent
turismo masivo: massive tourism
citar: to arrange
visitas: visits
granjas: farms
pueblos indígenas aislados: isolated indigenous towns
bosques tropicales: tropical forests
diversos miradores: diverse viewpoints
cuevas: caves
dormir bajo las estrellas: to sleep under the stars

mercado: market
no sólo...sino también: not only ... but also
vehículos todo terreno: all-terrain vehicles
navegar: to navigate
ríos guatemaltecos: Guatemalan rivers
barca: boat
recuerde/recordar: remember/ to remember
guías bilingües: bilingual guides
alimentados/alimentar: fed/to feed
entrenados/entrenar: trained/to train
amar: to love

consejos prácticos: practical advice
botas de equitación: horseback riding boots
pantalones largos: long pants
gafas de sol: sunglasses
prismáticos: binoculars
ropa para lluvia: rain clothing
sobre todo: above all
deseo de disfrutar: a desire to enjoy
viaje relajado: relaxed travel, trip
parajes inolvidables: unforgettable places

El senderismo en el Perú
PERÚ

Seguir senderos zigzagueantes, pasar por **angostos puentes abismales hechos de soguillas**, **cruzar** ríos **caudalosos**, **atravesar** desiertos, ascender montañas, **bajar colinas** o **abrirse paso** por una tropical **selva** son solamente algunas de las emociones que **nos ofrece** el senderimo en la increíble geografía peruana.

El Perú, **mítico país** de los incas, **no sólo** es conocido por su **milenaria** cultura y sus fabulosas construcciones prehispánicas **sino** que, gracias a la incomparable belleza de sus paisajes, es también un **auténtico edén** para los **caminantes**. Este país sudamericano es excelente para los amantes del senderismo ya que cuenta con elementos **de sobra** para la práctica de este deporte: una **costa bañada de tranquilas aguas**, una sierra cruzada por montañas, varios ríos y una selva amazónica.

Las **sendas** del Perú ofrecen **interminables** alternativas y muchas combinaciones **geniales** para caminantes de **todos los niveles** de experiencia. **Existen** caminos con diferentes grados de dificultad para este deporte. Uno puede **recorrer** senderos **apacibles** o atravesar desiertos, **llanuras**, **cañones**, **cerros**, **bosques**, **cataratas** y selvas. **Todo depende del** grado de aventura, **riesgo** y emoción que **desee** experimentar. Otra gran alternativa es **seguir** el famoso Camino Inca.

---

senderismo: trekking
seguir: to follow
senderos: paths
angostos: narrow
puentes: bridges
abismales: enormous
hechos de soguillas: made of small ropes
cruzar: to cross (a river)
caudalosos: abundant, plentiful
atravesar: to cross (the desert)
bajar: to go down
colinas: hills
abrirse paso: to open one's path
selva: jungle
nos ofrece/ofrecer: it offers us/ to offer

mítico país: mythical country
no sólo… sino: not only … but
milenaria: thousand-year-old
auténtico edén: authentic paradise
caminantes: walkers
de sobra: more than enough
costa bañada de tranquilas aguas: coast bathed by calm waters

sendas: paths
interminables: endless
geniales: brilliant
todos los niveles: all levels
existen/existir: they exist/to exist
recorrer: to travel
apacibles: mild, calm
llanuras: plains
cañones: canyons
cerros: hills
bosques: forests
cataratas: waterfalls
todo depende del: it all depends on
riesgo: risk
desee/desear: one wishes/to wish
seguir: to follow

Los incas **no conocieron** el **caballo** y **tampoco** la **rueda** por **lo que hicieron a pie** todo viaje o recorrido. Este pueblo fue caminante por excelencia. Como toda gran civilización, los andinos contaban con una **compleja red de caminos** que llegaron a **alcanzar** 16.000 kilómetros.

Los incaicos **construyeron trochas** y senderos de **piedra** que **cruzaban** montañas, **sitios desolados** y frías **punas**. Estas **vías peatonales** variaban en **calidad y tamaño**. Algunas sendas podían ser de seis u ocho metros de **ancho** y otras de sólo un metro de **anchura**. Generalmente estas rutas se hacían en **línea recta**, aunque sí contaban con **escalinatas**, veredas **inclinadas** y **túneles abiertos** en roca viva.

El **tramo** más conocido de esta **arteria** de comunicaciones fue el llamado Camino Inca que **se encuentra** en el Cuzco. **Fue descubierto** por Hiram Bingham entre 1913 y 1915. Este famoso **trayecto nace** en el kilómetro 88 de la **línea férrea** que va de la ciudad del Cuzco a Machu Picchu, desde donde uno baja del tren y parte a pie. La versión clásica de esta caminata puede **durar** cuatro días, pero existen otras alternativas que duran uno o dos días de viaje.

Actualmente **decenas** de **miles** de turistas llegan cada año a Cuzco para recorrer este paso. La **riqueza** de la flora y fauna, los exquisitos paisajes a 4.000 metros de altura, los senderos rodeados de vegetación selvática y los **escondidos restos** arqueológicos incaicos que se encuentran por el itinerario son sólo parte de esta experiencia para el caminante. Sin duda, el **premio** más fabuloso es **concluir** esta aventura llegando a las ruinas de Machu Picchu, la **joya** arqueológica de América.

---

no conocieron/conocer: they didn't know/to know
caballo: horse
tampoco: neither
rueda: wheel
lo que hicieron/hacer: they made it/to make
a pie: on foot
compleja: complicated
red de caminos: road network
alcanzar: to reach

construyeron/construir: they built/to build
trochas: narrow trails
piedra: rock
cruzaban/cruzar: they crossed/to cross
sitios desolados: desolate places
punas: bleak, desolate plateau
vías peatonales: pedestrian routes
calidad: quality
tamaño: size
ancho: wide
anchura: width
línea recta: straight line
escalinatas: steps
inclinadas: inclined, slanted
túneles abiertos: open tunnels

tramo: section, stretch
arteria: main road, artery
se encuentra/encontrarse: it is located/to be located
fue descubierto/descubrir: it was discovered/to discover
trayecto: route
nace/nacer: it starts, it begins/to start, to begin
línea férrea: rail line, railway
durar: to last

decenas: ten, group of ten
miles: thousands
riqueza: wealth
escondidos/esconder: hidden/to hide
restos: remains
premio: award, prize
concluir: to conclude
joya: jewel

Examina tu comprensión

El arte de imitar a los pájaros, página 128

1. ¿Qué cursos especiales son necesarios para volar en parapente en Argentina?

2. ¿Qué tiene de único la rampa de despegue de Cuchi Corral?

3. ¿Dónde termina el vuelo y qué puede hacer uno allí?

Acampando en San Felipe, página 129

1. ¿Dónde está ubicado San Felipe?

2. Aunque San Felipe tiene hermosas playas, ¿qué tipo de tierra rodea esta área?

3. Las noches en San Felipe son unos de los mejores momentos para observar ¿qué cosa?

Surfing en Costa Rica, página 130

1. ¿Qué condiciones hacen que surfear en Costa Rica sea ideal?

2. ¿Qué meses son los mejores para el surf?

3. ¿Qué consejo dan al final del artículo?

El fútbol, página 132

1. ¿Cuál es uno de los regalos favoritos de cumpleaños para niños pequeños en Argentina?

2. ¿Qué cosa es popular los domingos en Argentina?

3. ¿Qué emociones genera el fútbol?

Test your comprehension

El jai alai, página 134

1. ¿Cuál es el origen del término Jai Alai?

2. ¿Cuáles son las características principales del juego?

3. ¿Las reglas de Jai Alai son similiares a las de qué otro deporte?

Sierra Nevada, el paraíso blanco, página 136

1. ¿En qué estaciones se puede esquiar en la Sierra Nevada?

2. ¿Cómo se marcan los senderos para indicar niveles?

3. ¿Qué otras actividades se pueden disfrutar en la montaña?

El senderismo en el Perú, página 138

1. ¿Qué hace que el Perú sea un lugar excelente para el senderismo?

2. El tipo de trek que elija depende ¿de qué tipo de cosas?

3. ¿Qué hace que el pueblo sea un excelente lugar para caminantes?

4. Hacer el famoso Camino del Inca puede llevar ¿cuántos días?

La música es el arte más directo,
entra por el oído y va al corazón.

Magdalena Martínez

Música

estilos: styles

tan populares: so popular

han saltado fronteras: they have
   crossed borders (literally: jumped)

importar: to matter

fácilmente: easily

reconocible: recognizable

debido a: due to

en cuanto a: regarding

creencia: belief

se trata de/tratarse: it is about/
   to be about

parecido: similar

nos recuerda/recordar: it reminds us
   of /to remind

rallador de queso: cheese grater

cara: face

adoran/adorar: they adore/to adore

cualquier lugar: anywhere

en cuanto a: regarding

temas: topics

versan/versar: they are about/
   to be about

originariamente: originally

género: genre

fuera dado a conocer/dar a conocer:
   it was released/to release

medios de comunicación: media,
   means of communication

base: basis

actual: current

focos: centers

por la tarde: in the evening

más tarde: later

comenzaron/comenzar: they began/
   to begin

acelerar: to accelerate

nuevo paso de baile: new dance step

pasó a ser/pasar a ser: it became/
   to become

Bailando al son de merengue
REPÚBLICA DOMINICANA

Estos dos **estilos** de música dominicanos **tan populares han saltado fronteras** y ahora nos invitan a bailar sin **importar** dónde estemos.

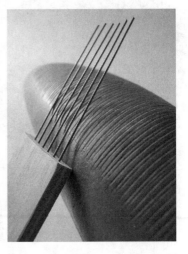

El merengue es **fácilmente reconocible debido a** su ritmo rápido de 2/2 y 2/4. Hay varias opiniones **en cuanto a** sus orígenes, pero la **creencia** más común es que **se trata de** una combinación de elementos africanos y europeos. Los instrumentos utilizados para el merengue son el melodeón (instrumento **parecido** al acordeón), la güira (cuya apariencia **nos recuerda** a un **rallador de queso**), y la tambora (un tambor de doble **cara**). Los dominicanos **adoran** el merengue y es normal verles bailando y cantando este ritmo en **cualquier lugar**.

En cuanto a la bachata, este estilo tiene un ritmo más melancólico de 4/4 y los **temas** que trata **versan** sobre la vida rural y las relaciones entre hombres y mujeres. **Originariamente**, y antes de que este **género fuera dado a conocer** por la industria discográfica y los **medios de comunicación,** los tríos y cuarteros de guitarra (**base** de la **actual** bachata), servían como informales **focos** de reunión en casas y patios, normalmente los domingos **por la tarde**. Durante los años 60, este estilo estaba clasificado como una subcategoría de la música de guitarra, pero algunas décadas **más tarde**, sus músicos **comenzaron** a **acelerar** el ritmo y se creó un **nuevo paso de baile**. Fue así como la bachata **pasó a ser** considerada música de baile.

Los instrumentos musicales
VENEZUELA

Venezuela tiene una tradición muy **rica** en lo que **se refiere** a música, danza y fiestas populares, ya que en todas estas expresiones **se mezclan** la tradición indígena, afro-venezolana y **criolla**. Esa **suma** de varias culturas hace que el **resultado** sea un **legado verdaderamente próspero**. Si hablamos de música, Venezuela **se destaca** por el gran **desarrollo** que cada comunidad hizo de los instrumentos musicales artesanales y tradicionales utilizados para acompañar bailes y cantos en celebraciones, fiestas y ceremonias religiosas. **Se pueden encontrar** más de 100 tipos, subdivididos en **instrumentos de viento** o aerófonos, de **cuerda** o **cordófonos**, los **construidos** con una membrana o membranófonos y los idiófonos.

Algunos ejemplos de aerófonos son: la **flauta** en diferentes formas y materiales; una trompeta construida con una **concha de caracol marino llamada** guarura con un orificio en la parte superior que **le sirve** de **boquilla**; el ovevi mataeto, hecho con un **cráneo de venado** con **cuernos**, **recubierto** con **cera** negra y un solo orificio en la base para emitir el **soplo**; y el isimoi o pito grande, una especie de clarinete hecho con un **tubo grueso** de **hoja de palmera**. **Dentro de** los cordófonos existen, entre otros, el arpa aragüeña con 35 cuerdas; el bandolín o mandolina que es un **laúd** con ocho cuerdas; y el cuatro venezolano, una guitarra pequeña de cuatro cuerdas que se usa en **casi todas** las festividades religiosas y **profanas**. El furruco es un membranófono hecho con una **lata** y una membrana de cuero **atada** y **tensada** con cuerdas, que **se frota** con un **palo** hasta transmitir una vibración o **sonido**. La mina y la curbata son tambores hechos con un **tronco de aguacate** y una membrana de cuero de **venado**, que **se ejecutan** siempre juntos y acompañan el canto y el baile que **se realizan** durante la celebración de la fiesta de San Juan Bautista en la región de Barlovento. Los idiófonos son instrumentos musicales cuyo sonido se produce por la vibración del **propio** material del que **se componen** al ser **golpeados**, **rascados** o **frotados**. En este caso, los distintos tipos de maracas son usadas en fiestas y principalmente en **rituales chamánicos**. **Dan ganas de tocar algo**, ¿no?

---

rica: rich
se refiere/referirse: it refers/to refer
se mezclan/mezclar: they mix/to mix
criolla: Creole
suma: addition
resultado: result
legado: legacy
verdaderamente: truly, really
próspero: prosperous, successful
se destaca/destacar: it stands out/ to stand out
desarrollo: development
se pueden/poder: they can/can
encontrar: to find
instrumentos de viento: wind instruments
cuerda: string
cordófonos: stringed instruments
construidos/construir: built/to build

flauta: flute
concha de caracol marino: conch sea shell
llamada/llamar: called/to call
le sirve/servir: it serves as/to serve
boquilla: mouthpiece
cráneo de venado: deer skull
cuernos: horns
recubierto/recubrir: covered/to cover
cera: wax
soplo: blow
tubo grueso: thick tube
hoja de palmera: palm leaf
dentro de: inside
laúd: lute
casi todas: almost all
profanas: secular
lata: can
atada/atar: tied/to tie
tensada/tensar: tightened/to tighten
se frota/frotar: it is rubbed/to rub
palo: stick
sonido: sound
tronco de aguacate: avocado tree trunk
venado: deer
se ejecutan/ejecutar: they are played/ to play, to perform
se realizan/realizarse: they take place/ to take place
propio: own
se componen/componerse: they are made of/to be made of
golpeados/golpear: beaten/to beat
rascados/rascar: scratched/to scratch
frotados/frotar: rubbed/to rub
rituales chamánicos: shamanic rituals
dan ganas de tocar algo: it makes you want to play something

se suele/soler: it is usually/to be usually

gitano: gypsy

palmas: clapping, the act of clapping following the rhythm of flamenco

zapateao: flamenco expression meaning to tap one's feet

ciertamente: certainly

símbolos típicos: typical symbols

se podría decir: one could say

apariencia: appearance

se manifiesta en/manifestarse: it is demonstrated by/to demonstrate

cante: singing

sin embargo: nevertheless

lo hace/hacer: it makes it/to make

sentimiento: feeling

en realidad: in fact

en los que: in which

se hace referencia/hacer referencia: it is mentioned/to mention

claro que: of course

lugar de nacimiento: place of birth

raza gitana: gypsy race

procedente de: from

estudiosos: specialists

consideran/considerar: they consider/ to consider

mezcla de: mixture of

de lo que hoy llamamos: of what we call today

judía: Jewish

musulmana: Muslim

debido a: due to

durante casi: for almost

en definitiva: in short

la mayor parte de: most of

principal: main

precursor: predecessor

les rodeaba/rodear: it surrounded them/to surround

El arte flamenco
ESPAÑA

La palabra "flamenco" **se suele** identificar con una guitarra, el pueblo **gitano**, las **palmas** y el **zapateao**. **Ciertamente**, todos estos son **símbolos típicos** del flamenco, aunque **se podría decir** que son sólo la **apariencia**. El flamenco es mucho más, es un arte que **se manifiesta en** el baile, en el **cante** y la guitarra. **Sin embargo**, en mi opinión, hay algo no tangible que **lo hace** muy especial: el **sentimiento**.

Sobre los orígenes del flamenco existe una gran controversia pues, **en realidad**, los textos más antiguos **en los que se hace referencia** a este arte son del siglo XVIII. Aunque está **claro que** su **lugar de nacimiento** fue Andalucía, existen varias teorías sobre sus creadores. Una

de ellas identifica a la **raza gitana**, que llegó a la Península Ibérica **procedente de** la India en el siglo XIV, aproximadamente. Otros **estudiosos consideran** que el flamenco es una **mezcla de** todas las culturas existentes en el sur **de lo que hoy llamamos** España, la bizantina, la **judía** y la **musulmana**. Otras teorías hablan del origen musulmán, **debido a** la dominación árabe del sur **durante casi** ocho siglos. **En definitiva**, **la mayor parte de** las personas que han estudiado este tema opinan que el pueblo gitano fue el **principal precursor**, pero que su arte se vio muy influenciado por la cultura que **les rodeaba** en esa región de la Península.

En la historia del flamenco existen tres **puntos principales**, **relacionados** con las **ciudades** de Cádiz, Triana y Jerez de la Frontera, donde **nacieron** las principales escuelas. Aquí comienza este arte, **tal y como** se conoce hoy, pues hasta ese momento, el flamenco era algo popular, sin **reglas** fijas, **nacido** del sentimiento y para expresar emociones.

Al principio, el flamenco era **sólo** cante, **es decir**, no existía **ni** el acompañamiento de guitarra **ni** el baile. Sólo **se seguía** el ritmo con las palmas. **Posteriormente,** durante lo que se conoce como "la **edad dorada** del flamenco" entre la **última mitad** del siglo XIX y principios del XX, el flamenco **adoptó** su **forma actual** al **incluir** instrumentos y baile. **Empezaron** a **proliferar** los cafés cantantes, momento en el que nacieron todas las variantes de este hermoso arte. Estos cafés evolucionaron **a mediados** del siglo XX **hasta convertirse** en los actuales **tablaos**. Así, **poco a poco**, el flamenco se fue extendiendo internacionalmente hasta el punto de **ser mostrado** en festivales y teatros.

En el flamenco actual, el **papel** de la guitarra y del **guitarrista** puede ser **no sólo** de acompañamiento, **sino también** de solista. Es el caso del gran Paco de Lucía, o de Manolo Sanlúcar, **verdaderos** revolucionarios de la guitarra flamenca.

Así, algo tan popular en sus **comienzos** es **hoy en día** un arte único y universal.

puntos principales: main points
relacionados/relacionar: related/ to relate
ciudades: cities
nacieron/nacer: they were born/ to be born
tal y como: just as
reglas: rules
fijas: fixed
nacido: born

al principio: at first
sólo: only
es decir: that is to say
ni...ni: neither ... nor
se seguía/seguir: one would follow/ to follow
posteriormente: later, subsequently
edad dorado: golden age
última mitad: last half
adoptó/adoptar: it adopted/to adopt
forma actual: present, current form
incluir: to include
empezaron/empezar: they started/ to start
proliferar: to proliferate, to spread
a mediados: in the middle
hasta: until
convertirse: to become
tablaos: flamenco bars
poco a poco: little by little
ser mostrado/mostrar: to be shown/ to show

papel: role
guitarrista: guitarist
no sólo...sino también: not only ... but also
verdaderos: real, authentic

comienzos: beginnings
hoy en día: nowadays

El reguetón está "rankeao"
PUERTO RICO

El reguetón es un **nuevo estilo** de **música latina bailable** que nació en Puerto Rico hace aproximadamente 10 años. Es una **mezcla de** rap, hip hop y reggae **jamaiquino**, con la influencia de ritmos típicamente puertorriqueños como **la bomba y la plena**. **Posee el ritmo básico** del reggae y **algunas de** las tendencias vocales del hip hop. **Además**, incluye los sonidos de **tambores** derivados de la bomba y plena. **Esto lo hace** ser un ritmo bien **pegajoso** y de gran popularidad entre la juventud hispana.

El reguetón **se dirige** principalmente a los **jóvenes**. Sus **líricas exponen** la realidad de las **calles**, hacen críticas sociales y, **por supuesto**, **hablan del** amor y la pasión. **Algunas veces** es también **conocido** como *perreo*, **término alusivo** a **la manera** de bailarlo que **emplea movimientos de caderas** que **algunos consideran** eróticos.

El *perreo* **se baila pegando el cuerpo con otro**, ejerciendo diferentes movimientos y **rozando** de **frente, lado o espalda** a la otra persona. Se puede hacer el famoso paso de "**hasta abajo**" que consiste en mover la pelvis suavemente **hasta llegar al suelo**.

El reguetón también **promueve** un **estilo de vestimenta** y una nueva forma de expresión verbal. La moda del reguetón incluye **mahones de piernas anchas**, **camisetas tropicales** en tamaños grandes, **calzado deportivo** tipo canvas y en algunos casos **tatuajes** y *body piercing*.

---

nuevo estilo: new style
música latina bailable: danceable Latin music
mezcla de: mixture of
jamaiquino: Jamaican
la bomba y la plena: names of traditional dances
posee el ritmo básico: it has the basic rhythm
algunas de: some of
además: in addition
tambores: drums
esto lo hace/hacer: this makes/to make
pegajoso: clingy, close

se dirige/dirigir: it is directed/to direct
jóvenes: young people
líricas: lyrics
exponen/exponer: they expose/ to expose
calles: streets
por supuesto: of course
hablan del/hablar: they speak of/ to speak
algunas veces: sometimes
conocido/conocer: it is known/ to know
término alusivo: elusive term
la manera: the way
emplea/emplear: they use/to use
movimientos de caderas: hip movements
algunos consideran: some consider

se baila/bailar: is danced/to dance
pegando el cuerpo con otro: the body pressed against another body
ejerciendo/ejercer: exerting/to exert
rozando/rozar: touching/to touch
frente, lado o espalda: front, side or backside
hasta abajo: all the way down
hasta llegar al suelo: until arriving at the ground

promueve/promover: promotes/ to promote
estilo de vestimenta: style of clothes
mahones de piernas anchas: jeans with wide legs
camisetas tropicales: tropical t-shirts
calzado deportivo: sports footwear
tatuajes: tattoos

El reguetón también se caracteriza por tener una **jerga muy callejera**, **llena de** anglicismos y con un vocabulario propio que incluye **palabras** como:

- pichaera – ignorar
- guerlas o gatas – **muchachas**
- guillao – **orgulloso** y **presumido**
- flow – **estilo**
- yales – **mujeres**
- gata fina – una chica **conservadora**
- corillo – grupo de personas
- rankearse – **subir de categoría**
- **perrear**

El **gusto** por este peculiar ritmo **ha crecido enormemente** y está **alcanzando** ya un importante reconocimiento internacional. **Se ha hecho popular** en otras islas del Caribe y **naciones vecinas**, entre ellas la República Dominicana, Panamá, Nicaragua, Méjico, Colombia y algunas regiones de Cuba. **Ya ha comenzado a escucharse** en los Estados Unidos, particularmente en Florida, Nueva York y Miami **debido a** la gran concentración de puertorriqueños e hispanos **que habitan** en estas regiones.

En la actualidad, Tego Calderón, Daddy Yankee, Ivy Queen, Nikky Jam y Don Omar son algunos de los más importantes **exponentes** del reguetón en Puerto Rico y Latinoamérica. Sus **conciertos se llenan a capacidad** y sus discos **se venden** como **pan caliente**. **Definitivamente**, este **género** de rápido **crecimiento promete seguir cautivando** a muchos. **Es por esto** que hacemos **un llamado** a todas las *guerlas* y chicos **que quieran** *rankearse* para que **se unan** al *corillo* y **aprendan** a *perrear* al ritmo del reguetón.

jerga muy callejera: street slang
llena de: full of
palabras: words
muchachas: girls
orgulloso: proud
presumido: vain
estilo: style
mujeres: women
conservadora: conservative
subir de categoría: to reach a higher class
perrear: a term given by Puerto Ricans to the way reggaeton is danced

gusto: taste
ha crecido/crecer: it has grown/ to grow
enormemente: enormously
alcanzando/alcanzar: reaching/ to reach
se ha hecho popular: it has become popular
naciones vecinas: neighboring nations
ya ha comenzado a escucharse: it started to be listened to
debido a: due to
que habitan/habitar: that live/ to live

exponentes: advocates
conciertos: concerts
se llenan a capacidad: they fill to capacity
se venden/vender: they are sold/ to sell
pan caliente: hot bread
definitivamente: definitely
género: type of music
crecimiento: growth
promete/prometer: it promises/ to promise
seguir: to follow
cautivando: captivating/to captivate
es por esto: it is because of this
un llamado: a call
que quieran/querer: that want to/ to want to
se unan/unir: they join/to join
aprendan/aprender: they learn/ to learn

El tango: pasión en la pista
ARGENTINA

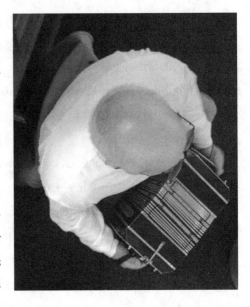

"Mi Buenos Aires **querido**, cuando yo **te vuelva a ver**, **no habrá** más **penas ni olvido**" **cantaba** Carlos Gardel. "El Zorzal" o "El Mudo", como **lo llamaban cariñosamente**, fue el **cantante** argentino más importante y una de las figuras más representativas del tango.

Además de baile, música, canción y poesía, el tango es sobre todo un fenómeno cultural y la **marca indiscutible** del ser **porteño**.

LOS COMIENZOS

Este género musical nació en la **ribera** del Riachuelo a **principios** de 1880 en un **escenario** particular. En esa **época**, Buenos Aires era una ciudad en expansión con un gran **crecimiento demográfico** producto de la inmigración de muchos **países** de Europa como Italia, España, Francia, Alemania o Polonia. Estos inmigrantes eran principalmente **hombres**: **marineros**, **artesanos**, **peones** y otros trabajadores que habían **abandonado** a sus familias **en busca de** nuevas y mejores posibilidades de vida en **otro** continente. Para **mitigar** su **soledad frecuentaban burdeles** y **lupanares**, donde diferentes **agrupaciones** de músicos **improvisaban** melodías con **flauta**, violín y guitarra.

---

pista: dance floor

querido: beloved

te vuela a ver: I see you again

no habrá/haber: there won't be/to be

penas: sorrows

ni olvido: nor oblivion

cantaba/cantar: he sang/to sing

lo llamaban/llamar: he used to be called/to call

cariñosamente: affectionately

cantante: singer

además de: besides

marca indiscutible: indisputable mark

porteño: inhabitant of Buenos Aires

los comienzos: the beginnings

ribera: riverside

principios: beginnings

escenario: place, scenario

época: time, period, age

crecimiento demográfico: population growth

países: countries

hombres: men

marineros: sailors

artesanos: craftsmen

peones: unskilled laborers

abandonado/abandonar: abandoned/to abandon

en busca de/buscar: in search of/to search

otro: another

mitigar: to alleviate

soledad: loneliness

frecuentaban/frecuentar: they frequented/to frequent

burdeles: bordellos

lupanares: brothels

agrupaciones: associations

improvisaban/improvisar: they improvised/to improvise

flauta: flute

Así **se empezó** a bailar el tango, al principio sólo entre hombres, y luego **junto a** las mujeres **del lugar**. Los primeros tangos **carecían de letra**, pero **posteriormente** algunos músicos **añadieron** canciones a los **acordes** que **describían** el ambiente en el que se encontraban, unas escenas a menudo un tanto obscenas o que **demostraban** poca educación. Por esto, y **debido a** su origen en los **ambientes prostibularios**, el tango **fue considerado** durante mucho tiempo una música prohibida.

LOS AÑOS DE GLORIA

Con el tiempo, los **lugares de baile fueron cambiando**. El tango llegó a los barrios y comenzó a bailarse en **salones públicos**, patios de casas particulares y **grandes galpones**. La década de 1940 **quedó grabada** en la historia del tango como su **época de oro**. El cantante **adquirió** más **protagonismo** en la orquesta, transformándose en un instrumento más de la misma. Y las letras **asumieron** un **nuevo perfil**: en sus versos le cantaban al amor y a la mujer en un tono diferente, más poético que en sus **inicios** y **exaltando** la ciudad, el barrio y los **protagonistas del baile**.

UN PRESENTE DE ÉXITO

Hoy, el tango **ha traspasado fronteras** y barreras culturales y su música y su baile **se disfrutan alrededor** del mundo. En casi todos los países existen academias o salones donde **avezados** bailarines demuestran sus habilidades y donde la música, seductora y melancólica, **les transporta** a otras épocas.

se empezó/empezar: they started/ to start

junto a: next to

del lugar: of the place

carecían de letra: they lacked lyrics

posteriormente: later

añadieron/añadir: they added/to add

acordes: chords

describían/describir: they described/ to describe

demostraban/demostrar: they demonstrated/to demonstrate

debido a: due to

ambientes prostibularios: brothel-like environments

fue considerado/considerar: it was considered/to consider

lugares de baile: dance places

fueron cambiando/cambiar: they started to change/to change

salones públicos: public ballrooms

grandes galpones: large sheds

quedó grabada/grabar: it stayed recorded/to record, to save

época de oro: golden age

adquirió/adquirir: it acquired/ to acquire

protagonismo: prominence

asumieron/asumir: they assumed/ to assume

nuevo perfil: new profile

inicios: beginnings

exaltando/exaltar: praising/to praise

protagonistas del baile: leading dancers

éxito: success

ha traspasado/traspasar: it has gone through/to go through

fronteras: borders

se disfrutan/disfrutar: they are enjoyed/ to enjoy

alrededor: around

avezados: experienced

les transporta/transportar: it transports them/to transport

actualmente: nowadays
unos de los bailes más típicos: one of the most typical dances
son conocidas: they are known
incluso: even
bailaores: dancers
Japón: Japan
ritmo: rhythm
sensualidad: sensuality
hacen que nuestros pies y brazos se muevan al ritmo: they make our feet and arms move to the rhythm
letras: lyrics
producen alegría/producir: produce joy/to produce
melancolía: sadness, melancholy
tantas emociones: so many emotions

veamos/ver: let's see/to see
brevemente: briefly
a partir de: apart from
fundación: the founding
Feria de Abril: April Fair
seguidilla: another genre of Spanish songs
fue llamada: it was named
más tarde: later
aparición: appearance
grabaciones de discos: record recordings
nuevos grupos: new groups

cruzaron las fronteras: they crossed the borders
El Adiós: The Goodbye
nacen nuevas sevillanas: new "sevillanas" are born
cada año: every year
mejor dicho: better if we said
no cambian mucho: they do not change a lot
regla general: general rule
cómo bailan los demás: how the others dance
perder la vergüenza: to lose one's inhibitions
pasarlo lo mejor posible: to enjoy it as much as possible
alma: soul

usted se divierte: you have fun
viendo y oyendo: watching and listening
aprender: to learn
seguramente: surely
manzanillas: a type of wine
harán que: they will make
se pierda la vergüenza: you lose your inhibitions

Las sevillanas
ESPAÑA

Las sevillanas son **actualmente unos de los bailes más típicos** de España, y **son conocidas** internacionalmente. ¡**Incluso** hay "**bailaores**" y "bailaoras" en **Japón**! Y es que las sevillanas son más que música y danza; su **ritmo** y **sensualidad hacen que nuestros pies y brazos se muevan al ritmo**; sus **letras producen alegría, melancolía, tantas emociones**.

Veamos brevemente la historia de las sevillanas. **A partir de** la **fundación** de la **Feria de Abril** de Sevilla, la **seguidilla** sevillana (posiblemente con orígenes en la antigua Castilla) **fue llamada** Sevillana. **Más tarde**, con la **aparición** de las **grabaciones de discos**, en los años 60, las sevillanas fueron conocidas en toda España, con **nuevos grupos** como "Los del Río" o "Los Marismeños".

Durante los años 80 y 90, las sevillanas **cruzaron las fronteras** españolas. Una de las más famosas es "**El Adiós**", de "Los amigos de Gines". Actualmente, **nacen nuevas sevillanas cada año**; **mejor dicho**, nuevas letras, pues la música y el ritmo, la base de las sevillanas, **no cambian mucho**. Una **regla general** para el visitante a la Feria de Abril en Sevilla es, primero, ver **cómo bailan los demás**, y luego, **perder la vergüenza** y **pasarlo lo mejor posible**. Esta es el **alma** de la Feria.

Usted se divierte viendo y oyendo a los demás, y viceversa. No es necesario **aprender** este baile en una academia, y **seguramente**, unas tapas y más de dos **manzanillas harán que**... ¡**se pierda la vergüenza**!

Es como una fiesta en familia, pero en un **entorno lleno de ritmo**, **palmas** y el color de los **trajes de faralaes**. Las sevillanas tienen un formato bien definido: **se componen de** 4 partes (La **Primera** o entrada, La **Segunda**, La **Tercera** y La **Cuarta**). **Cada una** de estas partes tiene 3 **versos** (o coplas). **A continuación** está la letra de una de las sevillanas más conocidas: El Adiós.

El Adiós
(La primera o entrada)
Algo se muere en el alma **cuando** un **amigo se va**

(La segunda)
Cuando un amigo se va
algo se muere en el alma
cuando un amigo se va
algo se muere en el alma
cuando un amigo se va

(La tercera)
cuando un amigo se va
y **va dejando** una **huella**
que no se puede borrar
y va dejando una huella
que no se puede borrar

(La cuarta)
No te vayas todavía,
no te vayas por favor
no te vayas todavía
que **hasta la guitarra mía llora**
cuando **dice** adiós.

En este caso, la letra es **triste**, **pues habla de** la **despedida** de un amigo.

En conclusión, la experiencia de **oír** una sevillana, y de **ver cómo se baila**, es **única**. Incluso para **aquellos que no hemos nacido rodeados** por esta forma de **vivir** la **vida**.

entorno: environment	
lleno de ritmo: full of rhythm	
palmas: clapping	
trajes de faralaes: typical dress with flounces and colors	
se componen de/componer: they are composed of/to compose	
primera: first	
segunda: second	
tercera: third	
cuarta: fourth	
cada una: each one	
versos: verses	
a continuación: next	

algo: something
se muere/morir: it dies/to die
cuando: when
amigo: friend
se va/ir: he/she goes away/to go
va dejando/dejar: he/she is leaving/ to leave
huella: trace
que no se puede borrar: that cannot be erased
no te vayas: don't go
hasta la guitarra mía: even my guitar
llora/llorar: it cries/ to cry
dice/decir: it says or tells/to tell

en este caso: in this case
triste: sad
pues habla de: as it talks about
despedida: farewell

oír: to listen
ver cómo se baila: to see how it is danced
única: unique
aquellos que no hemos nacido: those of us who weren't born
rodeados/rodear: surrounded/ to surround
vivir: to live
vida: life

El mariachi
MÉXICO

La música mariachi es una de las tradiciones más memorables de México. El nombre "mariachi" **viene** originalmente de los indios coca y significa "música". La música de mariachi es música folclórica de México y se considera una de las formas musicales más románticas del mundo. Un **conjunto** completo de mariachi tiene tres o más violines, dos **trompetas**, una guitarra, una **vihuela** y un guitarrón. **De vez en cuando** también se usan el **arpa** y la **guitarra de golpe**. El guitarrón es un **tipo** de instrumento **en forma de** guitarra pero con un **cuello corto** y una **barriga** grande en la **parte de atrás**. Este instrumento **toca** la parte de **bajo** y, **junto con** la vihuela, otra variante de la guitarra, **imparte** el ritmo distintivo del sonido mariachi **mientras** los violines, las trompetas y la guitarra tocan la melodía y la parte segunda o armonía. Normalmente, todos los músicos cantan pero a veces hay un solista.

La **vestimenta** del mariachi es de tipo **charro**, similar al **traje** que usan los **vaqueros** mexicanos pero mucho más elegante. Este traje típico normalmente está formado por **botas**, un **sombrero** grande, un **moño** o **corbata,** un **chaleco** o **chaqueta corta,** pantalones bien **ajustados** con una **correa ancha** y botonaduras o **botones brillantes** en los **lados** de los pantalones. Las bandas mariachi usualmente tocan en las **bodas, fiestas de cumpleaños, días festivos, serenatas** y servicios religiosos.

Algunas canciones populares de mariachi son: *Las Mañanitas, Cielito Lindo, México Lindo, Guadalajara, El Rey* y muchas más que **forman parte** del repertorio de cualquier grupo mariachi. Unos cantantes famosos de mariachi son Pedro Infante, Vicente Fernández, Javier Solís y Jorge Negrete. La música mariachi **ha sido** usada en muchas **películas** mexicanas y **aún se puede escuchar en vivo** en muchos restaurantes mexicanos.

---

viene/venir: it comes/to come
conjunto: band
trompetas: trumpets
vihuela: name of a small classical guitar used in mariachi bands
de vez en cuando: once in a while
arpa: harp
guitarra de golpe: Mexican variation of the Spanish guitar
tipo: kind
en forma de: with the shape of
cuello corto: short neck
barriga: belly
parte de atrás: back side
toca/tocar: it plays/to play
bajo: bass
junto con: coupled with
imparte/impartir: it gives/to give
mientras: while

vestimenta: clothes
charro: horseman
traje: costume
vaqueros: cowboys
botas: boots
sombrero: hat
moño: lace bow
corbata: tie
chaleco: vest
chaqueta corta: bolero jacket
ajustados: tight
correa: strap
ancha: wide
botones: buttons
brillantes: shiny
lados: sides
bodas: weddings
fiestas de cumpleaños: birthday parties
días festivos: holidays
serenatas: parties on the streets that take place at night

forman parte/formar parte: they are part of/to be part of
ha sido/ser: it has been/to be
películas: movies, films
aún: still
se puede/poder: one can/can
escuchar: to listen
en vivo: live

Los gamberros universitarios
ESPAÑA

Son la representación más **gamberra** de las universidades españolas, pero **a sus espaldas llevan** una tradición **centenaria**. Los **tunos**, **ataviados** con sus **capas** y sus **pantalones bombachos** negros, **llenan** con su **alegre** música la noche de las ciudades universitarias. Los tunos del siglo XXI son **herederos** de una antigua tradición que **se remonta** al siglo XIII. En el año 1212, bajo el **reinado** de Alfonso VIII, **se fundó** en Palencia el primer *Studium Generale*, **precedente** de las futuras universidades. A estos Estudios Generales, y a los que se crearon por todo el país, **acudían** también jóvenes de pocos **recursos económicos**, a los que se conocía como "sopistas".

Los sopistas eran estudiantes **pobres** que con su música, su **simpatía** y su **picardía recorrían** conventos, calles y plazas **a cambio de** un plato de sopa (de ahí proviene su nombre) y de unas **monedas** que **les ayudaran** a pagar sus estudios. Además de sus instrumentos siempre llevaban **consigo** una **cuchara** y un **tenedor de madera**, lo que **les permitía** comer en cualquier lugar donde tenían ocasión. Estos **cubiertos** de madera **siguen siendo** hoy en la **actualidad** el símbolo de todas las tunas universitarias.

Las tunas, **tal cual las conocemos** hoy en día, **aparecieron** en el siglo XVI ya que gracias a la creación de residencias universitarias para estudiantes pobres, los sopistas **dejaron de mendigar**. Las características de las tunas son muy particulares. Están integradas **únicamente** por hombres y su **vestimenta** es muy peculiar, toda negra y prácticamente idéntica a la de los estudiantes de las primeras universidades españolas. Cada miembro del grupo, que **suele estar formado** por unas ocho o diez personas, lleva un instrumento, a excepción del cantante principal. **Predominan** las guitarras, los **laúdes** y las **bandurrias**, aunque el instrumento más característico de las tunas es la **pandereta**. **La razón de ser** de estos grupos siempre **ha sido** la mujer; a ella **van dedicadas** todas sus canciones, todas sus **actuaciones**. Sin embargo, **conquistando** o sin conquistar **féminas**, el objetivo de las tunas es disfrutar de la compañía de los amigos y hacer de la noche una fiesta.

gamberra: mischievous
a sus espaldas: on their back
llevan/llevar: they carry/to carry
centenaria: hundred-year-old
tunos: members of a *tuna* (a *tuna* is a music group of university students)
ataviados: dressed
capas: capes, cloaks
pantalones bombachos: baggy pants
llenan/llenar: they fill/to fill
alegre: lively
herederos: heirs
se remonta/remontarse: it goes back/ to go back
reinado: kingdom
se fundó/fundar: it was founded/ to found
precedente: previous
acudían/acudir: they went/to go
recursos económicos: financial means

pobres: poor
simpatía: charm
picardía: craftiness
recorrían: they used to go around
a cambio de: in exchange for
monedas: coins
les ayudaran/ayudar: would help them/ to help
consigo: with them
cuchara: spoon
tenedor de madera: wooden fork
les permitía/permitir: it allowed them/ to allow
cubiertos: cutlery
siguen siendo/ser: they still are/to be
actualidad: nowadays

tal cual: the way
las conocemos/conocer: we know them/ to know
aparecieron/aparecer: they appeared/ to appear
dejaron de/dejar de: they stopped/ to stop
mendigar: to beg
únicamente: solely
vestimenta: clothing
suele estar formado: it usually consists of
predominan: they predominate
laúdes: lutes
bandurrias: a kind of wind instrument
pandereta: tambourine
la razón de ser: the objective
ha sido/ser: it has been/to be
van dedicadas: they are dedicated
actuaciones: performances
conquistando/conquistar: winning/ to win (hearts)
féminas: female, women

hoy en día: nowadays
constituye/constituir: it constitutes/to constitute
posee/poseer: it has/to have
distingue/distinguir: it distinguishes/to distinguish
países vecinos: neighboring countries
basado/basar: based/to base
se toca/tocar: it is played/to play
chico: name of one of the drums (literally: small)
repique: name of one of the drums (literally: peal of bells)
crean/crear: they create/to create
mantiene/mantener: it maintains/to maintain
toque creativo: creative touch
puede repetirse/repitir: it can be repeated/to repeat
conjuntos: band
decenas: tens
comienzos: beginnings
hogar: home

barrios: neighborhoods
al atardecer: at dusk
fines de semana: weekends
verano: summer
extraño: strange, foreign
se reúnen/reunirse: they gather/ to gather
convocatorias: calls (to a meeting)
se ha afincado/afincarse: it has established itself/to establish itself
han surgido/surgir: they have emerged/to emerge
aficionados: fans
dar rienda suelta: to give free rein to
ganas: desire
punto de encuentro: meeting point
esquina prefijada: prearranged corner
antemano: beforehand
se congregan/congregar: they congregate/ to congregate
propio: own
se juntan/juntarse: they get together/to get together
seguidores: followers, fans

calentar: to warm up
lonjas: strip of leather
alrededor: around
fogata: bonfire
recorrer: to visit, to go around
repitiendo/repetir: repeating/ to repeat

El candombe
URUGUAY

Hoy en día, el candombe **constituye** una de las expresiones musicales más particulares que **posee** el Uruguay y que lo **distingue** de los **países vecinos**. De origen africano, el candombe está **basado** en la percusión. **Se toca** con tres tambores, **chico**, **repique** y piano, que al ser tocados juntos **crean** el ritmo del candombe. El chico **mantiene** la métrica y el piano mantiene la base del ritmo, mientras que el repique le da el **toque creativo**. Este núcleo de tres tambores **puede repetirse** varias veces hasta formar **conjuntos** de varias **decenas**. Su combinación crea ritmos que invitan a bailar y que desde sus **comienzos** en su nuevo **hogar** americano estuvieron asociados con el carnaval.

En varios **barrios** de Montevideo, **al atardecer** y, sobre todo durante los **fines de semana** de **verano**, no es **extraño** escuchar grupos de personas que **se reúnen** a tocar candombe con sus tamboriles. Inicialmente, los barrios donde se realizaban estas **convocatorias** eran Barrio Sur y Palermo, donde la comunidad negra **se ha afincado** tradicionalmente. Más recientemente **han surgido** otros puntos en Montevideo donde **aficionados** al candombe se reúnen cada semana para **dar rienda suelta** a sus **ganas** de tamborilear. Generalmente, el **punto de encuentro** es en alguna **esquina prefijada** de la ciudad, a una hora y día determinados de **antemano**. Allí **se congregan** las personas, muchas de ellas cargando con su **propio** tamboril, aunque a menudo también **se juntan** vecinos curiosos y **seguidores** de esta expresión musical.

Después de **calentar** las **lonjas alrededor** de una **fogata**, comienzan a tocar y **recorrer** las calles, **repitiendo** así una costumbre que llegó a las costas del Río de la Plata gracias a los esclavos africanos.

Desde **principios** del siglo XIX, cuando los esclavos fueron introducidos al país por el puerto de Montevideo, la cultura africana **mantuvo** una **fuerte presencia** entre el **aluvión** de culturas de todo el mundo que **convergían** en la capital. **Sin embargo**, es difícil determinar con claridad los comienzos del candombe en el Uruguay. **Sin duda**, presente en las fiestas de los negros esclavos, el *candomblé* era parte danza y parte música, resultando un camino muy efectivo para que mantuvieran sus raíces africanas. Además de mantenerse vivo **dentro de** la comunidad negra, en la década de los años 40 el candombe comenzó a hacerse un lugar entre los ciudadanos uruguayos de otros grupos étnicos.

A este **cambio contribuyeron** artistas de otras **ramas** y **se manifestó**, por ejemplo, en los **cuadros** de uno de los pintores uruguayos más famosos, Pedro Figari. Este pintor **revalorizó** el carnaval tanto como a sus participantes y su música al **plasmarlos** en sus pinturas. Otro artista que **jugó un papel clave** en la expansión del candombe fue el músico Alfredo Zitarrosa, que en varios de sus temas hace referencia al candombe. En uno de ellos dice: "Para **ahuyentar** al Mandinga, macumba, macumbembé, hay que **tirar una flecha**, y bailar el *candomblé*." Así, esta expresión musical fue **poco a poco ganando** aceptación entre un **público más amplio**. Más tarde **aparecerían** otros músicos **destacados**, tales como José Carvajal, **más conocido como** "El Sabalero", que **compuso** temas de candombe **extremadamente** populares en la década de los años 60. Más recientemente, muchos otros músicos y cantautores uruguayos, como Jaime Ross, Rubén Rada o Fernando Cabrera, **se han incursionado** en el candombe. En los **últimos** 20 años, este ritmo musical ha **disfrutado** de un **auge creciente**, **gracias en parte a** la revalorización del carnaval uruguayo como **patrimonio** cultural nacional. **No sería de extrañar** que **de ahora en más**, el candombe **expanda** su **contagioso ritmo más allá de las fronteras** uruguayas.

principios: beginnings
mantuvo/mantener: it maintained/to maintain
fuerte presencia: strong presence
aluvión: downpour
convergían/converger: they converged/to converge
sin embargo: however
sin duda: without a doubt
dentro de: inside

cambio: change
contribuyeron/contribuir: they contributed/to contribute
ramas: lines of work, branches
se manifestó/manifestarse: it was shown/to be shown
cuadros: paintings
revalorizó/revalorizar: he revalued/to revalue
plasmarlos/plasmar: he captured them/to capture
jugó un papel clave: he played a key role
ahuyentar: to scare away
tirar una flecha: to shoot an arrow
poco a poco: little by little
ganando/ganar: winning/to win
público más amplio: a broader public
aparecerían/aparecer: they would appear/to appear
destacados: outstanding
más conocido como: better known as
compuso/componer: he composed/to compose
extremadamente: extremely
se han incursionado/incursionar: they have tackled (a subject)/to tackle
últimos: last
disfrutado/disfrutar: enjoyed/to enjoy
auge creciente: increasing peak
gracias en parte a: thanks in part to
patrimonio: heritage
no sería de extrañar: it would be hardly surprising
de ahora en más: from now on
expanda/expandir: it expands/to expand
contagioso ritmo: infectious rhythm
más allá de las fronteras: beyond the borders

instrumentos exóticos: exotic instruments

solemnidad evocativa: evocative solemnity

público selecto: select public

ritmo precolombino: precolumbian rhythm

vida del increíble hombre andino: life of an incredible Andean man

diversas etapas: diverse stages

se desarrollaron/desarrollar: it was developed/to develop

acompañadas de/acompañar: accompanied by, with/to accompany

varios tipos de ritmos: various types of rhythms

alegres: happy

tristes: sad

solemnes: solemn

guerreros: warlike

no se podían cambiar: could not be changed

dura: hard

faena: work

se aliviaba/aliviar: was relieved/to relieve

piezas: pieces

fecha: date

se convertía/convertía: it was changed/to change

dejaran/dejar: they left/to leave

caracterizaba: characterized

nueve flautas: nine flutes

amarradas: tied together

en fila: in line

hechas de carrizo: made of reed

confeccionada de arcilla: made of clay

plata: silver

carrizo: reed

huesos humanos: human bones

piel de puma: puma skin

marcar: to mark

también: also

caracol marino: marine snail

agudo: sharp, high-pitched

La música andina
PERÚ

Por sus **instrumentos exóticos** y su **solemnidad evocativa**, la llamada música de los andes tiene un **público selecto** en el planeta. Este **ritmo precolombino** de los quechuas y aymaras formó parte esencial en la **vida del increíble hombre andino**.

Las **diversas etapas** de la vida de los indígenas de los Andes **se desarrollaron acompañadas de varios tipos de ritmos**: alegres, tristes, solemnes, festivos o **guerreros**. Cada lugar u ocasión tenía sus propios cantos y bailes

que **no se podían cambiar**. Una **dura faena se aliviaba** con la ejecución de **piezas** musicales, y la celebración de una **fecha** festiva **se convertía** en motivo para que los indígenas **dejaran** por un momento esa melancolía que les **caracterizaba**.

LOS INSTRUMENTOS MUSICALES

El elemento más característico de esta melodía fue la zampoña, que era una especie de **nueve flautas amarradas en fila hechas de carrizo**. La quena era una flauta **confeccionada de arcilla**, **plata**, **carrizo** o de **huesos humanos**. En la percusión, el tambor, fabricado con **piel de puma** o piel humana, fue un elemento básico para **marcar** el ritmo. **También** existía el "pututo" o **caracol marino** que emitía un sonido **agudo** como de ultratumba, un sonido realmente mágico.

El arte musical andino precolombino no conoció los instrumentos de **cuerda** y su ritmo **estuvo basado** en la **escala pentatónica.**

Con la **llegada** de los españoles **se incorporó** a esta **orquesta** el **arpa**, y **nació** en estas **tierras** una **especie de** guitarra pequeña llamada "charango", hecha de la **concha del armadillo.**

LA ACTUAL MÚSICA ANDINA

Hoy la música de los Andes ya **no se conserva** "pura". Este concepto está **casi extinto**. Con el paso del tiempo **se añadieron** instrumentos europeos, **creándose** así una interesante fusión.

Hay abundantes grupos que aún **cultivan** este género con gran talento en Perú, Bolivia, Chile, Ecuador, Colombia y Argentina. Durante los años 60 y 70 muchos de estos grupos fueron **enviados** al exilio europeo por sus ideas socialistas o antimilitaristas. Ya en Europa, estos **sonidos** indígenas **atrajeron** la atención internacional. *El cóndor pasa*, creada en 1913 por el peruano Daniel Alomía Robles, es el **tema maestro** de la música andina. Paul Simon descubrió esta canción en París y **de ahí la hizo** conocida a todo el mundo en 1970.

La **complicada y hermosa ejecución** de *El cóndor pasa* es sólo un ejemplo del **reconocimiento** a este **género** musical indígena después de siglos de **haber sido marginado** por el **mundo occidental.**

cuerda: string
estuvo basado/basar: it was based/ to base
escala pentatónica: pentatonic scale

llegada/llegar: arrival/to arrive
se incorporó/incorporó: it was incorporated/to incorporate
orquesta: orchestra
arpa: harp
nació/nacer: was born/to be born
tierras: lands
especie de: sort of
concha del armadillo: shell of the armadillo

actual: current
no se conserva/conservar: is not kept/to keep
casi extinto: almost extinct
se añadieron/añadir: they were added/to add
creándose/crear: creating/to create

hay abundantes: there are a lot of
cultivan/cultivar: they cultivate/ to cultivate
enviados/enviar: sent/to send
sonidos: sounds
atrajeron/atraer: they drew (the attention of)/to draw
tema maestro: master piece
de ahí: from there
la hizo/hacer: he made it/to make

complicada y hermosa ejecución: complicated and beautiful execution
reconocimiento: recognition
género: genre
haber sido marginado: having been marginalized
mundo occidental: western world

Las danzas tradicionales
EL SALVADOR

El tigre, el **venado** y el **toro** no son sólo animales, **por lo menos** no en El Salvador. Aquí también son los nombres de **algunos** de los bailes tradicionales más populares que **forman parte** de la cultura, las raíces y las costumbres salvadoreñas.

El baile es una de las formas de expresión y comunicación más **bellas** y **estéticas**. Es **fuente** y emisión de energía, **conexión** con el mundo exterior e interior y una **forma de expresar** muchas emociones, principalmente **alegría** y **goce**. Desde tiempos **inmemoriales**, el hombre bailó, bailó para celebrar y **festejar**, para **invocar dioses** o para **cortejar**.

El Salvador, **como casi todos** los países de Centroamérica, es **rico** en danzas tradicionales, y **si bien** toda ocasión es buena para el baile, la mayoría de ellas **se representan** durante las fiestas de **Fin de Año**, **Año Nuevo** y fiestas patronales.

DANZA DEL TIGRE Y EL VENADO

Esta danza representa una **leyenda** del pueblo de San Juan Nonualco, en el departamento de La Paz. La historia **cuenta** que, **a mediados de** 1800, un **matrimonio** mayor **salió** a **cazar** un venado y al verse **amenazado** por la presencia de un tigre, **pidió auxilio** y **suplicó** al Señor de la Caridad, **patrono del municipio**, que los **salvara del peligro**.

Los **cazadores mataron** al tigre y en honor a este santo **se celebra** una danza en la que varios personajes representan aquel momento: el tigre **acecha** al venado y a la **pareja** bailando al **son** del tambor, mientras el matrimonio armado con **arco** y **flecha** baila también **alrededor** del tigre.

---

venado: deer
toro: bull
por lo menos: at least
algunos: some
forman parte: they are part of

bellas: beautiful
estéticas: aesthetic
fuente: source
conexión: connection
forma de expresar: form of expression
alegría: joy
goce: enjoyment
inmemoriales: immemorial
festejar: to celebrate
invocar: to invoke
dioses: gods
cortejar: to court, to woo

como casi todos: like almost all
rico: rich
si bien: although
se representan/representar: they are performed/to perform
Fin de Año: New Year's Eve
Año Nuevo: New Year's Day

leyenda: legend
cuenta/contar: tells/to tell
a mediados de: the middle of
matrimonio: married couple
salió/salir: went out/to go out
cazar: to hunt
amenazado/amenazar: threatened/to threaten
pidió auxilio: asked for help
suplicó/suplicar: begged, implored/to beg, to implore
patrono del municipio: patron saint of the town
salvara del peligro: to save from danger

cazadores: hunters
mataron/matar: they killed/to kill
se celebra/celebrar: is celebrated/to celebrate
acecha/acechar: lies in wait for/to lie in wait for
pareja: couple
son: sound, tune, melody
arco: arch
flecha: arrow
alrededor: around

El público observa cómo el tigre ataca a los viejos y aplaude cuando éstos **lo degüellan** y **reparten** las porciones del animal **entonando** frases humorísticas **dirigidas** a las personas del pueblo: "**Lo de adelante** para el **comandante**", "lo de atrás para el **juez de paz**", "la cabeza para Teresa" o "los **riñones** para los **mirones**".

LOS TOROS DE LA ASCENSIÓN

Esta tradición, también procedente de San Juan Nonualco, celebra el **hecho ocurrido** a un **personaje** llamado Isidro Labrador, que **se dedicaba** a la agricultura para **alimentar** a su familia. Un **Jueves de Ascensión** (día en el que se conmemora la **subida** de Cristo al **cielo**) Isidro **se disponía** a **labrar** la tierra y cuando **arreaba** a los **bueyes**, uno de ellos le dijo: "Isidro, hoy no trabajaremos, mañana sí". Él insistió pero **obtuvo** la misma **respuesta** y al darse cuenta de lo que se conmemoraba ese día, **se arrodilló** pidiendo perdón a Dios.

Basado en este suceso **se mantiene** la celebración del Jueves de Ascensión como el día dedicado a los toros. En todos los **barrios**, los habitantes **fabrican** un toro (**armazón** con **varas** de **bambú forradas** con **cuero** o **piel de toro** y en los extremos, **cuernos** y **cola**) que pasean por las calles, acompañados de música y **quema** de **pólvora**. En las **capillas** o ermitas se adornan altares y **se reza** el **rosario**. Luego de las **oraciones** y el baile, **se inician** competencias con los toros.

Éstos y otros tantos bailes y tradiciones mantenidos a lo largo de años reafirman el **compromiso** de **promover** las raíces del país.

lo degüellan/degollar: they beheaded him/to behead
reparten/repartir: they give out/to give out
entonando/entonar: singing, saying/to sing, to say
dirigidas/dirigir: addressed/to address
lo de adelante: in the front part
comandante: commander
juez de paz: justice of the peace
riñones: kidneys
mirones: curious people

hecho ocurrido: event that happened
personaje: character
se dedicaba/dedicarse: he was dedicated/to be dedicated
alimentar: to feed
Jueves de Ascensión: Ascension Day
subida: ascension
cielo: heaven
se disponía/disponerse: he got ready/to get ready, to prepare
labrar: to farm
arreaba/arrear: he was urging on/to urge on, to drive
bueyes: oxen
obtuvo/obtener: he got/to get
respuesta: answer
se arrodilló/arrodillarse: he knelt down/to kneel down

se mantiene/mantener: is kept/to keep
barrios: neighborhoods
fabrican/fabricar: they make/to make
armazón: shell
varas: rods, sticks
bambú: bamboo
forradas/forrar: covered/to cover
cuero: leather
piel de toro: bull skin
cuernos: horns
cola: tail
quema: burn
pólvora: gunpowder
capillas: chapels
se reza/rezar: it is said/to say
rosario: rosary
oraciones: prayers
se inician/iniciar: they start/to start

compromiso: commitment
promover: to promote

si no te asustan ... : if … don't scare you
ruidos: noises
noche: night
no necesitas/necesitar: (you) don't need/to need
tapones para los oídos: earplugs
prepárate para: (you) get ready for
redobles: drumrolls
se celebra/celebrar: is celebrated/to celebrate
no te extrañes: don't be surprised
al ver: if you see
desfile: parade, march
no solo... sino también: not only… but also
se tocan/tocar: are played/to play
tambores: drums
barriles: barrels, casks

existen/existir: there are/to be, to exist
algunas: some
se remontan al: date back to the
cuentan/contar: tell/to tell
panadero: baker
mientras llenaba/llenar: while (he) was filling/to fill
fuente: fountain, spring
cercana a: close to
iglesia: church
comenzó a cantar: (he) started to sing
jóvenes: young people
pasaba por allí/pasar: was passing by/to pass
empezó a acompañarlo: began to accompany him
tocando/tocar: beating/to beat
ocuparon/ocupar: occupied/to occupy
guerra: war
desfilaron/desfilar: paraded/to parade
por la ciudad: through the city
aguadoras: (female) water sellers
usaron/usar: used/to use
recogían/recoger: (they) collected/to collect
tamborileros: drummers
vestidos con: dressed with
trajes: suits, costumes
cocineros: cooks

en un principio: at first
formaba parte de: was a part of
hoy en día: today, nowadays
medianoche: midnight
obra: (a) work
continúan/continuar: (they) continue/to continue
desfilando/desfilar: marching/to march
barrios: neighborhoods
dura/durar: lasts/to last
termina/terminar: ends/to end
se cierra/cerrar: closes/to close
última: last
más antigua: the oldest

La Tamborrada en San Sebastián
ESPAÑA

Si no te asustan los **ruidos** de la **noche** de San Juan y **no necesitas tapones para los oídos** durante las Fallas en Valencia, **prepárate para** uno de los **redobles** más famosos de España. La Tamborrada de San Sebastián es la fiesta que **se celebra** en enero, precisamente el día de San Sebastián. Y **no te extrañes al ver** un **desfile** peculiar: durante la festividad **no solo se tocan** los **tambores**, **sino también** los barriles. ¿Por qué?

Existen diversas versiones sobre el origen de la fiesta. **Algunas se remontan** al siglo XVIII y **cuentan** la historia de un **panadero** que, un día, **mientras llenaba** los barriles de agua en una **fuente cercana a** la **Iglesia** de San Vicente, **comenzó a cantar**, y un grupo de **jóvenes** que **pasaba por allí** empezó a acompañarlo **tocando** sus barriles. Otra versión cuenta que los militares napoleónicos que **ocuparon** San Sebastián durante la **Guerra de la Independencia** (1808-1814) **desfilaron** en formación **por la ciudad** tocando los tambores. El desfile fue acompañado por **aguadoras**, quienes **usaron** como instrumentos los barriles en los que **recogían** el agua. Por eso, hoy, durante la fiesta, hay dos grupos: uno de **tamborileros vestidos con trajes** napoleónicos y otro de cocineros y aguadoras que tocan los barriles.

El primer desfile de la Tamborrada se celebró a finales del siglo XIX y, **en un principio**, **formaba parte de** los carnavales. **Hoy en día** la celebración empieza a la **medianoche** del 19 de enero en la Plaza de la Constitución. Varias sociedades gastronómicas y bandas comienzan tocando la Marcha de San Sebastián, **obra** del compositor Raimundo Sarriegui, y **continúan** durante todo el día tocando y **desfilando** por todos los **barrios** de la ciudad. La fiesta **dura** 24 horas y **termina** a las doce de la noche del 20 de enero en la Plaza de la Constitución. El círculo **se cierra** y la **última** composición tocada por la sociedad **más antigua** de la ciudad, la Unión Artesana, es la Marcha de San Sebastián.

Orishas: intermediarios de dios y músicos
CUBA

Los intermediarios de **dios** – La yoruba es una religión que **nace** en un pueblo de Nigeria, en el continente africano. De allí **llegó** a América de la **mano** de los europeos que **traían esclavos** africanos en sus **barcos**. Éstos, **para poder seguir viviendo a pesar de** la esclavitud, **trataron de mantener** sus costumbres, sus tradiciones y religión. Cuba, Brasil y Haití son algunos de los países americanos en donde las **creencias**, los **mitos** y los ritos religiosos yorubas **sobreviven** con **fuerza**.

La teología yoruba **cree** en la existencia de un sólo dios, **único** y omnipotente, "Olodumare", el cual **creó** todo **lo que existe**. **A partir de** él **se generaron** los "orishas", que son deidades o energías superiores de la naturaleza que **rigen** el **destino humano** y son intermediarios de dios, sus emisarios.

Existen más de 200 deidades orishas pero en América sólo **reconocen** treinta. **Algunos de ellos** son: Elleguá, el que tiene las **llaves** del destino; Oduduwa, orisha mayor que representa los misterios y secretos de la **muerte**; Obbatalá, dueño de los **sentimientos**, **sueños** y **pensamientos** humanos; Yemayá, **reina** de las **aguas saladas** y **dueña** de los **mares**; Oyá, dueña de las **centellas** y los **vientos**; Shangó, orisha del **fuego**, el **rayo**, el **trueno** y la **belleza viril**; Oshún, deidad del amor, la **paz**, la feminidad y la sexualidad, dueña de los **ríos**. En Cuba, la religión yoruba **se unió** con la católica, **dando lugar** a una nueva, **conocida como** Regla de Osha o Santería. **Hoy la misma** deidad africana **puede ser llamada** indistintamente por su nombre africano o católico, por ejemplo Shango es Santa Bárbara.

Los músicos – "Orishas" es una banda de músicos, representante por excelencia del hip-hop cubano en el **mundo**. Con cuatro **discos editados** y más de 800.000 copias en Europa, **ganaron varios premios**, entre ellos dos Grammys. Los integrantes de la banda son cubanos pero **viven fuera** de la isla **repartidos por** el continente europeo. Aún así la fuerza de sus raíces **vibra** en cada uno de sus temas musicales. **Según ellos mismos dicen**, sus canciones **abren caminos esperanzadores** y si **son casi dioses**, **habrá que creerles**.

dios: god
nace/nacer: is born/to be born
llegó/llegar: it arrived/to arrive
mano: hand
traían/traer: brought/to bring
esclavos: slaves
barcos: ships
para poder seguir viviendo: to be able to continue living
a pesar de: despite
trataron de mantener: tried to keep
creencias: beliefs
mitos: myths
sobreviven/sobrevivir: survive/to survive
fuerza: strength

cree/creer: believes/to believe
único: only
creó/crear: created/to create
lo que existe: that exists
a partir de: from
se generaron/generar: were created/to create
rigen/regir: run/to run, to control
destino humano: human destiny

reconocen/reconocer: are recognized/to recognize
algunos de ellos: some of them
llaves: keys
muerte: death
sentimientos: feelings
sueños: dreams
pensamientos: thoughts
reina: queen
aguas saladas: salt water
dueña: owner
mares: seas
centellas: sparks
vientos: winds
fuego: fire
rayo: bolt of lightning
trueno: thunder
belleza viril: manly beauty
paz: peace
ríos: rivers
se unió/unirse: joined/to join
dando lugar: making room, leading
conocida como: known as
hoy la misma: today the same
puede ser llamada: could be called

mundo: world
discos: CDs
editados: published
ganaron/ganar: won/to win
varios premios: several awards
viven fuera de: (they) live outside
repartidos por: scattered through
vibra/vibrar: vibrates/to vibrate
según ellos mismos dicen: according to what they ssay
canciones: songs
abren/abrir: open/to open
caminos esperanzadores: hopeful paths
son casi dioses: are almost gods
habrá que creerles: one might need to believe them

Examina tu comprensión

Bailando al son de merengue, página 144

1. ¿El merengue está influenciado por qué dos culturas?

2. ¿Qué instrumentos se utilizan en el merengue?

3. ¿Durante qué años este estilo de música fue clasificado como una subcategoría de la música con guitarra?

Los instrumentos musicales, página 145

1. ¿De qué materiales de origen animal están hechas la flauta y la trompeta?

2. ¿De qué tipo de hoja está hecho el tubo grueso del clarinete?

3. La mina y la curbata son tamborines hechos ¿de qué tipo de árbol?

El arte flamenco, página 146

1. El flamenco es un arte que se manifiesta de tres formas. ¿Cuáles son?

2. ¿Dónde nació el flamenco?

3. El flamenco comenzó como canto y evolucionó para incluir ¿qué cosa?

4. ¿Cuál es el papel de la guitarra y el guitarrista?

El reguetón está "rankeao", página 148

1. ¿El reguetón es una mezcla de qué influencias, ritmos y sonidos?

2. ¿Qué expresan las letras de reguetón?

3. ¿En qué lugar de los Estados Unidos se ha comenzado a escuchar reguetón?

Test your comprehension

El tango: pasíon en la pista, página 150

1. En 1880, ¿de qué países llegaban los inmigrantes a Buenos Aires?

2. ¿Cuáles fueron las principales ocupaciones de los inmigrantes?

3. ¿Dónde se bailaba el tango originalmente?

4. ¿En qué década se convirtió el tango en un baile más aceptado por todas las clases sociales?

El mariachi, página 154

1. ¿Cuál es el origen de la palabra mariachi y qué significa?

2. ¿Qué instrumentos forman parte de una banda de mariachi?

3. Describa el guitarrón.

El candombe, página 156

1. ¿Dónde y cuándo se puede escuchar candombe?

2. ¿Cuál es el origen del candombe y qué importancia tiene?

3. ¿En qué otras formas de arte ha aparecido representado el candombe?

La música andina, página 158

1. Los sonidos de la música andina evocan cinco ritmos. ¿Cuáles son?

2. ¿Cómo se construye una zampoña?

3. ¿Qué estadounidense hizo que la música andina se volviera conocida en los años 70?

Las buenas costumbres, y no la fuerza,
son las columnas de las leyes; y el ejercicio
de la justicia es el ejercicio de la libertad.

Simón Bolívar

Historia

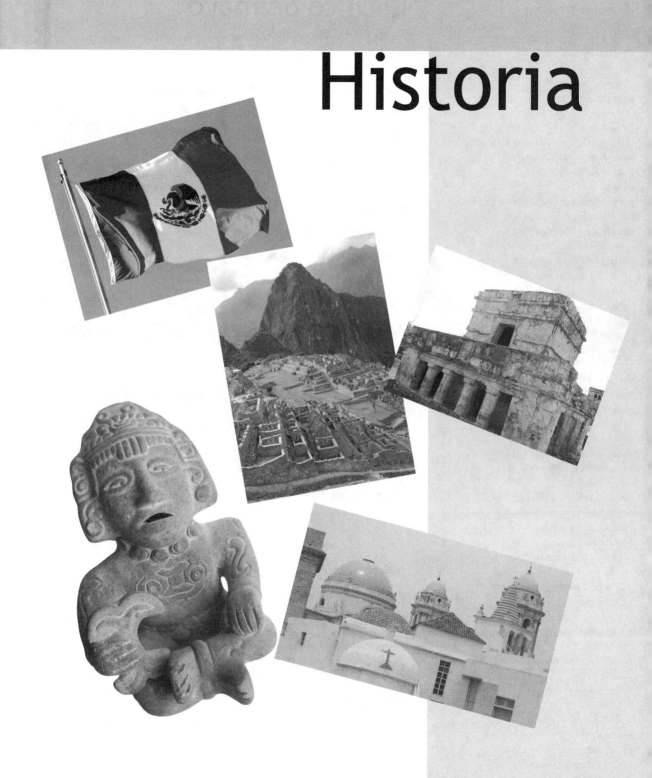

conmemora/conmemorar: commemorates/to commemorate

fecha muy importante: very important date

por todo México: everywhere in Mexico

pero especialmente: but especially, particularly

ciudad de: city of

últimos veinte años: last twenty years

han adquirido: have achieved

principalmente: mainly

de hecho: in fact

piensan/pensar: they think/to think

en realidad: in fact, actually

triunfo de: triumph of

ejército francés: French army

Batalla de Puebla: Battle of Puebla (The battlefield is now a park in Puebla with a statue of General Zaragoza riding horseback. But it is in the United States, not Mexico, where the celebration is more festive, consisting of parades, music, folklore, dances, and food.)

después: after

una larga lucha: a long battle

obtener la independencia de: to obtain independence from

primer: first

durante esta época: during this time

incurrió en grandes deudas: incurred great debts

otros países: other countries

e: and (before words beginning with *i* and *hi,* but not *hie*)

Inglaterra: England

inestabilidad política: political instability

por la cual estaba pasando: which Mexico was undergoing

en ese momento: then

impidieron/impedir: prevented/ to prevent

cumplir de inmediato: immediately fulfill

obligaciones financieras: financial obligations

actual: current

solicitó/solicitar: requested/to request

moratoria: moratorium

que fue aceptado por: that was accepted by

El cinco de mayo
MÉXICO

El cinco de mayo **conmemora** una **fecha muy importante** para los mexicanos. Las festividades de este día se celebran **por todo México, pero especialmente** en la **ciudad de** Puebla. En los **últimos veinte años**, las celebraciones del cinco de mayo **han adquirido** mucha popularidad en los Estados Unidos, **principalmente** en los estados de California,

Arizona, Texas y Nuevo México. **De hecho**, hay muchas personas que **piensan** que en este día se celebra la Independencia de México, que es el 16 de septiembre. **En realidad**, esta fecha conmemora el **triunfo de** los mexicanos sobre el **ejército francés** en la **Batalla de Puebla** de 1862.

En 1821, **después** de **una larga lucha** por **obtener la independencia de** España, se estableció el **primer** gobierno mexicano independiente. **Durante esta época**, el gobierno mexicano **incurrió en grandes deudas** con **otros países**, principalmente Francia **e Inglaterra**. La **inestabilidad política** y la situación económica **por la cual estaba pasando** México **en ese momento impidieron** que pudiera **cumplir de inmediato** con sus **obligaciones financieras**. El **actual** presidente, Benito Juárez, **solicitó** una **moratoria** para su deuda, **que fue aceptado por** Inglaterra y España.

Sin embargo, el gobierno francés **se mantuvo renuente** y **envió sus tropas** a la ciudad de México con la intención de **establecer allí su propio** gobierno monárquico. **Para llegar** a su destino, tenían que pasar **por el estado de** Puebla **donde las tropas mexicanas, bajo el mando del** general Zaragoza, **preparaban** su defensa.

Aunque el ejército mexicano **no aparentaba ser** lo suficientemente **fuerte** o **capacitado para destruir** las tropas francesas, el **ímpetu de su lucha** compensó sus limitaciones y **lograron vencer** al **poderoso** ejército europeo **a pesar de** que la **victoria** en esta batalla **no logró al final ganar la guerra**. Para los mexicanos la misma **simboliza** el valor, la determinación y el patriotismo del pueblo mexicano.

Las celebraciones de este día incluyen **desfiles militares** que **rinden homenaje a** todos los héroes **que perecieron por** la **libertad de** México. El desfile generalmente culmina en el Zócalo, la plaza central de cada pueblo, **donde jóvenes** y mayores **disfrutan** de las festividades. La fiesta incluye **juegos divertidos, corridas de toros**, deliciosos platos típicos de la cocina mexicana y **bandas de mariachis** que **alegran la velada** con su música y su **encanto**.

Al final de la noche, se oye la **pólvora de los fuegos artificiales** y un sinfín de **voces que exclaman con alegría** ¡Viva México! Este sentido **grito** refleja **el orgullo** que sienten los mexicanos por su **herencia** y el **espíritu festivo** de un pueblo que **celebra su libertad**.

historia   **169**

---

sin embargo: nevertheless
se mantuvo renuente: remained reluctant
envió sus tropas: sent its troops
establecer allí su propio: to establish its own
para llegar: in order to arrive
por el estado de: through the state of
donde las tropas mexicanas: where the Mexican troops
bajo el mando del: under the command of
preparaban/prepara: they prepared/ to prepare

aunque: although
no aparentaba ser: did not appear to be
fuerte: strong
capacitado para destruir: able to destroy
ímpetu de su lucha: impetus, momentum of their fight
lograron vencer: managed to defeat
poderoso: powerful
a pesar de: in spite of
victoria: victory
no logró al final ganar la guerra: did not in the end win the war
simboliza: symbolizes

desfiles militares: military parades
rinden homenaje a: pay tribute to
que perecieron por: who perished for
libertad de: freedom of
donde jóvenes: where young
disfrutan/disfrutar: they enjoy/ to enjoy
juegos divertidos: playing games
corridas de toros: bullfights
bandas de mariachis: mariachi bands
alegran la velada: cheer up the evening
encanto: charm

al final de la: at the end of the
pólvora de los fuegos artificiales: powder of the fireworks
voces que exclaman con alegría: voices that exclaim with joy
grito: shout
el orgullo: the pride
herencia: legacy, inheritance
espíritu festivo: festive spirit
celebra su libertad: celebrates its freedom

logró/lograr: he managed/to manage, to get

asimilar: to assimilate

conocimientos: knowledge

aportes: contributions

conquistaron/conquistar: they conquered/to conquer

crecimiento: growth

fue detenido/detener: it was stopped/to stop

respirar: to breathe

mayoría: majority

abarcó/abacar: it embraced/to embrace, to cover

imperio: empire

sobre todo: throughout all

leyenda: legend

que cuenta: that tells

lago: lake

amados: beloved

barreta: bar

hundieron/hundir: they sank/to sink

cerro: hill

fundaron/fundar: they founded/to found

sagrada: sacred

ombligo: center (literally: navel)

ciudad mágica: magical city

enseñó/enseñar: he taught/to teach

ganadería: cattle

cerámica: pottery

tejido: weaving

cocina: cooking, cuisine

alcanzó/alcanzar: reached/to reach

extraordinaria: extraordinary, exceptional

casi: almost

llevando con ello/llevar: taking with it/to take

adoración: worship

idioma: language

Los hijos del sol
PERÚ

Los incas fueron una magnífica civilización del siglo X que **logró asimilar** grandes **conocimientos** y **aportes** de las culturas que **conquistaron**. Aunque su **crecimiento fue detenido** por la invasión española en el siglo XVI, aún se puede **respirar** la gran influencia incaica en la **mayoría** de los países que **abarcó** este **imperio, sobre todo** en Perú.

Existe una **leyenda que cuenta** que el dios Inti sacó del **Lago** Titicaca, en Puno, a dos de sus **amados** hijos: Manco Cápac y Mama Ocllo. Ellos llevaban una **barreta** de oro que **hundieron** en el **cerro** Huanacaure. Aquí **fundaron** la maravillosa ciudad del Cuzco, la capital **sagrada** de los incas, a la que consideraban el **ombligo** del mundo. Esta **ciudad mágica** era el centro del imperio.

Manco Cápac, como primer inca, **enseñó** a los hombres la agricultura, la **ganadería** y la **cerámica**; y Mama Ocllo, a las mujeres, el arte del **tejido** y la **cocina**. Con el Inca Pachacútec, el imperio **alcanzó** una **extraordinaria** expansión por **casi** toda América del Sur **llevando con ello** la **adoración** al Inti, o Dios Sol y también el uso del **idioma** quechua.

Aunque **controlaron** todo el **actual Perú** y diversos territorios de Bolivia, Colombia, Ecuador, Argentina y Chile, los incas **respetaron** la cultura de los pueblos que conquistaban.

A pesar de que el Estado Inca mantenía **profundas** diferencias sociales y **utilizaba** el trabajo de la población **para su beneficio**, el pueblo **tenía asegurado** los **alimentos**, el **vestido** y la **vivienda**. Así, en una población de 12 millones no había **desocupación** ni **hambre**.

No existía **propiedad privada**, las tierras **pertenecían** al **emperador** y **eran administradas colectivamente** por **ayllus**, **quienes asignaban** a cada familia un **pedazo de tierra** para **cultivarla** para su propio **consumo** así como para dar **tributos** al rey. En las artes, las ciencias y la tecnología se alcanzó un alto nivel de desarrollo para la época, **destacando** principalmente en la **ingeniería** y la arquitectura. Los incas **construyeron** notables **palacios**, templos, canales, **puentes**, **fortalezas** y **caminos**.

Con la **muerte súbita** del **penúltimo** inca en 1526 el imperio fue dividido entre sus dos hijos Huáscar y Atahualpa, que **se enfrentaron** en una **guerra civil**.

En 1532, Atahualpa **derrotó** a Huáscar; pero ya el gran imperio se encontraba **debilitado** y **dividido sin estar preparado** para el **arribo** de los conquistadores españoles, que encontraron a su llegada una alta cultura.

controlaron/controlar: they controlled/to control
actual Perú: modern-day Perú
respetaron/respetar: respected/ to respect

profundas: deep
utilizaba/utilizar: it used/to use
para su beneficio: for its own benefit
tenía asegurado: they had guaranteed
alimentos: food
vestido: clothes
vivienda: housing
desocupación: unemployment
hambre: hunger

propiedad privada: private property
pertenecían/pertenecer: they belonged/to belong
emperador: emperor
eran administradas/administrar: they were managed/to manage
colectivamente: collectively
ayllus: kinship-based clan
quienes asignaban/asignar: who assigned/to assign, to allocate
pedazo de tierra: a piece of land
cultivarla: to cultivate it
consumo: consumption
tributos: tribute payments
destacando/destacar: emphasizing/ to emphasize
ingeniería: engineering
construyeron/construir: they built/ to build
palacios: palaces
puentes: bridges
fortalezas: fortresses
caminos: roads

muerte súbita: sudden death
penúltimo: next to the last
se enfrentaron/enfrentar: they faced each other/to confront, to face up to
guerra civil: civil war

derrotó/derrotar: he defeated/to defeat
debilitado: debilitated, weakened
dividido/dividir: divided/to divide
sin estar preparado: unprepared
arribo: arrival

toreo: bullfighting
se cree que/creer: it is believed that/
  to believe
tuvo lugar: took place
coronación del rey: crowning of the king
**después de la Reconquista de
  España:** after the Spanish Reconquest
se liberó/liberar: was freed/to free
poder musulmán: Muslim control
se hizo: became
varios reinados: various reigns
habituales: frequent
el papa: the Pope
las prohibió/prohibir: forbade them/
  to forbid
pues pensaba/pensar: as he thought/
  to think
el pueblo ignoró/ignorar: the people
  ignored/to ignore
continuó/continuar: continued/
  to continue
derogó el decreto: revoked the decree
asumiendo/asumir: accepting it/
  to accept

casi desaparece/desaparecer: nearly
  disappears/to disappear
ya que los toros: as the bulls
se utilizaban/utilizar: were used/to use
para alimentar: to feed
el conflicto terminó: the conflict ended
época: time
hoy en día: today, nowadays
se practica/practicarse: is practiced/
  to practice
desfile: parade

cuadrilla: team of the bullfighter
vestidos con trajes del siglo XVII:
  dressed in 17th-century costumes
para anunciar: in order to announce
al ruedo: into the ring
agita/agitar: waves/to wave
pañuelo blanco: white handkerchief
cada vez: each time
sale/salir: he exits/to exit
se ha matado al toro/matar: the bull
  has been killed/to kill
suena una trompeta/sonar: a trumpet
  is blown/to sound
participan/participar: they
  participate/to participate
pesan entre: they weigh between
nunca se han enfrentado a un hombre:
  they have never faced a man
si fuera así: if so
enbestiría/enbestir: may charge/
  to charge

La historia del toreo
ESPAÑA

¿Cuál es la historia del **toreo** en España? **Se cree que** la primera corrida de toros **tuvo lugar** en Verea, en la provincia de Logroño, en el año 1133, en la **coronación del rey** Alfonso VIII. **Después de la Reconquista de España** (en la que **se liberó** a la Península del **poder musulmán**) la fiesta del toreo **se hizo** popular en toda la geografía ibérica. Durante **varios reinados** las corridas fueron **habituales**, hasta que **el papa** Pío V **las prohibió**, **pues pensaba** que las corridas eran celebraciones primitivas. Pero **el pueblo ignoró** esta prohibición y **continuó** con su "fiesta". Más tarde, el papa Gregorio VIII **derogó el decreto, asumiendo** que era una fiesta del pueblo.

Varios siglos más tarde, con la Guerra Civil Española (de 1936 a 1939), el toreo **casi desaparece, ya que los toros se utilizaban para alimentar** a las tropas. Pero cuando **el conflicto terminó**, las corridas de toros fueron restablecidas. Algunos de los toreros más representativos de esta **época** son "Manolete" y Luis Miguel "Dominguín". **Hoy en día**, el toreo **se practica** también en otros países: Portugal, Ecuador, México, etc. Incluso en Japón o Estados Unidos (en California y otros estados del oeste).

Pero ¿cómo es una corrida de toros? La corrida de toros comienza con el "**desfile**" de los toreros y toda su **cuadrilla, vestidos con trajes del siglo XVII**, que saludan al presidente. **Para anunciar** la entrada del primer toro **al ruedo**, el presidente de la plaza **agita** un **pañuelo blanco**. **Cada vez** que el torero **sale** y cuando, finalmente, **se ha matado al toro, suena una trompeta**. En la corrida **participan** tres toreros (junto con sus cuadrillas) y seis toros. Cada torero torea dos toros, los cuales **pesan entre** 500 y 800 kilos. Estos toros **nunca se han enfrentado a un hombre. Si fuera así**, el toro **enbestiría** al hombre, no a la capa del torero.

Podemos diferenciar seis **etapas** durante la corrida de toros:

Primera etapa: Durante esta fase preliminar, los **capeadores** torean al toro, para **saber** si tiene las cualidades necesarias (su fuerza, inteligencia, agilidad, etc.). Si el toro no es aceptado, el presidente de la plaza agitará un **pañuelo verde**.

Segunda etapa: Los picadores, **montados en caballos protegidos, hacen que el toro les ataque**. Cuando esto **ocurre**, **le hunden las lanzas en el cuello** para **debilitar** sus músculos. **De esta forma** el toro **bajará la cabeza** y el torero **le dará el golpe de gracia** con más facilidad.

Tercera etapa: **Colocación** de las **banderillas** en el cuello del toro. El banderillero **lleva** una banderilla **en cada mano**, **corre hacia el toro** y **le coloca** las banderillas. **Su propósito** es **regular la embestida del toro**.

Ultima etapa: Llamada "suerte" o "tercio". **Comienza** cuando el torero **agita su gorro saludando** al presidente y **pidiendo permiso** para matar al toro. El torero usualmente **dedica** el toro a alguien del público. **Para atrae**r al toro, el torero **utiliza** distintos pases, usando **su capa y espada**.

La muerte del toro: Cuando el torero **cree que** el toro está **más débil**, **intentará darle el "toque de gracia"**, insertando la espada entre la vértebra cervical, directa al **corazón** del toro. Si el "**maestro**" **ha hecho una buena "faena"**, el público agitará pañuelos blancos. Esta es la **señal** para que el presidente **premie** al torero con una **oreja** o el **rabo** del toro. **Por otro lado**, si el torero **no consigue matar** al toro por su bravura, éste **será perdonado** y **se le permitirá vivir en paz**.

---

podemos diferenciar: we can differentiate
etapas: phases

capeadores: people who belong to the bullfighter's team
saber: to know
pañuelo verde: green handkerchief

montados en caballos protegidos: mounted on protected horses
hacen que el toro les ataque: they provoke the bull to attack them
ocurre/ocurrir: happens/to happen
le hunden las lanzas en el cuello: they plunge their lances into the bull's neck
debilitar: to weaken
de esta forma: this way
bajará la cabeza: will lower its head
le dará el golpe de gracia: will perform the coup de grace

colocación: placement
banderillas: barbed sticks
lleva/llevar: he carries/to carry
en cada mano: in each hand
corre hacia el toro: runs towards the bull
le coloca/colocar: places/to place
su propósito: his aim
regular la embestida del toro: to regulate the charge of the bull

comienza/comenzar: it begins/to begin
agita su gorro: shakes his hat
saludando/saludar: saluting/to salute
pidiendo permiso: asking for permission
dedica/dedicar: he dedicates/to dedicate
para atraer: to attract
utiliza/utilizar: he uses/to use
su capa y espada: his cape and sword

cree que/creer: he thinks/to think
más débil: weaker
intentará darle el toque de gracia: he will try to administer the "death stroke"
corazón: heart
maestro: master, a good bullfighter
ha hecho una buena "faena": he has given a good "faena" (performance)
señal: signal
premie: to award
oreja: ear
rabo: tail
por otro lado: on the other hand
no consigue matar: he is unable to kill
será perdonado/perdonar: will be spared/to spare
se le permitirá vivir en paz: the bull will be allowed to live in peace

La independencia de Colombia
COLOMBIA

conmemoran/conmemorar: they commemorate/to commerorate
sin embargo: nevertheless
marca/marcar: it marks/to mark
en realidad: in fact, actually
inicio: beginning
cuenta/contar: it tells/to tell
se iba a celebrar: was going to be celebrated
partidario: supporter

tienda: store
llamado/llamar: called/to call
prestara/prestar: lend him/to lend
florero: vase
adornar: to decorate
homenajeado: the one who they paid tribute to
monarquía: monarchy
reaccionó/reaccionar: he reacted/to react
de muy mala manera: in a very bad manner
criollos: creoles (of European descent born in a Spanish-American colony)
escuchar: to listen
se puso furioso/ponerse furioso: he became furious/to become furious
le dio una golpiza/dar una golpiza: he hit him/to hit
pelea: fight
aún: still
ilustre rol: illustrious, important role
placa: plaque
se lee/leer: it reads/to read
siguiente: following
se verificó/verificarse: it took place/to take place
reyerta: brawl, fight
entre: between
que dio principio/dar principio: it originated/to originate, to give birth (methaporically)

a pesar del: in spite of
ímpetu: energy
líderes políticos: political leaders
obtuvo/obtener: he obtained/to obtain

El 20 de julio los colombianos **conmemoran** el Día de la Independencia de Colombia. **Sin embargo**, esta fecha **marca en realidad** el **inicio** del proceso de independencia. **Cuenta** la historia que en este día **se iba a celebrar** un banquete en honor a Francisco Villavicencio, **partidario** de la independencia.

Antonio Morales fue a la **tienda** de un español **llamado** González Llorente para que le **prestara** un **florero** con el que **adornar** la mesa del **homenajeado**. Llorente, un fanático de la **monarquía**, **reaccionó de muy mala manera** e insultó a los **criollos**. Al **escuchar** sus insultos, Morales **se puso furioso** y **le dio una golpiza** a Llorente. La **pelea** se extendió por toda la plaza y se comentó por toda la capital. Esta tienda, que **aún** existe en la Plaza de Bolívar en Bogotá, es reconocida por su **ilustre rol** en el proceso de independencia y tiene una **placa** donde **se lee** la **siguiente** inscripción: "En este lugar **se verificó** la **reyerta entre** Morales y Llorente **que dio principio** a la Revolución del 20 de julio".

A pesar del ímpetu que ocasionó el famoso "incidente del florero de Llorente" y la influencia de **líderes políticos** como Antonio Nariño, no fue sino hasta el 7 de agosto de 1819, nueve años más tarde, que Colombia **obtuvo** su independencia con la batalla de Boyacá.

Los patriotas **carecían** de armas o uniformes pero con su determinación y fervor **lograron vencer** al **ejército español**. Bajo el **liderazgo** de Simón Bolívar **se creó** un nuevo estado llamado la Gran Colombia en el cual **se unieron** Venezuela, Panamá, Ecuador y Colombia. Sin embargo, a pesar de que Bolívar **asumió** la presidencia de la Gran Colombia, las **facciones políticas** comenzaron a **destruir** la unión de los países que muchos querían ver convertidos en estados **soberanos**. En el 1830, Venezuela y Ecuador **se convirtieron** en naciones independientes y en 1903 Panamá obtuvo finalmente su independencia.

En la actualidad, y a pesar de los conflictos políticos por los que pasa Colombia, el **pueblo siente gran orgullo** de su **patria**. Las celebraciones para el Día de la Independencia **abundan** en las ciudades del país. **Incluso se efectúan** paradas y **manifestaciones** por la **paz**. **Tanto** para los colombianos que viven en su país, **como** para los que residen en el **extranjero**, el 20 de julio es un día muy especial para **recordar** la creación de la república democrática que **les dio su libertad**.

carecían/carecer: they lacked/to lack
lograron/lograr: they managed/to manage
vencer: to defeat
ejército español: Spanish army
liderazgo: leadership
se creó/crear: was created /to create
se unieron/unir: united/to unite
asumió/asumir: he assumed/to assume
facciones políticas: political factions
destruir: to destroy
soberanos: sovereign
se convirtieron/convertirse: they became/to become

pueblo: people, town
siente gran orgullo/sentir orgullo: he is greatly proud/to be proud
patria: homeland
abundan/abundar: they abound/to abound, to be bountiful
incluso: even
se efectúan/efectuar: they carry out/to carry out
manifestaciones: demonstrations, rallies
paz: peace
tanto...como: both ... and
extranjero: foreigner
recordar: to remember
les dio su libertad: gave them their freedom

Vocabulario de la guerra

las fuerzas aéreas: air force

las fuerzas aliadas: allied forces

el ataque: attack

atacar: to attack

las fuerzas armadas: armed forces

el ejército: army

la batalla: battle

la batería: battery

estar en control: to be in control

sangriento: bloody

la bomba: bomb

bombardear: to bomb

el alto el fuego: cease-fire

el combate: combat

el conflicto: conflict

la muerte: death

destruir: to destroy

el gobierno: government

la granada: grenade

el helicóptero: helicopter

las hostilidades: hostilities

humanitario: humanitarian

derechos humanos: human rights

herir: to wound

herido: wounded

militar: military

la marina: navy

la paz: peace

el/la piloto: pilot

resguardar: to protect against

soldado: soldier

sacudir: to strike, to hit

las tropas: troops

antigüedad: antiquity
pueblos: people
consideraron: they considered/
   to consider
bandera: flag
profundo sentido: deep sense
pedazo de tela: piece of fabric
palo: pole
estandarte: banner
representaba/representar:
   it represented/to represent
pertenencia: belonging
diseño: design
conocemos/conocer: we know/
   to know
sufrió/sufrir: it suffered/to suffer
franjas: stripes
arriba: top, upper part
Patria Vieja: Old Homeland
fue izada/izar: it was hoisted/to hoist
poderes: powers
majestad: majesty
ley: law
fuerza: strength

usarse: to use
se adoptó/adoptar: it was adopted/
   to adopt
reemplazaba/reemplazar: it replaced/
   to replace
sangre vertida: spilled blood
campo de batalla: battlefield
nieve: snow
cordillera: mountain range
limpio: clean, clear
cielo: sky
sin embargo: however, nevertheless
pronto: soon
desapareció/desaparecer:
   disappeared/to disappear

actual: current
comienzos: beginnings
juramento: oath
hoy en día: nowadays
izada/izar: raised/to raise, to hoist
figuran/figurar: they appear/to appear
dispuestos/disponer: arranged/
   to arrange
cuadrado: square
estrella: star
velan/velar: they keep watch over/
   to keep watch over
en la actualidad: at the present time
corresponde: in accordance with
murieron/morir: they died/to die

Un símbolo de la nación
CHILE

Desde la **antigüedad**, los **pueblos consideraron** a la **bandera** como un objeto de **profundo sentido** simbólico y espiritual. La bandera era mucho más que un **pedazo de tela** con un **palo**; era el **estandarte** que **representaba** a la nación, un símbolo de **pertenencia** y de patriotismo. Hasta llegar al **diseño** que hoy **conocemos**, la bandera chilena **sufrió** tres transformaciones. La primera bandera se componía de tres **franjas** horizontales: azul la de **arriba**, blanca la del centro y amarilla la de abajo. Esta es conocida en la historia como la Bandera de la **Patria Vieja** y **fue izada** por primera vez en 1812. Para algunos representaba los tres **poderes** del estado: **majestad**, **ley** y **fuerza**.

En 1814 dejó de **usarse** y Chile estuvo un tiempo sin bandera propia hasta que en 1817 **se adoptó** una nueva insignia llamada Bandera de la Transición. Ésta tenía tres franjas: azul, blanca y roja (la roja **reemplazaba** a la amarilla de la bandera de 1812). Estos colores simbolizaban la **sangre vertida** por los hombres chilenos en el **campo de batalla**; el blanco, la **nieve** de la **cordillera** de los Andes; y el azul, el **limpio cielo** del país. **Sin embargo**, al igual que la de la Patria Vieja, esta bandera no tuvo legalización oficial y **pronto desapareció**.

La bandera **actual** se usó públicamente y por primera vez a **comienzos** de 1818 en la proclamación de la independencia y primer **juramento** de la bandera. **Hoy en día** es **izada** en todas las fiestas patrias. En esta bandera también **figuran** los colores azul, blanco y rojo, aunque **dispuestos** de manera distinta a la anterior: la parte superior con dos colores, azul y blanco, y la parte inferior con un solo color, rojo. El azul forma un **cuadrado**, cuyas dimensiones son un tercio del largo de la franja roja, y en el centro tiene una **estrella** que representa los poderes del Estado que **velan** por la integridad de la patria. **En la actualidad**, el día de la bandera se celebra el 9 de julio y **corresponde** a la conmemoración del Combate de La Concepción de 1882, en el que **murieron** más de 70 chilenos.

La bandera de México
MÉXICO

Las **banderas** son más que un simple **pedazo** de **tela** con colores; son el símbolo del país al que representan. Las banderas son la imagen de la unión de la nación, de sus ideales, de su historia y también de su cultura. **Por este motivo**, el **diseño**, los colores y el **escudo** con que están confeccionadas **son escogidos** para representar **algo específico** e importante de la **patria**.

La bandera mexicana está dividida en tres partes: una verde, una blanca y una roja. Cada color tiene un **significado** especial. La **franja** verde es la de la independencia y la **esperanza**. El centro blanco representa la **pureza** de los ideales de la nación. La parte roja de la bandera representa la **sangre** que los héroes nacionales **han derramado** por la patria. En el centro del área blanca de la bandera mexicana se encuentra el escudo nacional de México, un **águila** sobre un **nopal combatiendo** contra una **serpiente**. Este **emblema** representa la **fuerza** y la historia de México.

La **leyenda cuenta** que un día unos indios aztecas **llegaron** a un gran **valle** donde había una **laguna** con un **islote** pequeño **en el medio**. Allí observaron un águila sobre un nopal **florecido devorando** una **víbora**. Los indígenas tomaron esta imagen como una **señal** de los dioses y, por eso, **construyeron allí** Tenochtitlán, lo que **hoy en día** es la capital del país, México D. F. La bandera mexicana fue creada en 1821 después de la independencia de México. El 24 de febrero es un día nacional de fiesta por lo que se celebran muchos **desfiles** y otros eventos en honor a la bandera.

banderas: flags
pedazo: piece
tela: cloth
por este motivo: for this reason
diseño: design
escudo: coat of arms
son escogidos/escoger: they are chosen/to choose
algo específico: something specific
patria: homeland

significado: meaning
franja: stripe
esperanza: hope
pureza: purity
sangre: blood
han derramado/derramar: they have spilled/to spill
águila: eagle
nopal: prickly pear cactus
combatiendo/combatir: fighting/ to fight
serpiente: snake
emblema: emblem
fuerza: strength

leyenda: legend
cuenta/contar: tells/to tell
llegaron/llegar: they arrived/to arrive
valle: valley
laguna: small lake
islote: islet, small island
en el medio: in the middle
florecido: flowering
devorando/devorar: devouring/ to devour
víbora: viper
señal: sign
construyeron/construir: they built/ to build
allí: there
hoy en día: nowadays
desfiles: parades

San Juan
PUERTO RICO

*"En mi **viejo** San Juan…"* **Así comienza** una **canción famosa** que **se ha convertido** en **himno nacional** ya que **narra** la **angustia** y **esperanza** de quienes **nos encontramos lejos** de la isla.

San Juan, la capital de Puerto Rico, está **llena de** historia, **grabada** en sus **edificios antiguos** y sus **adoquines**. La ciudad original **fue fundada** en 1508 por Juan Ponce de León. **En aquel entonces se le conocía como** "Caparra". Un **año después**, Caparra fue **reubicada** al **oeste** del lugar original. La "ciudad **amurallada**", el viejo San Juan, **nace oficialmente** en 1521, **convirtiéndose** en la ciudad más antigua **bajo** la bandera estadounidense y la **segunda** de las Américas.

El área hoy conocida como San Juan se divide en tres partes: el Viejo San Juan, la playa y el **área hotelera**, aparte de otras comunidades como Río Piedras, Hato Rey y Santurce. Con su población de **cerca de medio millón de habitantes**, la ciudad es el **centro de procesamiento** más grande de la isla y su **puerto** el de más movimiento del Caribe. El puerto de San Juan es el segundo más grande de la región después de Nueva York. Pero, ¿cuál es la magia que esconde esta ciudad? A primera vista el **visitante siente** la influencia inmediata de los **ancestros españoles** aún **caminando** por sus **calles de adoquines**, **teñidos de azul** por el **pasar del tiempo**. Sus edificios coloniales hablan de **siglos lejanos**.

---

viejo: old
así comienza: so it begins
canción famosa: famous song
se ha convertido/convertir: has become/to become, to change
himno nacional: national anthem
narra/narrar: it narrates/to narrate
angustia: anguish
esperanza: hope
nos encontramos/encontrarse: we found ourselves/to find yourself
lejos: far away

llena de: full of
grabada: engraved
edificios antiguos: old buildings
adoquines: cobblestones
fue fundada/fundar: it was founded/to found
en aquel entonces: at that time
se le conocía como: it was known as
año después: year after
reubicada: relocated
oeste: west
amurallada: walled
nace/nacer: is born/to be born
oficialmente: officially
convirtiéndose: becoming
bajo: under
segunda: second

área hotelera: hotel area
cerca de medio millón de habitantes: nearly a half million inhabitants
centro de procesamiento: processing center
puerto: port, harbor
visitante: visitor
siente/sentir: he feels/to feel
ancestros españoles: Spanish ancestors
caminando/caminar: walking/to walk
calles de adoquines: cobblestone streets
teñidos de azul: dyed blue
pasar del tiempo: passing of time
siglos lejanos: centuries past

Estas estructuras son las que **rodean** las plazas donde jóvenes y adultos aún **se reúnen** a hablar, **escuchar** su música favorita o jugar un **partido de dominó**.

Entre las plazas preferidas de los puertorriqueños están la Plaza de San José, con su **estatua de bronce** en honor a Juan Ponce de León, La Plaza del Quinto Centenario, **celebrando** los 500 años del **descubrimiento** del **Nuevo Mundo** y la Plaza de Armas, con cuatro estatuas que representan las cuatro estaciones del año. **Yo prefiero** la Plazoleta de la Rogativa por el significado que **encierra**.

Se dice que en 1797 la **flota** británica llegó a la Bahía de San Juan para **atacar** y tomar posesión de la isla. Al verse **amenazados**, el gobernador **ordenó** una **rogativa** para **pedir la ayuda** de los santos. Las mujeres **organizaron** una procesión **repentina**. Caminaron por las calles de la ciudad **cargando antorchas** y **tocando campanas**. Ante la conmoción, los británicos **se retiraron pensando** que habían llegado **refuerzos**. Desde entonces **quedó demostrada** la **voluntad** y **valentía** de un pueblo cuando **se trata** de defender **lo suyo**.

San Juan también **cuenta con** infinidad de **parques** y **fortalezas**. Entre las mas conocidas se encuentra El Morro, con sus seis **niveles** a 140 pies sobre el **nivel del mar**. Esta **asombrosa** estructura es en realidad un **laberinto de túneles**, **calabozos**, **barracas** y rampas, rodeadas por las famosas **garitas** que se han convertido en símbolo nacional. A esto **se unen** las catedrales, los teatros y los museos donde se exhíbe la vida, historia, cultura y evolución de un pueblo, **mezcla de sangre** taína, española y africana.

Esto es San Juan de Puerto Rico, una ciudad antigua, rodeada de belleza natural. Este es el lugar a donde millones de puertorriqueños **esperan volver** algún día **cantando** la melodía de... *En mi viejo San Juan.*

Las ruinas de Tiwanaku
BOLIVIA

Parece mentira que luego de **tantos siglos**, tantos **sucesos** y tanta historia, parte de las ruinas de Tiwanaku **siga en pie**. **Si bien** el hombre **tuvo que ver** en su reconstrucción y posterior protección, **pasaron años**, décadas y hasta siglos para que estas cenizas **resurgieran** de sus **cenizas**.

Se trata de una antiquísima civilización cuyos **restos** aún **permanecen** en **forma megalítica** con inscripciones de símbolos que **todavía** hoy **siguen sin descifrar**. Según estudios arqueológicos **se calcula** que el origen de esta cultura **se remonta** al año 1600 AC.

Esta ciudad **desaparecida**, cuyas **milenarias** ruinas han sido **restauradas** en parte, está a sólo 72 kilómetros de la ciudad de La Paz, muy cerca del Lago Titicaca. Poco **se sabe** de ella y de su civilización, aunque historiadores y arqueólogos coinciden en que fue un gran centro urbano **sustentado** por un sofisticado sistema de agricultura en **terrazas** para producir **alimentos**, que **permitía satisfacer** las necesidades de consumo de toda esta ciudadela a semejante altura. También **destaca** por ser una metrópolis del **conocimiento** y de las ciencias ya que su pueblo, la cultura aymara, construyó monumentales **edificios** y templos con **grandísimos bloques de piedra orientados** de forma astronómica, perfeccionaron la técnica de la **momificación** y realizaron **hazañas sorprendentes** en el **campo de la medicina**.

Actualmente las ruinas de Tiwanaku están declaradas Patrimonio Histórico de la Humanidad por la UNESCO y están consideradas un **templo vivo** y un centro ceremonial por los descendientes del pueblo aymara, quienes todos los años **se dan cita** en el lugar para **rendir culto** o simplemente para **agradecer** y **acompañar** a sus ancestros. Y **no debe** ser casual que *Tiwanaku*, en **idioma** aymara, **quiera decir** "Ciudad de Dioses".

---

parece mentira: it seems unbelievable
tantos siglos: so many centuries
sucesos: events
siga en pie: it is still standing
si bien: even though
tuvo que ver: it had to do with
pasaron años/pasar (el tiempo): years went by/to go by
resurgieran/resurgir: they would revive/to revive
cenizas: ashes

se trata/tratarse: it is about/to be about
restos: remains
permanecen/permanecer: they remain/to remain
forma megalítica: megalithic form
todavía: still
siguen/seguir: they continue/ to continue
sin descifrar: not to decipher
se calcula/calcular: it is calculated/ to calculate
se remonta/remontarse: it goes back/ to go back, to date back

desaparecida/desaparecer: disappeared/to disappear
milenarias: thousand-year-old
restauradas/restaurar: restored/ to restore
se sabe/saber: it is known/to know
sustentado/sustentar: supported/ to support
terrazas: terraces
alimentos: food
permitía satisfacer: it allowed to meet
destaca/destacar: it stands out/ to stand out
conocimiento: knowledge
edificios: buildings
grandísimos: huge
bloques de piedra: stone blocks
orientados/orientar: oriented/to orient
momificación: mummification
hazañas: feats
sorprendentes: astonishing
campo de la medicina: field of medicine

templo vivo: live temple
se dan cita: they agree to meet
rendir culto: to worship
agradecer: to thank
acompañar: to accompany
no debe/deber: it must not/must
idioma: language
quiera decir/querer decir: means/ to mean
Ciudad de dioses: City of Gods

Una pieza de historia
HONDURAS

Se dice que hay evidencia de que existieron **tribus** maya en el oeste de Honduras. Pero fue Cristóbal Colón en 1502 quien primero **visitó** Trujillo y llamó al país Honduras debido a la **profundidad** del agua en la costa caribeña. La **herencia indígena** de Honduras está simbolizada por el nombre Lempira (**caballero** de las montañas), uno de los héroes nacionales **debido a** la batalla que organizó en los 1530 **contra** los españoles. Debido a la manera cruel en que **mataron** a Lempira, los hondureños **lo honraron** dándole ese nombre a su **moneda nacional.** Los españoles **llegaron** en 1525 y **denominaron** a Comayagua la capital en 1537. Fue 350 años más tarde, en 1880, cuando Tegucigalpa **se convirtió** en la capital. Debido al **oro** y la **plata encontrados** en Trujillo, holandeses y británicos **saquearon** la zona, y **no fue sino hasta** 1787 que los españoles **volvieron** a reclamar su espacio concentrándose en la zona central mientras los británicos **se enfocaron** en las costas.

En 1821 **se otorgó** la independencia a Honduras; luego de ser parte de México brevemente, **se unió** a la Federación Centro Americana. El conflicto entre liberales y conservadores llevó a Honduras a declararse nación independiente en 1838. **Desde ese entonces** ha habido **lucha de poderes**, cientos de **golpes de estado**, rebeliones e irregularidades electorales. Uno de los casos más relevantes fue de los americanos que **trataron** de **manera fallida** de obtener el control de Honduras en 1850. En 1913 los **bananos** eran el 66 por ciento de los productos de exportación del país, siendo el 75 por ciento de compañías americanas. En 1969 Honduras y El Salvador tuvieron una **guerra** (la Guerra del Fútbol) que **duró** 100 horas pero que **afectó** las relaciones entre estos **países vecinos.** En los años 80 Honduras fue **asilo** para los **Contra** cuando los sandinistas **derrocaron** al dictador nicaragüense. Tiempo después, el gobierno examinó el rol de la **base militar estadounidense, se negó** a **firmar** un **acuerdo, despidió** a los Contra de Honduras y Violeta Chamorro ganó las elecciones de Nicaragua en 1990.

se dice/decir: it is said/to say
tribus: tribes
visitó/visitar: he visited/to visit
profundidad: depth
herencia indígena: indigenous heritage
caballero: knight, horseman
debido a: due to
contra: against
mataron/matar: they killed/to kill
lo honraron/honrar: they honored him/to honor him
moneda nacional: national currency
llegaron/llegar: they arrived/to arrive
denominaron/denominar: they named/to name
se convirtió/convertirse: it was turned into/to turn into
oro: gold
plata: silver
encontrados: found
saquearon/saquear: they plundered/to plunder
no fue sino hasta: it was not until
volvieron/volver: they returned/to return
se enfocaron/enfocar: they focused/to focus

se otorgó/otorgar: it was granted/to grant
se unió/unirse: it joined/to join
desde ese entonces: since then
lucha de poderes: power struggle
golpes de estado: coups d'état
trataron/tratar: they tried/to try
manera fallida: unsuccessful way
bananos: bananas
guerra: war
duró/durar: it lasted/to last
afectó/afectar: it affected/to affect
países vecinos: neighboring countries
asilo: asylum
Contra: Somoza's National Guard
derrocaron/derrocar: they overthrew/to overthrow
base militar estadounidense: United States military base
se negó/negarse: he refused/to refuse
firmar: to sign
acuerdo: agreement
despidió/despedir: he fired/to fire

ha oído/oír: everybody has heard/ to hear
judíos: Jews
habitaron/habitar: they lived/to live
todavía: still
suelo: land
sin embargo: however
pocos: few
nos acercamos/acercarse: we get closer/to get closer

comienza/comenzar: it starts/to start
a principios: at the beginning
en ese entonces: then, at that time
fueron invadidos/invadir: they were invaded/to invade
conquistados/conquistar: conquered/ to conquer
territorio: land
llevaban/llevar: they took/to take
esclavos: slaves
naufragaron/naufragar: they were wrecked/to be shipwrecked
isla: island
pelearon/pelear: they fought/to fight
los unos contra los otros: one against the other
con el paso del tiempo: as time went by
aprendieron/aprender: they learned/ to learn
convivir: to live together
matrimonios: marriages
mixtos: mixed
así: this way
integrantes: members
fueron/ser: they were/to be
llamados/llamar: called/to call
desciende/descender: it descends from/to descend from

más adelante: further on
se apoderaron/apoderarse: they took possession/to take possession
pasó a ser/pasar a ser: it became/ to become
ayudados/ayudar: helped/to help
trataron de/tratar de: they tried to/to try to
mantener: to keep
aunque: even though
sin éxito: without success

Los garifunas
BELICE

Todo el mundo **ha oído** hablar alguna vez de los mayas, los aztecas, los **judíos**, los afroamericanos o de tantas otras culturas que **habitaron** algún día, y **todavía** lo hacen, **suelo** americano. **Sin embargo**, **pocos** conocen la cultura garifuna. En estas líneas **nos acercamos** a ella.

La historia de los garifunas **comienza a principios** del año 1600 en la isla de San Vicente, en el Caribe oriental, habitada **en ese entonces** por los indios arawaks. Estos **fueron invadi-**  **dos** y **conquistados** por otra tribu procedente de **territorio** norteamericano, los kalipunas, que asesinaron a los hombres arawaks y tomaron a sus mujeres como esposas. En 1635, dos buques españoles que **llevaban esclavos** nigerianos **naufraga- ron** cerca de la **isla**. Al principio, españoles, nigerianos y kali- punas **pelearon los unos contra los otros**, pero **con el paso del tiempo aprendieron** a **convivir** y se realizaron **matrimo- nios mixtos**, formándose **así** la comunidad garifuna. Sus **inte- grantes fueron** también **llamados** "caribes negros" (la palabra garifuna **desciende** probablemente del kalipuna).

Más adelante, los ingleses **se apoderaron** de San Vicente por lo que **pasó a ser** una colonia británica. Los "caribes negros", **ayudados** por los franceses, **trataron de mantener** el control independiente de la isla, **aunque sin éxito**.

En 1796, **ambos** "caribes" y franceses **se rindieron**. Los británicos deportaron a los caribes y **los dejaron** en la Isla de Roatán, **frente a** la costa de Honduras.

Los españoles, **arrebatando** la Isla de Roatán, **liberaron** a los garifunas de manos inglesas y **los llevaron** a trabajar a Trujillo, en el centro de España, como **agricultores** y en el **ejército**. Los primeros garifunas que llegaron a la costa de Belice fueron llevados por los españoles, a principios de 1800. **Al tiempo**, Belice fue ayudada por los británicos, quienes la llamaron la "Honduras británica". Los caribes que **continuaban** sirviendo en el ejército español se fueron moviendo **poco a poco hacia** el área de la "Honduras Británica" hasta que, después de la independencia centroamericana, un gran número de garifunas **huyó** hacia la costa de Belice. El 19 de noviembre se conmemora el Día del Acuerdo Garifuna, la mayor fiesta de esta comunidad.

A lo largo de todo el siglo XX, y **de forma gradual**, esta cultura **se esparció**, primero, por toda la costa de Belice y, **posteriormente**, por todo el mundo. Esto **dio como resultado** el **asentamiento** de pequeñas comunidades garifunas en otros lugares como Los Angeles, Nueva Orleans o Nueva York.

Su historia de **lucha** y trabajo ha hecho que la comunidad garifuna se caracterice, sobre todo, por su **fuerza** y su **voluntad** para **conseguir** lo que **se propone** y por defender lo propio. **Será por eso** que hoy la mayoría de ellos mantiene su música, su baile, su lengua, su religión y sus costumbres. **A pesar de** que esta cultura **se expandió** hacia otras ciudades y países, la mayor parte del pueblo garifuno reside todavía en Belice, un país donde **se entremezclan** culturas, lenguas y grupos étnicos que **conviven** en **armonía**, tolerancia y solidaridad.

ambos: both
se rindieron/rendirse: they surrendered/to surrender
los dejaron/dejar: they left them/ to leave
frente a: in front of

arrebatando/arrebatar: snatching/ to snatch
liberaron/liberar: releasing/to release, to free
los llevaron/llevar: they took them/ to take
agricultores: farmers
ejército: army
al tiempo: at the same time
continuaban/continuar: they kept/ to keep
poco a poco: little by little
hacia: towards
huyó/huir: they got away/to get away

de forma gradual: gradually
se esparció/esparcir: it was scattered/ to scatter
posteriormente: later
dio como resultado/dar: it gave as a result/to give
asentamiento: settlement

lucha: struggle
fuerza: strength
voluntad: willingness
conseguir: to reach
se propone/proponerse: (the community) intends/to intend
será por eso: maybe that is why
a pesar de: in spite of
se expandió/expandirse: it spread/ to spread
se entremezclan/entremezclarse: they mix/to mix, to mingle
conviven/convivir: they live/to live
armonía: harmony

Historia de la Virgen de Guadalupe
MÉXICO

Al norte de la actual Ciudad de México **se encuentra** el **cerro** del Tepeyac. **Se dice** que en **tiempos** prehispánicos **se veneraba** en ese **lugar** a una **diosa** indígena **llamada** Tonantzin, a quien **se consideraba** la madre de los dioses.

Tras la conquista, los **españoles establecieron** la capital de la Nueva España en **lo que fuera** la **antigua ciudad** de México-Tenochtitlán. Ésta **se conectaba** al cerro Tepeyac **por medio** de una **calzada**.

En el **siglo XVI se comenzaron a escribir** en **lengua** náhuatl, el **idioma** de los nahuas o aztecas, **millares** de **cantos**, **discursos**, narraciones y textos en general que **reflejaban** el **pensamiento** y la forma de expresión indígena.

Un ejemplo de estas **obras** es el Nican mopohua, un texto escrito en 1556 que **refiere** las **apariciones** de la Virgen de Guadalupe en el **mismo** cerro del Tepeyac. El texto **narra** el **encuentro entre** una noble señora de indescriptible **belleza** quien **se presenta a sí misma** como "la madrecita del dios verdadero, dador de la **vida**, inventor de la **gente**" y un **sencillo jornalero** llamado Juan Diego.

El texto pone como **fecha** de las apariciones el año de 1531. **Haciendo uso de** un hermoso lenguaje poético **lleno de** metáforas y **palabras** yuxtapuestas, **propio de** los **sabios** y **sacerdotes** del **antiguo mundo** náhuatl, **describe con lujo de detalle** los encuentros entre Santa María y Juan Diego.

se encuentra/encontrarse: is/to be (located, in a place)
cerro: hill
se dice/decir: it is said/to say
tiempos: times
se veneraba/venerar: was worshipped/ to worship, to venerate, to revere
lugar: place
diosa: goddess
llamada/llamar: called/to call
se consideraba/considerar: was considered/to consider

tras: after
españoles: Spaniards
establecieron/establecer: established/ to establish
lo que fuera: in what used to be
antigua ciudad: old city
se conectaba/conectar: connected/ to connect
por medio: through
calzada: road

siglo XVI: 16th century
se comenzaron a escribir: (they) started to write
lengua: language, tongue
idioma: language
millares: thousands
cantos: chants, songs, poems
discursos: speeches
reflejaban/reflejar: reflected/to reflect
pensamiento: thought, thinking

obras: works
refiere/referir: relates/to relate
apariciones: apparitions, appearances
mismo: same
narra/narrar: narrates/to narrate
encuentro: encounter
entre: between
belleza: beauty
se presenta a sí misma: introduces herself
vida: life
gente: people
sencillo jornalero: simple day laborer

fecha: date
haciendo uso de: using, making use of
lleno de: full of
palabras: words
propio de: typical of
sabios: wise men, sages
sacerdotes: priests
antiguo mundo: old world
describe/describir: describes/to describe
con lujo de detalle: in lots of detail

La virgen **deseaba** que **se le construyera** un templo en el cerro del Tepeyac para **desde ahí poder escuchar** el **llanto** de la gente, **protegerla** y **socorrerla** en sus **necesidades**. **Eligió** a Juan Diego como emisario ante el **obispo** de México. **Debido al** origen humilde de Juan Diego, el obispo **no dio** mucha credibilidad a sus palabras, pero **tras cierta** insistencia **le solicitó** una **señal**.

Tras ser informada del **hecho**, la virgen **pidió** a Juan Diego que **subiera** al cerro **para cortar** unas **flores**. El **terreno** era abrupto y árido y nada **crecía** allí, **menos aún** en esa época del año. Pero Juan Diego encontró el lugar **cubierto** de fragantes rosas y se las **llevó** a la virgen envueltas en su túnica. Tras **tocarlas** con sus **manos**, ella le pidió que las presentara al obispo. Cuando Juan Diego **abrió** su túnica **frente** al obispo **para mostrarle** las flores, **apareció** en la túnica misma, la imagen de la virgen. Dicho **milagro tuvo** tal efecto en el obispo, que éste inició de inmediato los **trabajos** de construcción del templo en el lugar **solicitado**.

Ya para mediados del siglo XVI, **algunos religiosos** se encontraban **muy consternados** por la relación que **se había establecido** entre la diosa indígena Tonantzin y la virgen, a quien **se la conocía como** Nuestra Señora de Guadalupe. La relación era tan evidente que los **nombres** a veces **se mezclaban** en Tonantzin Guadalupe. La influencia y devoción por la imagen **colocada** en el templo del Tepeyac eran ya tan grandes que **no hubo nada que hacer** al respecto.

La imagen de quien se conoce hoy como la Virgen de Guadalupe **se sigue venerando actualmente** en el Tepeyac. A través de los siglos, ella se ha convertido en símbolo de inspiración religioso, libertario, artístico e **incluso** de identidad nacional para México.

---

deseaba/desear: wanted/to want
se le construyera: was built (for her)
desde ahí: from there
poder escuchar: to be able to listen
llanto: cry
protegerla: protect them
socorrerla: help them
necesidades: needs
eligió/elegir: chose/to choose
obispo: bishop
debido al: due to
no dio/dar: didn't give/to give
tras cierta: after a certain
le solicitó: requested
señal: sign

hecho: incident
pidió/pedir: asked/to ask
subiera/subir: climb/to climb
para cortar: to cut
flores: flowers
terreno: land, piece of land
crecía/crecer: grew/to grow
menos aún: less so
cubierto: covered
llevó/llevar: took/to take
tocarlas: touching them
manos: hands
abrió/abrir: opened/to open
frente: in front of
para mostrarle: to show him
apareció/aparecer: appeared/to appear
milagro: miracle
tuvo/tener: had/to have
trabajos: works
solicitado: requested

ya para mediados: already towards mid-
algunos: some
religiosos: priests, members of a religious order
muy consternados: very worried
se había establecido/establecer: had been established/to establish
se la conocía como: was known as
nombres: names
se mezclaban/mezclar: got mixed/ to mix
colocada: placed
no hubo nada que hacer: there was nothing to be done

se sigue/seguir: continues to be/ to continue
venerando: venerated
actualmente: today
incluso: even

Viaje a una ciudad histórica de Uruguay

En el **ignorado norte** uruguayo, está el departamento de Tacuarembó. En **lengua** guaraní, "Tacuarembó" **quiere decir** "**río** de los juncos o cañaverales". Este departamento con forma de triángulo con base en el Río Negro es, **por lejos**, el más grande del **país**.

Historia y cultura: tango y **tren**

Tacuarembó **ha reclamado** un **lugar** en la muy controversial biografía del famosísimo **cantante** de tangos Carlos Gardel. Una de las versiones de la biografía **dice** que el **cantante nació** en una **estancia** en las **afueras** de la capital. Por esa **razón existe allí** el **Museo** Carlos Gardel. Inaugurado **hace** poco más de una década, **exhibe** documentos que **apoyarían** la versión del **nacimiento** de este **personaje** del tango.

En las afueras de la capital departamental también **se abrió** el Hotel Carlos Gardel. **Aprovechado** la controversia y el **reclamo** que **hace** Tacuarembó de ser la **cuna** de Gardel, **se creó** este hotel temático. **Decorado con ropas**, **joyas**, accesorios, **libros**, fotos y **afiches** del cantante y muchos otros elementos de **principios** del **siglo** XX, el hotel es un **homenaje** a Gardel y a todo **lo relacionado** al tango. **Incluso** las **habitaciones** están identificadas con los títulos de **canciones** de tango **muy conocidas**.

ignorado: ignored, disregarded
norte: north
lengua: tongue, language
quiere decir: means
río: river
por lejos: by far
país: country

tren: train
ha reclamado/reclamar: has claimed/ to claim
lugar: place
cantante: singer
dice/decir: says/to say
cantante: singer
nació/nacer: was born/to be born
estancia: ranch
afueras: outskirts
razón: reason
existe/existir: exists/to exist, to be
allí: there
museo: museum
hace: ago
exhibe/exhibir: exhibits/ to exhibit, to display
apoyarían/apoyar: would support/ to support
nacimiento: birth
personaje: celebrity, personality

se abrió/abrir: was opened/ to open
aprovechado: taking advantage of
reclamo: demand, claim
hace/hacer: makes/to make
cuna: cradle
se creó/crear: was created/ to create
decorado con/decorar: decorated with/to decorate
ropas: clothes
joyas: jewelry
libros: books
afiches: posters
principios: beginnings
siglo: century
homenaje: tribute
lo relacionado: related
incluso: even
habitaciones: rooms
canciones: songs
muy conocidas: well-known

La capital es una **ciudad pequeña** y modesta, pero otro punto de interés turístico es la **estación de trenes** que **se ha conservado** como era a **mediados** del siglo **pasado**. Fue allí que **se filmó** parte de la **película** "Corazón de fuego", también **conocida como** "**El último tren**". Esta co-producción uruguaya-española-argentina que **ganó premios** en el exterior, es una *road movie* con una locomotora como protagonista.

El **entorno** natural: **frescura** y **verdor**

A sólo unos 20 y tantos kilómetros de la ciudad **se encuentra** una **hermosa** zona natural conocida como el Valle Edén. La atracción **radica** en la vegetación autóctona y los **bellos paisajes** de **campos** decorados con **piedras**, **cerros**, ríos y **arroyos**. Allí **se puede visitar** un **salto de agua** que termina en un **pozo llamado** Pozo Hondo. Es posible **quedarse acampando** u **optar por alojarse** en la Posada Valle Edén, que también tiene restaurante.

Aún **más cerca** de la ciudad, está el Balneario Iporá. En ese parque se pueden **disfrutar** diferentes tipos de **playas**, dos **lagos artificiales** y otras instalaciones **para nadar** y **acampar**. Cuando **arrecia** el **calor** en **verano**, es una de las escapadas favoritas de los **lugareños**. El nombre Iporá también es de origen guaraní y significa "agua hermosa".

En una extensión de pocos quilómetros el **visitante puede recorrer** todas estas atracciones y disfrutar de **saber** que **ha sido de los pocos** en **descubrir** este **rincón** del Uruguay.

---

ciudad pequeña: small city
estación de trenes: train station
se ha conservado/conservar: has been maintained/to maintain
mediados: mid-
pasado: last
se filmó/filmar: was filmed/to film
película: movie
conocida como: known as
el último tren: the last train
ganó/ganar: won/to win
premios: awards

entorno: surroundings
frescura: freshness
verdor: greenness

se encuentra/encontrar: finds itself/ to find
hermosa: beautiful
radica/radicar: lies in/ to lie in
bellos paisajes: beautiful landscape
campos: fields
piedras: stones, rocks
cerros: hills
arroyos: creeks
se puede visitar: can be visited
salto de agua: spring, waterfall
pozo: well
llamado: called
quedarse acampando: to stay camping
optar por alojarse: to opt to stay

más cerca: closer
disfrutar: to enjoy
playas: beaches
lagos artificiales: artificial lakes
para nadar: to swim
acampar: to camp
arrecia/arreciar: intensifies/ to intensify, to get worse
calor: heat
verano: summer
lugareños: locals

visitante: visitor
puede recorrer: can visit
saber: knowing
ha sido/ser: has been/to be
de los pocos: among the few ones
descubrir: to discover
rincón: corner

Examina tu comprensión

El cinco de mayo, página 168

1. El Cinco de Mayo se celebra en todo México, pero especialmente ¿en qué ciudad?

2. Muchas personas creen que el Cinco de Mayo es el Día de la Independencia mexicana. ¿El verdadero Día de la Independencia cuándo es?

3. ¿Qué evento conmemora el Cinco de Mayo?

Los hijos del sol, página 170

1. ¿En qué siglo fueron invadidos los incas y por quién?

2. La leyenda de Cuzco describe la ciudad ¿como qué?

3. En 1526 el Imperio fue dividido, lo que dio lugar ¿a qué evento?

La independencia de Colombia, página 174

1. ¿Qué se iba a celebrar el 20 de julio?

2. ¿Cuántos años después de este evento llegó realmente la independencia a Colombia?

3. ¿Bajo el mando de quién fue obtenida la libertad?

Un símbolo de la nación, página 176

1. La bandera de Chile es más que un pedazo de tela. ¿Qué representa para la nación?

2. ¿Qué representan las tres franjas horizontales?

3. ¿Qué representa cada uno de los tres colores?

Test your comprehension

La bandera de México, página 177

1. Lista el significado de cada color de la bandera mexicana.

2. ¿Cuál es el emblema de la bandera mexicana y qué representa?

3. ¿Cuándo fue creada la bandera?

San Juan, página 178

1. ¿Quien fundó San Juan y cuál era el nombre original de la ciudad?

2. ¿Cuál es la plaza favorita de la ciudad y qué puede encontrar allí?

3. En 1797, la ciudad estaba bajo ataque. ¿Qué hicieron las mujeres de la ciudad?

Las ruinas de Tiwanaku, página 180

1. ¿Por qué los historiadores y arqueólogos piensan que este área podría haber sido un gran centro urbano?

2. ¿Qué maravillas científicas fueron descubiertas allí?

3. El pueblo aymara considera el área un templo ¿con qué objetivo?

Los garifunas, página 182

1. ¿Cómo se formó la comunidad garifuna?

2. ¿Quiénes liberaron a los garifunas de los ingleses?

3. A pesar de las luchas de los garifunas, la fuerza de su comunidad les ayudó a mantener ¿qué cinco elementos de su cultura?

La tierra que no es labrada llevará abrojos y espinas aunque sea fértil; así es el entendimiento del hombre.

Santa Teresa de Jesús

Geografía

El Parque Nacional Darién
PANAMÁ

Panamá es **reconocido mundialmente** por **poseer** su capital **rodeada** de **bosques tropicales caracterizados** por la **riqueza** de su biodiversidad. Es que en este país de América Central es posible **acceder** a parques nacionales a **tan sólo** 10 minutos del área urbana. La variedad de plantas y animales que **habitan** allí es difícil de **encontrar** en otras latitudes del mundo, y su abundancia y diversidad **ha imposibilitado** una **clasificación científica definitiva**.

El **mejor ejemplo** del exuberante y **complejo** ecosistema panameño **se encuentra** en la provincia de Darién, **ubicada** en el **extremo oriental** del país. El Parque Nacional Darién **fue creado** en 1980 y **constituye no sólo** el mayor parque del país, **sino** de toda Centroamérica. En 1981 la UNESCO declaró a este paraíso tropical Patrimonio Mundial de la Humanidad por el **valor** de su **ambiente diversificado** y por la riqueza cultural de las tribus aborígenes que allí habitan.

El área protegida del Parque Nacional Darién **atraviesa casi toda** la Provincia y **abarca** desde las costas del Pacífico hasta casi la costa del Mar Caribe. **A lo largo de** esta **superficie** de aproximadamente 579.000 hectáreas, un **manto forestal** de **bosques húmedos** tropicales **definen** el paisaje. **Precisamente**, es en este parque donde nacen los ríos Tuira, Balsas, Sambú y Jaque que luego **recorren** todo el territorio.

La **cordillera** y las **serranías** de la zona son de origen volcánico por lo que resulta interesante observar **piedras** y sedimentos de lava que dan cuenta de la intensa actividad de estos **gigantes de fuego** a lo largo del tiempo.

---

reconocido mundialmente: recognized worldwide

poseer: to have

rodeada/rodear: it is surrounded/ to surround

bosques tropicales: tropical forests

caracterizados: characterized

riqueza: wealth, richness

acceder: to access

tan sólo: just, only

habitan/habitar: they live/to live

encontrar: to find

ha imposibilitado: it has prevented/ to prevent

clasificación científica definitiva: definitive scientific classification

mejor ejemplo: best example

complejo: complex

se encuentra/econtrar: it is found/ to find

ubicada: located

extremo oriental: furthest eastern region

fue creado/crear: was created/to create

constituye/constituir: it constitutes/ to constitute

no sólo...sino: not only ... but also

valor: value

ambiente diversificado: diversified environment

atraviesa/atravesar: it goes over/ to go over

casi toda: almost all

abarca/abarcar: it spans/to span

a lo largo de: along

superficie: surface

manto forestal: forest mantle

bosques húmedos: humid forests

definen/definir: they define/to define

precisamente: precisely

recorren/recorrer: they go through/ to go through

cordillera: mountain range

serranías: mountainous areas

piedras: rocks

gigantes de fuego: giants of fire

Como se ha mencionado, también la riqueza cultural caracteriza al Parque Nacional Darién. En la región habitan tres grupos indígenas precolombinos: los Kunas, que **mantienen** poblaciones tradicionales al **pie** de la montaña **sagrada** Cerro Tarcuna; los Emberá, que **moran** en la **ribera** del Chocó; y los Wounaan, muy **cercanos** lingüísticamente y culturalmente a los Emberá. No obstante, también **cabe destacar** la presencia de poblaciones **afrodarienitas**. Estos grupos de **ascendencia** africana **han convivido** durante siglos con los indígenas de la región **creando** un mosaico etnocultural sin precedentes en Centroamérica.

A pesar de la riqueza y reconocimiento mundial del parque, los expertos de la zona **sostienen** que los **esfuerzos** para preservarlo **no han sido suficientes**. Entre los factores que lo **amenazan** se pueden **mencionar** el **avance de la agricultura**, el **manejo** poco responsable de las concesiones forestales, la **cacería** y la **pesca**, los residuos tóxicos, la introducción de especies **no originarias** y los **conflictos armados** del **país vecino**, Colombia.

Para la conservación de la diversidad de la región, los científicos **indican** que es **imprescindible** la regulación y control de la actividad agropecuaria y forestal y la **realización** y **profundización** de estudios de **impacto ambiental** y cultural **antes de proceder** a incorporar infraestructuras que podrían **alterar** el ecosistema.

Sin lugar a duda, la **estratégica ubicación** de este **pulmón** vegetal del Caribe lo convierte en un lugar de encuentro entre la riqueza natural y cultural de América Central y América del Sur. **¿Sabremos preservarla?**

mantienen/mantener: they maintain/ to maintain
pie: foot
sagrada: sacred
moran/morar: they live/to live
ribera: banks, riverside
cercanos: close
cabe destacar: it is worth pointing out
afrodarienitas: population of African descent from the Darien area
ascendencia: ancestry
han convivido/convivir: they have lived together/to live together
creando/crear: creating/to create

a pesar de: in spite of
sostienen/sostener: they maintain/ to maintain
esfuerzos: efforts
no han sido suficientes: they have not been enough
amenazan/amenazar: they threaten/ to threaten
mencionar: to mention
avance de la agricultura: advances of agriculture
manejo: management
cacería: hunting
pesca: fishing
no originarias: not originally from there
conflictos armados: armed conflicts
país vecino: neighboring country

indican/indicar: they indicate/ to indicate
imprescindible: essential
realización: carrying out
profundización: deepening
impacto ambiental: environmental impact
antes de proceder: before proceeding
alterar: to alter, change

sin lugar a duda: without a doubt
estratégica ubicación: strategic location
pulmón: lung
¿Sabremos preservarla?: Will we know how to preserve it?

Las islas Galápagos: The Galapagos
 Islands

localizadas/localizar: located/to locate

millas: miles

emergieron/emerger: they emerged/
 to emerge

como resultado de: as the result of

erupciones volcánicas submarinas:
 submarine volcanic eruptions

edades más antiguas: ancient period

sureste: southeast

edades más recientes: more recent
 period

noroeste: northwest

seis de los cuales: six of which

unidos formando: united forming

estas islas tienen una edad: these
 islands have an age

archipiélago: archipelago (a group of
 islands)

fue descubierto/descubrir: was
 discovered/to discover

obispo: Bishop

dio/dan: gave/to give

semejanza: similarity

caparazones: shells

tortugas: turtles

montura: saddle

silla: chair

cabalgar de mujeres: women to ride

fueron los primeros: were first

frecuentar: to frequent

era un lugar excelente: it was an
 excellent place

recuperarse: to recuperate

heridas: wounds

arreglar: to repair or fix

naves: ships

buscar agua: look for water

toma posesión: took possesion

derecho geográfico e histórico:
 geographic and historic right

Las islas Galápagos
ECUADOR

Las islas Galápagos están **localizadas** a 965 kilómetros (650 **millas**) de la costa del Ecuador. Las islas Galápagos **emergieron** del Océano Pacífico hace unos 6 millones de años **como resultado de erupciones volcánicas submarinas**. Las **edades más antiguas** de las islas están al **sureste**, mientras que las **edades más recientes** están al **noroeste**, donde también se encuentra toda la actividad volcánica, con ocho volcanes activos, **seis de los cuales** están **unidos formando** la isla Isabela, uno en la isla Fernandina y otro en la isla Marchena, **estas islas tienen una edad** de tres a cinco millones de años.

El **archipiélago fue descubierto** en 1535 por el **obispo** Fray Tomás de Berlanga, quien le **dio** el nombre de "Islas de los Galápagos" por la **semejanza** de los **caparazones** de las **tortugas** Galápagos con la **montura** o **silla** para **cabalgar de mujeres** de la época. Los piratas **fueron los primeros** en **frecuentar** las islas por 200 años pues este archipiélago **era un lugar excelente** para **recuperarse** de las **heridas** después de los combates, **arreglar** sus **naves** y **buscar agua** y comida para sus nuevos combates.

En el año 1832 el Ecuador **toma posesión** del archipiélago de Galápagos por **derecho geográfico e histórico**.

En el año 1835 llegó Charles Darwin para hacer investigaciones **para sus escritos** de la teoría del "Origen de las Especies" ya que las islas Galápagos eran el **escenario perfecto** para **comprender** los **cambios evolutivos** de las especies. Las islas Galápagos fueron declaradas Parque Nacional por **el gobierno** de Ecuador en 1936 para preservar la flora y la fauna de las trece islas más grandes, seis islas menores y más de cuarenta islas pequeñas **que conforman** el archipiélago.

En 1959 **se crea** la Fundación Charles Darwin para las islas Galápagos, **creada bajo los auspicios** de la UNESCO y de la Unión Mundial para Conservación. Esta fundación está dedicada a la conservación de los ecosistemas de Galápagos. La flora y la fauna **únicas** de las islas Galápagos **se deben a** diferentes factores como: el origen volcánico, la distancia **hacia el continente**, la dirección de los **vientos** y la **confluencia de** las **corrientes marinas** en donde se produce un **curioso fenómeno**: las aguas del norte son más calientes que la del sur (unos cinco grados centígrados) por lo que hace que en el norte **haya más vida marina**.

La fauna que se puede encontrar en estas islas es **la siguiente**: iguanas marinas, **leones marinos**, pingüinos, **cormoranes**, **garzas**, tortugas marinas, tortugas galápagos, iguanas terrestres, **pinzones**, **gaviotas**, flamencos, pelícanos, **focas**, albatros y **tiburónes ballena** que son **inofensivos para el hombre** ya que **sólo comen peces pequeños**. La flora que se puede encontrar en las islas es la siguiente: **manglar**, **cactus endémicos**, vegetación húmeda, **guaco** y desiertos con cactus.

También se encuentran **paisajes** únicos como **playas blancas**, **radiantes rocas basálticas** obscuras y sólidas, túnel de lava hacia el volcán Scalesiastewarth, que es un cráter, diferentes volcanes, **formaciones de lava y lagunas**.

El jurumí
PARAGUAY

La **diversidad genética** de las especies de nuestro planeta se encuentra **en peligro**. Si bien este **mecanismo ha sido**, y es, parte del **proceso evolutivo**, en los **últimos** 300 años es el hombre el que **se ha transformado** en la **principal amenaza**. **Actualmente**, algunos especialistas **estiman** que cada 15 minutos **desaparece** una especie.

"Jurumí" es el nombre en guaraní, la **lengua nativa precolombina**, del **oso hormiguero gigante**. Frecuentemente se encuentra en los **bosques espinosos** del Chaco paraguayo. Este típico **morador** de los bosques del Paraguay es un animal que puede llegar a **medir** hasta dos metros de largo y a pesar 40 kilos. Una de sus características más curiosas es su **lengua larga**, **fina** y **pegajosa**, que puede medir hasta 60 centímetros. Gracias a ella, le es posible **atrapar** todo tipo de insectos, fundamentalmente **hormigas** y **termitas**, y **deglutirlos** inmediatamente. Esta **estrategia de supervivencia** es muy **valiosa** para el ecosistema ya que así estos invertebrados están **controlados** y **no se vuelven plagas** para la región. **Aunque** esto **podría parecer** una cuestión menor, es de **suma importancia** ya que las termitas son **dañinas** en las zonas rurales. Su paso **transforma** los **suelos** y afecta el **desarrollo futuro** de la vegetación.

---

diversidad genética: genetic diversity
en peligro: in danger
mecanismo: mechanism
ha sido/ser: it has been/to be
proceso evolutivo: evolutionary process
últimos: last
se ha transformado/ transformar: it has been transformed/to transform
principal: main
amenaza: threat
actualmente: nowadays
estiman/estimar: they estimate/ to estimate
desaparece: disappears

lengua nativa: native language
precolombina: pre-Columbian
oso hormiguero gigante: giant anteater
bosques espinosos: pine forests
morador: dweller
medir: to measure
lengua: tongue
larga: long
fina: thin
pegajosa: sticky
atrapar: to catch
hormigas: ants
termitas: termites
deglutirlos/deglutir: swallow them/to swallow
estrategia de supervivencia: survival strategy
valiosa: valuable
controlados/controlar: controlled/to control
no se vuelven plagas: they don't become a plague
aunque: although
podría parecer: it could seem
suma importancia: extremely important
dañinas: damaging
transforma/transformar: it transforms/to transform
suelos: lands, grounds
desarrollo futuro: future development

Por otra parte, este oso hormiguero **se caracteriza** por su **escasa** visión y **audición**. **Sin embargo**, su **sentido del olfato** está **altamente** desarrollado y es el que **le permite conseguir** sus mejores **presas** y **subsistir a lo largo del** día.

El jurumí es un animal de **hábitos diurnos**. Por la noche, **duerme** al **aire libre** en **zonas descampadas**. Si bien **se le reconoce** como un animal **sumamente pacífico**, puede llegar a ser peligroso si es **atacado**, ya que cuenta con **garras afiladas** y **antebrazos fuertes**. Aunque es un animal solitario, se le puede ver en pareja durante el **período de cortejo**. La **hembra** del jurumí tiene una sola **cría** por año y el período de gestación es de 190 días. La cría nace en la **primavera** y es frecuente **verla montada** en la **espalda** de su madre. El **recién nacido** es **amamantado** durante seis meses y no estará en condiciones de subsistir independientemente hasta cumplir los 2 años. Si el **cachorro crece** en su ambiente natural suele llegar a vivir 14 años pero, si se desarrolla en **cautiverio**, puede **alcanzar** los 25 años.

Los enemigos naturales del jurumí son el jaguar y el puma. Sin embargo, entre las principales causas que **lo amenazan** hoy se encuentran la destrucción de su hábitat y la **cacería**. Esta última es una práctica tradicional en el Paraguay y en toda Suramérica. Por eso, si bien los **pobladores rurales destacan** la importancia de esta especie y la protegen, son los **cazadores furtivos** los que la ponen en peligro. Afortunadamente, tanto el **gobierno** del Paraguay como diversas organizaciones ecologistas locales **han emprendido** valiosas acciones para protegerla.

---

se caracteriza: it is characterized
escasa: poor
audición: hearing
sin embargo: however
sentido del olfato: sense of smell
altamente: highly
le permite conseguir: it allows it to obtain
presas: prey
subsistir: to live
a lo largo del: throughout

hábitos diurnos: daytime habits
duerme/dormir: it sleeps/to sleep
aire libre: outdoors
zonas descampadas: open areas
se le reconoce/reconocer: it is recognized/to recognize
sumamente: extremely
pacífico: peaceful
atacado/atacar: attacked/to attack
garras afiladas: sharp claws
antebrazos fuertes: strong forearms
período de cortejo: courtship period
hembra: female
cría: baby animal
primavera: spring
verla/ver: see it/to see
montada/montar: riding/to ride
espalda: back
recién nacido: newborn
amamantado: breast-fed
cachorro: baby, cub
crece/crecer: it grows up/to grow
cautiverio: captivity
alcanzar: to reach

lo amenazan/amenazar: they threaten it/to threaten
cacería: hunting
pobladores rurales: country dwellers
destacan/destacar: they emphasize/to emphasize
cazadores: hunters
furtivos: furtive
gobierno: government
han emprendido/emprender: they have undertaken/to undertake

departamento: department (state)
impresionante: impressive
llamado/llamar: called/to call
lo hace único: it makes it unique
cuencas hidrográficas: water basins
compuesta por: composed of
aves: birds
mamíferos: mammals
anfibios: amphibians
peces: fish
silvestre: wild
muy variada: very diverse
está formada por/estar formado por:
  it is made up of/to be made up of
bosques húmedos: rain forests
inundados/inundar: flooded/to flood
secos: dry
fue declarado/declarar: was declared/
  to declare
Patrimonio Mundial de la
Humanidad: World Heritage Site
Organización de las Naciones
  Unidas: United Nations

sobre el nivel del mar: above sea level
sede del gobierno central: central seat
  of the Government
se divide/dividirse: it is divided/
  to be divided
zonas geográficas diferentes: different
  geographic zones
zona subandina: the area under the
  Andes
zona amazónica: the area around the
  Amazon River
la capital más alta del mundo: the
  highest capital city in the world
alberga/albergar: it harbors/to harbor
se considera/considerar: it is
  considered/to consider
sitio arqueológico: archaeological site
habilidad artesanal: craft skills,
  artistry
conocimiento de la medicina
  tradicional: knowledge of
  traditional medicine

montañoso: mountainous
conviven/convivir: they coexist/
  to coexist
artesanía: handicrafts
fabrican/fabricar: they make/to make

Paisajes diversos
BOLIVIA

SANTA CRUZ Santa Cruz es un **departamento** muy importante en Bolivia porque tiene un reservorio natural **impresionante llamado** Noel Kempff Mercado. El parque tiene una gran diversidad que **lo hace único**, con ecosistemas naturales y **cuencas hidrográficas** y una fauna rica **compuesta por aves**, reptiles, **mamíferos**, **anfibios**, **peces** e insectos. Su flora **silvestre** es también **muy variada** y **está formada por bosques húmedos**, bosques **inundados**, bosques **secos** y sabanas. El reservorio de Noel Kempff Mercado **fue declarado Patrimonio Mundial de la Humanidad** por la **Organización de las Naciones Unidas** en el año 2000.

LA PAZ La Paz está situada al noroeste de Bolivia, a 3.649 metros **sobre el nivel del mar**, y es **sede del gobierno central**. La capital de Bolivia **se divide** en tres **zonas geográficas diferentes**. La zona del Altiplano, donde se encuentra el lago Titicaca, es la región más húmeda. La **zona subandina** es muy húmeda y tiene una vegetación exuberante. La **zona amazónica** también tiene una vegetación exuberante. La Paz es **la capital más alta del mundo** y **alberga** el centro ceremonial Tiahuanaco, que **se considera** el **sitio arqueológico** más importante de Bolivia. El grupo étnico mayoritario en esta zona son los aymaras y los quechuas, que se caracterizan por su **habilidad artesanal** y su **conocimiento de la medicina tradicional**.

COCHABAMBA Es esencialmente **montañoso** y se encuentra a 2.550 metros sobre el nivel del mar. En este departamento **conviven** diversos grupos étnicos como los cotas, los chius, los collas y los quechuas, quienes actualmente se dedican a la **artesanía** que **fabrican** con materiales de la región. Una de sus atracciones turísticas más importantes es una inmensa estatua de Jesús más alta que el Cristo del Corcovado de Río de Janeiro en Brasil.

Ofrece una **vista panorámica** de la ciudad increíble. Cochabamba es un departamento **agrícola**. Sus productos más importantes son: el **maíz**, el **trigo**, la **cebada**, el **lino**, la **avena**, la **papa**, las **hortalizas**, la **oca** y la fruta.

LAGO TITICACA   El lago Titicaca es el más grande de Sudamérica y tiene, además, la extensión de agua navegable más alta del mundo. Este lago, **compartido** por Bolivia y Perú, es semisalado y sus aguas tienen un **color azul muy particular**. Tiene 36 islas, varias penínsulas, **cabos** y el **estrecho** de Tiquina. En el lago se encuentran las islas del **sol** y la de la **luna**, famosa por su **leyenda** incaica y por sus importantes ruinas arquitectónicas. **De acuerdo** con la leyenda inca, por **mandato** del Dios Sol, Inti, de sus aguas **surgieron** Manco Kapac y Mama Ocllo, los **fundadores** del Imperio inca. Desde la Isla del Sol, que es muy pequeña, **se puede apreciar** una magnífica vista del lago y se puede ver el **monte** Illimani, donde están el Templo del sol y el Palacio Picolcayna. La Isla de la Luna tiene **playas desiertas** y ruinas incaicas, además de dos lagos. Huatajata es el lago **menor** y el Copacabana que es el **mayor**. Copacabana es muy interesante porque fue un centro ceremonial y de observaciones astronómicas. La fauna del lugar es variada y se encuentran **patos salvajes** y **truchas**.

SORATA   Es un pueblo pequeño **cerca** de La Paz que alberga **cuevas** y **grutas** con **aguas subterráneas calientes** (termas de aguas medicinales) y tiene un clima **templado** y **paisajes maravillosos** como las vistas de la Cordillera Real que están en las montañas Illampu.

TUPIZA   Tupiza está a unos cien kilómetros de la **frontera** con Argentina y al **sureste** de Potosí. Es un lugar muy atractivo con una flora y fauna únicas en Bolivia. La fauna que se encuentra es de aves, **perdices**, patos salvajes, alpacas, **vicuñas** y llamas. La flora del área está formada por **bosques de cactus**, muchos enormes con **flores rojas**, **sauces**, **álamos** y **matorrales**.

---

vista panorámica: panoramic view
agrícola: agricultural
maíz: corn
trigo: wheat
cebada: barley
lino: flax
avena: oats
papa: potato
hortalizas: vegetables
oca: Andean root vegetable

lago: lake
compartido/compartir: shared/ to share
color azul muy particular: particular blue color
cabos: cape
estrecho: strait
sol: sun
luna: moon
leyenda: legend
de acuerdo: according to
mandato: mandate
surgieron/surgir: they arose/to arise
fundadores: founders
se puede apreciar: it can be appreciated
monte: hill, small mountain
playas desiertas: deserted beaches
menor: smaller
mayor: greater
patos salvajes: wild ducks
truchas: trout

cerca: near
cuevas: coves
grutas: caves
aguas subterráneas calientes: hot subterranean waters
templado: mild
paisajes maravillosos: wonderful landscapes

frontera: border
sureste: southeast
perdices/perdiz: partridge
vicuñas: vicuna (relative of the camel)
bosques de cactus: cactus forests
flores rojas: red flowers
sauces: willow
álamos: poplars
matorrales: bushes

Paisajes, flora y fauna
VENEZUELA

Venezuela está en la **costa noroeste** de **Sudamérica**. Sus **países limítrofes** son Guyana al **este**, Brasil al **sur**, Colombia al **oeste** y al **norte** el **Mar Caribe**. La **superficie** del país es de 900,000 **kilómetros cuadrados** y está **dividida** en 23 **estados**. Venezuela tiene un **clima poco variado** debido a que está **cerca** del **ecuador**.

EL SALTO DEL ANGEL

El Salto del Angel está situado en el estado de Bolívar y es la **cascada más alta del mundo**. **Fue descubierta** por un **piloto norteamericano** alrededor del año 1920 **cuyo** nombre era Jimmy Angel y **se dice que él mismo le puso el nombre**. La **altura** del salto o cascada es de unos 900 **metros**, **superando** así a la de Tugala en Sudáfrica, que tiene 948 metros. Alrededor del salto **se puede encontrar** una abundante flora como **orquídeas**, palmeras y **lianas**.

LA **GRAN SABANA** La gran sabana está **dentro** del parque nacional Camaima al sur de Venezuela en el estado de Bolívar. En la gran sabana hay ríos y cascadas. También se encuentra una montaña que tiene una **cima plana y paredes verticales llamada** "Tepuy" que son **formaciones de piedras areniscas formadas** por la erosión.

---

paisajes: landscapes
costa noroeste: northwest coast
Sudamérica: South America
países: countries
limítrofes: bordering
este: east
sur: south
oeste: west
norte: north
Mar Caribe: Caribbean Sea
superficie: surface
kilómetros cuadrados: kilometers square
dividida/dividir: divided/to divide
estados: states
clima: climate
poco variado: little varied
cerca: near
ecuador: equator

cascada: waterfall
más alta del mundo: the highest in the world
fue descubierta/descubrir: was discovered/to discover
piloto norteamericano: North American pilot
cuyo: whose
se dice que él mismo le puso el nombre: it is said that he named it
altura: height
metros: meters
superando/superar: surpassing/ to surpass
se puede/poder: you can/can
encontrar: to find
orquídeas: orchids
lianas: liane (various woody climbing plants of tropical forests)

gran sabana: great plain
dentro: inside
cima plana y paredes verticales: flat top and vertical walls
llamada/llamar: called/to be called
formaciones de piedras areniscas: sandstone formations
formadas/formar: formed/to form

LOS ROQUES Es un archipiélago situado en el mar Caribe a unos 168 kilómetros del puerto de Caracas (la capital de Venezuela); por su **belleza** e importancia ecológica fue declarado parque nacional en 1972. Está formado por cincuenta islas diferentes. La más importante es el Gran Roque, el cual es un lugar muy interesante porque tiene una gran extensión de **mar tranquilo**. También hay lagunas, **cayos**, **playas con arenas blancas** y **aguas cristalinas**. Una de las atracciones turísticas de esta área es la variedad de su fauna marina, como **pulpos**, **tiburones**, **langostas**, **gaviotas** y **garzas**. En el sur está la **fundación científica** "Los Roques" que es una estación biológica dedicada a la preservación de la **tortuga verde**. También se puede encontrar una **extensa variedad de aves** y reptiles como iguanas, camaleones y salamandras.

MARGARITA Es una isla **situada** en el Mar Caribe al noroeste de Caracas. Se encuentran playas **con o sin olas**, grandes o pequeñas, **profundas o llanas**, **tibias o calientes**, con **viento** o sin viento. La isla fue descubierta por Cristóbal Colón, **quien le dio el nombre** Margarita. El área marina está formada por una **extensa barranca** de arena y un **conjunto** de lagunas **costeras** con formaciones de manglar. Un atractivo turístico de esta isla es que se pueden practicar todos los **deportes acuáticos**.

LOS LLANOS Los **llanos** se encuentran en el sur de Venezuela. Son extensas **sabanas** donde la vegetación y la fauna es muy variada.

El atractivo turístico más popular y **más visitado** es la **Cueva** del **Guácharo**, una formación natural donde están los guácharos y **pájaros** de **plumaje oscuro**. Allí se puede apreciar una galería de figuras de animales y **santos**, altares. La vegetación que caracteriza a esta zona es las sabanas, los **palmares**, los **bosques secos** y los bosques de galerías. Esta **zona se caracteriza** por la **cantidad** de animales que se pueden observar, como el **chigüire**, la **rana platanera**, el **venado**, la **baba**, el **pavón**, **culebras**, anacondas, tortugas, **zorros** y armadillos.

---

belleza: beauty
mar tranquilo: calm sea
cayos: coves
playas con arenas blancas: beaches with white sand
aguas cristalinas: crystalline waters
pulpos: octopus
tiburones: sharks
langostas: lobsters
gaviotas: gulls
garzas: herons
fundación científica: scientific foundation
tortuga verde: green turtle
extensa variedad de aves: extensive variety of birds

situada/situar: situated/to situate
con o sin olas: with or without waves
profundas o llanas: deep or flat
tibias o calientes: lukewarm, hot
viento: wind
quien le dio el nombre: who gave it the name
extensa barranca: extensive hill
conjunto: set
costeras: coastal
deportes acuáticos: aquatic sports

llanos: flat ground
sabanas: savanna, grassland

más visitado: most popular
cueva: cave
guácharo: oil bird
pájaros: birds
plumaje oscuro: dark plumage
santos: saints
palmares: palm groves
bosques secos: dry forests
zona se caracteriza: the zone is characterized
cantidad: amount
chigüire: rodent native to Venezuela
rana platanera: banana-tree frog
venado: deer
baba: small alligator
pavón: peacock
culebras: snakes
zorros: foxes

Las ballenas de Valdez
ARGENTINA

La Península de Valdez, **bañada** por el océano Atlántico, es uno de los santuarios ecológicos más importantes del mundo. Con 4.000 **kilómetros cuadrados** de **superficie** total, 110 kilómetros de costas a **mar abierto** y 150 kilómetros de costas a los golfos Nuevo y San José, **alberga** seis reservas naturales. Con **clima seco**, tiene **veranos** con **días calurosos** y **noches frescas**, e **inviernos** fríos con **pocas lluvias**.

El Istmo Carlos Ameghino es la **estrecha franja de tierra** que conecta la península con el continente, **a través de** la que se puede ver la fuerza de las **olas** del océano Atlántico **romper** contra los **acantilados** de la costa. Toda esta zona es muy rica en fauna marina: **delfines**, **lobos y elefantes marinos,** toninos y orcas son algunas de las **tantas especies** que pueden encontrarse. La familia de las **aves** también es **destacable**: desde **pingüinos** y **gaviotas**, hasta albatros y **palomas** antárticas.

Pero el **espectáculo mayor** que **ofrece** la naturaleza **gratuitamente**, año a año, es la reproducción y el **alumbramiento** de la ballena franca. De julio a diciembre, este **mamífero** llega en grupos a esta agua para **parir** sus **ballenatos**. En Puerto Pirámides, una pequeña **villa balnearia**, pueden verse desde la costa, pero para estar a muy pocos metros de ellas es necesario (¡y recomendable!) **tomar** una de las excursiones en **lancha** con las que cientos de turistas **se adentran** en las **aguas cristalinas**. Todos con cámara fotográfica **en mano quieren verlas saltar a pesar de** sus **toneladas** de peso. Ver el **chorro** por donde **expulsan** su **largo aliento**. **Escuchar** sus **alaridos**. Y ver su **gran aleta dorsal** y su **cola**. Algo que quizás vieron **alguna vez** en un libro, foto o video pero imposible de ver en un zoológico. La **única manera** de ver a la ballena franca **austral** es **en vivo y en directo** y Argentina ofrece esa oportunidad única.

bañada: surrounded
kilómetros cuadrados: square kilometers
superficie: surface
mar abierto: open sea
alberga/albergar: it houses/to house
clima seco: dry climate
veranos: summers
días calurosos: hot days
noches frescas: cool nights
inviernos: winters
pocas lluvias: little rain

estrecha: narrow
franja de tierra: strip of earth
a través de: through
olas: waves
romper: to break
acantilados: cliffs
delfines: dolphins
lobos y elefantes marinos: seals and sea lions
tantas especies: so many species
aves: birds
destacable: important
pingüinos: penguins
gaviotas: seagulls
palomas: pigeons

espectáculo mayor: greatest show
ofrece/ofrecer: it offers/to offer
gratuitamente: for free
alumbramiento: childbirth
mamífero: mammal
parir: to give birth
ballenatos: whale calf
villa balnearia: spa town
tomar: to take
lancha: motorboat
se adentran: they go deep
aguas cristalinas: crystal clear waters
en mano: in hand
quieren/querer: they love/to love
verlas saltar: to watch them jump
a pesar de: in spite of
toneladas: tons
chorro: spurt
expulsan/expulsar: they expel/to expel
largo aliento: long breath
escuchar: to listen
alaridos: screech
gran aleta dorsal: great dorsal fin
cola: tail
alguna vez: at some point, sometimes
única manera: unique way, manner
austral: southern
en vivo y en directo: live (live and direct)

La Reserva de El Vizcaíno
MÉXICO

A **primera vista** el **desierto** de la Península de Baja California **parece ser** uno de los lugares mas **desolados** y solitarios del mundo. **Sin embargo**, lo que **aparenta** ser un **lugar inhospitalario** es **en realidad** un **santuario biológico** para un gran número de plantas y animales. **Compuesta de** aproximadamente 2,540,000 hectáreas, La Reserva de la Biosfera El Vizcaíno es considerada el área protegida más grande de Latinoamérica. La reserva **se encuentra** en la parte norte del estado de Baja California Sur, México. Esta área **inmensa contiene** más de cuatrocientas especies de vegetales y más de trescientas especies de animales, **incluyendo mamíferos**, **aves**, reptiles y anfibios.

A pesar del **clima seco** y **árido** en el desierto, hay una variedad de plantas que **sobreviven abundantemente** en este ambiente. Entre ellas se encuentra el mesquite, **usado** por los nativos para hacer **fogatas**. También esta la pitaya con su **fruta deliciosa** y similar a la **tuna del nopal**. Otras plantas de esta zona incluyen el maguey que es un ingrediente importante del tequila, la biznaga y la savila con sus **propiedades curativas** y una variedad de otros cactus como la cholla y el cardón. **Algunos** de los animales en este desierto incluyen el coyote, la víbora de cascabel, el murciélago, varios tipos de venado y lagartijas **al igual que** el conejo silvestre, la ardilla, el borrego cimarrón con sus **cuernos enroscados**, el gato montés o puma y el zorrillo. Entre los **pájaros** de esta área están la **chuparrosa**, el cardenal, el pájaro carpintero, la paloma serrana, el gavilán, el aguila y el zopilote.

Aunque un lugar **caluroso** y con **poca agua**, el desierto de Baja California Sur es **hogar** para un gran número de diversas plantas y animales bien **adaptados** para vivir en este **ambiente duro**. **Gracias a** la reserva biológica **podrán seguir viviendo sin miedo** de la intervención humana.

---

primera vista: at first sight
desierto: desert
parece ser/parecer: it seems to be/ to seem
desolados: desolated
sin embargo: although, nevertheless
aparenta/aparentar: it looks like/ to look
lugar inhospitalario: inhospitable place
en realidad: in fact
santuario biológico: biological sanctuary
compuesta de: integrated by
se encuentra/encontrarse: it is located/to be located
inmensa: immense, huge
contiene/contener: it contains/ to contain
incluyendo/incluir: including/ to include
mamíferos: mammals
aves: birds

clima seco: dry climate
árido: arid
sobreviven/sobrevivir: they survive/ to survive
abundantemente: abundantly
usado/usar: used/to use
fogatas: bonfires
fruta deliciosa: delicious fruit
tuna del nopal: prickly pear fruits
propiedades curativas: healing properties
algunos: some
al igual que: just like
cuernos enroscados: curled horns, antlers
pájaros: birds
chuparrosa: hummingbird

caluroso: hot
poca agua: little water
hogar: home
adaptados: adapted
ambiente duro: hard (severe) environment
gracias a: thanks to
podrán seguir viviendo: they'll be able to go on living
sin miedo: without fear

gran altura: high altitude
humedad permanente: constant humidity
ofrecen/ofrecer: offer/to offer
ambiente: environment
para que ... alcance: for ... to reach
de hecho: in fact
orquídeas: orchids
se ha construido/construir: has been built/to build
orquideario: orchid garden
para poder preservar: to (be able to) maintain
difundir: to disseminate
riqueza: wealth
joya: jewel
lugar: place

crecen/crecer: grow/to grow
en algunos casos: in some cases
las vuelven: make them
comentan/comentar: comment/to comment
mientras las que: while those which
árboles: trees
las más conocidas: the best known
piedras: rocks, stones
suelo: ground, soil
las más vistosas: the most eye-catching
extrañas: strangest
sin dudas: without a doubt
al alcance de la mano: close at hand

respetuosos: respectful
valoran/valorar: (they) value/to value
cuidan/cuidar: take care of/to take care
recurso: resource
han formado/formar: have formed/to form
para protegerlas de: (in order) to protect them from
principales amenazas: main threats
talan/talar: cut down/to cut down
queman/quemar: burn/to burn

entre: between
hacen que ... se transforme en: turn ... into
verdadero: true
paraíso vegetal: plant paradise

de acuerdo a: according to
del lugar: local
ya han sido: there have already been
quedan/quedar: there remain/to remain
por clasificar: to be classified
a pesar de que: even though
poseen/poseer: have/to have
larga vida: long life
crecimiento: growth
se las considera: they are considered
tesoros: treasures
suman/sumar: add/to add
valor: value
paisaje: scenery, landscape

Orquideario
NICARAGUA

La **gran altura** y la **humedad permanente** de Miraflor **ofrecen** el **ambiente** ideal **para que** la flora de la reserva **alcance** su máximo esplendor. **De hecho**, existe tal diversidad de especies de **orquídeas** que **se ha construido** un **orquideario para poder preservar** y **difundir** la **riqueza** de esta **joya** natural del **lugar**.

En Miraflor estas flores **crecen** en lugares que, **en algunos casos**, **las vuelven** vulnerables. Los locales **comentan** que, **mientras las que** crecen sobre los **árboles** son **las más conocidas**, las que están sobre las **piedras** y el **suelo** son **las más vistosas** y **extrañas**. **Sin dudas**, en Miraflor las orquídeas están, literalmente, **al alcance de la mano**.

Los habitantes de la reserva son especialmente **respetuosos** y **valoran** y **cuidan** este **recurso** natural. Ellos **han formado** grupos especiales **para protegerlas de** sus **principales amenazas**: los traficantes inescrupulosos y quienes **talan** y **queman** indiscriminadamente los árboles.

Aunque es posible visitar el orquideario durante todo el año, es **entre** febrero y abril que el perfume y el color de algunas especies **hacen que** Miraflor **se transforme en** un **verdadero paraíso vegetal**.

De acuerdo a los expertos **del lugar**, **ya han sido** clasificadas más de 150 especies y **quedan** más de 50 **por clasificar**. **A pesar de que** las orquídeas **poseen** una **larga vida**, su **crecimiento** y reproducción son limitados. Por este motivo, **se las considera** como **tesoros** invaluables que **suman valor** y sofisticación al **paisaje** de la reserva.

Lluvia de ranas en El Yunque

PUERTO RICO

El coquí, la **ranita** que es símbolo de Puerto Rico, es un **pequeño anfibio** que **se encuentra** en **grandes cantidades** en el **Bosque** Nacional El Yunque y que **canta a coro durante la noche**. Su nombre **se debe a que** el **macho hace** una **llamada** de dos **sonidos** ("co"-"quí") **al croar**. Al hacerlo, su **cuerpo se llena de** aire **de tal modo que**… ¡**parece que va a estallar**! Pero, no. Continúa cantando y llenándose de aire, **una y otra vez**, durante toda la noche.

Se cuenta que el coquí es tan puntual **para iniciar** su canto todos los días, que **antiguamente** los **trabajadores** de la **caña de azúcar usaban** su croar **como señal de que** la **jornada de trabajo había terminado**.

El **fuerte** y particular sonido que **emite** el coquí al croar **puede hacer que** el turista que **recién llega** se cofunda **y crea** que **se trata del canto** de un **pájaro mediano o grande**. **Sin embargo**, el coquí **no supera** los 35 milímetros. Es que, ¿**quién podría imaginar** que una ranita tan pequeña **haga semejante barullo**?

En **temporadas** de **gran humedad** esta pequeña rana **trepa a** los **árboles**. Pero allí **la esperan** muchos predadores. Uno de ellos es la tarántula. Cuando llega el momento **de volver a casa**, los coquíes que **logran sobrevivir conocen** el **peligro** y **prefieren regresar evitándolo**. Por este **motivo** ellos **saltan juntos** de los árboles, y quien visita el bosque **puede ver** una auténtica "lluvia de ranas" en El Yunque.

---

ranita: little frog
pequeño anfibio: small amphibian
se encuentra/encontrarse: is found/ to be found
grandes cantidades: great numbers
bosque: forest
canta a coro: sings in chorus
durante la noche: at night
se debe a que: is due to the fact that
macho: male
hace/hacer: makes/to make
llamada: call
sonidos: sounds
al croar: when croaking
cuerpo: body
se llena de: fills with
de tal modo que: so that
parece que: it looks like
va a estallar: (it) is going to burst
un y otra vez: again and again

se cuenta que: they say that
para iniciar: to begin, to start
antiguamente: in the past
trabajadores: workers
caña de azúcar: sugar cane
usaban/usar: used to use/to use
como señal de que: as (the) sign that
jornada de trabajo: work day
había terminado/terminar: had ended/to end

fuerte: loud, strong
emite/emitir: emits/to emit
puede hacer que … se confunda: might cause … to get confused
recién llega: has just arrived
y crea: and to believe
se trata del/tratarse de: it is the/to be
canto: song
pájaro: bird
mediano o grande: medium(-sized) or large
sin embargo: (and) yet
no supera/superar: doesn't exceed/ to exceed
quién podría imaginar: who could imagine
haga/hacer: makes/to make
semejante barullo: such a racket

temporadas: times, seasons
gran humedad: great humidity
trepa a/trepar a: climbs/to climb
árboles: trees
la esperan/esperar: await it/to await
de volver a casa: to return home
logran sobrevivir: manage to survive
conocen/conocer: know/to know
peligro: danger
prefieren/preferir: (they) prefer/ to prefer
regresar: to go back
evitándolo: avoiding it
motivo: reason
saltan/saltar: jump/to jump
juntos: together
puede ver: can witness, can see

La laguna de San Ignacio
MÉXICO

maravilloso: wonderful
tiene lugar: it takes place
a lo largo: along
costa oeste: west coast
espectáculo: show
empieza/empezar: it begins/to begin
invierno: winter
ballenas grises: gray whales
comienzan/comenzar: they start/
  to start
viaje migratorio: migratory trip
templadas: warm
recorren/recorrer: they cover/to cover,
  to travel
millas: miles
científicos: scientists
abordan/abordar: they board/to board
barcos: boats
cerca: near

meta final: the finish line
lagunas: small lakes
calientes: hot
dan a luz: they give birth (literally: to
  give to the light)
crías: young
recién nacidas: newborn
miden/medir: they measure/
  to measure
alrededor de: about
pesan/pesar: they weigh/to weigh
libras: pounds
mamás: mothers
proveerán/proveer: they will provide/
  to provide
galones de leche por día: gallons of
  milk per day
contenido de grasa: fat content
aumenten/aumentar: they increase/
  to increase
gordura: fat
sobrevivir: to survive
heladas: frozen
verano: summer

Cada año hay un evento de la naturaleza **maravilloso** que **tiene lugar a lo largo** de la **costa oeste** de Norteamérica. Este **espectáculo empieza** en **invierno**, aproximadamente entre octubre y febrero. Las **ballenas grises comienzan** un **viaje migratorio** desde las aguas frías de Alaska y Canadá hasta las aguas **templadas** de México. Durante este viaje las ballenas **recorren** casi 5.000 **millas** y pueden ser observadas desde la costa. Muchos curiosos, y especialmente los **científicos**, **abordan barcos** para ver las ballenas desde más **cerca**.

La **meta final** de esta gran migración son las **lagunas** de Baja California en México. Allí, en  aguas más **calientes**, las ballenas **dan a luz** a sus **crías**. Las ballenas **recién nacidas miden alrededor de** 15 pies de largo y **pesan** unas 2.000 **libras**. Durante los primeros seis meses, las **mamás proveerán** hasta 50 **galones de leche por día** con un **contenido de grasa** del 56 por ciento, lo que hará que las crías **aumenten** de peso entre 60 y 70 libras al día. Esta **gordura** es necesaria para que las ballenas puedan **sobrevivir** en las aguas **heladas** del norte durante el **verano**.

Una de las lagunas más populares para las ballenas es la de San Ignacio. Esta laguna es muy importante para los científicos porque **ha tenido** poco **impacto humano** y **está protegida** por el gobierno de México como reserva natural.

En esta laguna se ha observado un fenómeno tan increíble que ni los científicos pueden explicarlo. Normalmente, cuando un animal **salvaje es seguido** por un humano, **se retira** y muchas veces **huye**. **Lo mismo** pasa con las ballenas grises en el mar. Pero en la laguna, por alguna **razón** que no comprendemos todavía, **parece** ser que estas ballenas no tienen miedo de la gente. Es más, **se acercan** a las **lanchas** y **dejan** que las personas **las toquen**. Es realmente un **acto sorprendente** y **único**, algo que **cambia** la vida de cualquier persona que **lo haya experimentado**.

Las ballenas grises son un gran **tesoro** de la Laguna de San Ignacio y **vale la pena** proteger estas magníficas criaturas y su laguna maravillosa para que puedan seguir **criando**, **creciendo** y viviendo como parte de nuestro gran sistema ecológico.

ha tenido/tener: it has had/to have
impacto humano: human impact
está protegida/proteger: it is protected/to protect

salvaje: wild
es seguido/seguir: it is followed/to follow
se retira/retirarse: it withdraws/to withdraw
huye/huir: it runs away/to run away
lo mismo: the same
razón: reason
parece/parecer: it seems/to seem
se acercan/acercarse: they get close/to get close
lanchas: motorboat
dejan/dejar: they let/to let
las toquen/tocar: they touch them/to touch
acto sorprendente: surprising act
único: unique
cambia/cambiar: it changes/to change
lo haya experimentado/experimentar: (any person who) has experienced it/to experience
tesoro: treasure
vale la pena/valer la pena: it is worth it/to be worth it
criando/criar: breeding/to breed
creciendo/crecer: growing up/to grow

CULTURE NOTE

Language has been a central issue in Puerto Rican education and culture since 1898. Until 1930 U.S. authorities insisted upon making English the language of instruction in the schools, the intent being to produce English-speaking persons of American culture in the same way this is done in the United States public schools. But strong resistance to the policy finally brought a change to the use of Spanish as the basic school language, with English becoming a second language studied by all. In 1991 the Puerto Rican legislature, following the lead of the pro-commonwealth Popular Democratic Party and the governor, Rafael Hernández Colón, endorsed a bill that made Spanish the island's official language, thus reversing a 1902 law that gave both Spanish and English official recognition. In 1993 Governor Pedro J. Rossello signed legislation restoring equal status to Spanish and English. It is estimated that Puerto Rico accounts for nearly 4 million of the 332 million who speak Spanish.

Examina tu comprensión

El Parque Nacional Darién, página 192

1. ¿Qué organización honró el parque por la diversidad de sus ambientes?

2. Describa la gente y las tradiciones que conforman la diversidad etno-cultural del parque.

3. ¿Cómo se conserva la diversidad de esta región?

Las islas Galápagos, página 194

1. ¿Qué evento natural resultó en la formación de las Islas Galápagos?

2. Los piratas fueron los primeros en frecuentar la isla porque era un lugar excelente ¿para hacer qué?

3. ¿Quién fue el inglés que estudió las Galápagos y escribió un libro acerca de la evolución? ¿Cómo se llama el libro?

El jurumí, página 196

1. ¿Qué es el jurumí?

2. ¿Cuál es la característica más curiosa del jurumí y para qué sirve?

3. ¿Cuál es el sentido más agudo del jurumí y por qué es importante?

4. ¿Cuáles son los enemigos que pueden contribuir a su extinción?

Paisajes diversos, página 198

1. ¿Qué hace que la reserva natural Noel Kempff Mercado sea única?

2. Describa las tres zonas de La Paz.

3. ¿Qué atracción turística se encuentra en Cochabamba?

4. Además de la vegetación, ¿qué otra cosa hace que Copacabana sea interesante?

Test your comprehension

Paisajes, flora y fauna, página 200

1. ¿Cuáles son las famosas cataratas de Venezuela y cómo se les dió el nombre?

2. ¿Qué son los tepuyes?

3. ¿Cuál es la isla más importante en Los Roques y por qué?

La Reserva de El Vizcaíno, página 203

1. ¿Cómo es el clima en El Vizcaíno?

2. ¿Cuáles son los usos de las plantas de mesquite y maguey?

Las ballenas de Valdez, página 202

1. ¿Cuál es el nombre del tramo de tierra que une la península con el continente?

2. ¿Cuál es el mayor espectáculo ofrecido allí?

3. ¿Qué partes de la ballena puedes llegar a ver?

La laguna de San Ignacio, página 206

1. ¿Cuándo comienzan su viaje las ballenas grises y cuántas millas recorren a lo largo de la costa?

2. ¿Por qué emigran las ballenas grises a México?

3. El alto contenido de grasas de la leche materna es necesario ¿para qué?

El amor es tan importante como la comida.
Pero no alimenta.

Gabriel García Márquez

Gastronomía

El dulce de papaya

PUERTO RICO

Cuando era niña, mi abuelo **solía cortar** los **tallos** del **árbol de la lechosa**. Los **limpiaba** y **me los daba** junto a un **vaso lleno de** agua con **jabón**. Yo me iba con mis tallos al **balcón** para **soplar burbujas** al aire. Este era uno de mis **pasatiempos** favoritos.

La lechosa es una fruta exquisita. El "dulce de lechosa" es muy popular en Puerto Rico. La fruta verde se **monda** y **luego se corta** en **pedazos finos**. Los pedazos **se hierven** y, **mientras** lo hacen, **se les añade azúcar** negra y **canela** hasta que la fruta esté suave. Cuando ya está **lista**, **se pone** en la **nevera**.

La mejor manera de comerla es **acompañada** con **queso blanco** de **leche de cabra**. Ésta es una receta de los abuelos que **aún se disfruta** en la mayoría de los **hogares** puertorriqueños así como en muchos de nuestros restaurantes típicos.

Prueben este delicioso **postre** y **tendrán** un **pedazo** de Puerto Rico en sus hogares.

---

cuando era niña: when I was a little girl
solía: used to
cortar: to cut
tallos: stems
árbol de la lechosa: papaya tree
limpiaba/limpiar: would clean/ to clean
me los daba/dar: give them to me/ to give
vaso: glass
lleno de: filled with
jabón: soap
balcón: porch
soplar burbujas: blow bubbles
pasatiempos: pastimes

monda/mondar: peel/to peel
luego se corta: then is cut
pedazos finos: thin pieces
se hierven/hervir: it is boiled/to boil
mientras: while
se les añade: (sugar) is added
azúcar: sugar
canela: cinnamon
lista: ready
se pone/poner: it is put/to put
nevera: refrigerator

la mejor manera: the best way
acompañada: along with
queso blanco: white cheese
leche de cabra: goat milk
aún se disfruta/disfrutar: is still enjoyed/to enjoy
hogares: homes

prueben/probar: try/to try
postre: dessert
tendrán/tener: have/to have
pedazo: piece

El mate

ARGENTINA

El mate es una infusión muy popular **entre** los argentinos. **Para prepararlo no se necesita más que yerba mate, bombilla**, un mate y agua. **Sin embargo, en realidad**, el mate es **más que eso**. Es un ritual, una tradición y una costumbre con un particular **significado que hacen** de esta **bebida algo** muy especial.

Hay distintas y **variadas** formas de **tomarlo**: con **azúca**r o **amargo**, muy caliente o frío con **jugo de naranja**, con una **cucharadita de café** o con **yuyos**. Pero **nunca debe hacerse** con **agua hervida** porque **se lava**.

Se toma **solo** o en **compañía**. O con la sola compañía del mate. Cuando **se pasa de mano en mano** debe **respetarse** la **ronda**, y **no decir** "gracias" hasta **llegar al punto** de **no querer más**. La yerba es lo único que hay siempre en todas las casas argentinas. Y **si un día** uno **se quedara sin yerba**, un **vecino amablemente le dará**.

El mate es **compañerismo**, es generosidad. Es la hospitalidad de la invitación. La **alegría** de la **charla compartida** o el **alivio** de **nunca sentirse** del **todo solo**. El mate **iguala**, **une** y **ayuda** a **sanar** los **corazones heridos**.

el mate: tealike beverage
entre: among
para prepararlo: to prepare it
no se necesita: you do not need
más que: more than
yerba mate: maté herb
bombilla: straw used to sip the mate
sin embargo: nevertheless
en realidad: in fact, actually
más que eso: more than this
significado: meaning
que hacen/hacer: that makes/to make
bebida: drink
algo: something

hay distintas: there are different
variadas: varied, assorted
tomarlo/tomar: drink it/to drink
azúcar: sugar
amargo: bitter
jugo de naranja: orange juice
cucharadita de café: a teaspoon of coffee
yuyos: medicinal herbs
nunca debe hacerse: it must never be made
aqua hervida: boiled water
se lava/lavar: it is washed/to wash

solo: alone
compañía: company
se pasa de mano en mano: it is passed from hand to hand
respetarse: to respect
ronda: round
no decir: do not say
llegar al punto: to reach the point
no querer más: not wanting more
si un día: if one day
se quedara sin yerba: you ran out of yerba
vecino: neighbor
amablemente: kindly
le dará: he will give it to you

compañerismo: companionship
alegría: happiness
charla compartida: shared conversation
alivio: relief
nunca sentirse: never feeling
todo solo: all alone
iguala/igualar: it equals/to equal
une/unir: it unites/to unite
ayuda/ayudar: it helps/to help
sanar: to cure, to heal
corazones heridos: broken hearts

El dulce de leche
ARGENTINA

Si bien muchos **sostienen** que el dulce de leche **nació** en **tierras** argentinas, su origen **no es bien conocido**. Chile, Perú y Uruguay **se disputan** también la **paternidad** de este **dulce**, uno de los **alimentos** más **arraigados** entre los **rioplatenses**. **Cualquier postre** o **torta rellena** con él **convierte** una **vulgar receta** en un **manjar** propio de **dioses**. **Se come** a cualquier hora, con **galletitas**, tortas, **tostadas, flanes**, con **panqueques** o, simplemente, a cucharadas. También se usa para la elaboración industrial de productos como **helados** y yogures.

Aunque es más fácil y rápido comprarlo en un supermercado, el dulce de leche **hecho en casa** es mucho más rico. Aquí va la receta:

Ingredientes:

2 litros de leche

1/2 kilo de azúcar

¼ **cucharadita** de bicarbonato de sodio

1 **chaucha** de vainilla (opcional)

Preparación:

Coloque todos los ingredientes en un **recipiente** grande, **preferentemente** de **cobre** o aluminio, **a fuego fuerte** hasta que **rompa a hervir**. **Revuelva evitando** que **se derrame**. Con el fuego un poco más bajo, **deje** hervir durante unas horas hasta que **tome** un color marrón acaramelado y comience a **espesar**. Baje el fuego al mínimo revolviendo **a menudo** con una **cuchara de madera**.

---

sostienen/sostener: they maintain/ to maintain
nació/nacer: it was born/to be born
tierras: lands
no es bien conocido/conocer: it is not well known/to know
se disputan/disputarse: they fight over/ to fight over
paternidad: paternity
dulce: cake, sweet
alimentos: foods
arraigados: deeply rooted
rioplatenses: from the region of the Río de la Plata
cualquier: any
postre: dessert
torta rellena: filled cake
convierte/convertir: it turns/to turn
vulgar: simple, common
receta: recipe
manjar: a delicious food or dish
dioses: gods
se come/comer: it is eaten/to eat
galletitas: small cookies
tostadas: toast
flanes: caramel custards
panqueques: pancakes
helados: ice cream

hecho en casa: homemade

cucharadita: teaspoonful
chaucha: vanilla bean

coloque/colocar: put/to put
recipiente: container
preferentemente: preferably
cobre: copper
a fuego fuerte: over high heat
rompa a hervir/hervir: it starts to boil/to boil
revuelva/revolver: stir/to stir
evitando/evitar: avoiding/to avoid
se derrame/derramarse: it spills/ to spill
deje/dejar: let/to let
tome/tomar: it takes/to take
espesar: to thicken
a menudo: often
cuchara de madera: wooden spoon

Para determinar **si está listo**, coloque un poquito de dulce en un plato y **fíjese** que **no se corra**. **Retire** del fuego y continúe revolviendo durante un rato hasta que **se entibie**.

UN DULCE CON HISTORIA

Algunos cuentan que la leche condensada fue la **antecesora** del dulce de leche. En la Francia de 1700, Napoleón Bonaparte **necesitaba encontrar** la **manera** de transportar más **fácilmente** la leche (elemento esencial para sus hombres en las **campañas militares**) sin que **se cortase**. Así, nació la leche condensada, que se obtiene también de la concentración **por acción del calor** de la **mezcla** de leche e **hidratos de carbono** (azúcar).

Sin embargo, según la tradición oral **bonaerense** el dulce de leche se originó algún día del año 1800 en una **estancia** del interior, donde Juan Manuel de Rosas, **jefe** de la Fuerza Federal y su opositor, el Comandante del **ejército** Unitario Juan Lavalle, **se encontraban** por motivos políticos.

La leyenda cuenta que una **criada** de Rosas estaba haciendo la lechada (leche caliente azucarada) para servir a su patrón, cuando al llegar Lavalle, **cansado** por el viaje, **se acostó** en un **catre** en el que usualmente **descansaba** Rosas. La criada, al encontrar ocupado el lugar por el **jefe enemigo**, **dio aviso** a la guardia **olvidando** la leche que hervía en la **olla** y **cuyo contenido se transformó** en la **mezcla** que hoy **se conoce como** dulce de leche.

quién no ha saboreado/saborear:
  who hasn't savored/to savor
puré de papas: mashed potatoes
al horno: baked
fritas: fried
ensalada: salad
platos: dishes
tubérculo: tuber
apareció/aparecer: it appeared/
  to appear
miles: thousands
cuenta con/contar con: it has/to have
variedades: varieties

según: according to
estudios: research, investigations
se cultivó/cultivar: it was farmed/
  to farm, to cultivate
muestras: samples
datan/datar: they date/to date
hallaron/hallar: they found/to find
cuevas: caves
ventanas: windows

forma parte/formar parte: it takes
  part/to take part
maíz: corn
se constituyó/constituirse: it set itself
  up/to set oneself up
alimentación: food
imperio: empire
leyendas: legends
reino: kingdom
esposa: wife, spouse
enseñar: to teach
cultivo: cultivation

no era conocido/ser conocido:
  it wasn't known/to be known
descubrimiento: discovery
lo llevaron/llevar: they took it/to take
se introdujo/introducir: it was
  introduced/to introduce
pasó/pasar: it moved/to move

La deliciosa papa
PERÚ

¿Quién no ha saboreado un **puré de papas**, unas papas **al horno**, unas papas **fritas** o una **ensalada** de papa? Todos estos **platos** están preparados con el **tubérculo** más famoso del mundo, la papa o patata, que **apareció** en este planeta hace **miles** de años y que, además, **cuenta con** más de 3.000 **variedades** en el Perú, su país de origen.

Según estudios científicos, este vegetal **se cultivó** cerca del Lago Titicaca, entre los territorios del Perú y Bolivia, unos 10.000 años atrás. Las **muestras** más antiguas **datan** del período neolítico, es decir, 8.000 años ante de Cristo, y se **hallaron** en unas **cuevas** llamadas Tres **Ventanas**, en la localidad de Chilca, a 65 kilómetros al sur de Lima.

Esta planta **forma parte** de la historia peruana y, junto con el **maíz**, **se constituyó** en la base de la **alimentación** del **imperio** incaico. Según una de las **leyendas** sobre la fundación de este **reino**, Manco Cápac, el primer Inca, junto con su **esposa** Mama Ocllo emergieron del Lago Titicaca para **enseñar** a los hombres el **cultivo** de este vegetal.

Este tubérculo **no era conocido** en Europa antes del **descubrimiento** de América. Los conquistadores españoles **lo llevaron** al viejo mundo en la segunda mitad del siglo XVI desde el Perú. España fue el primer país europeo donde **se introdujo** este alimento. Desde allí **pasó** a Italia, Francia, Alemania, Inglaterra y el resto de los países europeos.

Al principio, los europeos **se resistieron** a **comerla atribuyéndole** propiedades tóxicas. En Francia fue necesario que **el propio rey pusiera de moda** la flor de la papa en la corte, para **obligar** a los nobles a cultivarla en sus tierras.

Fue la **escasez** de alimentos en los años que precedieron a la Revolución Francesa, lo que **acabó imponiendo** su **consumo** en varios países europeos, **salvando** así a Europa de la **hambruna**.

LA GASTRONOMÍA PERUANA

La patata es uno de los ingredientes fundamentales de la **fina** gastronomía peruana. Entre los platos más exquisitos **sobresalen** la papa a la huancaína (papas **sancochadas cubiertas** con una salsa hecha de **queso fresco, aceite, ají** y **galleta remojada** en leche) y la ocopa (papas sancochadas **acompañadas** de **crema de almendras, huacatay**, queso fresco y leche). También **destacan** la papa **rellena** (papa sancochada **amasada** y rellena con **carne picada**, cebolla y **pasas** fritas en aceite bien caliente) y la causa (papa sancochada y amasada con un poco de aceite, limón y ají, y rellenada con **verduras, pollo** o **pescado**).

Quizás para el común de los **pobladores** del mundo este alimento de los incas sea algo simple y hasta **soso**, pero si visita Perú **se encontrará** con toda una tradición al **degustar** este tubérculo andino **lleno de** historia y **sabor**.

al principio: at the beginning
se resistieron/resistirse: they were reluctant/to be reluctant
comerla/comer: eat it/to eat
atribuyéndole/atribuir: attributing to it/to attribute
el propio rey: the king himself
pusiera de moda: to make fashionable
obligar: to force

escasez: scarcity
acabó/acabar: it ended/to end
imponiendo/imponer: imposing/ to impose
consumo: consumption
salvando/salvar: saving/to save
hambruna: starvation

fina: fine
sobresalen/sobresalir: they stand out/ to stand out
sancochadas: boiled
cubiertas: covered
queso fresco: fresh cheese
aceite: oil
ají: chili, red pepper
galleta: cookie
remojada: soaked
acompañadas: together with
crema de almendras: thick almond soup
huacatay: a Peruvian mint
destacan/destacar: they stand out/ to stand out
rellena: filled
amasada: mashed
carne picada: ground beef
pasas: raisins
verduras: vegetables
pollo: chicken
pescado: fish

pobladores: settlers
soso: tasteless
se encontrará/encontrar: one will find/to find
degustar: to taste
lleno de: filled with
sabor: flavor

papas: potatoes	
cocidas: boiled	
peladas: peeled	
cebollas verdes: green onions	
lavadas: washed	
rebanadas: slices	
huevo crudo: raw egg	
cucharada: spoonful	
perejil: parsley	
finamente picado: finely chopped	
taza: cup	
queso: cheese	
gratinado: grated	
al gusto: to taste	
pimienta negra: black pepper	

haga/hacer: make/to make
puré: puree
añada/añadir: add/to add
forme/formar: make/to make
mezcla: mixture
caliente: heat up
fuego medio-alto: medium-high heat
deben/deber: they must/must
quedar bien doradas: to be well browned
quemadas/quemar: burnt/to burn

betabeles: beets
diente de ajo: garlic clove
cucharadita: teaspoonful
jugo: juice
mitad: half

macere/macerar: crush/to crush
molcajete: a Mexican mortar and pestle made from basalt rock
corte/cortar: cut/to cut
agregue/agregar: add/to add
los demás: the rest
déjelo/dejar: let it/to let
refrigerar: to cool, to refrigerate
servir: to serve
póngalo/poner: put it/to put

Recetas con papas
MÉXICO

TORTA DE PAPA

Ingredientes:
2 ½ libras de **papas**, **cocidas** y **peladas**
2 **cebollas verdes**, **lavadas** y cortadas en **rebanadas**
1 **huevo crudo**
1 **cucharada** de **perejil finamente picado**
1 cucharada de aceite de olivo
1 **taza** de **queso gratinado**
Sal **al gusto**
Pimienta negra al gusto
Aceite de olivo para freír

Preparación:
Haga un **puré** con las papas. **Añada** el huevo, el perejil, la cebolla, el queso, la cucharada de aceite de olivo y la sal y la pimienta a su gusto. **Forme** la **mezcla** en cuatro hamburguesas. **Caliente** el aceite y fría la carne sobre **fuego medio-alto** en los dos lados. **Deben** de **quedar bien doradas** pero no **quemadas**.

ENSALADA DE PAPA CON BETABEL

Ingredientes:
4 papas medianas, cocidas y peladas
4 **betabeles** medianos, cocidos y pelados
1 **diente de ajo**
½ **cucharadita** de sal
¼ de taza de aceite de olivo
El **jugo** de la **mitad** de un limón
Pimienta negra al gusto

Preparación:
Macere el ajo con la sal en un **molcajete**. **Corte** las papas y los betabeles en rebanadas. **Agregue los demás** ingredientes y **déjelo refrigerar** una hora antes de **servir**. **Póngalo** en un platón bonito.

Ensalada de yuca

CUBA

Ingredientes:

2 **libras** de yuca

2 **dientes** de **ajo**

½ **cdta.** de sal

¾ **taza** de mayonesa

½ taza de cilantro **picadito**

7 **tomatines miniatura**

½ taza de **aceite de oliva**

3 **cdas.** de **jugo de naranja**

6 tazas de **lechugas**, **lavadas** y **bien secas**

Preparación:

Sancoche la yuca en agua con sal **hasta** que esté **blanda**. **Escurra** muy bien y **deje refrescar**. En una **vasija mezcle bien** la mayonesa con el **ajo machacado** y el jugo de naranja. **Al final**, se le **agrega el** aceite de oliva en chorrito y sal y pimienta **al gusto**. Esta salsa **se puede preparar** unas **horas antes**. Ahora **corte** la yuca en **trocitos** e incorporar en la salsa. Al final se le agrega el cilantro picadito. **Sirva sobre** las **hojas de lechuga** y **decore con** los tomatines.

libras: pounds
dientes: cloves
ajo: garlic
cdta.: cucharadita (teaspoon)
taza: cup
picadito: chopped
tomatines miniatura: cherry tomatoes
aceite de oliva: olive oil
cdas.: cucharadas (tablespoons)
jugo de naranja: orange juice
lechugas: lettuce
lavadas/lavar: washed/to wash
bien secas/secar: well dried/to dry

sancoche: parboil
hasta: until
blanda: soft
escurra/escurrir: drain/to drain
deje refrescar: let cool
vasija: pot, dish
mezcle bien/mezclar: mix well/to mix
ajo machacado: crushed garlic
al final: finally
agrega el/agregar: add the/to add
al gusto: to taste
se puede preparar: can be prepared
horas antes: hours before
corte: cut
trocitos: small pieces
sirva sobre: serve on
hojas de lechuga: lettuce leaves
decore con/decorar: decorate with/ to decorate

Vocabulario de la cocina

cocer al horno: bake
rociando: basting
albardilla: batter
punto de ebullición: boiling point
escaldar: scald
caldo: broth
chorrito: dash
cortar en cuadritos: dice
guarnición: garnish
escurrir: drain
cuajar: curdle
hacer puré: mash
glasear: glaze
rallado: grated

molido, pulverizado: ground
hierba: herb
herbario: herb garden
jengibre: ginger
albahaca: basil
laurel: bay leaf
romero: rosemary
nuez moscada: nutmeg
jugoso: juicy
congelado: frozen
barbacoa/parrillada: barbeque
batir: whisk
migas de pan: bread crumbs
pedazo grande: wedge

apagar: turn off
saltear: sauté
sazonar: season with salt
estofado: stew
cortado en cuatro: quartered
taza para medir: measuring cup
cucharones: ladles
papel de aluminio: aluminum foil
fregadero: kitchen sink
comedor: dining room
escoba: broom
congelador: freezer
lavaplatos: dishwasher
gabinete: cabinet

Camarones en salsa blanca
MÉXICO

La **primera vez** que fui a México con mi **esposo** estábamos **recién casados** y era febrero. El día de San Valentín **me llevó** a su restaurante favorito. **Se llamaba** El Rubí. ¡La **carta** era una delicia! ¡Camarones en salsa blanca! **Ese sigue** siendo **hoy en día** uno de mis platos favoritos.

Ingredientes:
12 camarones grandes sin pelar
½ **cucharadita** de sal
1 taza de agua
½ taza de **harina blanca**
8 onzas de **mantequilla salada**
½ taza de **vino blanco seco**
3 ¾ tazas de **leche fría**
1 **frasco mediano** de chile rojo dulce, **exprimido**, **cortado** en **rajas**
½ taza de **perejil**, **lavado** y picado
Sal y pimienta negra al gusto

Preparación:
En una **sartén grande derrita** la mantequilla a **fuego medio-alto** y **añada** la harina, **moviéndolo** todo hasta que **espese**. **Agregue** el vino y la leche fría y **siga removiendo** con el fuego algo más bajo. Continué **así** hasta que espese y **retírelo** del fuego. **Sazone** con sal y pimienta negra. **Mientras tanto**, caliente una taza de agua con media cucharadita de sal. **Cuando hierva**, añada los camarones y **déjelos hervir** durante un minuto. **Quítelo** del fuego y **enjuague** los camarones con agua fría. Quite la **cáscara** y **séquelos** con un **trapito de cocina**. Caliente el horno a 400 grados F. En una **cacerola de vidrio**, **ponga** la salsa blanca y los camarones, y **adórnelo** con las rajas de chile y el perejil. **Métalo** en el **horno** durante 10 minutos. **Se puede servir** con puntos de **pan tostado** y una ensalada.

---

camarones: shrimp
salsa blanca: white sauce
primera vez: first time
esposo: husband
recién casados: just married
me llevó/llevar: he took me/to take
se llamaba/llamar: it was called/to call
carta: menu
ese sigue/seguir: it continues to be, it still is/to continue
hoy en día: nowadays

cucharadita: teaspoon
harina blanca: white flour
mantequilla salada: salted butter
vino blanco seco: dry white wine
leche fría: cold milk
frasco mediano: medium-sized bottle
exprimido/exprimir: squeezed/ to squeeze
cortado/cortar: cut/to cut
rajas: pieces
perejil: parsley
lavado/lavar: washed/to wash

sartén grande: large frying pan
derrita/derretir: melt/to melt
fuego medio-alto: medium to high heat
añada/añadir: add/to add
moviéndolo/mover: stirring it/to stir
espese/espesar: it thickens/to thicken
agregue/agregar: add/to add
siga removiendo/remover: keep stirring/to stir
así: this way
retírelo/retirar: remove it/to remove
sazone/sazonar: season/to season
mientras tanto: in the meantime
cuando hierva/hervir: when it boils/ to boil
déjelos hervir: let it boil
quítelo/quitar: remove it/to remove
enjuague/enjuagar: rinse/to rinse
cáscara: shell
séquelos/secar: dry them/to dry
trapito de cocina: dishcloth
cacerola de vidrio: glass saucepan
ponga/poner: put/to put
adórnelo/adornar: decorate it/ to decorate
métalo/meter: put it inside/ to put inside
horno: oven
se puede/poder: you can/can
servir: to serve
pan tostado: toast

Carnitas
MÉXICO

Los domingos es típico **salir temprano** a comprar carnitas. El **olor** de estos **pedacitos** de **carne de puerco**, hechos en grandes **ollas de cobre**, es incomparable. Sin embargo, ¡yo **prefiero hacerlos** en mi cocina!

Ingredientes:

5 **libras** de carne de puerco **cortada en cubos** de tres **pulgadas**

2 libras de **manteca vegetal**

1 **cucharada** de sal

1 **cucharadita** de **pimienta molida fresca**

5 **dientes de ajo**

1 **cebolla** grande, **pelada** y **en cuartos**

3 **trozos** de naranja sin pelar

1/3 de **taza** de leche

Para servir: Guacamole y tortillas frescas y **calientes**

Preparación:

Ponga sal y la pimienta a la carne **por todos lados**. En una **sartén** grande o una **cacerola** grande (preferiblemente de **hierro**), **dore** la carne **a fuego alto** en la manteca ya **derretida** durante unos 20 ó 30 minutos. Es necesario mover la carne **de vez en cuando**. **Añada** la cebolla, la naranja y el ajo. **Baje** el fuego hasta el mínimo posible y **déjelo cocer** una hora. Ponga entonces la leche y **mueva** bien todos los ingredientes. Después de media hora, **apáguelo** y **saque** los pedazos de carne. **Sirva** la carne en un **platón bonito acompañada del** guacamole y **cómala** como tacos con las tortillas calientes después de **deshebrar** la carne. **¡Buen provecho!**

---

salir: to go out
temprano: early
olor: smell
pedacitos: little bits, small pieces
carne de puerco: pork meat
ollas de cobre: copper pots
prefiero/preferir: I prefer/to prefer
hacerlos/hacer: to make them/to make

libras: pounds
cortada en cubos: cut up in cubes
pulgadas: inches
manteca vegetal: vegetable fat
cucharada: spoonful
cucharadita: teaspoon
pimienta molida fresca: fresh ground pepper
dientes de ajo: cloves of garlic
cebolla: onion
pelada/pelar: peeled/to peel
en cuartos: in quarters
trozos: pieces
taza: cup
calientes: hot

ponga/poner: put/to put
por todos lados: everywhere
sartén: frying pan
cacerola: saucepan
hierro: iron
dore/dorar: brown/to brown
a fuego alto: on a high flame
derretida: melted
de vez en cuando: once in a while
añada/añadir: add/to add
baje/bajar: turn down/to turn down
déjelo cocer: let it cook
mueva/mover: move/to move
apáguelo/apagar: turn it off/to turn off
saque/sacar: take out/to take out
sirva/servir: serve/to serve
platón bonito: pretty plate
acompañada del: together with
cómala/comer: eat it/to eat
deshebrar: to shred
¡Buen provecho!: Enjoy your meal!

Sangría, la bebida del verano
ESPAÑA

Seguramente, **usted ha visto** en la **tienda** o supermercado sangría **embotellada**. **Y si le gusta** la sangría, ¿por qué no **prepararla** en casa? Esta bebida es popular y **refrescante**, y **puede servirse** con **casi cualquier plato**, para **comer** o para **cenar**. **A pesar de** sus **orígenes humildes** en España, es ahora una bebida **conocida en todo el mundo**. Sus ingredientes básicos son: **vino tinto**, **azúcar** y frutas. Pero si **usted quiere**, **también puede añadir** brandy, **ron** o Bacardi. El vino es Rioja tinto, pero también **se utiliza** cualquier vino tinto, **incluso** vino blanco.

La **receta no es siempre la misma**. **Podemos cambiar** las frutas, las **cantidad** de azúcar, el tipo de vino e incluso añadir, si queremos, el licor. ¡Puede ser **divertido** crear **nuestra propia** Sangría!

Ingredientes:
Una **botella** de Rioja u otro vino tinto
Azúcar **al gusto**
Un limón en **rodajas finas**
Una **naranja** en rodajas finas
Melocotón y/o **manzana cortados** en **pequeños trozos**
Gaseosa
Licor: al gusto (opcional)

Preparación:
Mezclar todos los ingredientes y **dejar reposar** unas horas en el **frigorífico**. Es importante que la **mezcla** repose unas horas, para que la mezcla tenga el **sabor adecuado**.

Después de ese tiempo, **agitar** y añadir el azúcar, el licor y la gaseosa, que puede ser de limón o naranja, pero es mejor la gaseosa **sin sabor**.

Cuando bebamos la sangría, añadir **hielo** y **servir lo más fría posible**.

---

seguramente: surely
usted ha visto: you have seen
tienda: store
embotellada: bottled
y si le gusta/gustar: and if you like/ to like
prepararla/preparar: prepare it/ to prepare
refrescante: refreshing
puede servirse: can be served
casi cualquier plato: almost any dish
comer: to have lunch
cenar: to have dinner
a pesar de: despite
orígenes humildes: humble origins
conocida en todo el mundo: known all around the world
vino tinto: red wine
azúcar: sugar
usted quiere/querer: you want/to want
también puede añadir: you can also add
ron: rum
se utiliza/utilizar: it is used/to use
incluso: even

receta: recipe
no es siempre la misma: is not always the same
podemos cambiar: we can change
cantidad: quantity
divertido: fun
nuestra propia: our own

botella: bottle
al gusto: as desired, to taste
rodajas finas: thin slices
naranja: orange
melocotón: peach
manzana: apple
cortados/cortar: cut/to cut
pequeños trozos: small pieces
gaseosa: bubbly water

mezclar: to mix
dejar reposar: let sit
frigorífico: refrigerator
mezcla: mixture
sabor adecuado: appropriate flavor

después de: after
agitar: to stir
sin sabor: flavorless

cuando bebamos/beber: when we drink/to drink
hielo: ice
servir lo más fría posible: to serve as cold as possible

La chicha
ECUADOR

La chicha es una **bebida alcohólica** que las comunidades indígenas **toman** todos los días. El **significado** de la chicha es comida, bebida, **hospitalidad** y también la **fuerza**.

Se prepara todos los días para que **permanezca fresca**. **Muy temprano en la mañana** las mujeres se van a **la chacra** con los niños para **sacar** la **yuca madura**. **Mientras** ellas trabajan cantan **"anent"** para que los niños **apren-dan la costumbre**. **Cuan-do llegan** a casa **meten los tubérculos** en **una olla** con un poco de agua **tapados** con **unas hojas** estén **cocinadas**.

Cuando están listas la mujer **saca** la olla de **la candela** y empieza a **aplastarlos** con el **"taink"**. Es mejor hacerlo cuando la yuca está caliente porque se **deshace fácilmente**. **Sin embargo**, el "alma" es la parte interna fibrosa; **hay que machacarla** muy bien. Cuando todo está machacado la mujer **vuelve a colocarla** en la olla y **la deja toda la noche fermentando**.

La mujer que la preparó también **la sirve en presencia de** su **marido**. Ella la mezcla bien con los dedos y es importante **no tocar** su mano **al coger** el **"pinink"**. **Rechazar** la chicha es **grave** porque significa **desprecio** o **desconfianza**.

¡**Acuérdense**, si usted visita el oriente, **prepárense para tomar** chica!

El turrón
ESPAÑA

Aunque el turrón **está disponible** todo el año, todos **lo comemos** en Navidad. **Digamos** que el turrón es **imprescindible** durante estas celebraciones. Hay muchos tipos de turrón: de **yema**, **coco**, chocolate, etc. Pero el turrón por excelencia es el turrón de almendra. Hay dos tipos de turrón de almedra: turrón de Alicante (**llamado también** "turrón **duro**") y turrón de Jijona (o "turrón **blando**"). **El primero** está **hecho con trozos** de almendras, y **el segundo** con almendras **molidas**.

Aproximadamente **un mes antes de Navidad**, todos los comercios tienen ya **a la venta** gran variedad de turrones. Pero este año **intentaremos** hacer **nuestro propio** turrón en casa.

Seguidamente encontrarás la receta del turrón de Alicante.

Ingredientes:
1 Kilo (2,20 **libras**) de **miel**
500 gramos (1,10 libras) de azúcar
2 **claras de huevo**
1,5 Kilos (3,30 libras) de almendras **tostadas** (Puedes tostarlas en el **horno**).
la **corteza de un limón**

Preparación:
Primero, **coceremos a fuego lento** la miel, en un **cazo**, **hasta que espese** (hasta que el agua **que contiene se evapore**). **A continuación** añadir el azúcar y **mezclar**. Se recomienda usar una **espátula de madera**.

Batir las claras de huevo **a punto de nieve** y **añadirlas** a la mezcla. **Remover con energía** durante **unos diez minutos** hasta que la mezlca **se oscurezca**. Añadir las almendras y la corteza de limón. Mezclar bien y cocer a fuego lento, **cuidando de** que **no se pegue**.

Seguidamente **verteremos** la mezcla en **moldes de madera forrados** con **papel vegetal**. Después de dos horas y media, el turrón estará listo. Conservar los trozos, cuando estén **completamente fríos**, en un **envase hermético**.

---

aunque: although
está disponible: it is available
lo comemos/comer: we eat it/to eat
digamos/decir: let's say/to say
imprescindible: essential
yema: egg yolk
coco: coconut
llamado también: also called
duro: hard
blando: soft
el primer: the first
hecho con trozos: made of pieces
el segundo: the second
molidas: crushed

un mes antes de Navidad: one month before Christmas
a la venta: on sale
intentaremos/intentar: we will try/ to try
nuestro propio: our own

seguidamente: next
encontrarás: you will find

libras: pounds
miel: honey
claras de huevo: egg whites
tostadas: toasted
horno: oven
corteza de un limón: lemon rind

coceremos a fuego lento: we will simmer
cazo: saucepan
hasta que espese: until it gets thick
que contiene: that it contains
se evapore/evaporarase: it evaporates/ to evaporate
a continuación: next
mezclar: to mix
espátula de madera: wooden spatula

batir: to beat
a punto de nieve: until stiff
añadirlas/añadir: add them/to add
remover con energía: to stir briskly
unos diez minutos: about ten minutes
se oscurezca: it gets dark
cuidando de: taking care
no se pegue/pegar: it does not stick/ to stick

verteremos/verter: we will pour/ to pour
moldes de madera: wooden molds
forrados: lined
papel vegetal: rice paper
completamente fríos: completely cold
envase hermético: airtight container

Tradicional comida
GUATEMALA

ARROZ CON LECHE

Ingredientes:
2 **tazas** de **arroz**
4 tazas de **leche**
2 **huevos**
1 ½ tazas de **azúcar**
1 taza de **pasas sin semilla**
4 **ramas** de **canela**
Agua

Preparación:
Lave el arroz. **Cocínelo hasta suavizarlo**. Ponga al **fuego** la leche, el azúcar y la canela. **Retírelo del fuego** cuando la leche **tenga el sabor de la** canela. **Cuélelo**. **Mezcle** la leche con una **batidora eléctrica** y **añada** los huevos. Mezcle el arroz con leche, el azúcar y la canela. **Ponga** al fuego y añada las pasas, **revolviendo** constantemente. Se **sirve frío o caliente**, adornado con **canela en polvo**.

LA FRITADA

Ingredientes:
1 Kg de **costilla de cerdo**
1/2 **taza de agua**
Sal
4 **dientes de ajo**
1 **cebolla blanca cortada en** 4 **trozos**
1 **ramita de apio**

Preparación:
En un **sartén grueso** poner todos los ingredientes, excepto la cebolla. **Cocinar** a **fuego alto**, dando **vueltas** a la **carne**, hasta que se **evapore toda el agua**. **Bajar** a llama media y **seguir friendo**, **aplastando** las **partes grasosas** de la carne, durante 25 a 35 minutos, **o hasta** que **se dore** en la **manteca que suelta**. **Añadir** el apio y la cebolla en los **últimos 15 minutos**. La fritada **debe estar muy dorada**, de color café. Típicamente se sirve con papas y **plátano maduro**.

tazas: cups
arroz: rice
leche: milk
huevos: eggs
azúcar: sugar
pasas sin semilla: seedless raisins
ramas: stalks (sticks)
canela: cinnamon

lave/llavar: wash/to wash
cocínelo hasta suavizarlo: cooking it until soft
fuego: heat
retírelo del fuego: remove from heat
tenga el sabor de la: tastes like, it has the flavor of
cuélelo: drain (sieve)
mezcle/mezclar: mix/to mix
batidora eléctrica: electric mixer
añada/añadir: add/to add
ponga/poner: put/to put
revolviendo/revolver: stirring/to stir
sirve frío o caliente: serve cold or hot
canela en polvo: ground cinnamon

costilla de cerdo: pork ribs
taza de agua: cup of water
dientes de ajo: garlic cloves
cebolla blanca: white onion
cortada en/cortar: cut in/to cut
trozos: pieces
ramita de apio: small stalk of celery

sartén grueso: heavy frying pan
cocinar: cook
fuego alto: high heat
vueltas/vuelta: turning/to turn
carne: meat
evapore toda el agua: all the water evaporates
bajar: lower
seguir friendo: continue frying
aplastando/aplastar: squashing/ to squash, to flatten
partes grasosas: greasy parts
o hasta: or until
se dore/dorar: it is brown/to brown
manteca que suelta: fat that it gives off
añadir: add
últimos 15 minutos: last 15 minutes
debe estar muy dorada: must be very browned
plátano maduro: ripe plantains

La "dieta mediterránea"

ESPAÑA

El concepto de "Dieta Mediterránea"... **¡está poniéndose de moda! Actualmente**, los mejores "maitres" de la cocina española **hablan de este tipo de dieta. Podemos encontrar** muchas páginas web que hablan sobre esta cocina, pero, ¿Cuál es el origen de la dieta mediterránea? Y ¿cuáles son sus **principales** características?

Sobre su origen, **cuando se estudiaron las costumbres alimenticias** de los países mediterráneos, (Grecia, Italia, Francia, España, etc.), **descubrieron** que en general **los habitantes de estas zonas** tenían un **bajo nivel de colesterol, comparados con** los **consumidores anglosajones**, centroeuropeos o norteamericanos, que **consumían** dietas **con más calorías**, más carnes, **grasas**, dulces y mantequilla. **Al contrario**, la dieta mediterránea **se basa** en los cereales, verduras, frutas, vino, pescados y... ¡también, pero **en menor cantidad**! Así, la dieta mediterránea **se ha creado a lo largo de los siglos**. Por ejemplo: los romanos y los griegos **nos dieron** "los tres productos mediterráneos", esto es, pan, vino y aceite de oliva. Más tarde, la cultura árabe nos dio la **berenjena**, la **alcachofa**, y muchas otras **hortalizas**. Y la dieta mediterránea también está influenciada por el descubrimiento de América: de allí **llegaron** el tomate, el **pimiento**, la patata o el maíz.

Ahora que ya sabemos sobre el origen de la dieta mediterránea, ¿Cuáles son sus características? Primero, es una dieta **saludable** y beneficiosa que previene las **enfermedades vasculares**, ya que **reduce** el nivel de colesterol. Segundo, el uso de aceite de oliva es muy importante. Tercero, gran consumo de productos vegetales y frutas. Cuarto, consumo **diario** de productos **lácteos** (yoghurt, leche, queso etc.) Quinto, consumo **semanal** de pescados. Sexto, consumo **mensual moderado** de carnes. Podemos encontrar la dieta mediterránea en **varios países**, y cada uno de estos países tiene **su propia** gastronomía basada siempre en este tipo de dieta.

Y ahora una nota personal: **No penséis** que esta dieta es **pobre en sabor o variedad**. Yo, **como seguidora** de esta cocina, **he probado** platos realmente deliciosos!

---

está poniéndose de moda: is becoming fashionable
actualmente: at present
hablan de este tipo de dieta: they talk about this type of diet
podemos econtrar: we can find
principales: main

cuando se estudiaron las costumbres alimenticias: when the nutritional customs were studied
descubrieron/descubrir: they discovered/to discover
los habitantes de estas zonas: the inhabitants from these areas
bajo nivel de colesterol: low cholesterol level
comparados con: compared with
consumidores anglosajones: Anglo-Saxon consumers
consumían/consumir: they consumed/to consume
con más calorías: with more calories
grasas: fat
al contrario: on the contrary
se basa/basarse: it is based
en menor cantidad: in less quantity
se ha creado/crearse: has been created/to create
a lo largo de los siglos: throughout the centuries
nos dieron/dar: they gave us/to give
berenjena: eggplant
alcachofa: artichoke
hortalizas: vegetables
llegaron/llegar: arrived/to arrive
pimiento: green pepper

ahora que ya sabemos: now that we already know
saludable: healthy
enfermedades vasculares: vascular illness
reduce/reducir: it reduces/to reduce
diario: daily
lácteos: dairy
semanal: weekly
mensual: monthly
moderado: moderate
varios países: several countries
su propia: its own

no penséis/pensar: do not think/to think
pobre en sabor o variedad: poor in flavor (taste) or variety
como seguidora: as a follower
he probado/probar: I have tasted/to taste

Un delicioso postre: flan de huevo
LATINOAMÉRICA

Uno de los **postres** más populares de Latinoamérica es el **flan de huevo**, aunque también **puede** ser de vainilla, chocolate, etc.... ¿Qué ingredientes **necesitamos** para esta receta?

Ingredientes:
1 **litro de leche**
7 **cucharadas grandes** de **azúcar**
1 **corteza de limón**
6 huevos
canela (un trozo pequeño)

Preparación:
Muy bien; **ahora**, **para preparar** el flan, **seguiremos los siguientes pasos**: Colocar la **bandeja del horno** a **altura media** y **precalentar** a 350ºF. **Hervir** la leche con el azúcar, la canela y la corteza de limón. Mientras **se calienta** la leche con los demás ingredientes, **batir** los huevos en un recipiente.

Mezclar la leche caliente con los huevos batidos. **Antes de verter la mezcla** en las **flaneras**, verter en ellas un poco de caramelo líquido. Pero **si no tenemos**, **podemos hacerlo así**: Mezclar **una taza pequeña** de azúcar con 1/3 de agua y calentar **a fuego lento hasta que** el azúcar **se disuelva**. **Subir el fuego** y **no remover** la mezcla, **hasta que tome un color ámbar oscuro**. Verter el caramelo inmediatamente en las flaneras. (Nota: Personalmente, **yo utilizo** caramelo líquido; **podéis comprarlo** en **cualquier tienda** y es **más útil que hacerlo en casa**.)

Verter la mezcla caliente de leche, azúcar, canela y corteza de limón en las flaneras caramelizadas. (**No llenarlas hasta arriba**.) Colocar las flaneras dentro de una **cacerola** con agua caliente. El agua caliente **debe llegar a media altura** de las flaneras. **Cocer** en el horno durante 30 minutos aproximadamente. **Para saber** cuándo está hecho el flan, introducir una **aguja de tejer** o un **tenedor**. **Si está limpio**, el flan está hecho. Sólo **tenemos que esperar** a que los flanes **se enfríen**.

postres: desserts
flan de huevo: egg custard
puede/poder: it can/can
necesitamos/necesitar: we need/to need

litro de leche: liter of milk
cucharadas grandes: large tablespoons
azúcar: sugar
corteza de limón: lemon peel
canela: cinnamon
un trozo pequeño: a small piece, portion

ahora: now
para preparar: to prepare
seguiremos los siguientes pasos: we will follow the following steps
colocar: to place
bandeja del horno: oven tray
altura media: in center of oven
precalentar: to preheat
hervir: to simmer
se calienta/calentarse: it gets warm/ to get warm
batir: to whisk

mezclar: to combine, mix
antes de verter la mezcla: before you pour the mixture
flaneras: bowls used to prepare flan
si no tenemos: we don't have
podemos hacerlo así: we can make it this way (or as follows)
una taza pequeña: a small cup
a fuego lento: over low heat
hasta que: until
se disuelva/disolverse: it dissolves/ to dissolve
subir el fuego: to increase heat
no remover: do not stir
hasta que tome un color ámbar oscuro: until it turns a deep amber color
yo utilizo/utilizar: I use/to use
podéis comprarlo: you can buy it
cualquier tienda: any store
más útil que hacerlo en casa: more useful than making it at home

no llenarlas hasta arriba/llenar: do not fill them to the top/to fill
cacerola: saucepan
debe llegar a media altura: must come halfway up
cocer: to cook
para saber: to know
aguja de tejer: knitting needle
tenedor: fork
si está limpio: if it is clean
tenemos que esperar: we have to wait
se enfríen/enfriar: they cool down/ to cool down

Examina tu comprensión

El dulce de papaya, página 212

1. Los niños en Puerto Rico utilizan los tallos de la papaya ¿para qué?

2. ¿Qué comida es un buen acompañamiento para el postre de papaya presentado en este artículo?

El mate, página 213

1. Nombre diferentes maneras de servir mate.

2. En Argentina, si un día te quedas sin yerba, ¿cuál es la solución?

3. ¿Cómo beneficia el mate el corazón?

La deliciosa papa, página 216

1. ¿Cuántas variedades de papa se originaron en el Perú?

2. ¿Qué es la papa a la huancaína?

Ensalada de yuca, página 219

1. ¿Cuántas libras de yuca se usan en una ensalada de yuca?

2. ¿Qué tipo de jugo se utiliza en una ensalada de yuca?

3. ¿Qué verdura se usa para decorar la ensalada?

Camarones en salsa blanca, página 220

1. ¿Cuál es el nombre del restaurante donde fue hecha esta receta?

2. ¿Qué tipo de licor es usado en este plato?

Carnitas, página 221

1. ¿Cuántos dientes de ajo son usados en esta receta?

2. ¿Qué tipo de carne es el ingrediente principal de este plato?

Test your comprehension

Sangría, la bebida del verano, página 222

1. ¿Cuál es el principal ingrediente de esta bebida?

2. ¿Qué frutas tiene esta bebida?

3. Después de mezclar el vino y las frutas, ¿cuánto tiempo debe esperar para que los sabores se mezclen?

La chicha, página 223

1. ¿Qué significado cultural se asocia a la chicha?

2. La chicha es una bebida alcohólica ¿hecha de qué?

El turrón, página 224

1. ¿Cuánta miel se usa para hacer el turrón de Alicante?

2. ¿El turrón es preparado un mes antes de qué celebración?

3. ¿Cómo se conserva el turrón?

La "dieta mediterránea", página 226

1. Cuando se estudiaron las costumbres nutricionales, ¿qué se descubrió acerca de aquellas personas que comían una dieta mediterránea tradicional?

2. Las personas que comen una dieta mediterránea, ¿consumen más o menos calorías que los que comen una dieta anglosajona?

Se necesitan dos años para aprender a hablar
y sesenta para aprender a callar.

Ernest Hemingway

Conversación

sin fines de lucro: non-profit
trabaja/trabajar: works/to work
salud: health
entrevista: interview
desarrollo: development
nos cuenta sobre: tells us about

después de realizar: after conducting
construyó/construir: built/to build
noroeste: northwest
por qué decidieron/decidir: why did
  you decide/to decide

para poder proveer: in order to provide
antes: before
tenían que viajar: had to travel
ciudad: city
para recibir: to receive
contador: accountant
había hecho/hacer: had done/to do
mejor: better
entonces: then
decidió/decidir: he decided/to decide
volver: to return
dedicó/dedicar: dedicated/to dedicate
vida: life
a ayudar: to help
ha motivado/motivar: has motivated/
  to motivate
a hacer lo mismo: to do the same

de avanzada: advanced, cutting edge
tratamientos complejos: complex
  treatments
muy capacitado: very qualified

pacientes: patients
necesitan/necesitar: need/to need
todo tipo de: all kinds of
algunos: some
sencillos: simple
sarampión: measles
mujeres embarazadas: pregnant
  women
vienen a/venir: they come to/to come
tener: to have
porque: because
quirúrgicas: surgical
además: in addition
se ofrece/ofrecer: it offers/to offer

Un ejemplo de salud sustentable
ECUADOR-ESTADOS UNIDOS

Andean Health & Development (AHD) es una organización **sin fines de lucro** que **trabaja** en el área de **salud** rural en América Latina. Una ejemplo de lo que hace es el hospital Pedro Vicente Maldonado (PVM). En esta **entrevista**, Laura Dries, Directora de Administración y **Desarrollo** de la organización, **nos cuenta sobre** la experiencia.

Think Spanish (TS): **Después de realizar** un estudio de salud, AHD **construyó** el hospital PVM en el **noroeste** de Quito. ¿**Por qué decidieron** construirlo allí?

Laura Dries (LD): **Para poder proveer** servicios de salud a ecuatorianos de las zonas rurales. **Antes**, los habitantes de esta comunidad **tenían que viajar** a la **ciudad para recibir** atención. David Gaus, un **contador** de Wisconsin, **había hecho** trabajo voluntario en esta zona y vio que era necesario un **mejor** sistema de salud. **Entonces decidió volver a** los Estados Unidos a estudiar medicina. **Dedicó** su **vida a ayudar** a personas de América Latina y **ha motivado** a muchos **a hacer lo mismo**.

TS: ¿Cuáles son las principales características de este hospital rural?

LD: Cuenta con tecnología **de avanzada** para poder realizar operaciones y **tratamientos complejos**. El personal está **muy capacitado** y tiene muy buena formación.

TS: ¿Cuáles son los servicios de salud que más se solicitan?

LD: Los **pacientes necesitan todo tipo de** tratamientos. **Algunos** de los problemas de salud más serios a menudo necesitan tratamientos **sencillos**: neumonía, diarrea, deshidratación y **sarampión**. Muchas **mujeres embarazadas vienen a tene**r a sus bebés. Otros pacientes vienen **porque** necesitan intervenciones **quirúrgicas** más complejas. **Además**, **se ofrece** atención médica de emergencia, rayos X, ultrasonido y servicios de farmacia.

TS: Los proyectos de cooperación internacional **suelen enfrentar barreras idiomáticas** y culturales. ¿Cuáles fueron los principales obstáculos de este **proyecto**?

LD: Muchos habitantes de zonas rurales **hablan lenguas** indígenas y **practican** medicina tradicional y religiosa. AHD **ha respetado** y **celebrado** esas diferencias trabajando **junto con** los residentes **para crear** un sistema de atención de la salud con **armonía** cultural.

TS: El hospital fue construido con donaciones de Estados Unidos y la **ayuda** del **gobierno** local. ¿Quiénes fueron los principales **donantes** y por qué **decidieron involucrarse** en este proyecto?

LD: La mayoría de los donantes fueron de Estados Unidos, motivados por el modelo de hospital 100% autosustentable. Nuestra organización es un ejemplo para el futuro de la salud global. Los donantes son profesionales del **campo** de la salud que **entienden** esto.

TS: El hospital se financia localmente y es sustentable. **¿Cómo lograron hacer** esto fuera posible?

LD: El hospital es autosustentable porque los pacientes **pagan** por la atención. Como la **calidad** de la atención es muy buena, los pacientes **están dispuestos a** pagar una pequeña suma. Las **empresas** locales y agencias asociadas también ayudan **a subsidiar** el costo de los servicios.

TS: **Después de** esta experiencia **exitosa**, ¿cuáles son los planes de AHD?

LD: ¡**Expandirse**! El modelo ha sido tan exitoso que **nos gustaría abrir nuevos** hospitales en **otros poblados empobrecidos**. La sustentabilidad de los hospitales es **realmente impresionante** y **demuestra** que **estamos haciendo algo bueno**, **a largo plazo** y que beneficia a la salud de la población de Ecuador.

Para más información **acerca de** AHD, por favor **visiten** el sitio www.andeanhealth.org. **Ha sido un placer compartir** esta experiencia con sus **lectores**. Muchas gracias.

suelen enfrentar:	are often faced with
barreras:	barriers
idiomáticas:	language
proyecto:	project
hablan/hablar:	speak/to speak
lenguas:	languages
practican/practicar:	they practice/ to practice
ha respetado/respetar:	has respected/ to respect
celebrado/celebrar:	celebrated/ to celebrate
junto con:	together with
para crear:	(in order) to create
armonía:	harmony
ayuda:	help
gobierno:	government
donantes:	donors
decidieron involucrarse:	they decided to get involved
campo:	field
entienden/entender:	they understand/ to understand
cómo lograron hacer:	how did you manage to make
pagan/pagar:	pay/to pay
calidad:	quality
están dispuestos a:	are willing to
empresas:	companies, businesses
a subsidiar:	to subsidize
después de:	after
exitosa:	successful
expandirse:	to expand
nos gustaría abrir:	we would like to open
nuevos:	new
otros:	other
poblados empobrecidos:	impoverished villages
realmente impresionante:	really impressive
demuestra/demostrar:	it proves/ to prove
estamos haciendo/hacer:	we are doing/to do, to make
algo bueno:	something good
a largo plazo:	long-term
acerca de:	about
visiten/visitar:	visit/to visit
ha sido un placer:	it has been a pleasure
compartir:	to share
lectores:	readers

padres: parents
hijos bilingües: bilingual children
me hablan de/hablar: talk to me
  about/to talk
criar: to raise, to bring up
idioma: language
de donde viven: from where they live
expuestos: exposed
marido: husband
no se mezclan: don't they get
  mixed up
hablar: (when) speaking

yo creo/creer: I believe/to believe
caso: case
se les mezcla: they get mixed up
bastante: quite a bit
casi siempre: almost always
tienen/tener: they have/to have
giros: expressions, turns of phrase
tiene seis años: is six years old
dice/decir: says/to say

cosa curiosa: curious thing
no lo utiliza: doesn't use it
lo dice/decir: she says it/to say
yo digo/decir: I say/to say
confundida: confused
no lo entiende/entender: she doesn't
  understand it/to understand
jamás: never
ha pronunciado/pronunciar:
  has pronounced/to pronounce

luego: then
no sabe conjugar/saber: (she) doesn't
  know how to conjugate/to know
fíjate: see, look
acabamos de: (we) just finished
  (doing something)
meses: months
yo pensaba/pensar: I was thinking/
  to think
iba a coger: she was going to pick
se iba a decantar: she was going to
  choose
a veces: sometimes
se confunde/confundirse: gets
  confused/to get confused

El desafío de criar hijos bilingües
ESTADOS UNIDOS

Think Spanish (TS): Los **padres** de **hijos bilingües me hablan** siempre **de** las particularidades de **criar** niños en más de un **idioma.** Para ti es aún más complicado, ¿no? Porque además del inglés **de**

donde viven, los niños están **expuestos** a tu español, de España y al español de tu **marido,** de Nicaragua. **¿No se mezclan** al **hablar?**

Paula (P): **Yo creo** que en mi **caso,** sí, **se les mezcla bastante.** Los dos creo que tienen más influencia castellana, de España, porque, bueno, básicamente estoy yo con ellos **casi siempre,** entonces **tienen** los **giros,** la "z". Anita, por ejemplo, que ya **tiene seis años, dice** la *zeta* como *zeta* no como *ese.*

TS: ¿Y además de la pronunciación?

P: Una **cosa curiosa** es que el *vosotros* y el *ustedes* **no lo utiliza. Lo dice** en inglés. Como **yo digo** "vosotros" y Carlos dice "ustedes" creo que está un poco **confundida, no lo entiende. Jamás ha pronunciado** "ustedes". A lo mejor habla sin el sujeto, dice: ¿Dónde están? ¿Quién? Papi y tú. Pero no dice "vosotros", "ustedes".

TS: Pero usa "están", no "estáis".

P: Sí, si lo usa, dice "están". **Luego** me dice en inglés "you", en castellano **no sabe conjugar.** Y **fíjate** que **acabamos de** estar en España casi dos **meses** y **yo pensaba** que **iba a coger** ya, que **se iba a decantar** por uno o por otro, y no. **A veces** dice "nosotros", **se confunde.**

TS: ¿Entonces **crees** que la influencia **más marcada** es la de España?

P: **No siempre**. A veces dice "acá", en vez de "aquí". Yo le digo "ven aquí", Carlos **diría** "ven acá". Ella **intercambia** esos dos cuando habla con su **hermano**. Pero es curioso porque cuando está conmigo me dice "aquí", pero cuando está con su padre le dice "acá". **Ya ha diferenciado**.

TS: ¿**Han tenido** otras influencias en cuanto a **lenguaje**?

P: **Pues sí**. Los amigos que hablan español son, **a ver**, hay unos que son mejicanos, hay otros que son de Colombia y hay otros que son paraguayos. A ella **se le pegan** todos los acentos. Entonces, cuando está con unos **habla así** y cuando está con otros **habla asá**. Por ejemplo, un año que **pasó** mucho **tiempo** con una amiguita suya que es de Paraguay, entonces ella hablaba como su amiga, un poquito con el acento.

TS: ¿Qué acento dirías que tiene?

P: Tiene un acento que **no se sabe** de dónde es. Cómo también estuvo en Perú, **ella cogió** mucho acento de Perú. Hablaba con el acento y el vocabulario de allí. Nosotros **volvimos** cuando tenía dos años y era una **cotorra**. Era casi una peruana más. En otras cosas tiene más influencia mía: dice "patatas", no "papas". La **comida** es lo que yo digo, **ella repite**. **Cada vez** que pasamos tiempo en España el acento **se le identifica mejor** pero **sigue teniendo** otros acentos. Y el "ok" lo usa siempre, es parte de su **vida**. No te dice "vale". Por eso, en España, a ella siempre le dicen: ¿De dónde eres?

TS: Será muy interesante ver cómo termina **desarrollando** el **manejo** del español. **Quizás termine construyendo** su **propio** español internacional.

P: **¡Ya veremos!**

---

crees/creer: do you believe/ to believe, to think
más marcada: more distinct, more marked

no siempre: not always
diría/decir: would say/to say
intercambia/intercambiar: swaps/ to swap
hermano: brother
ya: already
ha diferenciado/diferenciar: has differentiated/to differentiate

han tenido/tener: they have had/ to have
lenguaje: language

pues sí: well, yes
a ver: let's see
se le pegan/pegar: she has matched/ to match
habla así: talks this way
habla asá: talks that way
pasó/pasar: spent/to spend
tiempo: time

no se sabe/saber: one doesn't know/ to know
ella cogió/coger: she picked up/ to pick up
volvimos/volver: we returned/ to return
cotorra: parrot, chatterbox
comida: food
ella repite/repetir: she repeats/ to repeat
cada vez: each time
se le identifica mejor: is easier to identify
sigue teniendo: she keeps on having
vida: life

desarrollando: developing
manejo: use
quizás: perhaps
termine construyendo: she ends up building
propio: own

¡Ya veremos!: We will see!

¡Cuánto tiempo!: It's been so long!

¿Qué contás?: What's up?

te cuento/contar: let me tell you/ to tell

dentro de: in

semanas: weeks

viajando/viajar: traveling/to travel

voy a tener: I'm going to have

día libre: free day

me gustaría/gustar: I would like/ to like

saber: to know

puedo hacer/poder: can I do/ can, to be able to

vos has ido: you have been

veces: times

¿Qué me recomendás?: What do you recommend?

tercera: third

ciudad: city

tamaño: size

tiene/tener: it has/to have

pero: but

igual: all the same, anyhow

desarrollo: development

ofrecer: to offer

sin: without

locura: craziness

vos sabés/saber: you know/to know

me resulta: I find it

apabullante: overwhelming

a mí me parece: in my opinion

linda: pretty

pasear: visit

se extiende/extender: it stretches/ to stretch, to extend

a lo largo: along

río: river

ribera: bank

rambla: promenade

mercados: markets

recorras/recorrer: visit/to visit, to do

mañana: morning

viste/ver: did you see/to see

a mí me gusta/gustar: I like/to like

tiempo: time

Recomendaciones de un amigo
ARGENTINA

In some countries and regions in Latin America "vos" is used instead of "tú" for the 2nd person singular.

Alejandra (A): Hola, ¿Carlos? ¿Cómo estás?

Carlos (C): ¡Alejandra! **¡Cuánto tiempo! ¿Qué contás?**

A: **Te cuento** que **dentro de** dos **semanas** estoy **viajando** a Rosario, en la provincia de Santa Fe, por una conferencia. Pero **voy a tener** un **día libre** y **me gustaría saber** qué **puedo hacer. Vos has ido** muchas **veces**, ¿no? **¿Qué me recomendás?**

C: Bueno, como sabés, es la **tercera ciudad** argentina en cuanto a **tamaño. Tiene** poco más de un millón de habitantes, **pero igual** tiene un **desarrollo** y actividad suficientes como para **ofrecer** todos los atractivos de un centro urbano - **sin** la **locura** de Buenos Aires, que **vos sabés, me resulta** un poco **apabullante. A mí me parece** que es una **linda** ciudad para **pasear** porque **se extiende a lo largo** del **río** Paraná. La **ribera** y la **rambla**, los parques, centros culturales, **mercados** y ferias artesanales, son todas opciones agradables para que **recorras** en la **mañana**.

A: Sí, pero **viste** que **a mí me gusta** la historia. Y no tengo mucho **tiempo**, ¿qué puedo visitar?

C: **Entre** las atracciones históricas, **sobresale** el Monumento Nacional a la **Bandera**. Es el símbolo de Rosario y conmemora el lugar donde en **1812 se izó** por **primera vez** la bandera argentina. **Allí mismo podés subir** a una **torre** de 70 metros **de altura** y de allá **arriba vas a poder apreciar** las **vistas** de la ciudad. **Combinás paseo** e historia y **matás dos pájaros de un tiro**.

A: ¡**Me encantó**! Y de **tarde**, **si me da el tiempo**, me gustaría **ir de compras**. ¿**Alguna sugerencia**?

C: Tenés muchas opciones. Si es un día **lluvioso** o muy **caluroso**, mejor **andá** a uno de los cuatro shoppings: Rosario, Portal Rosario, Palace Garden o Del Siglo. Si el tiempo acompaña, **capaz preferís** ir a recorrer las **tiendas** que se encuentran en las **peatonales**, en las **calles** Córdoba y San Martín.

A: ¿Y a la noche?

C: Mirá, **no estoy seguro**, pero **fijate** en el hotel Pullman City Center. Es un hotel **cinco estrellas** con un casino enorme, **creo** que el más grande de América Latina, con tres **niveles**, más de dos mil **maquinitas tragamonedas**, etcétera, etcétera. **Te hacés una idea**. **No te lo digo** por los **juegos** porque **sé que a vos no te gustan**, pero sé que siempre hay espectáculos de buen nivel, **llevan cantantes** importantes, o hay demostraciones de **cocina** con los mejores chefs de la región.

A: ¡Eso sí me gusta! ¡Estupendo! Muchísimas gracias; **sabía que podía contar contigo**.

C: Por favor, **a las órdenes**. **A la vuelta llamame** y **contame cómo te fue**.

fomenta/fomentar: promotes/ to promote
desarrollo: development
capacidad: capability
empresarial: business
financiera: financial
país: country
nos contara/contar: tells us/to tell
sobre: about

pobreza: poverty

tienen que ver: they have to do
riqueza: wealth
tenemos/tener: we have/to have
rentista: person who lives off the income from investments
ingresos: income
injusta: unfair, unjust
existe una gran mayoría: there exists a big majority
empobrecida: impoverished

necesidades: needs
experimenta/experimentar: experiences/to experience

nosotros hemos diseñado/diseñar: we have designed/to design
apoyo: support
da respuestas: answers
servicios bancarios: bank services
eso hace que: as a consequence of that
tengan que recurrir a: they have to resort to
usureros: usurers (a person who lends money at high rates of interest)
pagar: pay
tasas: rates
hacemos lo posible/hacer: we make it possible/to make
para darle acceso: to give access
fondos rotatorios de crédito: rotating credits
más justas: more fair, more just

ofrecen/ofrecer: they offer/to offer

se trata de: it's about
aquellos que: those who
van a tener acceso a: are going to have access to
se enseña a/enseñar a: they teach to/ to teach to
mejor: better
contabilidad: accounting
atención al cliente: customer service
mercadeo: marketing

Para luchar contra la inequidad
VENEZUELA

Fudep es una organización venezolana que **fomenta** el **desarrollo** de la **capacidad empresarial** y **financiera** de las poblaciones más vulnerables del **país**. Entrevistamos a la Señora Mary Gloria Olivo, Directora General de Fudep, para que **nos contara sobre** el tema.

Think Spanish (TS): En su opinión, ¿cuáles son las causas estructurales de la **pobreza** en Venezuela?

Mary Gloria Olivo (MGO): **Tienen que ver** con la inequidad en la distribución de la **riqueza**. Dependemos del petróleo y **tenemos** una economía **rentista**, pero la distribución de los **ingresos** es totalmente **injusta**. Por eso **existe una gran mayoría empobrecida** y sin oportunidades.

TS: ¿Cuáles son las principales **necesidades** financieras que **experimenta** una persona en situación de pobreza en Venezuela y qué hacen ustedes para responder a esas necesidades?

MGO: **Nosotros hemos diseñado** programas de atención e intervención en las comunidades. Por ejemplo, el programa de **apoyo** y fomento empresarial **da respuestas** a quienes están excluidos de la economía formal y no tienen acceso al financiamiento ni a productos y **servicios bancarios**. **Eso hace que tengan que recurrir a usureros** y **pagar** exorbitantes **tasas** de interés, haciendo imposible que salgan de la pobreza. Por eso **hacemos lo posible para darle acceso** a esa población a **fondos rotatorios de crédito** en condiciones **más justas**.

TS: ¿En qué consiste la educación financiera que **ofrecen**?

MGO: **Se trata de** cursos elementales para **aquellos que van a tener acceso a** nuestros fondos de crédito. **Se enseña a** administrar **mejor** el crédito, cuáles son los productos bancarios que existen, nociones básicas de **contabilidad**, administración, acceso al sistema bancario, **atención al cliente**, **mercadeo**, etc.

TS: ¿Qué productos financieros **ponen a disposición**?

MGO: En este momento **trabajamos** con cuatro bancos: Citibank, Bolívar Banco, Confederado y Banpro. Con ellos **hemos hecho convenio para que**, **una vez que quienes participan** en nuestros programas **demuestran** que sus proyectos y **emprendimientos están bien encaminados**, **puedan tener** acceso al banco.

TS: ¿Qué tipo de emprendimientos desarrollan estas poblaciones?

MGO: Aquí la economía informal **mueve** la base de la economía del país. Estos emprendedores, como otros emprendedores de países en vías de desarrollo, **se encuentran** principalmente en el área del **comercio**, la manufactura, la **artesanía**. En este momento, estas son las áreas en las que más **se generan** emprendimientos.

TS: **Además del** programa de **apoyo** a la microempresa, ¿qué otros programas desarrollan en este momento?

MGO: Tenemos varios programas **en marcha**, que **responden a** diferentes necesidades. En el programa de microempresas, tenemos a cuatro mil participantes a **nivel** nacional.

TS: ¿Cuáles son los **logros** más importantes de FUDEP?

MGO: El primer logro es la credibilidad que tenemos en las comunidades en las que estamos trabajando. Este es un **logro clave** ya que las comunidades **optan por seguir** trabajando con nosotros. **El contar con** la credibilidad de **los más pobres** y necesitados de Venezuela, significa que la **alianza** que **hemos hecho con** ellos es efectiva.

TS: Muchas gracias, ¿**desea agregar algo más**?

MGO: No, gracias a ustedes por esta oportunidad de **contarles lo que hacemos**.

---

ponen a disposición: you make available to

trabajamos/trabajar: we are working/ to work
hemos hecho convenio: we have made an agreement
para que: so that
una vez que: once
quienes participan/participar: those who participate/to participate
demuestran/demostrar: prove/ to prove
emprendimientos: undertakings
están bien encaminados: are on the right track
puedan tener/poder: they can have/ can

mueve/mover: moves/to move
se encuentran/encontrarse: are found/ to be found
comercio: trade, commerce
artesanía: crafts
se generan/generar: are generated/ to generate

además del: in addition to
apoyo: help, support

en marcha: in motion
responden a/ responder a: respond to/ to respond to
nivel: level

logros: achievements

logro clave: key achievement
optan por/optar: they choose/ to choose
seguir: to continue
el contar con: having
los más pobres: the poorest (people)
alianza: alliance
hemos hecho con/hacer: we have made with/to make

desea/desear: do you wish/to wish
agregar: to add
algo más: anything more

contarles: to tell you
lo que hacemos/hacer: what we do/ to make, to do

estuve leyendo/leer: I was reading/ to read	
me mandaste/mandar: you sent me/ to send	
había oído/oír: I had heard/to hear	
sobre: about	
verdad: truth	
no tenía idea/tener: I had no idea/ to have	
tratar: to treat	
me queda una duda: there's still something I don't understand	
conoces/concer: know/to know	

Think Spanish (TS): Hola Juan Carlos. **Estuve leyendo** las páginas web que **me mandaste**. Muy interesante. **Había oído sobre** la ayahuasca, pero la **verdad** es que **no tenía idea** de su uso medicinal para **tratar** adicciones y problemas emocionales y psicológicos. Pero **me queda una duda**, ¿qué es exactamente la ayahuasca? Tú que **conoces** más del tema...

cocción: cooking	
liana: vine	
hoja: leaf	
se combinan/combinar: are combined/to combine	
tienen/tener: they have/to have	
poder: power	
estados: states	
ha sido usado/usar: has been used/ to use	
cientos: hundreds	
miles: thousands	
años: years	

Juan Carlos (JC): Es una **cocción** de dos plantas, una **liana** y una **hoja**, que **se combinan** y **tienen un poder** de producir **estados** de introspección y visiones. **Ha sido usado** por **cientos** o **miles** de **años**.

cómo te enteraste/enterarse: how did you find out/to find out

TS: ¿**Cómo te enteraste** de su uso?

primera vez: first time	
2001: dos mil uno	
creo/creer: I think/to think	
trabajaba/trabajar: was working/ to work	
selva: forest, jungle	
tratando/tratar: treating/to treat	
me dijo/decir: told me/to tell, to say	
iban a hacer: they were going to do	
me invitó/invitar: invited me/to invite	
me dio curiosidad: it peaked my curiosity	
ver: to see	

JC: La **primera vez** que participé en una ceremonia de ayahuasca fue en el **2001**, **creo**. Un amigo que **trabajaba** en la **selva** peruana **tratando** a pacientes con adicciones **me dijo** que **iban a hacer** una sesión en Lima y **me invitó** a participar. **Me dio curiosidad** por **ver** la ceremonia, los rituales, pero fui con mucho escepticismo.

me quedé muy impresionado: I was very impressed	
tuve/tener: I had/to have	
no pude hacerlo: I couldn't do it	
hasta: until	
me llevé/llevar: I took with me/to take	
hermano: brother	
mujer chamán: shaman woman	

Me quedé muy impresionado por la experiencia y por el significado de las visiones que **tuve**, pero **no pude hacerlo** de nuevo **hasta** el 2011. Ese año fui al Perú y **me llevé** a mi **hermano** a la selva de Iquitos a participar en una ceremonia con una **mujer chamán**.

consisten/consistir: do (they) consist/ to consist	
¿Qué propósito tienen?: What is their purpose?	

TS: ¿Y en qué **consisten** las ceremonias? **¿Qué propósito tienen?**

JC: Es una forma de conectarte con tu **mundo** subconsciente y **limpiarte** mental y físicamente. Es muy importante **hacerlo** con un **curandero** que **puedas confiar**. Hay distintas formas de **conducir** la ceremonia. La forma tradicional, en la selva peruana, es en la **noche**, **a oscuras**, con mucho respeto. **Recomiendan** una preparación de al menos una **semana antes**: **no tomar** alcohol, **grasas**, condimentos, sal, **carne de cerdo**. **Dicen** que es la forma que tu **cuerpo lo va a recibir mejor**. Tomas la cocción y el efecto dura unas tres o cuatro horas a lo mucho.

TS: ¿Y cuál es el resultado?

JC: Cada persona tiene distintas formas de experimentarlo. No es raro tener visiones, **entendimiento** de experiencias que en forma consciente no tienes la **facilidad** de **entenderlas**. Eliminas todas esas **capas** que **nos ponemos encima** y **haces contacto** con tu persona interna. No funciona como por arte de magia, sino que **te muestra** el **camino**. **Me permite entender** como **voy a proceder**, pero **depende de mí hacer** esas **cosas**, hacer ese **seguimiento**.

Siempre me sorprendo del potencial. Es más intenso que cualquier terapia, más profundo, uno siempre está consciente de lo que **está pasando**. No es como que estás **drogado** o **borracho**, **recuerdas** perfectamente **lo que ha sucedido**.

TS: ¿Por qué **crees** que **no ha sido** más **utilizado**?

JC: La **gente** no entiende, tiene **prejuicios contra** los indígenas. Siempre está la arrogancia de la cultura occidental, de creer que porque **construimos** cosas materiales tenemos más **conocimiento** que otras culturas.

TS: Gracias por **compartir** tu experiencia. Será interesante ver si las investigaciones que **se están llevando a cabo** sobre el tema hacen que la práctica se extienda y **logre ayudar** a más personas.

---

mundo: world
limpiarte: to clean yourself
hacerlo: to do it
curandero: healer
puedas confiar/poder: you can trust/ can
conducir: to conduct
noche: night
a oscuras: in the dark
recomiendan/recomendar: is recommended/to recommend
semana antes: week before
no tomar: not to drink
grasas: fats
carne de cerdo: pork meat
dicen/decir: they say/to say
cuerpo: body
lo va a recibir: will receive it
mejor: better

entendimiento: understanding
facilidad: gift, capacity
entenderlas: to understand them
capas: layers
nos ponemos encima/poner: we put on ourselves/to put
haces contacto/hacer: you make contact/to make
te muestra: it shows you
camino: way
me permite entender: allows me to understand
voy a proceder: I will proceed
depende de mí: it's up to me
hacer: to do
cosas: things
seguimiento: follow up

siempre: always
me sorprendo: I'm surprised
está pasando: is happening
drogado: drugged
borracho: drunk
recuerdas/recordar: you remember/ to remember
lo que ha sucedido: what has happened

crees/creer: do you think/to think
no ha sido utilizado: hasn't been used

gente: people
prejuicios contra: prejudices against
construimos/construir: we build/ to build
conocimiento: knowledge

compartir: (for) sharing
se están llevando a cabo: are being carried out
logre ayudar: manages to help

El sueño de la casa propia

CUBA

La **noticia** que muchos **esperaban fue anunciada a fines de** 2011: una **ley** finalmente autoriza a **ciudadanos** y residentes cubanos **a comprar y vender inmuebles**, un **cambio** drástico dentro del régimen comunista. **Para saber más** sobre el impacto que esta nueva ley **tendrá** en los habitantes de la **isla**, **entrevistamos** a Chen Lizra, experta en cultura cubana y autora del libro *My Seductive Cuba* (Mi Cuba seductora), una **guía del país** "**desde dentro**".

Think Spanish (TS): ¿Qué **nos puede decir** de la nueva ley sobre la **propiedad privada**?

Chen Lizra (CL): **Desde** 2010, Raúl Castro, Presidente del Consejo de Estado de Cuba, ha implementado cambios en la economía cubana **para mejorar** la situación del país. **Desde reducir** el número de **empleados estatales hasta dar** más **libertad** a los ciudadanos **para que tuvieran** sus propios **negocios**, Raúl **buscó** estimular la economía y **actualizar** la situación existente. Uno de los **pasos** que **tomó** fue **permitir que** los cubanos **puedan** comprar y vender casas. Antes, sólo **podían hacer permutas** (intercambios de casas del **mismo valor**) o vender **al gobierno**.

TS: ¿**Cómo cree** que la nueva ley **afectará** el **día a día** de los cubanos?

CL: Les permitirá **hacer cosas** que antes **no podían**. Pero también puede generar situaciones conflictivas. Por ejemplo, ¿qué **sucede** en casos donde dos familias **están compartiendo** una misma casa pero esta **pertenece** sólo a una de ellas? Cuando esta nueva ley **entre en efecto**, la familia propietaria podría vender la casa y **echar** a la otra familia. ¿**Adónde va entonces** esta otra familia?

---

noticia: news
esperaban/esperar: were waiting for/ to wait for
fue anunciada/anunciar: was announced/to announce
a fines de: at the end of
ley: law
ciudadanos: citizens
a comprar y vender: to buy and sell
inmuebles: real estate (property)
cambio: change
para saber más: to know more
tendrá/tener: will have/to have
isla: island
entrevistamos/entrevistar: we interviewed/to interview
guía del país: country guide
desde dentro: from the inside

nos puede decir: can you tell us
propiedad privada: private property

desde: since
para mejorar: to improve
desde reducir: from reducing
empleados estatales: state employees
hasta dar: to giving
libertad: freedom
para que tuvieran/tener: so that they could have/to have
negocios: businesses
buscó/buscar: sought to/to seek
actualizar: update, upgrade
pasos: steps
tomó/tomar: he took/to take
permitir que... puedan: to allow ... to (be able to)
podían hacer permutas: could do swaps
mismo valor: same value
al gobierno: to the government

cómo cree/creer: how do you think/ to believe, to think
afectará/afectar: will affect/to affect
día a día: day to day

hacer cosas: to do things
no podían/poder: were not able to do/ can, to be able to
sucede/suceder: happens/to happen
están compartiendo/compartir: are sharing/to share
pertenece/pertenecer: belongs/ to belong
entre en efecto: goes into effect
echar: evict
adónde va entonces: where does ... go, then

Actualmente **no hay suficientes viviendas**. Es común que **gente** que **se casa se quede a vivir** en la casa de los **padres** de uno de ellos; hay incluso **parejas** que se divorcian y **siguen viviendo juntas** porque no tienen adónde ir. Y no todos tienen el dinero para comprar casas. Será muy interesante ver cómo **se va a implementar** el tema de la vivienda, cuáles serán las repercusiones, cómo se van a resolver los conflictos que **surjan**. **¿Empezarán a aparecer** personas **sin techo**? **Hasta ahora**, en Cuba no había gente que **viviera en la calle**, algo que **los enorgullecía**. ¿Cambiará eso con la nueva ley?

TS: ¿Qué otras cosas ve usted que **deben ocurrir** en Cuba para que la transición a una economía de propiedad privada sea **exitosa**?

CL: Es **demasiado pronto** para saber qué **sucederá**. La nueva ley **otorga** a las personas más libertad y oportunidades, pero es un tema muy complejo que genera muchas preguntas. ¿Cómo se hace la transición de un **mercado** totalmente controlado a un mercado **abierto**? Lo que es claro es que la economía tiene que cambiar para que la gente tenga más dinero y pueda comprar casas.

TS: Para los ciudadanos y residentes cubanos habrá una restricción **en cuanto al** número de casas: **se podrá tener** una propiedad para residir y otra para vacaciones. ¿Qué pasa con los **extranjeros**?

CL: Existen megaproyectos de compañías internacionales **para construir** propiedades **de alquiler** para **veraneo** o **campos de golf**. **Aunque** ninguno de estos proyectos **ha pasado a** la **etapa** de construcción, los cambios que han **ocurrido** en este **último año indican** que **se están considerando seriamente** estos **emprendimientos**. **Por primera vez se ha autorizado** el **arrendamiento de tierras** por 99 años. Eso antes no era posible.

TS: **Debe ser** extremadamente **enriquecedor** poder vivir **de cerca** este proceso histórico que se está **produciendo** en Cuba. **En nombre de** los **lectores** de ThinkSpanish, **le agradezco que compartiera** parte de su experiencia con nosotros.

no hay suficientes: there isn't enough
viviendas: housing
gente: people
se casa/casarse: get married/to get married
se quede a vivir: stays living
padres: parents
parejas: couples
siguen viviendo juntas: keep on living together
se va a implementar: will be implemented
surjan/surgir: arise/to arise
empezarán a aparecer: will there begin to appear
sin techo: homeless (without roof)
hasta ahora: up until now
viviera en la calle: living on the streets
los enorgullecía: they were very proud

deben ocurrir: have to happen
exitosa: successful

demasiado pronto: too soon
sucederá/suceder: will happen/ to happen
otorga/otorgar: gives/to give, to grant
mercado: market
abierto: open

en cuanto al: regarding the
se podrá tener: will be possible to have
extranjeros: foreigners

para construir: to build
de alquiler: rental
veraneo: summer vacation
campos de golf: golf courses
aunque: although
ha pasado a/pasar a: has gone on to/ to go on to
etapa: stage
ocurrido/ocurrir: occurred/to occur
último año: last year
indican/indicar: indicate/to indicate
se están considerando/considerar: are being considered/to consider
seriamente: seriously
emprendimientos: undertakings
por primera vez: for the first time
se ha autorizado/autorizar: has been authorized/to authorize
arrendamiento de tierras: land leasing

debe ser: it must be
enriquecedor: enriching
de cerca: up close
produciendo: taking place
en nombre de: on behalf of
lectores: readers
le agradezco que compartiera: I thank you for sharing

Examina tu comprensión

Un ejemplo de salud sustentable, página 232

1. ¿Para qué se creó la organización Andean Health & Development?

2. ¿Qué servicios de salud ofrecen?

3. ¿Cuáles son algunas de las barreras que enfrentan al practicar la medicina en áreas rurales?

El desafío de criar hijos bilingües, página 234

1. ¿El uso de qué pronombres personales le resulta más difícil de descifrar a Anita?

2. Nombra al menos 4 influencias lingüísticas a las que ha estado expuesta la niña del artículo.

3. ¿En qué tipo de vocabulario se nota claramente la influencia de la madre?

Recomendaciones de un amigo, página 236

1. ¿A qué ciudad está viajando Alejandra? ¿De qué tamaño es esa ciudad?

2. ¿Cuál es el significado histórico del Monumento Nacional a la Bandera y qué puede uno hacer allí?

3. ¿Qué sugiere Carlos que haga en un día lluvioso o de mucho calor?

Para luchar contra la inequidad, página 238

1. Mary Gloria Olivia dice que hay dos aspectos causantes de la pobreza en Venezuela. ¿Cuáles son?

2. En Venezuela, ¿cuáles son las necesidades financieras principales de una persona viviendo en la pobreza?

Test your comprehension

Sabiduría indígena, página 240

1. ¿Qué elementos se combinan para hacer la ayahuasca?

2. Una vez combinados tienen el poder de producir ¿qué cosa?

3. ¿Cuál es el propósito de la ceremonia?

El sueño de la casa propia, página 242

1. La ley anunciada a fines de 2011 permite que los ciudadanos ¿hagan qué?

2. ¿Qué pasos tomó Raúl Castro para estimular la economía?

3. ¿Qué conflicto se ha generado?

La cultura es la buena educación del entendimiento.

José Vasconcelos

Costumbres

Tiendas de productos alimenticios
ESTADOS UNIDOS

Una de las formas **más fáciles** de **acercarnos** a una nueva cultura es **a través de** su **comida**. **A menudo podemos acceder** a esta comida **sin tener** que **trasladarnos** a otro **país** ni saber demasiado del **idioma**. Más económico, educativo e interesante **que ir** a un restaurante, es ir a una tienda especializada en productos de una región. Allí podemos **descubrir** productos y **marcas** que **ni siquiera** sabíamos que existían y **ver lo que** la **gente** realmente **compra** y consume en sus **casas**.

Por suerte, en Estados Unidos, es muy común encontrar tiendas con productos de América Latina. ¿Por qué no **nos acompañas** a una **visita guiada** de una tienda de productos latinoamericanos?

En general, **encontrarás** los productos organizados por regiones. De la región **sur seguramente verás yerba mate**, generalmente importada de Argentina o Brasil. **Si tienes suerte** podrás encontrar **mates** y **bombillas**. ¿Qué más? **Abre** el freezer **para buscar** las **tapas de empanadas** y de **pascualinas**.

De la región del altiplano **llegan** productos tan **dispares** como **pisco**, mermelada de **saúco** y té de achiote o de coca. Hay otros productos, que con sus variaciones, son comunes a varias regiones; por ejemplo, los **alfajores** y el **chimichurri**.

Si buscas productos del norte, vas a encontrar tortillas de **maíz**, **queso fresco**, **latas** de **frijoles refritos**, muchos tipos diferentes de chiles, gran variedad de tabasco y otras salsas picantes, **mezclas** de especias para condimentar. Los productos mexicanos **suelen ser** los más abundantes.

Anímate a ir a una tienda latinoamericana **cerca** de tu casa y explorar los productos que allí **ofrecen**. ¿**Conoces** todos los productos? ¿Sabes cómo se usan? ¿**Te animas** a preparar un **plato típico** latinoamericano con los productos que allí encuentres?

---

más fáciles: easiest
acercarnos/acercarse: approaching/to approach
a través de: through
comida: food
a menudo: often
podemos/poder: we can/can, to be able to
acceder: access
sin tener: without having
trasladarnos: to move, go
país: country
ni saber: nor knowing
demasiado: much
idioma: language
que ir: than going
descubrir: discover
marcas: brands
ni siquiera: didn't even
ver lo que: see what
gente: people
compra/comprar: buy/to buy
casas: homes

por suerte: luckily
nos acompañas: do you go with us
visita guiada: guided visit, tour

encontrarás/encontrar: you'll find/to find
sur: south
seguramente verás: you'll probably see
yerba mate: maté tea
si tienes suerte: if you're lucky
mates: gourds
bombillas: metal straws
abre/abrir: open/to open
para buscar: to look for
tapas de empanadas: ready-made dough for typical Latin American turnovers
pascualinas: spinach pie

llegan/llegar: arrive/to arrive
dispares: different
pisco: grappa-like drink
saúco: elderberry
alfajores: biscuits filled with jam or caramel and covered with chocolate
chimichurri: type of hot sauce

maíz: corn
queso fresco: fresh cheese
latas: cans
frijoles refritos: refried beans
mezclas: mixtures
suelen ser: usually are

anímate a ir: dare to go
cerca: close
ofrecen/ofrecer: offers/to offer
conoces/conocer: do you know/to know
te animas/animar: do you dare/to dare
plato típico: traditional dish

Programas de televisión
ESTADOS UNIDOS

¿**Quieres practicar** español **fuera de** clase y **no sabes** cómo? Nada **más fácil**: **enciende** la televisión, **busca** un canal **de habla hispana** y **escucha**. **No sólo aprenderás** nuevas **palabras** y su pronunciación, **sino que te enterarás** de lo que **está ocurriendo** en los diferentes **países** y **descubrirás** múltiples facetas de **cada** cultura.

Los programas de **noticias** son un buen **lugar** por donde **empezar**. ¿Por qué? Porque el español que **usan** los informativistas es el **más cercano** al **estándar**. ¿Qué **quiere decir eso**? Significa que los informativistas son **entrenados para reducir** su acento original y **hacerlo** más neutro. De esta forma **no se puede** identificar realmente **de dónde vienen** y **cualquier oyente**, **ya sea** hondureño, cubano, boliviano o argentino, **lo podrá comprender** sin problemas. Con ese **mismo propósito** el **lenguaje** utilizado en los informativos **deja de lado** expresiones coloquiales, **modismos** locales y otros **rasgos** que puedan ser considerados específicos de una región.

Para practicar un lenguaje más coloquial, **nada mejor** que los programas de **entretenimiento**. Allí **se dan** muchas más interacciones **entre** las personas y **te enteras** quiénes son los **personajes** populares o famosos.

Finalmente, están las telenovelas. Es un fenómeno cultural **muy extendido** en enormes sectores de la población de todos los países latinoamericanos. En general, están producidas en los países más grandes. Las telenovelas de México, Venezuela y Argentina **se ven** en todo el continente. En menor medida, se ven novelas chilenas o colombianas. **Si bien se trata de obras** de ficción, puedes **rescatar** aspectos de la **vivienda** y la **vestimenta**, costumbres, relaciones, valores y muchos otros elementos que **reflejan** la realidad de cada país, región o sector social. ¿**Quién dijo** que la televisión no es educativa?

---

quieres practicar: do you want to practice
fuera de: outside
no sabes/saber: you don't know/to know
más fácil: easier
enciende/encender: turn on/to turn on
busca/buscar: look for
de habla hispana: Spanish-speaking
escucha/escuchar: listen/to listen
no sólo...sino que: not only ... but
aprenderás/aprender: you will learn/ to learn
palabras: words
te enterarás/enterarse: you'll find out/ to find out
está ocurriendo: is happening
países: countries
descubrirás/descubrir: you'll discover/ to discover
cada: each

noticias: news
lugar: place
empezar: to begin
usan/usar: they use/to use
más cercano: closest
estándar: standard
quiere decir eso: does that mean
entrenados: trained
para reducir: to reduce
hacerlo: to make it
no se puede: it's not possible
de dónde vienen: where they come from
cualquier oyente: any listener
ya sea: whether
lo podrá comprender: will be able to understand
mismo propósito: same purpose
lenguaje: language
deja de lado: leaves aside
modismos: idioms
rasgos: characteristics, features

nada mejor: nothing better
entretenimiento: entertainment
se dan/darse: take place/to take place
entre: between
te enteras/enterarse: you find out/ to find out
personajes: characters

muy extendido: very widespread
se ven/ver: are seen/to see
si bien: even though
se trata de: they are
obras: works
rescatar: to rescue, to pick out
vivienda: housing
vestimenta: clothing
reflejan/reflejar: reflect/to reflect
quién dijo/decir: who said/to say

El mes de la herencia hispana
ESTADOS UNIDOS

Desde 1988, del 15 de setiembre al 15 de octubre de **cada año**, **se festeja** en Estados Unidos el **mes** de **la herencia hispana**.

¿De qué se trata? En este mes **se busca honrar** a todas aquellas personas de origen hispano que **han contribuido** con el **país** de una u otra forma.

¿Por qué **se celebra** en setiembre? La elección de esa **fecha se debe** en parte a que **entre** el 15 al 18 de setiembre se festeja el día de la independencia en varios países centroamericanos, en México y en Chile.

¿Quiénes son esas personas a **las que honramos**? **Incluso si nos vamos** muy **atrás** en **el tiempo podemos encontrar** políticos hispanos **sirviendo** al país, en el Congreso y el Senado. En 1822 Joseph Marion Hernández **entró** al Congreso como representante de Florida. En 1876 y 1879 Romualdo Pacheco representó a California. **Ya** en el **siglo** XX, Octaviano Larrazo fue electo para el **Senado** en 1928. **Más adelante**, Dennis Chávez, de Nuevo México, **serviría** en el Senado por un largo período: entre 1935 y 1962.

Acercándonos aún más a **nuestros días**, podemos **ver** que también **hubo** hispanos **ocupando altos cargos** en **lo que hoy** es la Administración Federal de Aviación, el **gabinete** y los ministerios de Transporte, de **Desarrollo** Urbano y **Vivienda** y de Justicia.

Glosario:

desde: since
cada año: every year
se festeja/festejar: it is celebrated/ to celebrate
mes: month
herencia hispana: Hispanic heritage

¿De qué se trata?: What is it about?
se busca honrar: tries to honor
han contribuido/contribuir: have contributed/to contribute
país: country

se celebra/celebrar: is celebrated/ to celebrate
fecha: date
se debe/deberse: is due to/to be due to
entre: between

las que honramos/honrar: that we honor/to honor
incluso: even
si nos vamos/ir: if we go/to go
atrás: back
tiempo: time
podemos/poder: we can/can, to be able to
encontrar: find
sirviendo: serving
entró/entrar: entered/to enter
ya: by
siglo: century
Senado: Senate
más adelante: later on
serviría/servir: would serve/to serve

acercándonos: coming closer, approaching
nuestros días: our days
ver: see
hubo: there were
ocupando: occupying
altos cargos: high positions
lo que hoy: what today
gabinete: office
desarrollo: development
vivienda: housing

Las **mujeres no se quedan atrás**: Antonia Coello Novello fue la primera hispana y la primera mujer en **ocupar** el cargo de Directora General de **Salud Pública** en 1990. Y en 2009 Sonia Sotomayor **fue nombrada** Juez Asociada de la Corte Suprema de Justicia.

Además de la política, ¿en qué otros **ámbitos se destacaron** los hispanos? **No debemos olvidar** los ámbitos militar y científico. **Dentro de este último** podemos **nombrar** a los astronautas Franklin Chang-Díaz y a Ellen Ochoa o a los **ganadores** del Premio Nobel: Luiz Walter Álvarez en 1968 en **física** y Severo Ochoa en 1959 en medicina.

Dentro de las artes encontramos hispanos en todas las áreas: literatura, música, **cine** y televisión. **Seguro** que todos **han oído hablar de** Carlos Santana, y **si le preguntan** a sus **padres** o **abuelos**, **seguro** que **saben** a quién **me refiero si menciono** a Richie Valens. ¿Sofía Vergara, Alexis Bedel, Cameron Díaz? Hispanas.

No vamos a poder cubrir todas las áreas de actividad, pero **creo** que **nadie ignora** que muchos **jugadores de béisbol** son hispanos. **Por supuesto**, también hubo hispanos famosos en otros **deportes** como fútbol y boxeo. Y **de más está decir** que los **empresarios** hispanos **se cuentan por montones**. ¿**Te animas** a **descubrir** otros hispanos que **hayan dejado** una **huella** en el país?

mujeres: women
no se quedan atrás: do not lag far behind
ocupar: occupy
Salud Pública: Public Health
fue nombrada/nombrar: was named/to name

además de: in addition to, other than
ámbitos: fields, spheres
se destacaron/destacarse: stood out/ to stand out
no debemos olvidar: we shouldn't forget
dentro de: in, within
este último: the latter
ganadores: winners
física: physics

cine: cinema, film
seguro: certainly
han oído hablar de: have heard about
si le preguntan/preguntar: if you ask/ to ask
padres: parents
abuelos: grandparents
seguro: for sure
saben/saber: (they) know/to know
me refiero/referirse: I'm referring to/ to refer to
si menciono/mencionar: if I mention/ to mention

no vamos a poder cubrir: we won't be able to cover
creo/creer: I think/to think
nadie ignora: nobody ignores
jugadores de béisbol: baseball players
por supuesto: of course
deportes: sports
de más está decir: needless to say
empresarios: entrepreneurs
se cuentan por montones: are lots, are many
te animas/animarse: do you dare/ to dare
descubrir: to discover
hayan dejado/dejar: have left/to leave
huella: mark

El Día de los Muertos
ESTADOS UNIDOS

entre: between
tal como: as
se celebra/celebrar: it is celebrated/ to celebrate
habla/hablar: talks/to talk
actitudes: attitudes
hacia: towards
muerte: death
espeluznantes: horrific, horrifying
se ven/ver: are seen/to see
reflejan/reflejar: reflect/to reflect
miedo: fear
ser perseguido: to be chased
espíritus vengativos: vindictive spirits
mundo: world
se llena/llenar: gets filled/to fill
caras monstruosas: monstrous faces
heridas sangrientas: bleeding wounds
colores oscuros: dark colors
ambientes lúgubres: gloomy atmospheres

reina/reinar: reigns/to reign
reflejando: reflecting
alegría: joy
compartir: (of) sharing
recordar: remembering
seres queridos: loved ones
han pasado a mejor vida: have passed on to a better life
se suele decir: it's usually said
se decora/decorar: one decorates/ to decorate
esqueletos danzan: skeletons dance
calaveras sonríen: skulls smile

hace un par de años: a couple of years ago
me invitó/invitar: invited me/to invite
se realizaba/realizar: was taking place/ to take place
barrio: neighborhood
quienes quisieran: those who wanted
asistir: to attend
velas: candles
homenajearlos: to pay homage to them
me sorprendió/sorprender: I was surprised/to surprise
llegar: to arrive
comida y bebida: food and drinks
cálido: warm
mundo: world
se concibe/concebir: is conceived/ to conceive

La diferencia **entre** el Día de los Muertos **tal como se celebra** en México y la fiesta de Halloween **habla** de diferentes **actitudes hacia** la **muerte**. Las imágenes **espeluznantes** que **se ven** durante Halloween **reflejan** el **miedo** de **ser perseguido** por **espíritus vengativos**. El **mundo se llena** de **caras monstruosas**, **heridas sangrientas**, **colores oscuros**, **ambientes lúgubres**.

Por el contrario, en las celebraciones del Día de los Muertos **reina** la exuberancia de color y el humor, **reflejando** la **alegría** de **compartir** y **recordar** aquellos **seres queridos** que "**han pasado a mejor vida**", como **se suele decir**. **Se decora** con colores primarios, los **esqueletos danzan**, las **calaveras sonríen**.

Hace un par de años, una amiga boliviana **me invitó** a participar en un festejo que **se realizaba** en un restaurante del **barrio** para el Día de los Muertos. Se invitaba a **quienes quisieran** a **asistir** con fotos, **velas**, flores y objetos que recordaran a sus seres queridos para **homenajearlos** y celebrar su vida. **Me sorprendió llegar** a un local que estaba totalmente decorado donde se compartió **comida y bebida** en una ambiente jovial y muy **cálido**. ¡Un **mundo** de diferencia con la forma violenta y terrorífica con que **se concibe** la muerte en Halloween!

Si no tienes la suerte de **recibir** una invitación para **asistir** a una celebración de este tipo, **nada te impide armar** tu **propio** altar. La costumbre de **crear** un altar que honre a nuestros **antepasados** no es exclusiva de México. **Puedes tomar** elementos que representen tus orígenes o los de la persona a la que homenajeas e incorporarlos al altar para **darle** un **toque especial**.

Una manera de **conocer más a fondo** este **enfoque** más alegre hacia la muerte, es asistir a eventos que **se organizan** en varios pueblos y ciudades de los Estados Unidos en esa **fecha**, que **toman** elementos del festejo tradicional mexicano pero con **aportes** e influencias regionales.

En Tucson, Arizona, la procesión de todas las **almas**, **se viene realizando desde** 1990. En San Francisco se celebra el Día de los Muertos en el Parque Garfield y **algunos** centros culturales y **museos**. En Los Ángeles, un centro comunitario méxico-americano incorpora elementos políticos a las representaciones tradicionales. En el **pueblo** de Missoula, Montana, se realiza un **desfile** al que asisten esqueletos gigantes, calaveras **de poncho y sombrero de ala ancha** y otros **personajes** curiosos.

Averigua en tu comunidad **si alguien** celebra el Día de los Muertos y **participa**. Y **si nadie lo hace**, ¡organiza tu propio evento para el Día de los Muertos!

---

si no tienes la suerte: if you're not lucky enough
recibir: to receive
asistir: to attend
nada te impide/impedir: nothing prevents you/to prevent
armar: (from) building
propio: own
crear: (of) creating
antepasados: ancestors
puedes tomar/poder: you can take/ can, to be able to
incorporarlos: incorporate them
darle: give it
toque especial: special touch

conocer: (of) knowing
más a fondo: more in depth
enfoque: approach
se organizan/organizar: are organized/ to organize
fecha: date
toman/tomar: they take/to take
aportes: contributions, input

almas: souls
se viene realizando: has been taking place
desde: since
algunos: some
museos: museums
pueblo: town
desfile: parade
de poncho y sombrero de ala ancha: dressed with a poncho and a wide brimmed hat
personajes: characters

averigua/averiguar: find out/ to find out
si alguien: if somebody
participa/participar: participate/ to participate
si nadie lo hace/hacer: if nobody does it/to make, to do

Estados Unidos con salsa

ESTADOS UNIDOS

Mucha **gente alrededor del mundo** asocia América Latina con un **baile** en particular: la salsa. La realidad es mucho más **compleja**, ya que hay muchos **lugares** de América Latina donde tradicionalmente **no se baila** salsa, **mientras** existen otros lugares, por ejemplo Estados Unidos, donde la salsa es tremendamente popular. **Tanto es así** que dos de los **estilos** de salsa que **se enseñan comúnmente** en los cursos de salsa son el estilo de Nueva York y el de Los Ángeles. **Pero no tienes que ir** a estas **ciudades para enamorarte de** la salsa; **por suerte**, Estados Unidos **está lleno de** salsa.

¿**Qué puede ofrecer** la salsa al estudiante de español? La salsa es **indiscutiblemente** una **manera** muy **divertida de aproximarse a** América Latina y al español. **A través de** la música, la **letra** de las **canciones** y el **nombre** de los **pasos, uno se acerca poco a poco** a la cultura hispana. **Además**, por su aspecto social, es una **forma de conocer** latinos o **conectarse con** otra gente que **habla** español. **Ni qué decir del aporte** que **hace** a la **salud**: ¡bailar salsa es un **gran ejercicio**!

¿Dónde **se puede aprender** salsa? **Lo mejor** es ir a un club de salsa. Allí, **no es extraño que al comienzo de la noche se ofrezca gratis** una media hora de clase, en la que **se demuestran** los pasos básicos. De esta manera, **incluso** la persona que va **por primera vez** puede **divertirse**.

---

gente: people
alrededor del: around
mundo: world
baile: dance
compleja: complex
lugares: places
no se baila/bailar: is not danced/ to dance
mientras: while
tanto es así: so much so
estilos: styles
se enseñan/enseñar: are taught/ to teach
comúnmente: commonly, frequently
pero no tienes que ir: but you don't have to go
ciudades: cities
para enamorarte de: to fall in love with
por suerte: luckily, fortunately
está lleno de: is full of

qué puede ofrecer: what can it offer
indiscutiblemente: unquestionably
manera: way
divertida: fun
de aproximarse a: of approaching
a través de: through
letra: lyrics
canciones: songs
nombre: name
pasos: steps
uno se acerca... a/acercarse a: one gets ... closer to /to get closer to
poco a poco: little by little
además: besides
forma: way
de conocer: to meet
(de) conectarse con: to connect with
habla/hablar: speak/to speak
ni qué decir del: not to mention the
aporte: contribution
hace/hacer: makes/to make
salud: health
gran ejercicio: great exercise

se puede aprender: is it possible to learn
lo mejor: the best (thing)
no es extraño: is not uncommon
que...se ofrezca/ofrecer: for them to offer/to offer
al comienzo de la noche: early in the evening
gratis: free (of charge)
se demuestran/demostrar: are shown/to show, to demonstrate
incluso: even
por primera vez: for the first time
divertirse: have fun

¿**Y si uno quiere** aprender salsa **en serio**? En ese caso, lo mejor es **tomar** cursos en academias de baile: existen en todas partes de Estados Unidos, **no sólo** en las grandes ciudades. **Hay que** investigar un poco y **no tener miedo de probar** diferentes estilos, **escuelas** y profesores, **hasta encontrar lo que uno buscaba**.

¿Adónde puede uno ir **si ya ha completado** todos los cursos que **se dan** en el lugar donde **vive**? Los **congresos** o festivales de salsa son el lugar perfecto **para ampliar horizontes**. Muchos de los mejores instructores a **nivel** nacional e incluso **mundial asisten a** estos congresos, y es una gran oportunidad para probar nuevos estilos o **descubrir un paso nuevo**. También se puede aprender mucho **en poco tiempo**, ya que las clases **toman forma de talleres** que se dan a todos los niveles **durante** todo el día. En las noches se organizan **fiestas bailables** en las cuales los instructores hacen demostraciones artísticas en **espectáculos** coreografiados y con **trajes de baile** especiales.

¿Dónde se puede **ir a ver** salsa de primera categoría? La Federación Mundial de Salsa, una organización **fundada** en **2001** en Miami, **dirige** el **Concurso** de Salsa Mundial, donde **cada año se otorga** el título de **campeón** mundial a los mejores bailarines de salsa en varias categorías. **De entre todas** estas categorías también **se elige** el campeón mundial indiscutible de salsa. Pero si no puedes asistir a ese evento, **cualquier** tipo de campeonato o competición **será** una buena oportunidad para ver maravillosos espectáculos de salsa.

y si uno quiere/querer: and if one wants/to want
en serio: seriously
tomar: to take
no sólo: not only
hay que: one has to
no tener miedo de: not be afraid to
probar: try
escuelas: schools
hasta encontrar: until one finds
lo que uno buscaba: what one was looking for

si ya ha completado/completar: if (one) has already completed/to complete
se dan/dar: are given/to give
vive/vivir: (one) lives/to live
congresos: conferences
para ampliar horizontes: to broaden horizons
nivel: level
mundial: world (adjective)
asisten a/asistir a: they attend/to attend
descubrir: to discover
un paso nuevo: a new step
en poco tiempo: in a short time
toman forma de/tomar: take the format of/to take
talleres: workshops
durante: during
fiestas bailables: dance parties
espectáculos: shows
trajes de baile: dance costumes

ir a ver: go to see
fundada/fundar: founded/to found
2001: dos mil uno
dirige/dirigir: runs/to run
concurso: competition
cada año: each year
se otorga/otorgar: is awarded/to award
campeón: champion
de entre todas: among all
se elige/elegir: is chosen/to choose
cualquier: any
será/ser: will be/to be

huella: footprint, mark
más extendido: most widespread
en el exterior: abroad
podría explicarse por: could be explained by
tan orgullosos: so proud
quizás: perhaps
se deba a que: is due to the fact that
al ser: being
mayor estado: biggest state
país: country
de hecho: in fact

quienes saben un poco/saber: those who know something/to know
acerca de: about
según: according to
menudo: often
se define/definirse: defines itself/ to define oneself
en contraposición a: in contrast to
(lo más) cercano: closest
podrían aventurar: could venture, could put forward
sienten/sentir: feel/to feel
de acentuar: to emphasize
su pertenencia a: the fact that they belong to
de distanciarse de: to distance themselves from
raíces: roots
vecino: neighbor
sur: south

sea como fuere: be that as it may
inconfundibles: unmistakable
pasado hispano: Hispanic past
en reclamar: to claim
corona: crown
lo controló/controlar: controlled it/ to control
hasta: up until
aún hoy en día: even today
habla/hablar: speaks/to speak
al restante: the remaining
se le escape/escapar: misses/to miss, to escape
mundo: world
sin embargo: nevertheless
se vuelve/volverse: it becomes/ to become
si se pone atención al: if one pays attention to the
nombre: name
varios lugares: several places

La huella del español por Texas
ESTADOS UNIDOS

El cowboy texano probablemente sea el estereotipo del americano **más extendido en el exterior**. Esto **podría explicarse por** el ferviente patriotismo del que los texanos están **tan orgullosos**. O **quizás se deba a que**, **al ser** el segundo **mayor estado** del **país** en extensión y población, Texas es **de hecho** una gran parte de Estados Unidos.

Pero **quienes saben un poco acerca de** las teorías de la construcción de la identidad (**según** las cuales un grupo a **menudo se define en contraposición a** lo más similar o **cercano**) **podrían aventurar** que una explicación podría ser la mayor necesidad que los texanos **sienten de acentuar su pertenencia a** los Estados Unidos y **de distanciarse de** sus **raíces** hispanas o diferenciarse de su **vecino** del **sur**.

Sea como fuere, hay huellas **inconfundibles** del **pasado hispano** de Texas. Como todos saben, España fue el primer país europeo **en reclamar** para su **corona** el territorio y México **lo controló hasta** 1836. **Aún hoy en día**, el 27% de la población **habla** español. **Al restante** 73% quizás **se le escape** esa conexión con el **mundo** hispano, que **sin embargo se vuelve** muy evidente **si se pone atención al nombre** de **varios lugares** de la región.

El famoso **Río** Grande, en la **frontera** con México, habla, obviamente, de su **tamaño**. Y, para quienes saben español, está **clarísimo** que **resulta** redundante **decir** el Río Grande River, **¿no les parece?** Otro de los principales ríos en el estado es el Río **Colorado** – un nombre que **a todas luces describe** su color. Y el Río Brazos, **¿por qué llevará** ese nombre? ¿**Se animan a plantear** una hipótesis?

Algunos elementos geológicos de la región **también** llevan nombres en español y son **altamente** descriptivos. **Tal es el caso** de la **meseta** de **Llano Estacado** o la **Falla Balcones**.

Las **ciudades reflejan asimismo** su herencia hispana: la **segunda** ciudad **más grande** del estado, San Antonio, y otras **más pequeñas**, como El Paso. En estos dos casos es relativamente **fácil adivinar** qué **significan** sus nombres, pero usar la pronunciación correcta en español es un poco **difícil** cuando uno **está acostumbrado a escuchar** esos nombres pronunciados en inglés. ¿**No creen**?

Hasta algunos de los huracanes que **azotan** Texas periódicamente tienen nombres en español: el Huracán Carla de 1961 y el Huracán Alicia, en 1983.

¿Qué otros lugares en Estados Unidos **muestran** la relación con el español? Algunos de los más obvios son **Los Ángeles**, **Nevada** y, **como ya vimos**, Colorado. ¿Se animan a **hacer** una lista más completa?

---

río: river
frontera: border
tamaño: size
clarísimo: very clear
resulta/resultar: (it) is/to be
decir: to say
¿no les parece?: don't you think (so)?
colorado: red
a todas luces: evidently
describe/describir: describes/ to describe
por qué llevará: why might it have
se animan a/animarse a: do you dare to/to dare to
plantear: propose

también: also
altamente: highly
tal es el caso: such is the case
meseta: plateau
llano estacado: staked plain
falla balcones: balconies fault

ciudades: cities
reflejan/reflejar: reflect/to reflect
asimismo: likewise
segunda: second
más grande: biggest
más pequeñas: smaller
fácil: easy
adivinar: to guess
significan/significar: mean/to mean
difícil: difficult
está acostumbrado a escuchar: is used to hearing
no creen/creer: don't you think/ to think

hasta: even
azotan/azotar: batter/to batter

muestran/mostrar: show/to show
los ángeles: the angels
nevada: snowy, snow-capped
como ya vimos/ver: as we have already seen/to see

piensan en/pensar: think of/to think
pedacito: little piece
se ha identificado a/identificar:
  has been identified/to identify
recién: only
últimos: last
diez años: ten years
ha ido aumentando/aumentar:
  has been increasing/to increase
cantidad: number, amount
provienen de/provenir de: come
  from/to come from
duplicado: doubled
en lo que va de siglo: so far this
  century
si bien: even though
alrededor de: around, about
más ha crecido/crecer: has grown the
  most/to grow
según: according to

siendo tantos los…que: since so
  many …
se instalaron/instalarse: settled/
  to settle
descubrir: (for me) to discover
conocía a/conocer a: (I) knew/
  to know
a través de: through
redes: networks
me volví a conectar: (I) reconnected
conocido mío: acquaintance of mine
que hacía casi 15 años que no veía:
  whom I hadn't seen in almost 15 years

mantuvimos/mantener: we had/
  to have
me contó/contar: he told me/to tell
decidió irse: he decided to leave
al Norte: to the United States
  (literally: to the North)
feliz: happy
de haberse mudado a: of having
  moved to
como te podrás imaginar: as you can
  imagine
fácil: easy
tiene ya cierta edad y: is already a
  certain age and (has)
dejar todo: to leave everything behind
empezar: to start
nuevamente: again
de cero: from scratch
al principio: in the beginning

La cara latina de Miami
ESTADOS UNIDOS

Hay muchos que **piensan en** Miami como un **pedacito** de América Latina en Estados Unidos. Pero tradicionalmente **se ha identificado a** Miami principalmente con cubanos y puertorriqueños. **Recién** en los **últimos diez años ha ido aumentando** la **cantidad** de latinoamericanos que **provienen de** otras regiones. Tal es el caso de los uruguayos, quienes han más que **duplicado** su número **en lo que va de siglo**. **Si bien** en números totales no son muchos —**alrededor de** veinte mil—, los uruguayos son la comunidad latinoamericana que **más ha crecido** en el estado de Florida en la última década, **según** censos locales.

Siendo tantos los uruguayos **que se instalaron** en Miami, no fue raro **descubrir** que **conocía a** uno de ellos personalmente. **A través de** las **redes** sociales en internet, **me volví a conectar** con un **conocido mío que hacía casi 15 años que no veía** y que ahora reside en Miami.

En una conversación que **mantuvimos** por teléfono, **me contó** que **decidió irse al Norte** en un momento de crisis económica. Hoy, instalado en Miami, está **feliz** con su decisión **de haberse mudado a** los Estados Unidos. "**Como te podrás imaginar**, no fue una decisión **fácil**", me comentó. "Cuando uno **tiene ya cierta edad y** una familia, no es fácil **dejar todo** y **empezar nuevamente de cero**. Ahora estamos muy contentos, pero **al principio** fue difícil".

En efecto, **rehacer** la **vida** en un nuevo país **implica superar** numerosos obstáculos. Una **mudanza** internacional tiene un costo considerable. A eso **se le debe agregar**  el estrés de comunicarse en otro **idioma**, **aprender** costumbres nuevas y adaptarse a una sociedad y cultura distintas. El proceso es **aún** más difícil porque en general **no se cuenta con** el **apoyo** de **familiares** ni amigos.

Como respuesta a la **necesidad** de tantos compatriotas y **para paliar** esas dificultades, **han surgido** servicios y programas de apoyo. **A fines del año pasado se lanzó** la **Tarjeta** Consular Uruguaya para los residentes de Florida y **otros estados**. Este documento **sirve para verificar** la identidad de la persona **en el momento de acceder a servicios médicos** y **financieros** o **llevar a cabo trámites** en instituciones públicas.

También **se han organizado talleres gratuitos** para ofrecer apoyo psicológico y un espacio de reflexión. Así **se intenta** facilitar la transición, **mejorar** la **calidad de vida** de los migrantes y **lograr** una reinserción **exitosa** en su **nueva patria**.

en efecto: in fact
rehacer: to rebuild
vida: life
implica/implicar: entails/to entail
superar: overcoming
mudanza: move
se le debe agregar: must be added
idioma: language
(de) aprender: (of) learning
aún: even
no se cuenta con/contar con: one doesn't have/to have
apoyo: support
familiares: relatives

como respuesta a: in response to
necesidad: need
para paliar: to mitigate, to ease
han surgido/surgir: have arisen/ to arise
a fines del año pasado: at the end of last year
se lanzó/lanzar: was launched/ to launch
tarjeta: card
otros estados: other states
sirve para verificar: can be used to verify
en el momento de acceder a: when accessing, when obtaining
servicios médicos y financieros: medical and financial services
llevar a cabo trámites: (when) processing documents

se han organizado/organizar: have been organized/to organize
talleres gratuitos: free workshops
se intenta/intentar: they are trying to/to try to
mejorar: to improve
calidad de vida: quality of life
lograr: to achieve
exitosa: successful
nueva patria: new homeland

Guayaberas

Las guayaberas son una **prenda masculina** favorita en **algunos lugares** tropicales y **costeros** de Latinoamérica tales como Cuba, República Dominicana, Puerto Rico, México, Panamá, Venezuela, la región **Caribe** de Colombia, la costa ecuatoriana, e **incluso** en la región andaluza de España, las **islas Canarias** y Filipinas.

Hechas en **lino** o **algodón** son **camisas** que **se abrochan** con **botones a** todo **lo largo del frente** y que **se llevan sueltas por encima** del **pantalón**. **Cuentan con** un **cuello alto, bolsillos grandes, alforzas** o **pliegues** verticales y **bordados**.

Su origen **se remonta** a la Cuba colonial. **Cuenta** la **leyenda** que en la provincia de Sancti Spíritus, a la **orilla** del **Río** Yayabo, un **hombre pidió** a su **esposa** que **le confeccionara** una prenda **tipo gabán** lo suficientemente **cómoda** como **para trabajar** en el **campo**, con una pieza de lino **que acababa** de **recibir** de España. **Ello explicaría** el origen de su **nombre**. **Se piensa que** fue inicialmente yayabera, en honor al río **junto al** cual **surgió**, pero también existen numerosas **fuentes que** dicen que los **amplios** bolsillos de la nueva prenda eran muy útiles **para cargar** las guayabas que los hombres **cortaban después** del trabajo **camino hacia** sus casas, y que por ello, las camisas **empezaron a llamarse** guayaberas.

---

prenda masculina: piece of clothing for men
algunos lugares: some places
costeros: coastal
incluso: even
islas Canarias: Canary Islands

hechas: made
lino: linen
algodón: cotton
camisas: shirts
se abrochan/abrocharse: are buttoned/to button, to fasten
botones: buttons
a ... lo largo del: along the, on the
frente: front
se llevan/llevar: are worn/to wear
sueltas: loose
por encima: over
pantalón: pants
cuentan con/contar con: have/to have
cuello alto: high collar
bolsillos grandes: big pockets
alforzas: pleats
pliegues: folds
bordados: embroidery

se remonta/remontarse: dates back/ to date back, to go back to
cuenta/contar: says/to say, to tell
leyenda: legend
orillas: margins
río: river
hombre: man
pidió/pedir: asked/to ask
esposa: wife
le confeccionara: to make for him
tipo: type
gabán: overcoat
cómoda: comfortable
para trabajar: to work
campo: country, fields
que acababa de recibir: had just received
ello explicaría: that would explain
nombre: name
se piensa que: it is believed that
junto al: by the
surgió/surgir: appeared/to appear
fuentes: sources
amplios: ample, spacious
para cargar: to carry
cortaban/cortar: cut/to cut
después: after
camino hacia: on their way to
empezaron a llamarse: (they) began to be called

Puesto que inicialmente su uso **se popularizó** entre los guajiros o campesinos cubanos, **se tendía a menospreciar** a quien la usara, pero **con el paso del tiempo** se le ha considerado **ropa de etiqueta** para eventos especiales, e incluso a las **de manga larga** se les **ha empleado** como sustituto al **saco** o **chaqueta** en **lugares calientes**.

Las guayaberas también tienen una historia política asociada a ellas, **durante** el tiempo de la revolución cubana, los guerrilleros independentistas **llamados** mambises **comenzaron** a **portarlas** como un símbolo de rebelión. **Para facilitar** el uso del machete, que **tornaron** de **herramienta** de trabajo en **arma principal**, le **añadieron** dos **cortes laterales** que **se han mantenido** como parte del diseño. Tras el triunfo de la revolución, las guayaberas **se convirtieron** en el atuendo nacional de la isla y fueron adoptadas por **funcionarios gubernamentales** a partir de los **años cuarenta**.

Las guayaberas **llegaron** a México a través de la península de Yucatán y del Puerto de Veracruz y de inmediato **ambos lugares** las **integraron** a su **vestuario** tradicional regional. Pronto su demanda fue tan grande que **tuvieron que** establecer sus propios centros manufactureros donde perfeccionaron su confección e incluso introdujeron pequeñas variantes **para darles un toque local**.

Actualmente a las guayaberas también **se las conoce como** cubanas, chabacanas y guayabanas en otras partes de Latinoamérica.

---

puesto que: given that
se popularizó/popularizarse: became popular/to become popular
se tendía a: there was the tendency to
menospreciar: (to) look down on
con el paso del tiempo: with time
ropa de etiqueta: formal wear
de manga larga: long-sleeved
ha empleado/emplear: have been used/to use, to employ
saco: coat
chaqueta: jacket
lugares calientes: hot places

durante: during
llamados: called
comenzaron/comenzar: began/ to begin
portarlas: to wear them
para facilitar: to facilitate
tornaron: turned into
herramienta: tools
arma principal: main weapon
le añadieron: (they) added to it
cortes laterales: slits on the sides
se han mantenido/mantener: have been kept/to keep, to maintain
se convirtieron/convertirse: became/ to become
funcionarios gubernamentales: government employees
años cuarenta: 1940s, the Forties

llegaron/llegar: arrived/to arrive
ambos: both
lugares: places
integraron/integrar: integrated/ to integrate
vestuario: wardrobe
tuvieron que: (they) had to
introdujeron/introducir: introduced/ to introduce
para darles: to give them
un toque local: a local touch

actualmente: nowadays
se las conoce como/conocer: are known as/to know

Talavera poblana
MÉXICO

En la **ciudad** de Puebla, capital del **estado** que **lleva** el **mismo nombre**, **se elabora** una cerámica **vidriada** y **esmaltada**, de influencias árabes, que fue importada desde España a México en la **segunda mitad** del **siglo** XVI por los **frailes dominicos**.

La cerámica poblana **se bautizó con el nombre** de Talavera porque **se piensa** que los primeros **maestros ceramistas llegados a** la Nueva España, y que **se establecieron** en Puebla, eran de Talavera de la **Reyna** en España, una población **ubicada** en la provincia de Toledo. El nombre **le quedó**, también, por la **similitud** de **estilo** que **existe entre** la cerámica **creada** en esa localidad española y **la hecha** en Puebla.

Debido a su ubicación geográfica en un **punto estratégico** entre el puerto de Veracruz (que era la **puerta de entrada** de todos los productos **venidos de** Europa) y la capital de la Nueva España, Puebla **se convirtió en la época virreinal** en un importante centro comercial y cultural. Los españoles que se establecieron allí **quisieron construir** una ciudad **a imagen y semejanza** de sus ciudades de origen, y **por lo tanto**, **se dispusieron a embellecerla** con sus **artes y oficios**.

Los maestros **loceros** españoles **encontraron en las cercanías de** Puebla los materiales necesarios para producir cerámica de **buena calidad**. Ello **les facilitó** la introducción de una técnica **heredada de** los árabes, un tipo de **loza cubierta de arcilla blanca** y **barnizada** con **estaño**, que era popular en Europa desde el siglo XII, pero **desconocida** en América.

---

ciudad: city
estado: state
lleva/llevar: has/to have, to carry
mismo nombre: same name
se elabora/elaborar: is produced/ to produce, to make
vidriada: glazed
esmaltada: enameled
segunda mitad: second half
siglo: century
frailes dominicos: Dominican friars

se bautizó con el nombre de: was given the name
se piensa/pensar: it is believed/ to believe, to think
maestros ceramistas: master ceramists
llegados a: who made it to
se establecieron/establecerse: settled/ to settle
reyna: queen (old spelling of "reina")
población: town
ubicada: located
le quedó: stuck
similitud: similarity
estilo: style
existe/existir: there is/to be, to exist
entre: between
creada/crear: created/to create
la hecha/hacer: the one made/to make

debido a: due to
punto estratégico: strategic point
puerta de entrada: gateway
venidos de/venir: coming from/ to come
se convirtió … en/convertirse en: became … /to become
en la época virreinal: in the time of the viceroyalty
quisieron/querer: wanted/to want
construir: to build
a imagen y semejanza de: in the image and likeness of
por lo tanto: therefore, hence
se dispusieron a/disponerse a: set out to/to set out to
embellecerla: beautify it
artes y oficios: arts and crafts

loceros: pottery makers
encontraron/encontrar: found/to find
en las cercanías de: in the vicinity of
buena calidad: good quality
les facilitó: made easier for them
heredada de: inherited from
loza: china, crockery
cubierta de: covered with
arcilla blanca: white clay
barnizada: glazed
estaño: tin
desconocida: unknown

En las colonias españolas, **dicha** técnica **se aplicó** principalmente a la elaboración de cerámicas utilitarias, como **jarras**, **jarrones**, **pilas de agua**, **platones**, **tibores**, **ollas**, **bandejas**, **macetas**, figuras religiosas y **azulejos**. Las piezas eran decoradas con motivos florales, animales, y **personajes** y **paisajes** de influencia morisca, italiana y china.

Para el siglo XVII, la producción de cerámica era tan abundante que fue necesario establecer regulaciones **para controlar** su producción, calidad y decorado. Así fue cómo **se fundó** el **gremio** de loceros de la Nueva España. Ello **contribuyó a que** el vidriado de las piezas se conservara uniforme, **terso** y brillante, y de un **hermoso blanco lechoso**. También **se delimitó** el uso de los colores al azul, amarillo, verde, anaranjado y negro, aunque el diseño más tradicional fue siempre el de **azul cobalto sobre blanco**.

El azulejo de Talavera **se hizo** tan popular en la arquitectura religiosa y civil **poblana** que **aún actualmente** es considerado como la firma característica de la ciudad. **Tras enfrentar** muchos problemas en el siglo XIX, la talavera poblana **resurgió** recientemente con un **nuevo brío**. Ello **llevó a** la promulgación de la declaratoria gubernamental de Denominación de Origen (D.O.), una validación de calidad que sólo **se otorga** a los **talleres** que conservan la producción artesanal tradicional. Ésta **implica** un total de seis procesos, que **pueden llevar hasta** seis meses. **Para empezar**, una **mezcla** de **barros** blanco y negro **se amasa** con los **pies** y **se somete** a un proceso de deshidratación. Luego, se hace el **moldeado** de **cada pieza** en **tornos manuales**. Finalmente, llega el turno de la decoración, **hecha a mano** con **esmaltes** y colores minerales producidos por los **mismos alfareros**, y el **horneado** doble, que **se lleva a cabo antes y después de** la aplicación del decorado.

La talavera poblana **conjunta** tradición con diversidad y **engalana** con la belleza de sus formas los aspectos más básicos de la **cotidianidad**.

---

dicha: said
se aplicó/aplicar: was applied/to apply
jarras: pitchers
jarrones: vases
pilas de agua: sinks
platones: platters
tibores: large jars
ollas: kitchen pots
bandejas: trays
macetas: flowerpots
azulejos: tiles
motivos florales: flower motifs
personajes: characters
paisajes: landscapes

para controlar: to control
se fundó/fundar: was founded/ to found
gremio: guild
contribuyó a que … se conservara: help maintain
terso: smooth
hermoso blanco lechoso: beautiful milky white
se delimitó/delimitar: was delimited/ to delimit
azul cobalto sobre blanco: cobalt blue on white

se hizo/hacerse: became/to become
poblana: from Puebla
aún actualmente: still today
tras enfrentar: after facing
resurgió/resurgir: reemerged/ to reemerge
nuevo brío: new vigor
llevó a/llevar: led to/to lead
se otorga/otorgar: is given/to give
talleres: worshops
implica/implicar: entails/to entail
pueden llevar hasta: can last up to
para empezar: to begin with
mezcla: mixture, blend
barros: clays
se amasa/amasar: is mixed/to mix
pies: feet
se somete a/someterse a: undergoes/ to undergo
moldeado: molding, modeling
cada pieza: each piece
tornos manuales: hand-operated (potter's) wheels
hecha a mano: handmade
esmaltes: enamels
mismos alfareros: potters themselves
horneado: firing (in the kiln)
se lleva a cabo: is done
antes y después de: before and after

conjunta/conjuntar: combines/ to combine
engalana/engalanar: adorns/to adorn
cotidianidad: everyday life

Examina tu comprensión

Tiendas de productos alimenticios, página 248

1. ¿Cuál es uno de los modos más fáciles de acercarse a una nueva cultura?

2. ¿Qué alimentos de Argentina o Brasil podría usted encontrar?

3. ¿Qué alimentos de México podría usted encontrar?

Programas de televisión, página 249

1. ¿Qué puede usted aprender de la televisión en español?

2. ¿Qué tipo de programa de televisión es un buen lugar para empezar a aprender?

3. ¿Qué se puede aprender viendo telenovelas?

El mes de la herencia hispana, página 250

1. ¿De qué se trata el mes de la herencia hispana?

2. ¿Qué estadounidense de origen hispano fue designado juez en la Corte Suprema de Justicia?

3. ¿Qué estadounidenses de origen hispano ganaron el Premio Nobel y por qué?

El Día de los Muertos, página 252

1. ¿Cuál es la diferencia entre los festejos de Halloween y los del Día de los Muertos?

2. ¿Qué se recuerda y qué se suele decir durante el Día de los Muertos?

3. ¿Cómo se celebra el Día de los Muertos?

Test your comprehension

Estados Unidos con salsa, página 254

1. ¿Qué aspectos de la salsa ayudan a que las personas se aproximen a la cultura hispana?

2. ¿Dónde se puede aprender salsa?

3. ¿Y si uno quiere aprender salsa en serio?

La huella del español por Texas, página 256

1. ¿Qué porcentaje de la población de Texas habla español?

2. ¿Qué punto de referencia, denominado por su tamaño, se encuentra en la frontera entre Estados Unidos y México?

3. ¿Cuál es el nombre de la segunda ciudad más grande de Texas?

La cara latina de Miami, página 258

1. Muchas personas piensan en Miami ¿como qué?

2. ¿Qué implica rehacer la vida en un nuevo país?

3. ¿Qué es la Tarjeta Consular Uruguaya?

Respuestas

Cultura

Los vejigantes, página 4 1. Africa 2. los moros y cristianos 3. coco **De tapeo, página 6** 1. acudir en grupo, pedir varias tapas para comerlas con el resto, beber un vinillo para alegrar el alma y hablar sin parar 2. la provincia de Cádiz 3. tapar la copa con una loncha de jamón arruinaría el vino 4. chocos, patatas bravas, aceitunas rellenas, boquerones, croquetas, champiñones al ajillo, embutido, pescaíto frito, sepia a la plancha, gambas, tigres, bombas, chistorra o pulpo a la gallega **La siesta en Argentina, página 8** 1. la palabra siesta proviene del latín sixta, que significa "la sexta hora del día" 2. recuperar energías, descargar ansiedades, desbloquear la mente y estimular la creatividad, previene el envejecimiento y alarga la vida 3. entre 15 y 30 minutos diarios y nunca más de 40 **Pescando con "caballos", página 10** 1. rústicos botes hechos de caña llamados "caballitos de totora" 2. más de 1.200 años 3. el escaso interés de las nuevas generaciones, la actual presencia de barcos arrastreros, la acelerada urbanización de Huanchaco **Los alebrijes, página 12** 1. madera, de cartón y de papel maché. 2. suelen mezclarse dos o más animales, ejemplares de las clásicas tortugas, mariposas, escorpiones y sapos 3. la leyenda de Pedro Linares **La pollera panameña, página 14** 1. la pollera montuna es la de vestir de diario o de trabajo; la pollera de encajes es la que se usa para festejos o motivos importantes 2. desde un fino alambre enroscado hasta escamas de pescado y seda 3. chapines, pueden ser de satén o terciopelo 4. algunos reconocen sus raíces en España **El gaucho, página 16** 1. la libertad y la individualidad 2. le servían como arma y como herramienta de trabajo 3. un pantalón de pierna ancha ajustado a la cintura con una faja o cinto, una camisa y pañuelo al cuello, un sombrero de ala ancha **El rodeo y los "huasos", página 19** 1. el duro trabajo de los campesinos y su necesidad de ordenar el ganado 2. la capacidad, fortaleza física y destreza

Viaje

El barrio gótico de Barcelona, página 30 1. una antigua ciudad romana 2. Puente de los Suspiros 3. ¡el calzado cómodo es esencial! **Colonia del Sacramento, página 32** 1. ropa confeccionada con lana o cuero, posavasos de cuero repujado o una caja de alfajores, guantes y gorro de lana, juguetes de madera 2. salir, con el mate bajo el brazo, a caminar por el puerto en compañía de amigos o familia **Verano en enero y febrero, página 34** 1. minifaldas, escotes y Bermudas 2. caminar la rambla, a la vera del mar, sentarse a mirar las destrezas de los surfistas o tirarse como un lagarto al sol; va a los espectáculos teatrales o disfrutando de un café en algunas del las terrazas al aire libre 3. Mar del Plata 4. Pinamar y Cariló; combinan la playa con el bosque, la arena amarilla con la madera oscura de los árboles crean un aire más sensorial **Mallorca y sus castillos, página 36** 1. conocidas por su belleza, playas, sol y diversión; Mar Mediterráneo 2. En el siglo XIX, tuvieron que limpiar la fachada del castillo, pues había sido quemado como método de desinfección para acabar con una plaga de peste **Un paraíso en el Caribe, página 38** 1. montañas, semidesérticas, bosques tropicales, playas 2. Casa de Campo 3. no hay serpientes venenosas ni insectos cuya picadura o aguijón sean una amenaza vital **Varadero, arenas blancas, página 40** 1. fondos marinos 2. Bahía de Cochinos 3. la Cueva de Ambrosio se encuentran dibujos rupestres, La Casa de la Cultura es posible ver obras de teatro y espectáculos, Museo Municipal de Varadero se exhiben piezas claves de la cultura y la historia. **El turismo rural, página 43** 1. el entorno, la ausencia de multitudes, el relax y la posibilidad de practicar actividades como hacer rutas en bicicleta y visitar una granja 2. las casas rurales y los hoteles rurales 3. escribiendo en un buscador las palabras "casa rural" o "turismo rural" **San Miguel de Allende, página 44** 1. Estados Unidos y Canadá 2. español y arte **Tulum, la ciudad sobre el mar, página 45** 1. sacerdotes, matemáticos, ingenieros o astrónomos; se los consideraba seres superdotados

Tradición

Chichicastenango, página 57 1. Santo Tomás 2. "Palo Volador" 3. el manuscrito del Popol Vuh **La Pachamama, página 58** 1. "pacha" significa universo, mundo, tiempo, lugar y "mama" significa madre 2. cigarrillos, hojas de coca, alcohol, cerveza y vino 3. la alegría y los deseos e intenciones de cada asistente **Una Navidad en Paraguay, página 61** 1. verano 2. una flor típica del lugar: la flor del cocotero **La gritería, página 62** 1. los cohetes esporádicos y los fuegos artificiales 2. "¿Quién causa tanta alegría?"; "La concepción de María" **Gaspar, Melchor y Baltasar, página 64** 1. hierba fresca y agua para los camellos 2. abre las puertas de la Fortaleza y, entre música y comida típica, honra a todos los niños **7 de julio San Fermín, página 66** 1. Ernest Hemingway; The Sun also Rises 2. más de 400 años 3. las ferias comerciales con pregón, actuaciones musicales, torneo, teatro y corrida de toros **¡Viva el novio! ¡Viva la novia!, página 68** 1. encontraron su coche lleno de globos 2. un antiguo convento rehabilitado 3. un vals **Castillos en el aire, página 70** 1. unas torres humanas de más de 15 metros de altura 2. los mayores en la base y los más jóvenes en la cima 3. unos pantalones blancos ajustados, una faja alrededor del cuerpo de color negro, una camisa holgada del color distintivo de la "colla" y un pañuelo rojo en la cabeza

Answers

Celebración

La Mamá Negra, página 80 1. para venerar a la Virgen de la Merced o Santísima Tragedia y por la independencia 2. una muñeca negra representando a su hija 3. seres que realizan exorcismos para limpiar las almas 4. el ángel de la estrella que representa al ángel Gabriel; el rey moro que simboliza la llegada de los españoles a Ecuador; el capitán símbolo del ejército **El Día de los Muertos, página 82** 1. un espejo que refleja la forma en que uno ha vivido 2. "El muerto al cajón y el vivo al fiestón". 3. calaveritas de azúcar y huesos hechos de la misma masa **Festeja su independencia, página 84** 1. Fiestas Patrias 2. una semana, comenzando el 18 3. tocaban sus instrumentos para atraer compradores a las mesas cubiertas con tortas, licores y otras delicias, bailan cumbias, polcas y cuecas, se ofrece una gran variedad de comidas típicas que incluye el asado, las empanadas y la chichi 4. "El palo ensebado"; un palo de madera de 5 a 6 metros de alto enterrado en la tierra, que se unta con grasa y que debe ser trepado por los competidores que, resbalando una y otra vez, luchan por alcanzar el premio que está en la cima **¡Menudo tomate!, página 86** 1. un puesto de verduras y frutas en los alrededores con las cajas expuestas en la calle para su venta, por lo que los implicados en la tangana cogieron tomates y empezaron a tirárselos unos a otros 2. 120 toneladas; una hora 3. se reúnen para tomar juntos un gran desayuno y coger fuerzas para la lucha **La Virgen de la Candelaria, página 90** 1. 2 de febrero y se prolonga durante 15 días; en honor a la Virgen de la Candelaria 2. Capital del Folklore Peruano; esta fiesta está llena de símbolos y manifestaciones artístico-culturales de la cultura quechua, aymara y mestiza 3. estadio Enrique Torres Bellón; bandas musicales y danzas folklóricas **La Pascua y Semana Santa, página 92** 1. El viernes Santo se rememora la crucifixión. En algunas se practica el ayuno, algunos lo consideran un día de silencio y reflexión 2. El sábado está dedicado al lamento por la muerte de Cristo. **La fiesta con más Gracia, página 94** 1. Los vecinos, reciclan objetos y periódicos, botellas de plástico, vasos de yogur, alambres, cajas de cartón o hueveras 2. la más original, la mejor iluminada, la que más ecológica y la más bella; las calles agraciadas hace que sean estas vías las más visitadas y, en consecuencia, las que más bebidas venden y dinero recaudan. **El carnaval de Cádiz, página 96** 1. el mes de febrero 2. se remontan al siglo XVI, cuando la ciudad tenía uno de los puertos marítimos más importantes del mundo 2. Los orígenes se remontan al siglo XVI, los gaditanos copiaron el carnaval de Venecia y con el tiempo, lo adaptaron a sus propias costumbres. 3. el concurso oficial de canciones and baile

Personas

La magia de García Márquez, página 106 1. estudiar derecho 2. novela de suspenso 3. periodismo 4. Kafka, Faulkner, Virginia Wolf y Hemingway **Diego Rivera, página 108** 1. Frida Kahlo 2. murales a las calles, a los techos y paredes de edificios públicos 3. la historia de México 4. revolución social mexicana, resistencia a la opresión extranjera, la valoración del indígena, sus raíces, el pasado y el futuro de su país **Frida Kahlo, página 110** 1. no pudo tener hijos y dolor físico la acompañó en todo momento 2. autorretratos 3. Diego Rivera; Nueva York **Celia Cruz, página 112** 1. niños, adoptó a centenares de ahijados 2. la primera mujer hispana en el Carnagie Hall. 3. un tumor cerebral **Rubén Diarío, página 113** 1. gran poeta y escritor **El Che Guevara, página 114** 1. la miseria dominante entre las masas y la omnipresencia del imperialismo 2. Che fue ejecutado por soldados bolivianos en La Habana. **Unamuno, el eterno poeta, página 116** 1. sus ideas políticas 2. recuerdos de su amor y sus crisis personales en torno a la religión **Andrés Segovia, página 118** 1. cuatro años; 16 años 2. La guitarra no podía producir suficiente sonido como para llenar el salón. Segovia perfeccionó su técnica experimentando con maderas y diseños nuevos, para aumentar la amplificación natural de la guitarra. 3. su transcripción del Chaconne de Bach **Galeano, página 120** 1. la historia de América a través de pequeñas historias y personajes, muchos reales y otros míticos 2. caminando a lo largo de la rambla, disfrutando del aire y del mar

Deportes

El arte de imitar a los pájaros, página 128 1. no hay que hacer ningún curso especial para el primer vuelo 2. la rampa de despegue es un antiguo mirador sagrado 3. Río Pintos; uno puede refrescarse en sus cálidas aguas **Acampando en San Felipe, página 129** 1. al norte del estado de Baja California, cerca de Mexicali 2. árido y caliente desértico 3. uno de los mejores lugares para observar las maravillas celestiales **Surfing en Costa Rica, página 130** 1. aguas cálidas, unas 700 millas de costa, gente amable y unos precios razonables 2. diciembre hasta abril 3. ¡No es una buena idea guardar en el salpicadero del auto nuestro reloj, pasaporte u otros objetos valiosos antes de ir al agua! **El fútbol, página 132** 1. una pelota de fútbol o la camiseta de algún equipo 2. para un picadito con los amigos, para una ida al campo en grupo o, simplemente, para juntarse a ver por televisión al equipo de sus sueños 3. tensión, alegría, amargura, llanto y gritos **El jai alai, página 134** 1. una palabra de origen vasco que significa "fiesta alegre" 2. la acción y la velocidad 3. tenis **Sierra Nevada, el paraíso blanco, página 136** 1. todo el invierno y hasta bien entrada la primavera, a veces incluso hasta el mes de mayo 2. con colores 3. montar a caballo o hacer rutas en bicicleta de montaña **El senderismo en el Perú, página 138** 1. una costa bañada de tranquilas aguas, una sierra cruzada por montañas, varios ríos y una selva amazónica 2. grado de aventura, riesgo y emoción que desee experimentar 3. Los incas no conocieron el caballo y tampoco la rueda por lo que hicieron a pie todo viaje o recorrido 4. cuatro días

Respuestas

Música

Bailando al son de merengue, página 144 1. africanos y europeos 2. el melodeón, la güira, la tambora 3. los años 60 **Los instrumentos musicales, página 145** 1. una concha de caracol marino y un cráneo de venado 2. hoja de palmera 3. tronco de aguacate **El arte flamenco, página 146** 1. el baile, el cante y la guitarra 2. Andalucía 3. el acompañamiento de guitarra 4. acompañamiento y de solista **El reguetón está "rankeao", página 148** 1. hip hop, reggae, con la influencia de la bomba y la plena 2. la realidad de las calles, hacen críticas sociales y, por supuesto, hablan del amor y la pasión 3. Florida, Nueva York y Miami **El tango: pasión in la pista, página 150** 1. Italia, España, Francia, Alemania o Polonia 2. marineros, artesanos, peones y otros trabajadores 3. ambientes prostibularios 4. la década de 1940 **El mariachi, página 154** 1. indios coca y significa música 2. violines, dos trompetas, una guitarra, una vihuela y un guitarrón 3. un tipo de instrumento en forma de guitarra pero con un cuello corto y una barriga grande en la parte de atrás **El candombe, página 156** 1. en varios barrios de Montevideo, al atardecer y, durante los fines de semana de verano 2. la cultura Africana, mantener la cultura en Montevideo 3. los cuadras **La música andina, página 158** 1. alegres, tristes, solemnes, festivos o guerreros 2. nueve flautas amarradas en fila hechas de carrizo 3. Paul Simon

Historia

El cinco de mayo, página 168 1. Puebla 2. 16 de septiembre 3. del triunfo de los mexicanos sobre el ejército francés **Los hijos del sol, página 170** 1. siglo XVI, española 2. consideraban el ombligo del mundo 3. una guerra civil **La independencia de Colombia, página 174** 1. un banquete en honor a Francisco Villavicencio 2. nueve años más tarde 3. Simón Bolívar **Un símbolo de la nación, página 176** 1. pertenencia y patriotismo 2. los tres poderes del estado: majestad, ley y fuerza 3. roja es la sangre vertida por los hombres chilenos en el campo de batalla, el blanco es la nieve de la cordillera de los Andes, y el azul es el limpio cielo del país **La bandera de México, página 177** 1. verde es la de la independencia y la esperanza, blanco representa la pureza de los ideales de la nación, roja representa la sangre que los héroes nacionales han derramado por la patria 2. un águila; representa la fuerza y la historia de México 3. 1821 **San Juan, página 178** 1. Juan Ponce de León; Caparra 2. la Plaza de San José; una estatua de bronce en honor a Juan Ponce de León 3. Ellas organizaron una procesión repentina. Caminaron por las calles de la ciudad cargando antorchas y tocando campanas. **Las ruinas de Tiwanaku, página 180** 1. por un sofisticado sistema de agricultura en terrazas para producir alimentos 2. grandísimos bloques de piedra orientados de forma astronómica, perfeccionaron la técnica de la momificación y realizaron hazañas sorprendentes en el campo de la medicina 3. un lugar para rendir culto o simplemente para agradecer y acompañar a sus ancestor **Los garifunas, página 182** 1. Con el paso de tiempo, los españoles, nigerianos, se aprendieron a convivir y se realizaron matrimonios mixtos 2. Los españoles 3. música, baile, lengua, religión y costumbres

Geografía

El Parque Nacional Darién, página 192 1. UNESCO 2. Los tres grupos indígenas precolombinos, los kunas, que mantienen poblaciones tradicionales al pie de la montaña sagrada Cerro Tarcuna; los emberá, que moran en la ribera del Chocó; y los wounaan, muy cercanos lingüísticamente y culturalmente a los Emberá. 3. los científicos indican que es imprescindible la regulación y control de la actividad agropecuaria y forestal **Las islas Galápagos, página 194** 1. erupciones volcánicas submarinas 2. recuperarse de las heridas después de los combates 3. Charles Darwin; "Origen de las Especies" **El jurumí, página 196** 1. el oso hormiguero gigante 2. lengua larga, fina y pegajosa; atrapar todo tipo de insectos, estrategia de supervivencia es muy valiosa para el ecosistema 3. sentido del olfato; le permite conseguir sus mejores presas y subsistir a lo largo del día 4. el jaguar y el puma y los cazadores **Paisajes diversos, página 198** 1. ecosistemas naturales y cuencas hidrográficas y una fauna rica 2. La zona del Altiplano donde se encuentra el lago Titicaca es húmeda. La zona subandina es muy húmeda y tiene una vegetación exuberante. La zona amazónica también tiene una vegetación exuberante. 3. una inmensa estatua de Jesús 4. centro ceremonial y de observaciones astronómicas **Paisajes, flora y fauna, página 200** 1. El Salto del Angel, un piloto norteamericano Jimmy Angel 2. formaciones de piedras areniscas formadas por la erosión 3. el Gran Roque; porque tiene una gran extensión de mar tranquilo **Las ballenas de Valdez, página 202** 1. Istmo Carlos Ameghino 2. la reproducción y el alumbramiento de la ballena franca 3. gran aleta dorsal y su cola **La Reserva de El Vizcaíno, página 203** 1. clima seco y árido 2. mesquite es usado por los nativos para hacer fogatas; el maguey que es un ingrediente importante del tequila **La laguna de San Ignacio, página 206** 1. octubre y febrero; 5.000 millas 2. aguas más calientes, las ballenas dan a luz a sus crías. 3. Esta gordura es necesaria para que las ballenas puedan sobrevivir en las aguas heladas del norte durante el verano.

Answers

Gastronomía

El dulce de papaya, página 212 1. para soplar burbujas al aire 2. queso blanco de leche de cabra **El mate, página 213** 1. con azúcar o amargo, muy caliente o frío con jugo de naranja, con una cucharadita de café o con yuyos 2. un vecino amablemente le dará 3. ayuda a sanar los corazones heridos. **La deliciosa papa, página 216** 1. 3.000 2. papas sancochadas cubiertas con una salsa hecha de queso fresco, aceite, ají y galleta remojada en leche **Ensalada de yuca, página 219** 1. 2 libras 2. jugo de naranja 3. los tomatines **Camarones en salsa blanca, página 220** 1. El Rubí 2. vino blanco seco **Carnitas, página 221** 1. cinco 2. carne de puerco **Sangría, la bebida del verano, página 222** 1. vino tinto 2. limón, naranja, melocotón, manzana 3. unas horas **La chicha, página 223** 1. comida, bebida, hospitalidad y también la fuerza 2. la yuca madura **El turrón, página 224** 1. 1 Kilo (2,20 libras) 2. Navidad 3. en un envase hermético **La "dieta mediterránea", página 226** 1. bajo nivel de colesterol 2. menos

Conversación

Un ejemplo de salud sustentable, página 232 1. Para poder proveer servicios de salud a ecuatorianos de las zonas rurales 2. pneumonía, diarrea, deshidratación y sarampión, mujeres embarazadas, intervenciones quirúrgicas, atención médica de emergencia, rayos X, ultrasonido y servicios de farmacia 3. barreras idiomáticas y culturales **El desafío de criar hijos bilingües, página 234** 1. ustedes (América Latina) y vosotros (España) 2. española, nicaragüense, inglesa, peruana, (también mejicana, colombiana, paraguaya) 3. vocabulario relacionado a la comida **Recomendaciones de un amigo, página 236** 1. Rosario, la tercera ciudad más grande argentina 2. conmemora el lugar donde en 1812, la bandera se izó por primera vez; podés subir a una torre de 70 metros de altura 3. ir de compras **Para luchar contra la inequidad, página 238** 1. la inequidad en la distribución de la riqueza 2. Nosotros hemos diseñado programas de atención e intervención en las comunidades **Sabiduría indígena, página 240** 1. una liana y una hoja 2. tienen un poder de producir estados de introspección y visiones 3. formar de conectarte con tu mundo subconsciente y limpiarte mental y físicamente **El sueño de la casa propia, página 242** 1. a comprar y vender inmuebles 2. buscó estimular la economía y actualizar la situación existente 2. no hay suficientes viviendas, parejas que se divorcian y siguen viviendo juntas porque no tienen adónde ir

Costumbres

Tiendas de productos alimenticios, página 248 1. a través de su comida 2. mates y bombillas, tapas de empanadas y de pascualinas 3. tortillas de maíz, queso fresco, latas de frijoles refritos, muchos tipos diferentes de chiles, tabascos, salsas picantes, y mezclas de especias para condimentar. **Programas de televisión, página 249** 1. nuevas palabras y su pronunciación, lo que está ocurriendo en los diferentes países y facetas de cada cultura 2. los programas de noticias 3. la vivienda y la vestimenta, costumbres, relaciones, valores y muchos otros elementos que reflejan la realidad de cada país **El mes de la herencia hispana, página 250** 1. honrar a todas aquellas personas de origen hispano que han contribuido con el país, los estados unidos 2. Sonia Sotomayor 3. Luiz Walter Álvarez en 1968 en física y Severo Ochoa en 1959 en medicina **El Día de los Muertos, página 252** 1. diferentes actitudes hacia la muerte, Halloween reflejan el miedo de ser perseguido por espíritus vengativos. Día de los Muertos reina la exuberancia de color y el humor, reflejando la alegría de compartir y recordar aquellos seres queridos. 2. recordar aquellos seres queridos que "han pasado a mejor vida" 3. armar tu propio altar, ir a un evento, organiza tu propio evento **Estados Unidos con salsa, página 254** 1. a través de la música, la letra de las canciones y el nombre de los pasos 2. un club de salsa 3. tomar cursos en academias de baile **La huella del español por Texas, página 256** 1. 27% 2. Río Grande 3. San Antonio **La cara latina de Miami, página 258** 1. Miami como un pedacito de América Latina en Estados Unidos 2. un costo considerable, estrés de comunicarse en otro idioma, aprender costumbres nuevas y adaptarse a una sociedad y cultura distintas 3. Es un documento, sirve para verificar la identidad de la persona en el momento de acceder a servicios médicos y financieros o llevar a cabo trámites en instituciones públicas.

Audio Recordings

Recordings of the following sixty-five passages are available via the online and mobile McGraw Hill's Language Lab app (see page iv for details).

Cultura
1.	Los vejigantes	page 4
2.	De tapeo	page 6
3.	El rodeo y los "huasos"	page 19
4.	Boticas mexicanas	page 20
5.	Un país lleno de música	page 22
6.	Piedras misteriosas	page 24

Viaje
7.	El barrio gótico de Barcelona	page 30
8.	Un paraíso en el Caribe	page 38
9.	Cali, ¡qué ciudad!	page 42
10.	San Miguel de Allende	page 44
11.	Vinos y Bodegas	page 46
12.	Bocas del Toro	page 48
13.	Isla de Taquile	page 50

Tradición
14.	La Pachamama	page 58
15.	Una Navidad en Paraguay	page 61
16.	Gaspar, Melchor y Baltasar	page 64
17.	La leyenda de la Colosuca	page 72
18.	Día Internacional del Libro	page 73
19.	Otávalo	page 74

Celebración
20.	El Salvador del Mundo	page 81
21.	Festeja su independencia	page 84
22.	El baile del palo de mayo	page 88
23.	Un lento retorno	page 93
24.	La fiesta con más Gracia	page 94
25.	Noche del fuego en Salamina	page 100
26.	San Pedro de Macorís	page 101

Personas
27.	La magia de García Márquez	page 106
28.	Rubén Darío	page 113
29.	Andrés Segovia	page 118
30.	Galeano	page 120
31.	María Félix	page 122

Deportes

32.	Acampando en San Felipe	page 129
33.	Surfing en Costa Rica	page 130
34.	Conociendo Guatemala a caballo	page 137

Música

35.	Bailando al son de merengue	page 144
36.	El mariachi	page 154
37.	La Tamborrada	page 162
38.	Orishas	page 163

Historia

39.	Un símbolo de la nación	page 176
40.	La bandera de México	page 177
41.	Las ruinas de Tiwanaku	page 180
42.	La Virgen de Guadalupe	page 184
43.	Viaje a una ciudad histórica	page 186

Geografía

44.	El jurumí	page 196
45.	Orquideario	page 204
46.	Lluvia de ranas en El Yunque	page 205
47.	La laguna de San Ignacio	page 206

Gastronomía

48.	El mate	page 213
49.	Camarones en salsa blanca	page 220
50.	La chicha	page 223

Conversación

51.	Un ejemplo de salud sustentable	page 232
52.	El desafío de criar hijos bilingües	page 234
53.	Recomendaciones de un amigo	page 236
54.	Para luchar contra la inequidad	page 238
55.	Sabiduría indígena	page 240
56.	El sueño de la casa propia	page 242

Costumbres

57.	Tiendas de productos alimenticios	page 248
58.	Programas de televisión	page 249
59.	El mes de la herencia hispana	page 250
60.	El Día de los Muertos	page 252
61.	Estados Unidos con salsa	page 254
62.	La huella del español por Texas	page 256
63.	La cara Latina de Miami	page 258
64.	Guayaberas	page 260
65.	Talavera poblana	page 262